THE SYSTEM OF INDUSTRIAL RELATIONS
IN GREAT BRITAIN

THE SYSTEM OF
INDUSTRIAL RELATIONS
IN
GREAT BRITAIN

H. A. CLEGG

Professor of Industrial Relations
University of Warwick

BASIL BLACKWELL
OXFORD
1972

Reprinted 1973

ISBN 0 631 14610 5

Printed in Great Britain by Western Printing Services Ltd, Bristol
and bound by Kemp Hall Bindery, Oxford

PREFACE

The original *System of Industrial Relations in Great Britain*, consisting
of six contributions edited by Allan Flanders and myself, was
published in 1954 and ran through five reprints. It has long been
evident that much of it is out of date and the decision to rewrite
it completely was taken as long ago as 1961. At that time the plan
was for a book in three sections, one each by Allan Flanders and
myself and the third, dealing with labour law, by Otto Kahn-
Freund. But there were delays due to other obligations, both
academic and public, and there were changes in plan. It became
evident that labour law warranted a separate volume of its own.
In the end we decided that I should go ahead alone.

This volume has little in common with the original beyond its
subject and the title. There have been many important developments in the subject-matter since 1954, and meanwhile the study
of industrial relations has advanced considerably, requiring new
treatment of old themes. The title, however, is still apt and may be
more fitting than before, for a single author has the opportunity
to adopt a more systematic approach than six contributors.

On the other hand there is the disadvantage that a book from a
single pen must reflect its author's biases and limitations. Because
of this, topics which should form part of a textbook on British
industrial relations are excluded or inadequately treated. In
addition the reader may find that questions which seem to him of
importance are not raised, or, if they are, they remain unanswered.
The explanation in most instances is that I would have been glad
to give the answer if I had known what it was, but I did not, and
I have tried to cut down idle speculation.

I owe thanks to many people who have helped me, above all to
Allan Flanders with whom I have worked and exchanged ideas
for more than twenty years. He read the whole book in draft
and made many helpful suggestions, as did another former
Oxford colleague, Alan Fox, and two current Warwick colleagues,
William Brown and Richard Hyman. Otto Kahn-Freund read

and commented upon Chapter 9. None of them has any responsibility for the errors, misconceptions and infelicities which remain. There are many other students of industrial relations from whom I have learned much, first among them William McCarthy. And there are many practitioners to whom I owe a debt of gratitude for taking a hand in my education, among whom I must name David Basnett, Richard O'Brien and Sir Jack Scamp. Thanks are also due to Nuffield College, Oxford, and the University of Warwick, and to the Leverhulme Trustees and the Clarkson Trustees, for their support of several research projects whose results lie behind a good deal of what I have written. Mrs. Yates, Mrs. Powell and Mrs. Heape typed almost innumerable drafts with patience and good humour. George Bain, John Birch and Michael Mellish helped me with the proofs.

A first draft of Chapter 1 was delivered as the T. H. Searls Memorial Lectures at the University of Hull in 1968.

September 1969   H. A. Clegg

PREFACE TO THE SECOND EDITION

It is too early to attempt a major revision of a textbook only two years after its appearance, particularly when its subject matter is, in many respects, little changed. On the other hand, it would be unthinkable to allow a reprint to come out without regard for the vast changes in the legal framework of industrial relations accomplished by the Industrial Relations Act, 1971. Consequently the first eleven chapters reappear unaltered, except for the correction of a few slips, but the final chapter (formerly "The Reform of Collective Bargaining") has been entirely rewritten as "The Reform of Industrial Relations" to include the Act. It follows that the first sections of Chapter 9 ("The State in Industrial Relations: the Traditional Pattern") still outline British labour law as it had developed before the Act, leaving the changes wrought by the Act to the final chapter.

I owe thanks to George Bain, William Brown, John Corina, Allan Flanders, Otto Kahn-Freund, Richard Hyman and Michael Mellish for reading the new chapter in draft, and for their many helpful comments and suggestions.

January 1972   H. A. Clegg

CONTENTS

LIST OF TABLES

WORK GROUPS AND SHOP STEWARDS

THE NATURE OF THE SUBJECT

What is industrial relations? Evidently it is concerned with strikes, with negotiations between unions and employers, and with government intervention in strikes and negotiations. The press, radio and television constantly remind us of that. But this is not enough to define the subject-matter of an academic study. What is it that professors of industrial relations are employed to investigate and teach? The answer which is now generally given is that they deal with the rules which govern employment. Sometimes these are described as the rules which regulate jobs, so that industrial relations could be briefly defined as the study of job-regulation.

These rules are of more than one kind. There are rules or norms which regulate pay, the length of the working day, overtime and holidays and the way in which a job should be done or the time it should take. These are called *substantive rules*. There are other rules which regulate the way these substantive norms are made, and the ways in which they can be challenged, interpreted and applied. These are *procedural rules*. It is also possible to separate out the arrangements for dealing with breach of substantive and procedural rules under the heading of *disciplinary rules*. Thus industrial relations encompasses the rules governing employment together with the ways in which the rules are made and changed and their interpretation and administration.

There are three well-known ways in which employment rules can be made and administered. It can be done by managers. It is widely supposed that in the early days of industrialisation factories, mines, railways and offices were run by autocratic managers whose word was law. This is generally called *employer regulation*. When a union (or unions) establishes a foothold some of the rules may be made by agreement between manager and unions, with joint arrangements for revision and interpretation. This is called *collective bargaining*, or sometimes bilateral or joint regulation in contrast to the unilateral regulation of managers acting on their own. Firms may join together in an employers' association to bargain with unions, and the resulting agreements will then apply to all the firms in the association, but this is still collective bargaining. The third method is *statutory regulation*. The state can intervene by laying down legal rules governing aspects of employment in particular classes of undertaking, or throughout the country. These rules can prescribe rates of pay, hours of work, standards of safety and so on, and statutory arrangements may be made for their enforcement and interpretation.

There are, however, complications. The state can also intervene as a third party in collective bargaining. It may for instance oblige unions and employers to make use of arbitration if they cannot reach agreement on a particular rule; or it may give statutory force to a rule on which unions and employers have agreed, thus taking upon itself the task of enforcing a collective agreement. Besides this, some students of industrial relations emphasise *joint consultation* as an alternative method of arriving at decisions which is neither autocratic management nor collective bargaining. In joint consultation managers given information to representatives of their workers and discuss their plans with them but retain the sole responsibility for the final decision.

The rules governing employment, and the ways in which they are made and interpreted, cannot be understood apart from the organisations which take part in the process. Consequently industrial relations includes the study of trade unions, employers' associations, management and the state institutions concerned with the regulation of employment. These bodies are the sources of authority in industrial relations and it is therefore essential to consider the ways in which they come to decisions, and the extent to which they can make their decisions effective. Wherever there are separate sources of authority there is a possibility of conflict, and when organisations are in conflict they may apply pressure, or sanctions, or persuade each other to make concessions. The most notable form of conflict in industrial relations is the strike. Industrial relations therefore includes the study of industrial conflict, how it arises, what pressures are used and how it can be contained.

Each employee is likely to be affected by a considerable number of rules, and the complex of rules within a particular plant can be regarded as a system. Some of the rules will apply to all those who work in the plant, and others to particular departments such as the tool-room or the packing department. Still others will apply to particular classes of employee, such as fitters or foremen. The system in the plant as a whole is likely to reveal certain characteristics when compared with other systems. It may be centralised, with most decisions referred to the plant managers, or it may be decentralised with many decisions left to the departments. It may be prone to conflict with frequent disputes over what the rules should be and how they should be interpreted, or it may run smoothly. Some of the rules will almost certainly come from outside. If the plant is one of several owned by a single company, some rules may be company-wide. In Britain many collective agreements between one or more employers' associations and the relevant unions cover the whole of an industry. Each industry can therefore be seen as having its system of regulating employment, with the complex of rules in each company or plant forming a sub-system within it. The characteristics of one industry-wide system can then be compared with those of others.

There are also rules and general characteristics which apply in a number of industries, or to all of them. The most obvious of these are the legal rules affecting employment which form part of the law of the land. But there are other common features deriving from our history, from our experience of two centuries of industralisation, from past attempts to deal with industrial problems, and from the values that our society has developed in the process. It is the assumption of this book that an understanding of industrial relations in this country requires an appreciation of a system of industrial relations peculiar to Britain, with its own sub-systems in each industry and each plant and with trade unions, employers' associations, methods of collective bargaining and labour law all differing in many respects from those to be found in other countries. Many people would like to reform this system, and it is in fact now changing at quite a pace, but the ways in which it is likely to develop, and the ways in which it might be altered, can only be understood by those who have grasped the nature of the system.

Until recently most students of industrial relations would have considered the main elements of their subject to be employer regulation, collective bargaining, state regulation and state intervention in collective bargaining, together with the managements, unions, employers' associations and state institutions which make and administer the rules, so that the British system would consist of a particular mixture of these three types of rules, and a special set of relationships between these four types of organisation. But in recent years it has become evident that there is another important method of regulating employment which has no accepted name, but may perhaps be called "worker regulation"; and another type of organisation which plays an important part in the making and administration of rules affecting employment, namely the work group. In order to describe and analyse the British system of industrial relations, therefore, it is necessary to explain what worker regulation means, and to say what work groups are.

CUSTOM AND WORKER REGULATION

Through much of the nineteenth century custom was the most important authority in British industrial relations. Employers took workers on at the rate of wages customary for that trade in the town or district, and expected them to work for the customary hours and under the customary conditions. If the employer broke with custom his workers could be expected to object. Some of the early unions sprang up as the protectors of the customs of the trade against innovating employers. Perhaps the most imposing of all unions in the first half of the century was the Operative Builders' Union, covering all the building crafts and labourers too, which flourished in 1831–3. In 1833 the union launched a campaign against the new system of "general contracting". It had previously been usual for the customer to deal separately with the master craftsmen of the various building trades, but with the industrial revolution had come the master builder who tendered a general estimate for the erection of a complete building. At first sight it appears that this was a quarrel between two types of employer, and the men would have done better to concentrate on demands for higher pay and a shorter working day regardless of the status of their employer. In fact, however, the building workers were protecting their own interests by protecting the customs of their trades. According to G. D. H. Cole, their objection to the new system was "partly because it tended to deprive them of the chance of becoming masters, and partly because the 'general contractor' was apt to be intolerant of the traditional rules and customs of the various trades, which the small masters, being themselves mostly apprenticed craftsmen not far removed in status from the skilled workmen, were accustomed to observe".[1] Nineteenth-century crafts protected their customs with the tenacity that twentieth century trade unionists might be expected to devote to resisting a wage cut; and for much the same reason.

As trade unions became stronger, some of the rules which they tried to impose on employers lost any appearance of custom, and became direct trade union decisions, although they might still be described as the "customs of the trade." The members of a union branch or district, or of a union as a whole, would decide on the minimum rate of wages, the hours of work and the other conditions on which they would permit themselves to accept work. These decisions were then regarded as binding on the members, who were expected to insist upon their observation in any shop in which they were employed. In some instances they were formally embodied in the union rules. The Typographical Association's rule-book, for example, included instructions on the wages and conditions its members were to accept until 1921, although by that time most of these rules were negotiated with the employers before they were enforced.[2]

In some industries collective bargaining began as an attempt to change these customs. When members of the Amalgamated Society of Engineers or the Amalgamated Society of Carpenters and Joiners were dissatisfied with their pay they would apply to the employers in their town or district for an advance. Discussion might lead to an agreement to advance the customary rate by, say, $\frac{1}{4}$d. or $\frac{1}{2}$d. an hour, without any explicit agreement as to what that rate should be.

The next stage, naturally enough, was to make agreements on rates of wages and hours of work and to extend them to deal with overtime, shiftwork and later with holidays and other matters, so that the province of custom was gradually taken over

---

[1] G. D. H. Cole, *Attempts at General Union*, 1953, pp. 104–5.
[2] A. E. Musson, *The Typographical Association*, 1954, p. 387.

by collective bargaining. Some matters, however, continued to be controlled by "custom and practice". This was so with many of the rules governing apprenticeship. Even today when collective agreements generally deal with the pay of apprentices and with the period and method of their training, the type of work reserved for members of a given craft is often left to custom. Similarly in industries, such as steel, in which promotion to skilled process jobs is by seniority, not by apprenticeship, the seniority rules are not agreements but customs.

When Dr. W. E. J. McCarthy brought out his book on *The Closed Shop in Britain* in 1964, many students and practitioners of industrial relations were surprised at his estimates that about two out of five of Britain's trade unionists had no choice but to remain union members if they wanted to keep their jobs.[1] They expected the proportion to be very much less than this because they knew that formal agreements on the subject are confined to a few areas of employment, notably coalmining, docks and co-operative societies. McCarthy's surveys revealed, however, that although less than three-quarters of a million trade unionists were covered by formal agreements of this kind, more than three million of them worked in informally recognised closed shops or in closed shops where the employer's co-operation was grudging and rested ultimately on the knowledge that the workers in the departments concerned would refuse to work with a non-unionist.[2] Dr. McCarthy's findings, which have been supported by subsequent surveys and are now generally accepted, drew attention to the importance of worker regulation in maintaining the closed shop; and this conclusion applies to the regulation of many other aspects of industrial relations. However, now that trade unions have come to rely primarily on collective bargaining, worker regulation is the business of work groups rather than of the unions as such.

THE WORK GROUP

Men and women form groups at work, as they do outside it, for all manner of purposes. They chat together, take tea-breaks and meal breaks together, exchange cigarettes and newspapers, lend each other money and help each other with their work. If work

[1] pp. 30-4.   [2] *Ibid.*, pp. 52-3, 62-4.

groups have no other objectives but these they are of no direct interest to the student of industrial relations. It is when they act together to make or to influence rules governing their employment that work groups enter into the field of industrial relations.

The work group first became a subject of academic inquiry in the most famous investigation ever conducted into industrial relations on the factory floor. This was a study carried out by a group of Harvard research workers at the Hawthorne plant of the Western Electric Company in Chicago. They observed the behaviour of two groups of workers in the plant over a period of years during the late nineteen-twenties and the early nineteen-thirties. The first was a group of girls engaged on relay assembly and the second a group of men in what was called the "bank wiring room". These bank wiremen had their own idea of a day's work, lower than the firm's "bogey", and its observance was supported by sarcasm, by ridiculing offenders against it, by "binging" them—that is hitting them hard on the upper arm— or by ostracism. "The men had elaborated spontaneously and quite unconsciously", reported the investigators, "an intricate social organisation around their collective beliefs and sentiments."[1] The bank wiremen made use of a provision in the incentive system of payment which permitted the submission of claims for "daywork allowances" for delays in work due to factors outside the workers' control. Workers had considerable discretion in making these claims and excessive claims could be embarrassing to supervisors who were responsible for smooth production. This practice was further evidence of a social organisation among the bank wiremen which "served to protect the group from outside interference by manifesting a strong resistance to change".[2] The standards and beliefs of the group cut across the intentions and instructions of management and the investigatiors therefore emphasised the importance of the "informal organisation", as they called it, of the group in contrast to the "formal organisation" laid down in the rules and policies of the company.

Two notable points about the inquiry and its findings are that it was conducted in a non-union factory and during the worst economic depression ever experienced, when it would be reasonable

[1] F. J. Roethlisberger and W. J. Dickson, *Management and the Worker*, 1939, p. 524.
[2] *Ibid.*, p. 525.

to suppose that the collective strength of workers had fallen to its lowest point.

The Hawthorne investigations led to the development of a whole philosophy of "human relations in industry", associated with the name of Elton Mayo, much of it now discredited. Its more valuable legacy was a tradition of empirical research in industrial sociology. A series of subsequent investigations in the United States and elsewhere has established that the behaviour of the bank wiremen was by no means exceptional. Group restrictions on output are common among male workers. They are supported by group sanctions, and groups seek to protect themselves against outside interference. The informal organisation of the group is therefore often in conflict with the formal organisation of the undertaking. All this is as true in Britain as it is in the United States. One important study of output limitations in Britain is Professor Lupton's *On the Shop Floor.*[1] The Devlin report on the docks drew attention to the practice of "welting" in the Liverpool docks, or "spelling" in the port of Glasgow, whereby the two halves of a gang of dockers take turns to rest from work throughout the working day. This example of output limitation was dependent entirely upon work group enforcement, for the leaders of the Transport and General Workers at Liverpool and of the Scottish Transport and General Workers in Glasgow were at one in condemning it. "They blame the employers, with some justification, for having allowed the situation to become as bad as it is."[2]

The importance of work groups in British industrial relations has also been emphasised by the development of "productivity bargaining". Productivity agreements, according to the National Board for Prices and Incomes, are agreements in which workers undertake "to make a change, or a number of changes, in working practice that will lead . . . to more economical working; and in return the employer agrees to a higher level of pay or other benefits".[3] Attempts to negotiate changes in work practices have demonstrated the degree to which work groups control these practices. In his account of the negotiation of the most famous of

[1] Published in 1963.

[2] *Final Report of the Committee of Inquiry under the Rt. Hon. Lord Devlin into certain matters concerning the Port Transport Industry,* Cmnd. 2734, 1965, pp. 16–19.

[3] National Board for Prices and Incomes, *Productivity Agreements,* Report No. 36, Cmnd. 3311, 1967, p. 1.

British productivity agreements, the "Blue Book Agreement" at the Esso refinery at Fawley, Allan Flanders noted that the refinery management "overlooked, until it was forced to take note of it, ... the informal structure of organisation which is intermediate between the unions and the men as individuals—the work group based on similarity of occupation, function and status". Changes in work practices "acceptable to the various crafts on the shop floor were formulated and agreed" only when working parties of managers and shop stewards were set up to work out what the changes should be.[1] The full-time officers could do no more than decide what the unions would be willing to accept.

After examining a number of productivity agreements the National Board for Prices and Incomes concluded that: "Methods of work and traditional practices cannot be changed by decision of an industry or a company but only by the men who do the work". The Board found the Fawley experience had been repeated elsewhere. The application of a productivity agreement at selected sites in I.C.I. was seriously delayed because "the first occasion on which local managers, shop stewards and employees received definite information about the proposals was when the agreement, already signed, was distributed to them". It was only after this that top managers and union leaders realised the extent to which the application of the agreement depended upon "negotiation with committees of shop stewards within the plant about re-organisation of work".[2]

THE WORK GROUP AND COLLECTIVE BARGAINING

Productivity bargaining helps to demonstrate the degree to which work groups were in control of work practices before a productivity agreement was signed. It also shows that work groups may play an important part, not only in direct worker regulation of industrial relations, but also in regulation by collective agreement, for it appears to be impossible, in many instances, to negotiate successful productivity agreements without bringing work groups into the negotiations. However, productivity bargaining is a comparatively recent development in Britain and gives no guide to the part played by work groups in traditional

[1] Allan Flanders, *The Fawley Productivity Agreements*, 1964, pp. 139–41.
[2] *Productivity Agreements*, pp. 33, 37.

collective bargaining. On that point other evidence must be found.

The first systematic studies of work group participation in collective bargaining were made in the United States, and drew attention to the process which Professor Kuhn has entitled "fractional bargaining".[1] North American collective agreements in manufacturing industry generally cover a single plant or a single company. They normally settle most issues of joint concern to the company and union for a period of time, often two or three years. From time to time new issues crop up during the life of the agreement which require a supplementary agreement, but otherwise dealings between the two sides for the term of the agreement are supposed to be confined to the administration and interpretation of its clauses through a "grievance procedure" established for the purpose. In fact, however, groups of workers often seek additional concessions for themselves during the life of the agreement, which may involve bending the agreement rather than applying it. Moreover, although the understanding between the union and the company is that they are free to use sanctions against each other only when the agreement comes to an end or over issues to which it does not apply, groups widely resort to pressures to achieve their aims. They may, for example, limit their output to the extent of a "slowdown", imperilling the completion of vital orders on time, or disrupting the work of other departments; or they may flood the procedure with fabricated grievances. Managers can retaliate if they choose, by "cracking down" through strict supervision, or by procrastination in dealing with grievances that really bother members of the group. The balance of power may be tested by an unofficial or "wild cat" strike in breach of procedure. All this is not administration or interpretation. It is bargaining, not between the union and the company, but between managers and supervisors on the one hand and a work group on the other.

Professor Kuhn describes at length a case in which the men engaged on one process in a rubber plant felt they should have had a more generous pay allowance for a period when their machine was out of action. There was no question but that the allowance was in accordance with the agreement, so that a claim through the grievance procedure stood no chance of success by itself, but the

[1] James Kuhn, *Bargaining in Grievance Settlement*, 1961.

men wanted more. They therefore tried to push the foreman into a concession by building up another grievance over handling hot "treads" to the extent that he feared a stoppage. When management still insisted on dealing with the claim through the grievance procedure the men brought forward a number of other claims to make it appear that life would be much easier for management if the original claim could be settled.[1]

Fractional bargaining is another instance of contrast between formal and informal organisation. This time, however, the contrast is not between the informal work group and the formal structures of management and of the union. It is between the formal bargaining arrangements of the company and the union on the one hand and the informal bargaining of managers and work groups on the other.

We have examples of fractional bargaining in Britain. From 1950 until 1967 the Ford Motor Company maintained a pay structure for manual workers of three grades for men and one for women. These rates were negotiated with the unions. In addition merit allowances could be paid to individuals on management's assessment of their worth, and after the introduction of the pay structure one or two groups received additional allowances for abnormal working conditions. Other groups sought similar allowances. In 1965 an allowance to paint sprayers which ultimately led to a strike was followed by further allowances to other groups. Meanwhile the merit payment system was under strain. The toolmakers demanded an allowance for using their own tools although it is the custom of their trade for men to supply their tools. They threatened to leave their tools at home. The settlement was to pay a uniform merit increase in place of a tool allowance, clearly contrary to the principles of the scheme. Shortly afterwards the company decided that it was time to devise a new pay structure.

Clearcut company agreements like Ford's are, however, comparatively rare in Britain. Most industry-wide agreements leave room—sometimes a great deal of room—for local adjustment, so that bargaining by work groups can be regarded as legitimately supplementing the formal agreements rather than in conflict with them. In car factories covered by the industry-wide engineering agreements the submission of claims for special allowances for

[1] *Ibid.*, pp. 62–70.

uncongenial conditions or tool allowances, like those in the Ford Company, would be nothing out of the ordinary. What is the extent of bargaining of this kind? Information about the work of shop stewards can provide a clue to the answer.

THE SHOP STEWARD IN COLLECTIVE BARGAINING

The results of various studies of the part played by shop stewards in British industrial relations were brought together in a research paper published by the Royal Commission on Trade Unions and Employers' Associations.[1] Subsequently the Government Social Survey undertook a number of sample surveys into work-shop industrial relations for the Commission.[2] Generally they confirm and amplify the conclusions of the first paper, although on a few points these require revision in the light of the more ample evidence of the surveys.

One conclusion which required no revision was that shop stewards are "essentially shop-floor bargainers, using all the opportunities presented to them to satisfy their members' grievances and claims". They negotiate "over a wide variety of issues, from the level of piecework earnings to non-financial questions such as discipline and conditions of work. On the whole they tend to be most prominent and influential where they can secure a measure of influence over earnings", but "even where earnings are not determined at shop-floor level they can usually find plenty to do, unless special arrangements are made to curtail and restrict their activities".[3]

The subsequent surveys confirmed the extent of shop-steward bargaining. Over half of the sample of 1200 shop stewards said that they negotiated over wage issues as a standard practice, and more than half the remainder that they did so sometimes; half said that they settled hours of work as a standard practice and another quarter that they did so sometimes. Among those who dealt regularly with hours of work over two-thirds discussed and settled the level of overtime and over two-thirds discussed and

[1] W. E. J. McCarthy, *The Role of Shop Stewards in British Industrial Relations*, Royal Commission Research Paper No. 1, 1966.

[2] W. E. J. McCarthy and S. R. Parker, *Shop Stewards and Workshop Relations*, Royal Commission Research Paper No. 10, 1968, and Government Social Survey, *Workplace Industrial Relations*, 1968.

[3] *The Role of Shop Stewards in British Industrial Relations*, p. 30.

settled the distribution of overtime.[1] Taken together these replies suggest that many shop stewards have a very considerable influence over the earnings of those they represent, and they were confirmed by the survey of works managers and personnel managers, the majority of whom said that they negotiated with stewards on wage issues, and on hours of work.[2]

In addition, between 20 and 30 per cent of shop stewards said they dealt as a standard practice with redundancy, with suspensions and dismissals, with the manning of machines, with the introduction of new machinery and new jobs and with the distribution, the pace and the quality of work, and many more that they did so sometimes. Here again the extent of shop-steward activity was confirmed by the managers. Such matters as these are rarely covered by formal collective agreements in this country. Consequently, whereas on pay and hours the shop steward's work might be considered to be supplementary to the industry-wide agreements, on these issues he has to establish his position for himself.

THE SHOP STEWARD AND HIS UNION

Before trying to assess the importance of the work group in industrial relations from the activities of the shop steward, we must know more about the shop steward: who he is; whom he represents; how he is chosen; and under whose authority he acts. Once more the Royal Commission's studies provide much of the evidence.

In most workshops and many offices where there is a fair degree of trade union organisation it is the practice, in most industries, for trade union members to choose one of their number as their representative and spokesman. A variety of titles is used for the post, but by the far the most common is shop steward. Where there is more than one union in the workshop, and particularly where the several unions represent different classes of worker, say fitters, electricians, and semi-skilled workers, each is likely to have its own shop steward. This is not the universal rule, however, for in some plants, including Ford factories, stewards are chosen to represent all workers in the shop regardless of union; and it seems that many stewards sometimes act on behalf of other unions' members as well as their own.[3]

[1] *Workplace Industrial Relations*, pp. 29–30.   [2] *Ibid.*, pp. 79–80.   [3] *Ibid.*, p. 20.

In some unions, such as the Transport and General Workers, the rules allow for the election of stewards either at the workshop or in the branch, but workplace elections generally outnumber branch elections by nearly five to one.[1] In industries in which the branch normally covers a single place of work, such as the bus industry, the shop steward may be a branch officer; and in some unions much of the work carried on elsewhere by shop stewards is the responsibility of the branch secretary or president, as in many of the civil service unions. In some industries works committee representatives elected by all the workers, whether union members or not, are accepted as union shop stewards. This is the case with the members of Local Departmental Committees, as they are called, on the railways. In other industries there are separate elections to the two posts, but often the same man or woman holds both of them.

As a consequence of these differences and the great range in size of plants and workshops, the constituency of a steward can vary from several hundreds to two or three. Indeed where there is only one member of a given craft in the workshop he might claim to be his own shop steward. In the Royal Commission's sample the average number of members for whom the "ordinary" stewards (that is, excluding senior stewards) were responsible was sixty.[2]

In the same sample almost 30 per cent had originally been chosen in a contested election, 55 per cent in an uncontested election and the remainder with no form of election at all. Where there was voting a show of hands was more than twice as frequent as a ballot. About two-thirds said that in practice they had to stand for re-election every year or two years, and a further 15 per cent that technically they should do so; but 70 per cent of those who had stood for re-election had never been opposed and only 15 per cent were regularly re-opposed.[3]

Competition for the post of shop steward is thus not very keen and once chosen shop stewards are fairly secure. A high proportion, 40 per cent, had to be persuaded to take the job, but 58 per cent had wanted it, and 81 per cent found it rewarding and satisfying once they had tried it.[4] Moreover, an earlier survey suggested that the post of shop steward is more attractive than that of branch secretary. In a sample of stewards 86 per cent thought that

[1] *Ibid.*, p. 14.   [2] *Ibid.*, p. 16.   [3] *Ibid.*, p. 14.   [4] *Ibid.*, p. 42.

there would be someone else to take their place if they resigned. Only 55 per cent of a sample of branch secretaries thought that there would be anyone to take over from them if they resigned.[1]

On the average shop stewards spent about six hours a week on union business, about two hours of their own time and four of their working time. In more than four cases out of five no pay was lost because of this, as the employer was willing to continue full pay for union work in working time. The remainder probably consisted mainly of pieceworkers, many of whom may have received a fallback rate and not their average earnings while on union business in the factory. About half had the loss made good in some way. Some of them received a commission from the union for collecting subscriptions. In some factories the stewards raise their own funds from the members for compensating stewards for loss of pay and for other purposes. Otherwise, the steward's branch may compensate him.[2] In 1962 the General and Municipal Workers authorised branches to raise a levy for this purpose.

In plants with several stewards, one of them generally acts as senior shop steward, or convener of stewards; and in large plants with two or more unions, each union may have its own senior steward. In the Royal Commission's sample 22 per cent described themselves as senior stewards. On the average they were responsible for 350 members each, although for most of the 350 their responsibility was indirect, through a subordinate steward. They spend more of their time on union business than ordinary stewards; and some of them occupy all or most of their working time with union business. One per cent of the Royal Commission's sample of shop stewards came into this category.[3] Since the number of shop stewards in Britain is about 175,000,[4]

---

[1] H. A. Clegg, A. J. Killick and Rex Adams, *Trade Union Officers*, 1961, pp. 126–8, 164–5.   [2] *Workplace Industrial Relations*, pp. 16–17.   [3] *Ibid.*, p. 16.

[4] There are two methods of estimating the total number of shop stewards in the country. The first is to take the totals from individual unions which keep records of stewards and plus them up to take account of unions which do not. Using this method the Trades Union Congress estimated "at least 200,000" stewards in 1960 (*Annual Report*, 1960, p. 128) and the same method would now yield about 225,000. The other method is to discover by sampling the average number of members for whom stewards are responsible, and to divide total trade union membership by this figure. This yields a lower total. The first estimate on this basis was 90,000 (*Trade Union Officers*, p. 153). It was certainly far too low. The Royal Commission was able to get closer to the mark. Their sample of stewards drawn from union records turned out to include almost 20 per cent who were

it follows that the total number of full-time shop stewards in the country may be not far short of two thousand. This can be compared with a total of about three thousand full-time officers in British trade unions in 1961,[1] and probably a rather higher figure today.

What do the unions expect of their shop stewards? First of all they expect them to recruit. Although junior full-time officers are still called "organisers" in many unions, most of them have little time for organising work.[2] Such organising work as they are able to fit in is probably directed to breaking new ground. Branch secretaries might also be expected to recruit, but most of them are overburdened part-time clerical workers fully occupied with the branch minutes, records, correspondence and finance, with too little time for even more urgent tasks than organising.[3] Accordingly in plants where there are shop stewards their unions rely upon them to contact and enrol new employees and to persuade non-unionists within the plant to change their minds.

Secondly, stewards are supposed to see that their members remain union members in good standing, and many of them are expected to conduct inspections of union cards for this purpose.

The stewards' third service to their unions is the collection of trade union subscriptions, although in many unions, according to the rules, it is not their job. In the Transport and General Workers and the General and Municipal Workers, and in other unions, collecting stewards are appointed by the branch for this purpose; but in many instances the two posts are held by the same person. Seventy per cent of the General and Municipal Workers' shop stewards in the Royal Commission's sample collected union dues. Until recently the Amalgamated Engineering Union required dues to be paid personally at a branch meeting;[4] but in fact many of the union's shop stewards collected dues from their constituents and paid them in to the branch secretary on their constituents' behalf. An earlier survey suggested that only 20

not currently acting as stewards so that the 225,000 is reduced to nearer 180,000. On the other hand the survey of union members showed that 80 per cent had stewards, and with a constituency of 55 this gives a total of 168,000 (*Shop Stewards and Workshop Relations*, p. 15).

[1] Clegg, Killick and Adams then estimated that there were about 2500–2600 full-time officers, as defined in union rule-books, and a further 400 full-time branch secretaries in unions whose rules regard such branch secretaries as "lay" members. (*Trade Union Officers*, 38–9, 92–4.)   [2] *Ibid.*, pp. 43–5.   [3] *Ibid.*, pp. 117–25.

[4] Since January 1969 the branches have been empowered to appoint collectors.

per cent of the members of the Amalgamated Engineering Union paid their dues personally at branch meetings.[1] Overall about a half of the stewards in the Royal Commission's sample collected subscriptions, but they may have handled more than half the total income.[2]

There is, however, an alternative: the "check-off", the deduction of union dues by the employer in order to transfer them in bulk to the union. Until recently this practice was rare in Britain and unpopular with many unions,[3] but in the last few years opinions have changed. An inquiry conducted for the Royal Commission suggests that the dues of 20 per cent of British trade union members are collected in this way, mainly in the public services and nationalised industries.[4] But the check-off has so far done relatively little to relieve the shop steward of this task in private manufacturing industry.

The fourth service which stewards provide is communication between the member and his union. Complaints about the failure of members to attend branch meetings are almost as old as trade unionism, but average attendance today, at below 10 per cent,[5] is probably lower than in earlier periods. As the movement has grown in size the proportion of enthusiasts in the total may be expected to have diminished. There are also other signs of the decay of the branch. A number do not meet as often as prescribed in the rules, and a few not at all,[6] and in some unions a fair

---

[1] A survey conducted by H. A. Clegg, E. E. Coker and W. E. J. McCarthy whose results have never been published separately, but many of whose findings are quoted in *The Role of Shop Stewards in British Industrial Relations*, where this figure and a brief summary of the survey's methods are set out on p. 39.

[2] *Workplace Industrial Relations*, p. 16.

[3] A common explanation of trade union reluctance to ask for the check-off is that it would break the one regular contact between most members and their shop steward or branch secretary. Two-thirds of the stewards who collect say that it is a very useful way of keeping contact with the members. (*Ibid.*, p. 16.) Such evidence as there is, however, suggests that the check-off allows more time to attend to members' problems. (*Trade Union Officers*, pp. 224–5.)

[4] A. I. Marsh and J. W. Staples, "Check-off Agreements in Britain", in *Three Studies in Collective Bargaining*, Royal Commission Research Paper No. 8, 1968, pp. 48, 58.

[5] Probably the most detailed survey of branch attendance is the Clegg, Coker and McCarthy survey which put average attendance at branch meetings at 5 per cent in the General and Municipal Workers and 9 per cent in the Engineers, and attendance at the biggest meeting of the year at 13 per cent and 16 per cent respectively.

[6] In the General and Municipal sample studied by Clegg, Coker and McCarthy, 5 per cent of branches had held no meeting during the previous year, 2 per cent only one meeting and 4 per cent only two.

proportion of branches have to be run by full-time officers in their spare time because no member can be persuaded to take on the job of branch secretary.[1]

The Royal Commission asked union members where they got information about what was happening in their unions. Union journals were mentioned by 41 per cent of the sample, the shop steward by 40 per cent, circulars by 36 per cent, notice boards at work by 30 per cent and branch meetings by 20 per cent. After that came "talk at work" (14 per cent) and "meetings at work" (8 per cent). Over half of those who saw their journal got their copy from their steward (54 per cent), and presumably it is usually the steward who hands round circulars and sees that notices are posted on the board.[2] Whatever may have been true in the past, the steward is now the main means of union communication.

These four services make shop stewards an indispensable element in union administration. Without their stewards most unions would cease to recruit, lose existing members, face a financial crisis and lack any effective means of communication with their members. Nevertheless the steward's duties are not set out clearly in most union rule books. Indeed many smaller unions do not mention shop stewards in their rule books at all,[3] although most of the major unions do so. Where stewards are mentioned, the rules commonly provide for their appointment or election, usually without specifying the method; lay down the body—in many instances the district committee—to whom they are responsible; and say something about the steward's duty to recruit and retain members. They may mention the collection of subscriptions by stewards, but they are just as likely to prescribe that subscriptions should be handled in some other way. In addition, most major unions now give their shop stewards further guidance in a *Shop Steward's Handbook*. These stress the importance of the shop steward's job and his responsibility to approach new employees, to hold card inspections, to try to achieve 100 per cent membership, and to keep members informed on union business.

Rule books are also reticent on the representative and bargain-

---

[1] *Trade Union Officers*, pp. 45–6.

[2] *Workplace Industrial Relations*, p. 122.

[3] B. C. Roberts, *Trade Union Government and Administration*, 1956, p. 65, found that only a third of his sample of 134 rule books (including those of most major unions) mentioned shop stewards; another third mentioned collectors or collecting stewards. The proportion providing for shop stewards may have risen since then.

ing duties of shop stewards. The Transport and General Workers' rules do not mention them, nor do those of the Shop, Distributive and Allied Workers. Where rules touch on these duties, they do so lightly. The Engineers, for example, merely warn their stewards not to interview employers except in the presence of a witness. *Handbooks* go a little further. They may emphasise the importance of dealing promptly with grievances, of discovering whether they are genuine and of checking whether the shop steward can deal with them himself or should hand them on to his branch or full-time officer. But when it comes to telling the steward what issues he is competent to handle and exactly how he should deal with them, the *Handbooks* generally refer the steward to the procedural agreement in force in his industry.

This in its turn may be a poor guide to the stewards' authority. Some important industries, such as local government, make no room at all in their procedure for shop stewards. There is provision for works committees whose members can deal with certain matters, and shop stewards are likely to be elected to the committees. But where he is not elected to the committee, or no committee is set up, the shop steward has no formal authority to deal with grievances. The building employees officially recognised shop stewards only in 1964, although they had operated on building sites for many years.

In engineering shop stewards have been recognised since 1917 when they were given wide scope to raise grievances. The agreement dealing with manual workers lays down that:

"a. A worker or workers desiring to raise any question in which they are directly concerned shall, in the first instance, discuss the same with their foreman.

"b. Failing settlement, the question shall be taken up with the Shop Manager and/or Head Shop Foreman by the appropriate Shop Steward and one of the workers directly concerned.

"c. If no settlement is arrived at the question may, at the request of either party, be further considered at a meeting of the Works Committee [consisting of not more than seven representatives of the Management and not more than seven shop stewards]. At this meeting the O.D.D. [full-time trade union officer] may be present, in which case a representative of the Employers' Association shall also be present."

Thereafter the procedure provides for taking unsettled questions through further stages to a central conference between the Engineering Employers' Federation and the union or unions.

Thus an engineering shop steward is entitled to raise any question in which one or more of his constituents is directly interested, provided that it cannot be settled between the foreman and the man or men concerned. This gives the steward wide scope, and leaves the limits of his authority quite open. They depend upon the extent to which foremen and managers are prepared to settle issues with him, as they must also do in an industry where shop stewards are not officially recognised. Most managers seem to be ready to deal with stewards. In its surveys the Royal Commission asked works managers and personnel managers whether they preferred to deal with stewards or full-time officers over an issue which either was competent to settle. In plants with stewards, 70 per cent of the works managers preferred to deal with them, as did 74 per cent of the personnel managers.[1]

The Shop Steward and the Work Group

The preference of managers for dealing with shop stewards can be understood if the stewards are seen as the representatives of their constituents rather than as the agents of their unions; for these constituents are the employees whom managers have to manage. If the shop steward acts on their behalf with no more than relaxed and general guidance from his union and from formal agreements then the manager is likely to see his advantage in securing a settlement with the shop steward.

The printing industry provides unusually clear evidence on the relationship between the steward, the work group and the union. In printing the equivalent of the shop steward is the "father of the chapel". The chapel originated as an informal association of members of a given trade—compositors or bookbinders for example—working in a printing shop. It can be traced back for several centuries and antedates printing trade unionism. Recognis-

[1] *Shop Stewards and Workshop Relations*, p. 35.

ing its strength the printing unions incorporated the chapel into their branch structure. In this industry therefore the role of the shop steward as representative of the work group preceded his post as a union officer.

It is also significant that unofficial work group representatives can play an important part in industrial relations even where unions refuse them recognition and support. In the docks, for instance, the Devlin Committee reported that there were at that time (with some exceptions) no shop stewards. All negotiations and grievance handling was supposed to be carried out by full-time union officers. In fact most of the functions of a shop steward were performed by the "ganger", although he was regarded by managers as responsible for supervising the work of the gang. "In some instances . . . the ganger himself is a casual worker. If so, he may be chosen by his gang (or succeed to the job by virtue of seniority), and his long-term interest lies only with the gang and not with the employer. Thus, although he is responsible for supervising the work of his gang, he is also its representative in the first stage of any negotiations with management on a dispute concerning members of the gang and their work . . . He is therefore likely to take their point of view in any dispute with management, and as their leader must be their spokesman. Even where the ganger . . . is a permanent employee he appears to fulfil this dual function."[1]

A similar ambiguity exists in coal-mining, where colliery negotiations are supposed to be handled by the branch, but chargemen are chosen by faceworking and ripping groups[2] in many parts of the country to look after their interests. "Management recognised the chargemen to the extent of paying them an extra five shillings a day and maintaining that they should assume some responsibility for production." In one colliery their functions were found to be "to allocate stints amongst their particular face groups, to act as unofficial checkers of their group's wages, to act as spokesmen when grievances occurred and to influence the kind of action to be taken over these grievances". The branch secretary claimed that "because the management paid the chargemen 5s. per

---

[1] *Final Report*, pp. 10–11.

[2] These were the main piece-working groups in the industry. Since the national power-loading agreement of 1966 most faceworkers and many rippers have been transferred to day rates.

B

day extra the men did not regard them as union representatives". The research workers conducting this inquiry thought this last statement to be of "doubtful validity".[1]

What about the majority of industries in which unions give recognition to stewards? The leading authority on the printing chapel, Dr. A. J. M. Sykes, argues that the relationship between the father of the chapel and chapel members in printing is very different from that between the steward and his constituents in other industries. The chapel, he says, is a "group-centred" institution in which the chapel father is strictly subordinated to the decisions and customs of the group, whereas "the shop steward is expected to act as a *leader* rather than as a delegate, and, once elected, the initiative lies in his own hands".[2]

The contrast which he draws is far too sharp. Not every chapel is wholly group-centred. In the London newspaper trade and in magazine printing in London, where chapels are often larger than elsewhere in the country, some chapel fathers appear to exercise considerable leadership. Before the Royal Commission a spokesman of the International Publishing Corporation reported that many fathers of chapels did "almost no work" for the employer, and might have a "tremendous influence . . . in the negotiations in the chapel . . ."[3] Pressed on this point, the witness said that it was "extraordinarily difficult to get at the facts", but quoted the instance of a "militant FOC"[4] on whom the management could make "no impression . . ., and we had numerous stoppages". He was replaced by a "statesmanlike FOC . . . whom we found we could talk to, we could explain a situation, with the result that trouble immediately disappeared from that chapel . . . I can only assume that the difference lay 100 per cent or nearly 100 per cent in the chairmanship of the FOC."[5]

Equally, however, the Royal Commission's surveys do not support the view that the shop steward outside printing is usually the "*leader* rather than the delegate and, once elected, the initiative lies in his own hands".

Trade union members were asked whether their stewards generally decided themselves what action should be taken over a

[1] W. H. Scott, Enid Mumford, I. C. McGivering, J. M. Kirby, *Coal and Conflict*, 1966, pp. 154–7.
[2] "The Cohesion of Trade Union Workshop Organisation", *Sociology*, May, 1967.
[3] *Minutes of Evidence*, Qs. 9291–9292.   [4] Father of Chapel.   [5] *Minutes of Evidence*, Qs. 9327–9328.

complaint or a claim, or the decision was generally taken by a majority of the members. Two-thirds of the sample said that the majority generally decided, and only 22 per cent said that the decision was generally the steward's.[1] The shop stewards themselves were asked: "Do you feel that you can *always* get your members to see things your way, where a particular dispute arises, and get them to do what you believe to be right?" Less than half replied that they could, and the proportion did not vary very much from one union to another.[2]

Case-studies supply further evidence. In his study of industrial relations in a car plant Dr. Garfield Clack described a series of stoppages in which "the unrest was on the shop floor. The stewards attempted to act constitutionally. . . . When this failed and their members took strike action, they attempted to obtain a return to work. They were under pressure from their members, and their leadership appeared reluctant."[3] Generalising on this and other evidence Dr. Clack and his colleagues have invented the title of the "unofficial-unofficial" strike, the strike without the sanction either of the union as such or of the shop stewards, which they say "in the motor car industry . . . appears to be becoming the norm".[4] The Royal Commission's sample of managers held that shop stewards were less militant than their members.[5] When trade union members were asked how ready their stewards were to urge strikes or similar action when trying to get managers to agree over a dispute, almost three-quarters replied "not at all ready", and only 4 per cent said "very ready".[6]

Circumstances and personalities make for wide variations in the relationship between the shop steward and his constituents, but the evidence suggests that the shop steward is mainly dependent on them for his authority in collective bargaining. In some instances, such as the docks and coalmining in the past, the work group's part in collective bargaining has not been recognised by the union and the group has operated outside the union machinery. Elsewhere the shop steward provides a link between the group

[1] *Workplace Industrial Relations*, p. 120.   [2] *Ibid.*, p. 38.
[3] Garfield Clack, *Industrial Relations in a British Car Factory*, 1967, p. 61.
[4] H. A. Turner, Garfield Clack, Geoffrey Roberts, *Labour Relations in the Motor Industry*, 1967, p. 223.
[5] Forty-six per cent of works managers thought shop stewards less militant than their members; 16 per cent more militant; and 38 per cent thought they were about the same (*Workplace Industrial Relations*, p. 85).   [6] *Ibid.*, p. 130.

and the union, but even so it is not the union which gives the steward his position in collective bargaining. Accordingly the important position of the steward in collective bargaining in Britain is evidence of the importance of the work group in collective bargaining.

However, all this assumes that the shop steward is the representative of a single and clearly defined group of workers who are in the habit of acting together over a whole range of matters affecting their work. This can happen, but it is by no means universal, perhaps not even general, for two reasons. The first is that even where such "primary" work groups can be clearly identified, the shop steward's constituency may include several of them. A study by J. F. B. Goodman and T. G. Whittingham found that in a sample of nineteen stewards the median number of groups per steward was five. "One steward represented ten different primary groups and another nine and, excluding those, the mean average was three."[1] The second reason is that it is not always possible to pick out clearly defined work groups.

Take a bus garage. Normally a driver and conductor work together as a team but both of them are also part of larger groups. Drivers have interests in common and for some purposes all the drivers may be said to constitute a single work group, and all the conductors another. Alternatively, since many busmen work on shifts, the drivers and conductors on one shift may have their own view of a particular issue. At other times the whole of the road-operating staff may act as a single unit. There is still the inside staff, consisting of skilled mechanics, semi-skilled workers, cleaners and so on, each forming a group of their own for some purposes, perhaps coming together for others. Usually there is a single union delegate or representative for the operating staff, and one or more shop stewards for the inside staff.

As Goodman and Whittingham observe, "it is more plausible to count shop stewards as leaders of work *groups* rather than as work *group* leaders". Perhaps it is even more apt to see them as leaders of complexes or coalitions of work groups. Thus individual groups may act on their own, perhaps contrary to the advice of their steward and the wishes of other groups within his constituency, or all the groups may act together under his

[1] J. F. B. Goodman and T. G. Whittingham, *Shop Stewards in British Industry*, 1969, p. 74.

leadership, while for other purposes many work groups may coalesce behind a committee of stewards, or even contrary to the wishes of the stewards' committee. Where worker regulation extends over a considerable area of employment without any direct support from trade unions, as with welting or spelling in the docks, it seems sensible to regard the practice as the product of a coalition of work groups each following the same custom. Unofficial strikes of any size might also be regarded as evidence of work group coalition, as could shop stewards' committees formed without union backing—for example the "combine" committees which bring together shop stewards from the several factories of a major company.

The docks also provide instances of a different kind of work group. Before decasualisation in 1967 the organisation of dock work tended to divide dockers into four categories. There were the permanent workers employed as a nucleus by some employers. The others were employed only when there was work for them. Otherwise they earned attendance money for reporting to see whether work was available and were guaranteed a minimum "fall-back" each week. Some of them, the "regulars", sought security in attaching themselves to a particular employer, or to one of his foremen, and expecting work whenever he had it to offer. The "drifters" were generally the poorer and older workers, not in much demand and glad to make up a gang wherever there was an opportunity to do so. Finally the "floaters" sought to exploit the opportunities of casual employment by pursuing the best jobs—generally those with the highest piecework earnings or the greatest likelihood of weekend overtime—and avoiding the worst jobs.

For most purposes the work group in the docks is the gang. Permanent workers and regulars belonged to gangs, drifters and floaters shifted from gang to gang and might therefore be said not to belong to any work group. However, the floaters formed a fraternity. In 1951 in Manchester "two-thirds of them live[d] in the dock community and form[ed] an integrated and dominating group", and identified "themselves with dock workers as a whole, accepting with enthusiasm the ideas and values associated with dock work."[1] They had a common interest in preserving the opportunities for high earnings on some jobs. They were

[1] University of Liverpool, *The Dock Worker*, 1954, p. 79.

attached to the casual system which they exploited, supporting any action which resulted in the undermining of the permanent gang structure. They valued the Dock Labour Board which provided a minimum standard of security, not so much for that as because they saw it as something wrested from the employers and as a champion in their struggles with their employers.[1] In this their interest differed from that of the regulars who were ready to welcome an extension of the system of permanent employment. The floaters also tended to dominate in union affairs. Thus they might be said to form a group. Although a very different sort of group from the gangs, the fraternity of floaters arose out of the organisation of work and could therefore be described as a work group. It undoubtedly played an important part in industrial relations.

THE BEHAVIOUR OF WORK GROUPS IN INDUSTRIAL RELATIONS

Although Sykes's sharp distinction between the behaviour of printing chapels and work groups in other industries must be rejected, it does not follow that all work groups behave alike. Clearly they do not. Professor Lupton's *On the Shop Floor* is a study of work groups in two factories, one an electrical engineering shop employing men and one a waterproof garment workshop employing women. There were work groups at both places in the sense that cliques formed, and common attitudes and beliefs were observed, but the men in the electrical engineering shop had devised their own methods of controlling work practices, output and pay, whereas the women in the clothing factory had not done so. Equally differences can be found within factories as well as between them. In most factories of any size it seems that one or more groups have a reputation for sustained activity in the industrial relations field, while others are considered quiescent.

Generally it seems that work group activity is much lower among women and white collar employees than among male manual workers. If the number of unofficial strikes were taken as an index of work group action (on the assumption that official strikes are evidence of formal trade union action) then women and white collar employees strike much less frequently than male

[1] *Ibid.*, pp. 80–1.

manual workers, and when white collar employees do strike it is likely to be on union instructions.[1] Overtime bans, common among many groups of male manual workers, are also likely to be rare among women and white collar employees, for both work far less overtime than do male manual workers.[2] Moreover, if they work less overtime, then they are less likely to exercise work group control over the amount and distribution of overtime earnings.

There is a now a fair accumulation of studies of work group behaviour. The United States lead the field, and the most detailed and comprehensive investigation is the *Behaviour of Industrial Work Groups* by Professor Leonard Sayles.[3] Some of Sayles's findings can help to account for the difference between men and women, and between manual and white collar employees. He noted that work group activity tended to be low among the lowest grades of manual workers, and explained that these groups consisted of "young newcomers, low seniority employees, persons marking time until seniority brings them promotions, unambitious individuals and workers who intend to remain only until they can find better jobs".[4] Such groups are not predisposed to planned collective activity. Because women are concentrated in lower grades, tend to be less career-minded than men, and have a considerably higher rate of turnover than men, work groups of women are more likely than groups of men to come into this category.

Another of Sayles's findings is that, on the whole, larger groups were "associated with more concerted activity".[5] Despite the great concentration of white collar workers in public administration and financial undertakings, generally speaking white collar workers are employed in much smaller groups than manual workers. The main areas of employment for women are the white collar field (including distribution), catering and miscellaneous services, all of them employments in which the size of establishments is relatively small. Sayles also found that "adjacently located employees who operated different kinds of machines or performed different tasks were not prone to associate in a pressure group to attain mutual goals. They do not have

---

[1] The most strike-prone group of white collar workers in Britain are the draughtsmen, who rarely strike without official backing (see pp. 299–300). [2] See pp. 183, 214.
[3] Published in 1958. [4] *Behaviour of Industrial Work Groups*, p. 55. [5] *Ibid.*, p. 57.

enough in common". On the other hand where members of a group were engaged on closely similar jobs there seemed to be a "resonance effect" or a "mutual reinforcement of the sentiments each holds individually".[1] This helps to explain why active groups tend to be found in larger establishments in which it is more likely that considerable numbers will be employed on closely similar jobs.

OBJECTIVES

The behaviour of a work group must depend upon the objectives which the group is trying to reach. The most universally recognised objective of collective industrial action is the maintenance and improvement of the position of those concerned in terms of pay and conditions of work. Maintenance and improvement might be measured in absolute terms, but most students of industrial relations think that relative positions exercise most influence on behaviour. This is Sayles's view. The most active work groups, he says, are those of "ambiguous" status in the plant, whose members feel that in some respect their position is not as high as it should be in relation to that of other workers. Whereas "the highest prestige groups in the plant are so favoured in their various endowments that they are less likely to exhibit open pressure tactics".[2] Since Sayles confined his investigation to manual work groups, this verdict assumes that manual workers are more influenced by comparisons with other groups of manual workers than by comparisons with white collar workers or managers. Otherwise they would not be likely to see themselves as the "highest prestige" groups.

Sykes stresses another objective, the maintenance and strengthening of group cohesion. For him the main instrument for this purpose is insistence on equal treatment for members of the group. "The subordination of the individual to the authority of the association is vital for its unity of action: equality before the authority is an essential condition for accepting subordination".[3] Equality, however, is restricted to full members of the group. Sykes's printing craft groups relegate the junior worker to the position of an acolyte and the labourer to a permanently inferior position.

[1] *Ibid.*, pp. 57–60.   [2] *Ibid.*, p. 55.   [3] *loc cit.*.

Cohesion is also promoted by protecting the individual member of the group from interference or punishment by supervisors or managers. This aspect of group behaviour was noted in the Hawthorne bank-wiring room study, which also emphasised the tendency of the group to resist change. Change may, of course, promise advantages or disadvantages to members of the group. Often it will mean advantages for some and disadvantages for others. If so, the carrying out of the change will upset the social structure and cohesion of the group, and challenge its ability to protect those of its members who suffer as a consequence. A typical example would be a redundancy in which the membership of a work group is split, those who stay receiving higher pay, the rest losing their jobs.

An improved position and strengthened cohesion are rational objectives of group behaviour. There is, however, no reason why groups should be more uniformly rational than the individuals who compose them. A common motive for both individual and group action is the need to express frustration, and this motive is in evidence in some unofficial strikes.

VALUES AND SANCTIONS

Whether group objectives are rational or not, the support which group members give to them will be influenced by the value they place on collective action. It is generally held that manual workers value solidarity more highly than do white collar employees, and working class culture may therefore help to explain the relatively high level of group activity among manual workers. Some communities are especially imbued with class feeling which may help to reinforce group solidarity among work groups within the community. Mining villages are often quoted as examples. Trade unions promote collective action, so that trade union membership may both indicate belief in solidarity and help to strengthen it. Trade union membership among manual workers in Britain is a little over 50 per cent compared with rather less than 30 per cent among white collar employees. Among men it is rather more than 50 per cent compared with about 25 per cent among women.[1] These figures help to explain the relatively low level of group activity among white collar employees and women.

[1] See p. 61.

Apprenticeship offers especially favourable conditions for indoctrination in group values. "The apprentice is attached to older men for the purpose of technical instruction and he remains in the same works for several years in a relationship to the older men of pupil to teacher. During this time the apprentice receives not only technical instruction from the tradesmen but also informal instruction in the customs and traditions of his trade, his trade union, and his particular works and work group. In this way apprenticeship acts as a social as well as a technical system of training".[1] This factor also affects the comparison with women and white collar employees. When they leave school "only some 7 per cent of girls enter apprenticeships (hairdressing predominantly) compared with 43 per cent of boys".[2] Apprenticeship is much more rare among white collar workers than among manual workers.

Group cohesion can also be reinforced by sanctions. These are not confined to trade union work groups. Most of the common sanctions—ridicule, censure, mild physical violence and ostracism—were at the command of the Hawthorne bank wiremen. But it is possible for trade union branches or districts to use their power to fine or even to expel in order to punish offences against group standards. Eleven per cent of a sample of nearly five hundred trade union members questioned in one of the Royal Commission's surveys personally knew of cases in which discipline had been applied by their unions, and some of the offences were against group standards. One instance was that of a man "working more overtime than allowed".[3]

BARGAINING STRENGTH

The ability of a group to achieve its objectives depends on the willingness of managers to make concessions, which may be called the group's bargaining strength. An important element in bargaining strength is the difficulty which managers face in replacing the members of the group. Thus group bargaining strength is high in periods of full employment when almost all grades of labour are scarce as is shown by the high level of work

---

[1] Sykes, *loc. cit.*
[2] Royal Commission on Trade Unions and Employers' Associations, 1965–8 (henceforth the Royal Commission) *Report*, Cmnd. 3623, p. 91.   [3] *Ibid.*, p. 168.

group activity in both world wars and in the years since the second world war. As between different groups bargaining strength is generally related to skill. Generally speaking, the more skilled the worker the greater the difficulty of replacing him.

What is skill? In Britain we often equate skilled work and craftsmanship, the skilled worker and the craftsman. Although this usage goes back to the industrial revolution and beyond, it is a prodigal source of confusion. In the past, skill generally meant the practised ability to perform a difficult task, or group of tasks; more recently technical knowledge has come to constitute a greater part of many skills. For the purpose of industrial relations, on the other hand, a craft is a social institution based upon a set period and form of training, and the reservation of certain jobs for those who are undergoing or have completed that training. There have always been some jobs which have been regarded as skilled but have not been subject to an apprenticeship, such as the mule-spinners in cotton or the first hands in the various branches of the steel industry. Today their number is probably increasing, and as a broad generalisation the senior grades of process workers in most industries are skilled but not apprenticed. On the other hand the social institution of the craft can be established without a high degree of skill, and can certainly persist long after the job has lost most of its requirement for skill. It is arguable that this is true of many if not most of the craft jobs in engineering, shipbuilding, printing and building. So long as these jobs are reserved for craftsmen, however, the bargaining strength of the work groups employed on them is buttressed by scarcity due, not only to skill, but also to the social institution of the craft. It is, moreover, a principle of most crafts that the apprenticed worker (provided he has the appropriate trade union card) is capable of performing any of the tasks reserved for that craft in any factory or in any industry. This last point is of great importance to those crafts employed in maintenance work whose labour is in demand in virtually every industry in the country. Consequently the social institution of the craft not only strengthens the craftsman's hold on his existing job but widens the range of alternative jobs. The process worker's skill usually has no market outside his own industry, and in some instances he has to start again at the bottom of the ladder if he moves outside his own company or even his own factory.

There are, however, a number of other influences at work. Technological development can affect the demand for a particular skill, and therefore its bargaining strength whether or not it is organised as a craft. In recent years this has been demonstrated by certain grades of white collar employees, notably computer-programmers.

Bargaining strength, moreover, is not simply a matter of scarcity of labour. Some relatively unskilled grades can exercise considerable bargaining strength because of a strategic position in the production process from which they can quickly bring a whole department or a whole factory to a standstill. Sayles instances cranemen and internal transport drivers.

Another factor is the vulnerability of the employer. If a colliery is stopped for a day or two the loss of output can probably be made good during the next few days. If an air-line is stopped for a day or so its passengers turn elsewhere. In a newspaper strike the loss of revenue for the duration of the stoppage may be less important than the loss of readers which it might take months to recover. A stevedoring company in the docks may lose relatively little through a strike, for it saves the wages which are its major cost, but the shipper with a perishable cargo may bring pressure to bear for a quick settlement in a dock dispute and thus reinforce the bargaining strength of the dockers.

Finally, the readiness of managers to make concessions is not necessarily determined only by a careful calculation of consequences of rejecting a group's demands. They may find it easier to sympathise with some groups than with others. It seems that managers in steel plants are more ready to appreciate the production workers' point of view than that of the craftsmen, whom they regard as "ancillary workers". Although mechanisation has increased the numbers and importance of the craftsmen, "this is only being recognised slowly and grudgingly by the firm and by the other unions, and they are still regarded as a 'necessary evil' ".[1]

PAY SYSTEMS

Perhaps the most obvious of the circumstances which must affect the way work groups go about achieving their objectives, and the

[1] W. H. Scott, J. A. Banks, A. H. Halsey, T. Lupton, *Technical Change and Industrial Relations*, 1956, pp. 153-5, 279.

likelihood of achieving their objectives, is the system of wage payment in use and the way it is applied.

Overtime payment provides a simple example. If managers show themselves ready to use overtime, work groups can increase their members' earnings by limiting output during normal hours so as to increase overtime. At the same time overtime working threatens the cohesion of the group. If some members of the group work more overtime than others, their earnings are higher and the others have a grievance. In a survey of workshop bargaining, McCarthy and Coker found that "the most common cause of grievances and claims arising out of hours of work concerned overtime. In all the workplace situations studied grievances had arisen over the uneven distribution of overtime."[1] Accordingly, following the principle of equality between members of the group, there is pressure for the equal distribution of overtime. Sykes found a variety of printing chapel rules intended to ensure equality of overtime. One simple rule is that if anyone in the section is to work overtime then the whole section must work overtime. Another is to set a limit to the amount of overtime which no member of the group is to exceed until every member of the group has had the opportunity to work that number of hours.[2]

Payment-by-results systems present a more complicated challenge. Since some workers are more productive than others, payment related to output yields a variation of earnings within the group. But that is not all. Unless the members of the group are all permanently engaged on the same job, piecework prices or bonus values have to be set for more than one job. Even where great care is taken by the use of work-study techniques to ensure that the same effort yields the same pay some jobs are likely to bring more pay than others, and where less care is used the variation between "tight" and "loose" prices is likely to be greater. This is another source of inequality. Where "group bonus" is used, so that the earnings of the group are divided equally, or according to grade, among the members of the group, these difficulties can be avoided so long as the group for payment purposes is the same as the work group which normally exercises collective control over industrial relations. But where there is

---

[1] *The Role of Shop Stewards in British Industrial Relations*, p. 12.
[2] *loc. cit.*

individual piecework or group bonus is paid to small sections of workers, variation in earnings can foster jealousies.

Consequently some groups try to equalise earnings by setting a limit on output or a limit on earnings, like the bank wiremen in the Hawthorne plant. This seemed to the Harvard investigators to be irrational behaviour, the more so because of the explanation offered by members of the group. They said that it protected them against the risk that high output would lead to a reduction in the incentive values and therefore in their earnings. In fact there was no evidence of rate-cutting in the firm. However, if the practice is seen as a means of protecting the unity of the group, then it is rational; but perhaps the risk of rate-cutting is a more acceptable excuse for the members of the group to offer outsiders, and to put to new members of the group as a reason for their compliance with the group's practices.

However, equalisation of earnings is not the sole objective of work groups in dealing with payment by results. Groups also wish to increase their members' earnings, and this may be done by haggling over the values fixed for particular jobs, and over the allowances to be paid when for some reason normal earnings cannot be reached. Earnings may also be affected by the way in which jobs and times are recorded, and the group may wish to protect its members' opportunity to "fiddle the system". But exploitation of these possibilities may add to the likelihood of differences in earnings between members of the group. If so, the principle of equality may be abandoned in the interests of higher earnings.

Both overtime and payment by results present the work group with another challenge—insecurity of earnings. A reduction in output normally brings a cut in overtime. The reduction in earnings is proportionately greater than the reduction in hours because overtime is paid at premium rates. The group can attempt to protect itself by insisting that overtime hours should continue to be worked, or at least paid, regardless of the need for them, or by stretching out the job further than ever so that the extra hours are still needed. Fluctuations in output have a direct effect on the earnings of the worker paid by results, but his pay-packet can vary for other reasons also. A shift from a "loose-rated" job to a "tight-rated" job may prevent him reaching his expected level of pay. Where waiting time is paid at a considerably lower level than production time there is another cause of insecurity. The remedy is variously described as "banking" or "using the back of the book". Some of the "tickets" recording the completion of jobs are stored for "cashing" in what would otherwise be a week of low earnings. This can help to even out short-run fluctuations in pay.

MANAGEMENT CONTROL AND TECHNOLOGY

The ability of work groups to exploit the opportunities of a payment system or to protect their members against its adverse consequences depends on managerial controls and the rigour with which they are operated. If managers insist on a weekly check on overtime in every section and a close inspection of the reasons for it, then work group control over the volume and distribution of overtime is impossible. The use of "banking" to even out fluctuations in piecework earnings also depends on lax control or connivance. The National Board for Prices and Incomes found that in some instances "it was the foreman and chargehand who undertook the necessary manipulation of records" and "in a Midlands factory the management had an informal agreement under which work tickets would be accepted for payment purposes up to four weeks after the work had been completed".[1] Where work study is used to guide foremen or ratefixers on the prices or values that should be placed on piecework jobs, the upward movement of earnings—apart from general increases in pay—depends on their willingness to disregard the results of work study, or conceivably on the willingness of work study engineers to falsify their own results.

The need for complex and detailed production controls can arise from the method of production itself. Sayles tried to show that many of the differences in group behaviour within a plant are the consequence of the work which members of the group perform and its part in the whole production process. But differences in the level of work group activity are observable not only within plants but also between plants and between industries. Joan Woodward offers an explanation for many of these differences, so far as they occur in manufacturing industry. She classifies production systems into three types: unit and small-batch

[1] *Payment by Results Systems*, Report No. 65, Cmnd. 3627, 1968, p. 28.

production to customers' orders, including the making of proto-types; large-batch and mass production, which she classifies together and in which she includes assembly line work; and process production, by which she means the continuous flow production of liquids, gases and crystalline substances and also the batch production of chemicals. She argues from a survey of a hundred firms that the organisation of a firm is shaped by its system of production. The main contrast is between the small batch and process production systems on the one hand, and the large batch or mass production systems on the other. In the last two systems there is a tendency to more rigid organisation and a clear-cut definition of duties, along with elaborate production control procedures, whereas in the small batch and process systems organisation is flexible and the exercise of control is a relatively easy matter. This has its consequences for industrial relations, since the "intractable problems of human relations were concentrated in the technical area where production control procedures were most complex, and sometimes more rigorously applied".[1]

More recently, John Goldthorpe and his colleagues have shown that it would be a mistake to regard the system of production as the sole determinant of the industrial relations of the plant. In three plants in Luton they found favourable attitudes to manage-ment among workers employed in a wide variety of production systems. This they explained as the consequence of an "instru-mental orientation to work. . . . To the extent that workers define their employment as essentially a means of acquiring a certain standard and style of living outside of work, it is clearly possible for them to take a negative view of the work-tasks they actually perform while at the same time appreciating a firm which offers pay and conditions that can bring a valued way of life within their grasp."[2] The organisation of production is not the only factor at work.

Besides the organisation of production the organisation of formal collective bargaining is also relevant. A detailed and precise system of formal collective bargaining between union and management leaves the work group little room to act on its own except through fractional bargaining. Equally the scope of agree-

[1] Joan Woodward, *Industrial Organisation: Theory and Practice*, 1965, pp. 180–1.
[2] John H. Goldthorpe, David Lockwood, Frank Bechhover, Jennifer Platt, *The Affluent Worker: Industrial Attitudes and Behaviour*, 1968, pp. 79–80.

ments can have an effect. Where the range of issues is narrow, the work group is impelled towards activity on its own if it is to have an effect on matters outside the agreement.

WORK GROUPS IN LABOUR HISTORY

There is one final question to be considered. If work groups play such an important part in contemporary British industrial relations; if the study of their behaviour is so important for the understanding of British industrial relations; then why is the work group found so rarely in the writings of labour historians? Work groups and shop stewards might of course be expected to be more powerful and more in evidence during the last thirty years of full employment than in most earlier periods, and therefore to receive less attention from historians than from students of contemporary industrial society. But this should be no more than a matter of emphasis. The Hawthorne inquiry showed a work group exercising considerable strength and cohesion in the depths of a depression.

One answer is that the work group and its effects could become evident only to an investigator scrutinising behaviour in the factory as closely as does the modern industrial sociologist. The historian is at a disadvantage in tracing elements in the social structure which went unnoticed by contemporaries. This, however, is too easy an answer. If it really was of importance during the nineteenth century, for example, the work group would surely have left some trace, for it was a period for which we have ample records and the writings of contemporary observers of industrial affairs.

In fact the work group of the nineteenth century has left some traces, and not only in the chapels of the printing industry. It is not true that, as one historian has put it, "shop stewards had only rarely existed before the war, as the employers would refuse to tolerate union activities within the factory premises".[1] The checkweighman of the coalmining industry, whose position was safeguarded by the Coal Mines Act of 1860, performed many of the functions of a shop steward, or of a senior shop steward. The steel industry's equivalent of the shop steward was written into the north-east coast Conciliation Board in 1869. In the engineering

[1] Henry Pelling, *A History of British Trade Unionism*, 1963, p. 151.

industry, shop steward organisation had reached such a pitch by 1897 that the employers' leader complained that "in every shop and in every department there have been for years, what are known as 'shop stewards', members of the A.S.E.,[1] whose duty it is to see that the rules, written and unwritten, of their society are carried out, and he is a brave employer who dares say 'nay' to their demands".[2] The number and scope of shop stewards in engineering were further extended by the spread of piecework during the last decade of the nineteenth century and the early years of the present century. G. D. H. Cole noted that "special 'Workshop Committees' or 'Piece-work Committees' sprang up for the purpose, among others, of considering all [piecework] prices before any man was allowed to accept them".[3]

In many unions collecting stewards exercised the functions of shop stewards. In September 1889 the collecting stewards of the National Union of Gasworkers and General Labourers at the South Metropolitan Gasworks secured an oral agreement with the chairman of the company that "non-union men and union men cannot work in the same gang, provided that the men would accept non-union gangs in the same retort-house", and then within a month persuaded every stoker into the union.[4] Just before the 1914–18 war an organiser of the Workers' Union wrote:

"It is to the Collector that the Union principally looks for the maintenance of the strength of the Union, in his shop or section of the shop. Upon the Collector rests the responsibility of advice in the first instance, in those emergency difficulties which occasionally spring up in even the best shops; and upon him frequently falls the duty of acting as spokesman for the others, in discussion with Foreman or Works Manager."[5]

These are odd gleanings from sources most of which were not primarily concerned with the development of work groups and their representatives. There must be other sources waiting to be

---

[1] The Amalgamated Society of Engineers, forerunner of the Amalgamated Union of Engineering and Foundry Workers.

[2] Colonel Dyer in *Cassius Magazine*, November 1897.

[3] G. D. H. Cole, *Workshop Organisation*, 1923, p. 15.

[4] *Royal Commission on Labour*, C–6894–IX, 1893, Qs. 26790–99. The union's grip on the South Metropolitan works was broken during a strike in the following winter.

[5] *The Workers' Union Record*, January 1914, quoted in Richard Hyman, *The Workers' Union*, Oxford D. Phil. thesis, 1968.

tapped by historians who know what they are looking for. Consequently the history of the work group in British industrial relations may yet be written.

FULL EMPLOYMENT AND INDUSTRIAL STRUCTURE

The influence of the work group in industrial relations is, then, not a recent development. It goes back to the industrial revolution and beyond. But it is powerfully affected by the level of employment. When jobs are easy to come by, and managers are looking for more labour, workers can have a larger say in job-regulation if they choose to act collectively. At the same time they are less in need of the external protection of a trade union, if they have one, and better able to act for themselves. Consequently the heroic age of work group action in Britain came with the first world war, and the thirty years of full employment since the outbreak of the second have brought the work group and the shop steward steadily into greater prominence. The study of British industrial relations today is to a considerable extent the study of how a system of industrial relations fashioned at a time of unemployment, or fluctuating employment, has reacted to a long period of full employment. A high level of demand for labour has influenced pay systems. Overtime has flourished; payment by results has extended; and earnings from payment by results have swollen. This has presented work groups with a challenge and an opportunity.

However, full employment has not been the only influence at work on the power of the work group. Changing technology and increasing capitalisation have strengthened the bargaining power of small groups in many industries. Continuous growth in the size of firms has emphasised the importance of job-regulation within the firm at the expense of collective bargaining at industry level and thus brought many decisions nearer to the work group. Society now recognises many issues which were once within the undisputed province of the manager as suitable for joint regulation. Redundancy and discipline are two such issues. Work groups have been pioneers in asserting the workers' right to share in decisions made upon them.

Most of the remaining chapters of this book explore these changes, the decline in industry regulation, the effect of full employment on pay structures, the influence of the size of the firm on industrial relations, the effect of full employment on the size, number and form of strikes, and finally the consequences of these various developments for state intervention in industrial relations. But the next two chapters deal with trade unions. The members of most work groups which exercise authority in industrial relations are also trade union members, and most shop stewards are trade union officers. The formal machinery of collective bargaining depends on the trade unions. When top managers, employers' associations and government officials take part in industrial relations they generally deal with the full-time officers of trade unions. Consequently the strange and complex organisation of British trade unions remains one of the most important parts of the British system of industrial relations.

CHAPTER 2

TRADE UNION STRUCTURE

PRESENT STRUCTURES

In the study of organisations the word "structure" generally means the relationship between the parts of an organisation, but in relation to trade unions it has a special meaning. It is usually confined to the coverage of trade unions by industry or by grade of worker, and the relationship between different grades or industries within a union. The relationship between the various decision-making bodies within a union is called trade union government, and regarded as a separate topic. This usage is followed here, for even when it is narrowly defined in this way British trade union structure is a complex subject which needs to be treated on its own.

In the past, three categories have generally been used to analyse trade union structures: craft, industrial and general. Craft unions are those which organise workers practising a particular skill, or practising any one of a group of related skills, wherever they may work. Industrial unions are those which organise all workers in a given industry, whatever the job they perform. General unions are those which organise workers regardless of skill or industry, or at least workers of various grades in a number of industries.

There have always been difficulties in using these terms. As already noted, although the word "craft" is commonly used to describe a skilled occupation which recruits and trains by means of an apprenticeship system, there are also skilled trades in which skills are learned on the job, and promotion takes men stage by stage from labourer to the highest level of skill. Thus in the past the mule-spinner in cotton was promoted from the ranks of the "big piecers", or senior assistants, who were in turn promoted from the ranks of the "little piecers", or junior assistants; and in the days of steam trains, engine cleaners waited for vacancies in the ranks of firemen, and firemen in the ranks of engine drivers. Unions of apprenticed craftsmen could control the supply of skilled labour by limiting the number of apprentices. Even if the employer were able to increase the number of apprentices, this would affect the size of the skilled labour force only several years ahead. On the other hand the cotton master or the railway company could increase the skilled labour force at once by promoting piecers or engine cleaners. Consequently the spinners and the drivers organised the junior grades into their trade unions so as to have their potential competitors under their control, and only a minority of union members worked at fully skilled jobs. Even so these unions have often been classified as craft unions. However, where a union organised on this principle covers most of the workers in an industry, it can also be classified as an industrial union. An example is our major steel union, the British Iron, Steel and Kindred Trades Association, which has long considered itself an industrial union, although there are a number of other unions in steel.

Industrial unionism—organisation by industry—has been advocated as the ideal form of trade union organisation since the turn of the century. However, enthusiasts have had to face the question: "What is an industry?" Is it to be defined by the product, as in the car industry, or by the material, as in the cotton industry, or by the process, as in the engineering industry? Are the railway workshops part of the railway industry or of engineering? Moreover, the complications have increased over the years. In the past some unions which regarded themselves as industrial organisations neglected the fact that small groups of maintenance workers were members of their appropriate craft unions, only to discover subsequently that technical change had greatly increased the proportion of maintenance workers. Similarly white collar employees were once regarded as beyond the scope of trade unionism; but as white collar trade unionism has become more palatable many groups of white collar workers have joined trade unions of their own, further undermining the claims of "industrial" unions to their title.

If general unions are defined as unions which are not confined to skilled workers, nor to a single industry, then this term also is of little use in analysing British trade union structure. For most major British unions spill over the boundaries of both skill and industry. Nevertheless there are many important structural differences between them. The only way to understand union structure is, therefore, to examine each union in turn. Classification is of little use.

TABLE I

MEMBERSHIP OF MAJOR BRITISH TRADE UNIONS

	Membership end 1968
Transport and General Workers Union	1,476,000
Amalgamated Union of Engineering and Foundry Workers	1,136,000
General and Municipal Workers' Union	798,000
National and Local Government Officers' Association	373,000
Electrical Electronic Telecommunication Union/Plumbing Trades Union	365,000
National Union of Mineworkers	344,000
Union of Shop, Distributive and Allied Workers	311,000
National Union of Public Employees	283,000
Society of Graphical and Allied Trades	229,000
National Union of Railwaymen	199,000
	5,514,000

The ten unions whose membership figures are given in Table I include between them 62 per cent of the total membership of the Trades Union Congress, which is approaching 9 million. If the 287,000 members of the National Union of Teachers,[1] the largest union not affiliated to Congress, are added to theirs, the eleven unions include almost 58 per cent of the total membership of trade unions in Britain, which is about 10 million. Accordingly, although an examination of their structures cannot tell us much about the structure of the 550 British trade unions, it can reveal the structures within which most British trade unionists have to operate.

Two pairs can be picked out of the list. The first of them is the Transport and General Workers and the General and Municipal Workers, the two avowedly general unions. Whom do they organise?

[1] On a basis of the examination of the rules and accounts of this union, the Chief Registrar of Friendly Societies has formed the opinion that it is not a trade union, but a professional association. Its behaviour, however, is manifestly that of a trade union. (Royal Commission, *Minutes of Evidence*, Q. 1414.)

In some instances they approximate fairly closely to an industrial union for a particular industry. In the oil industry, for example, the Transport and General Workers represent all the drivers, process workers and vehicle maintenance workers (including skilled fitters and electricians, although a few of these belong to the Engineers or the Electricians). Skilled maintenance workers in the refineries are represented by their own unions, but to the extent that clerical and supervisory workers belong to trade unions they are members of the white collar section of the Transport and General Workers Union. The union has an almost equally comprehensive grip on the bus industry, although it does not organise the majority of skilled vehicle maintenance staff, and both the General and Municipal Workers and the National Union of Railwaymen organise relatively small groups of busmen. The nearest approach of the General and Municipal Workers to a similiar position is in the gas industry. They organise the majority of the production workers and the largest section of craftsmen, the gas fitters; but the Transport and General Workers also have a sizeable membership among production workers, other skilled maintenance workers are in their separate unions, and most white collar workers are in the National and Local Government Officers' Association.

The situation in gas is not very different from that in a group of industries where the two unions organise production workers, and probably some of the white collar workers where they belong to unions, but leave the skilled maintenance workers to their separate unions. Food manufacture, chemicals and rubber manufacture provide three examples. In chemicals and rubber manufacture, however, the two unions compete with small so-called industrial unions for chemical workers and rubber workers. In the steel industry, by contrast, the British Iron, Steel and Kindred Trades Association (102,000) organises the majority of the process workers, and many white collar workers, leaving only a minority interest to each of the general unions.

In one or two industries, such as shipbuilding and building, where skilled craftsmen still perform much of the production work, the two general unions approximate to "labourers' unions" catering for labourers and craftsmen's assistants, although independent semi-skilled tasks are emerging, especially in building, and they also cater for these.

Engineering is an instance where this process has developed so far that the two general unions have long ago grown from labourers' unions into production workers' unions, but they now compete in this field with several former craft unions who have opened their ranks to non-apprenticed workers. These include the Engineers, the Electricians and the Vehicle Builders (72,000).

These several structural situations do not exhaust the variety to be found in the two general unions, but they cover the vast majority of their members. These are spread over all but one or two of the industrial groups in the Standard Industrial Classification listed in Table II (page 59).

The second pair is the Amalgamated Union of Engineering and Foundry Workers and the Electrical Electronic Telecommunication Union/Plumbing Trade Union. Both of them are also to be found in almost every industrial group in the Standard Classification. In one instance, electrical contracting, the Electricians perform the job of an industrial union, for there is no other union catering for manual workers there, whether skilled or not. In nearly all the industries in which the two general unions act as production workers' unions, the Engineers and the Electricians organise the skilled maintenance workers who fall within their scope. Between them they include the majority of skilled maintenance men. The minority is scattered over a number of other unions such as the Boilermakers (122,000), the Metal Mechanics (45,000), the Woodworkers (174,000) and the Building Trade Workers (69,000).

More and more the two unions, and especially the Electricians, have tended to recruit less-skilled workers who serve as "mates" for their craft members. In the engineering industry generally the Engineers open their ranks to workers of all grades of skill, and the Electricians recruit on the same generous scale in electrical engineering and electricity supply. So that although they started at the opposite end of the hierarchy of skill from the two general unions, the Engineers and Electricians now overlap with them more and more.

Finally both unions, again like the general unions, are showing an increasing interest in extending their membership among white collar employees. Here their chief concern is to maintain their control over members promoted to supervisors or to the rapidly expanding ranks of the technicians.

The rest of the unions listed in Table I have to be taken one by one. The Mineworkers come closer to being an industrial union than any other major British union. They have few members, mainly coke workers, outside the employment of the National Coal Board, and they include the vast majority of the Coal Board's employees—all manual workers, most clerical workers, and some supervisory workers, although most of these belong to a separate union. Their unchallenged position among manual workers in the industry has been achieved by making special arrangements with the Engineers, the Electricians and the two general workers unions, all of which have some thousands of members whom the Mineworkers represent in all industrial matters leaving friendly benefits and administrative matters to their existing unions.

The National and Local Government Officers' Association began its life as an organisation for the white collar employees of local authorities—administrative, professional, technical and clerical, and ranging from clerical assistant to town clerk. They were introduced into other fields by the nationalisation of a number of industries and public services, which brought together undertakings in private ownership and undertakings previously municipally owned. Now the union organises in the National Health Service, the gas industry, the electricity supply industry and the road passenger transport industry, but in none of these does it have the complete coverage of white collar workers which it has achieved in local government. Other organisations also cater for professional and technical staffs in hospitals and electricity supply, and to some extent for administrative and clerical staffs as well.

The Union of Shop, Distributive and Allied Workers is primarily a shop assistants' and shop managers' union, with the majority of its members in co-operative societies, most of which impose a closed shop. In addition, however, it has a considerable membership spread over a range of manufacturing industries. This is partly because of the wide manufacturing interests of the Co-operative Wholesale Society. But it also derives from an amalgamation, shortly after the first world war, between one of the unions which subsequently merged into the Shop, Distributive and Allied Workers and a Warehouseman's and General Labourers' Union which organised a number of factory trades, particularly in Liverpool and South Lancashire. Consequently the union now works alongside the two general unions in chemicals, rubber, several food manufacturing industries and elsewhere.

The National Union of Public Employees is primarily a union for manual workers among the "non-trading" services of the local authorities and in the National Health Service, although it also recruits white collar workers. It is another contender for the title of "industrial union" but in both services it competes with the two general unions, and in the National Health Service with the Confederation of Health Service Employees (75,000) as well. The Confederation also claims to be an industrial union.

The Society of Graphical and Allied Trades is a recent amalgamation of two unions in the paper and printing group of industries. Both of them organise unskilled, semi-skilled and process workers in various parts of the group, and also clerical, supervisory and administrative staffs. One of them also brought with them a group of apprenticed craftsmen, the skilled bookbinders. Most of the apprenticed craftsmen in the printing industry are, however, in unions of their own, the largest being the National Graphical Association (107,000), another recent amalgamation, whose main section of members is the compositors.

Since its formation in 1913 the National Union of Railwaymen has proclaimed itself to be an industrial union for railway workers. The majority of the footplate staff, however, remain with the Associated Society of Locomotive Engineers and Firemen (32,000) and the majority of clerical, administrative, supervisory and technical staff are members of the Transport Salaried Staffs Association (70,000). Besides these important limitations to their claim to the status of an industrial union within the railway industry, the Railwaymen followed the former railway companies in a number of ventures outside the railways themselves, and have remained there. They organise most of the semi-skilled and unskilled workers in the railway workshops which might be regarded as part of the engineering industry, busmen in several bus companies which were once railway-owned, and dockers in railway-owned or formerly railway-owned docks.

This completes a brief survey of the structure of the unions listed in Table I, but four more points must be made to give even a first impression of the structure of British unions.

The first is that, excluding maintenance work, there are in

addition to printing three other important industries with a number of unions organising apprenticed craftsmen: construction, engineering and shipbuilding. In construction, the major unions are the Amalgamated Society of Woodworkers, which also includes a small section of allied process workers, and the Amalgamated Union of Building Trade Workers, which is primarily a bricklayers' union but includes a considerable number of less-skilled building workers in competition with the general unions. In addition, both unions have in membership considerable numbers of "skilled" carpenters and bricklayers who did not in fact serve an apprenticeship. Both of them organise outside construction. The Woodworkers cover carpenters working in engineering, shipbuilding and other industries. The Building Trade Workers include bricklayers who line and re-line steel furnaces and maintenance bricklayers in other industries. The majority of engineering craftsmen are organised by the Engineers and the Electricians but there is almost a score of other unions catering for craftsmen other than fitters, turners and electricians. Many of them also organise in the shipbuilding industry where the largest union is the Amalgamated Society of Boilermakers, Shipwrights, Blacksmiths and Structural Workers. Its largest section of members, however, is the welders, most of whom work in engineering or other industries outside the shipyards.

Secondly, there are a few other unions which can make nearly as good a claim to the title of "industrial" union as the Mineworkers. The most important of these are: the National Union of Agricultural and Allied Workers (115,000), although it competes with the agricultural trade group of the Transport and General Workers; the National Union of Tailors and Garment Workers (111,000); and the National Union of Boot and Shoe Operatives (70,000).

Thirdly, government service requires a paragraph to itself. The Union of Post Office Workers (192,000) and the Post Office Engineering Union (106,000) will cease to be civil service unions when the Post Office becomes a public corporation, and several smaller unions of postal employees will go with them. In the rest of the civil service, manual workers are for the most part covered by the unions which cater for their occupation outside, shipbuilding unions in the dockyards, engineering unions in the ordnance factories, printing unions in the Stationery Office and so on. Among clerical, supervisory, technical, professional and administrative staff, some unions cater for particular grades regardless of department, the largest of which is the Civil and Public Services Association (174,000), and others cater for particular departments like the Ministry of Labour Staff Association (14,000) and the Inland Revenue Staff Federation (47,000). Finally there is the Civil Service Union (28,000) which is almost a "general" union for civil servants.

Fourthly there is the white collar sector of private industry. Here the major unions straddle industrial boundaries. The two well-organised occupations are journalists and draughtsmen. About half of the latter are members of the Draughtsmen and Allied Technicians (76,000), the great majority being employed in engineering. The Association of Scientific, Technical and Managerial Staffs (101,000) also caters for technicians but in addition has a considerable number of foremen and some managers in membership. For non-technical white collar workers there is the Clerical and Administrative Workers' Union (86,000). The clerical and supervisory trade group of the Transport and General Workers has its own title for the sake of employers who do not like their white collar staff to be in the same organisation as their manual workers. By changing this title to the Association of Clerical Supervisory and Technical Staffs it has recently announced its intention of competing across the whole field. In many industries other predominantly manual unions also compete for supervisors, technicians and sometimes for clerical staff.

THE ORIGINS OF BRITISH TRADE UNION STRUCTURE

How did this strange and complex structure come to be? A clue might be found in George Woodcock's dictum that "structure is a function of purpose",[1] which implies that understanding of a union's objectives is necessary to comprehend the forms of organisation which it has adopted. But what are the objectives of trade unions? In this context the Webbs' famous definition of a trade union as "a continuous association of wage-earners for the purpose of maintaining or improving the conditions of their working lives"[2] does not help. This may be the purpose of a trade union, or

[1] Trades Union Congress, *Annual Report*, 1962, p. 298.
[2] *History of Trade Unionism*. 1920, p. 1.

the purpose of workers in joining trade unions, but no special form of organisation follows from it, until the methods by which a particular union seeks to achieve the general objective are known.

Trade unions can do nothing to maintain or improve the conditions of their members unless they can exercise some control over those conditions. Consequently the link between the general purpose and the particular form of organisation might be the method by which a trade union tries to regulate the conditions of its members' working lives. In addition to that, men are interested not only in the consequences of the rules which govern their working lives but also in how those rules are made. They want to have a say in the matter. And trade unions allow workers to share in decisions affecting their working lives so long as the unions can exercise an influence on those decisions. For this reason also it might be the method of regulation which shapes the organisation. The traditional union of apprenticed craftsmen, for example, attempted to dictate the terms on which its members should be employed. This it did by trying to ensure that all apprenticed craftsmen were in the union and that certain jobs were performed only by apprenticed craftsmen. Then, so long as its members refused employment except on the union's terms, its power to regulate was assured.

Most craft unions sought as far as possible to impose standard pay and conditions throughout the trade. Their method of operation was a form of worker regulation as described in the last chapter, and therefore had a good deal in common with work group methods which regulate workshop matters through "custom and practice", and ensure the loyalty of group members by providing them with equal treatment and equal protection. The aim of the traditional craft union could be seen as the fashioning of a single massive work group co-terminous with the trade, its authority dependent on the united action of its members in imposing standard terms on the trade, and its unity supported by the equal treatment and protection they received from the union. This method dictated union structure. All members of the craft must be in the union and semi-skilled workers and labourers must be excluded, although apprentices might be admitted as junior members.

Trades in which the skilled jobs were reached by a series of promotions through subordinate posts could not copy these methods in all respects. Their unions could try to insist on common terms for all skilled men, but success depended on their ability to force the employers to follow the prescribed "promotion ladder", and to make sure that subordinate workers did not reach skilled jobs except by climbing the ladder according to the rules. Accordingly they also tried to make the work group co-extensive with the "craft", but only by organising their semi-skilled subordinates, who outnumbered them, into a subsidiary group.

Few unions completely achieved the ideal. Unions of apprenticed craftsmen might find it politic to admit some members who had not "served their time". Except in localised trades, pay and conditions of employment usually varied from place to place, and in areas in which a union was weak it might have to admit a number of exceptions to its supposedly universal practices. There were also variations in structure. The Engineers and the Boilermakers each found it possible to include several separate crafts within their ranks. Even more important for what it foreshadowed for the future was the structure of the Cardroom Amalgamation in cotton. This included, within a single union, several groups of skilled men with their own controls over entry to their trades, and also the semi-skilled women, who formed the majority of the operatives in the preparatory section of the cotton industry where the union organised, but did not compete for the men's jobs. These arrangements demonstrated that a trade could exercise effective control over the conditions of its members without the support of a union co-terminous with the trade. It could regulate its affairs within a union covering several different trades, or within a union which included groups of workers organised on quite a different basis.

One of the influences at work in these developments was collective bargaining which grew in importance in the second half of the nineteenth century. This substituted joint regulation with employers for unilateral regulation by the union and thus limited the unions to what the employers would agree; but it had the enormous advantage that once a joint rule was agreed the unions could expect the assistance of the employers in its enforcement. Originally collective bargaining applied mainly to changes in pay and normal hours of work, and employers usually wished to operate these changes throughout their plants at an agreed date. Accordingly the several groups of employees in a single plant or industry were under pressure to work together in negotiating with employers, whether or not they came from different trades, and whether they were skilled or not. A group which tried to insist on complete autonomy might find that its pay and conditions were being regulated by the other groups without its consent.

However, before following through the effect of collective bargaining on union structure, there are further consequences of organisation by trade to be mentioned. Although unions of apprenticed craftsmen may never have constituted a majority of British trade unionists they exercised a domination over British industry in the nineteenth century probably greater than that of craft unions in any other country, then or since; and their strength enabled them to bequeath two great legacies to the trade union movement today.

Firstly, because their grip extended to members of their trades almost wherever they could be found, skilled maintenance workers were organised in craft unions right across industrial boundaries, presenting a barrier to comprehensive industrial unionism. Secondly, their concern to preserve the purity of their craft principles meant that they neglected the less skilled workers in their own industries. Even when new techniques enabled these workers to replace craftsmen, it was still left to others to organise them—if they could. Hence there developed labourers' unions.

Labourers' unions became general unions because the beginnings of stable organisation among the less-skilled workers in the craft industries coincided with the development of mass production techniques in a whole range of industries and services. With no principles of organisation to restrict them, the "new unions" of 1889 developed their characteristic alliance of labourers in craft industries with production workers in previously unorganised industries and services, which remains one of the bases of general unionism today. However, after the boom of 1889 was past the new unions remained small and fragile for twenty years, and an altered approach from the craft unions might have brought a new trade union structure. At no point between 1892 and 1910 could the new unions have resisted rationalisation of trade union structure, had anyone seriously proposed it. But in 1911 there began a decade of change and growth in British unions which pushed membership up from 2·5 millions to 8 millions over ten years. Naturally it was in the areas of employment in which they had been weakest in 1910 that the unions grew most rapidly, and these were the areas to which the general unions laid claim. From barely a hundred thousand members in 1910 they rose to 1·5 millions a decade later. By this time there were few industries in which one or more of them had not achieved a sizeable membership.

Paradoxically, it was during this period of growth that the doctrine of industrial unionism was being propagated with great enthusiasm throughout the British trade union movement, mainly by left-wing groups such as the syndicalists and the industrial unionists. Many of them had little use for collective bargaining, and preferred unions to impose their terms on employers. But since they proposed to do this industry by industry, they wanted the union to be co-extensive with industry, not with a particular trade. They foresaw a future in which workers would run their own industries, and industrial unions seemed to be the ideal organisations for that purpose. For many of them the means to take over an industry was a strike of all workers in the industry, and an industrial union appeared to be the best means to organise an industry-wide strike. Many more moderate trade unionists were also convinced of the superiority of industrial unionism, but they saw it as an instrument for collective bargaining; for bargaining was coming to be conducted more and more at industry level, industry by industry.

However, they all misread the signs. Workers did not take over their industries, and collective bargaining flourished despite the complexity of union structure. It proved possible for several unions, in some instances a dozen or more, to co-operate in industry bargaining and on occasion to organise an industry-wide strike. In some respects industry bargaining even confirmed and strengthened existing trade union structure. It involved employers recognising certain unions as the appropriate representatives of of workers in their industries. Inevitably unions were recognised on the basis of their existing membership. Accordingly, after the rapid extension of industry bargaining at the end of the first world war, unions not only happened to be where the upsurge of war and boom had swept them. They also had a right to be there, a right recognised by the appropriate employers' association. One

c

or more general unions were involved in most of the Joint Industrial Councils established at that time, and the new Whitley system of settling pay and conditions in the civil service gave official blessing to the interwoven pattern of class and departmental civil service unions.

When the craft unions at last decided to act, they were too late. In 1926 the Engineers resolved, not for the first time, to open their ranks to all classes of male engineering workers, and this time the decision was effective. Within a few years they were recruiting energetically among less skilled workers in the rapidly growing car industry, followed by other sections of engineering. During the second world war they made women eligible for membership, and recruited vigorously among women munitions workers. One by one, other unions of apprenticed craftsmen followed the same path, including the Electricians, the Vehicle Builders, the Foundry Workers and the Building Trade Workers. Having learned their lesson too late to prevent the growth of the general unions, these craft unions applied it when it was bound to bring a further complication in union structure. But it did not lead, as industrial unionists and syndicalists had hoped, to the destruction of the barriers between the skilled and the less skilled in one united and egalitarian organisation. On the contrary, the unions followed the path pioneered by the Cardroom Amalgamation and retained within themselves groups of craftsmen who imposed their restrictions on jobs and on access to jobs even against the new recruits, while negotiating along with them for changes in rates of pay and hours of work.

Accordingly it was evident that direct worker regulation no longer required organisation by trade. Worker regulation could be left to separate groups within the union and was therefore compatible with almost any form of trade union organisation. Similarly it had become clear that collective bargaining was compatible with almost any form of organisation, and could even serve to sustain apparently irrational structures. Consequently, since neither method determined the form of organisation a union must take, structure was open to the influence of the organisational needs and wishes of groups and individuals within the unions.

In any organisation there is likely to be a good deal of opposition to change, and especially to rationalisation. In a trade union, rationalisation can mean transferring members between branches or merging branches, with consequent loss of commission and status by branch secretaries. It may bring transfers between districts or mergers of districts leading to the abolition of district posts and the disbanding of district committees. Rights of representation at conference, elections to the executive and the chance of success in competing for full-time posts may all be affected. Since the losses are evident and gains hypothetical, organisational interests at the lower levels of trade unionism generally support inertia. However, things may be different at the top. Full-time officers of declining unions may want a merger to protect their offices and pensions. Trade union leaders are respected for the votes at their command, and the quickest route to a larger membership is amalgamation. In addition trade union members can be persuaded to support amalgamation on the grounds that a bigger organisation will protect their interests better, will offer them more secure financial benefits and will provide more adequate services. Consequently the structural history of British trade unions during the present century records long periods of rigidity interspersed with bursts of amalgamation. The first came soon after the first world war, its most notable products being the Transport and General Workers in 1921 and the General and Municipal Workers in 1924. The second began during the nineteen-sixties. There is, however, no particular reason why expansion aimed at more votes, a bigger organisation, financial security and improved services should follow any particular occupational or industrial lines. The Transport and General Workers' Union was originally conceived as a means of rationalising the transport unions, but in the event, and especially after its merger with the Workers' Union in 1929, the transport sections were outnumbered by its manifold interests elsewhere.

With the growth of white collar employment the organisation of white collar employees was already an important issue in the trade union world by the end of the first world war, and it has become steadily more important since then. From the beginning every type of union structure was in use. The Draughtsmen adopted a craft organisation and applied craft methods. For many years the National Association of Local Government Officers (as it then was) organised all white collar employees in a single service. Civil service associations organised mainly by occupation, whether across the service, or department by department. The Clerical and Administrative Workers organised in a range of white collar occupations over a number of industries. The Transport and General Workers organised white collar workers in many occupations and industries in a section of a general workers' union. All these unions flourished as did others with still further structural variations. Consequently the extension of trade unionism among white collar employees did nothing to discipline the variety of trade union organisation. On the contrary, it added to the range of variation.

It seems therefore that the link between purpose and structure is weak. A trade union does not have a single overriding purpose. It aims to serve its members' interests but it also has organisational objectives. It serves its members' interests by regulating industrial relations, but structures have been adapted only slowly to changing methods of regulation, and it is now evident that the various methods of regulation can be used effectively by unions with very different structures. Different groups within a union may have differing interests and different organisational objectives. Consequently unions are liable to a variety of pressures pushing them towards different structural forms, and it is not surprising that British unions, with aims and methods changing over the years, have produced a bewildering variety of structure.

However, it also appears that today, in contrast to earlier periods, one form of organisation can serve a union's needs almost as well as another. If so it would appear that unions might be moulded into a simpler structural pattern by a powerful central authority. The Trades Union Congress is not as powerful as some central federations overseas, but it has some authority in this field. Its Disputes Committee, set up after the reorganisation of 1921, hears complaints from one union against another, usually arising out of the "poaching" of members, or the pursuit of negotiating rights in another union's territory. The committee acts first as a mediator, and then, if no agreement emerges, issues an award. Over the years its decisions have established a body of case-law, codified in the "Bridlington" principles of 1939, which suggest that no union should accept a member of another union without inquiry, and that except by agreement no union should start organising activities in an establishment in which another union has a majority of the workers in membership and negotiates for them. This second limitation applies also where a union is trying to organise "in face of exceptional difficulties" and has not succeeded in winning over a majority, and even if it once had a majority but has lost it.[1]

Generally speaking these principles prevent new unions breaking in to add to the complexity of trade union structure. They do not, however, prevent unions which have a foothold from expanding at the expense of other unions. The most dramatic evidence of this was the rise of the National Union of Public Employees from 10,000 members in 1933 to a quarter of a million today, the majority of them among the manual employees of local authority non-trading service where the General and Municipal Workers once held a comfortable majority. Equally they did not prevent craft unions opening their ranks to less-skilled workers. Most important of all, however, the Bridlington principles only try to "set agreed limits to inter-union competition. . . . They do not stretch to any positive powers to pursue rationalisation."[2]

Congress has from time to time debated the rationalisation of trade union structure, and the General Council has prepared several reports on the subject. All of them have been cautious documents. Reviewing them in 1963 the Council noted that "at the end" they had "always contented themselves with giving general approval to all efforts to achieve greater unity and with offering the General Council's help to reach amalgamation or arrangements for closer unity in particular cases", and went on to "consider how best to stimulate and to guide the process of piecemeal and *ad hoc* developments by which changes in the structure of unions have come about in the past".[3]

Some central trade union bodies abroad face structural complications which have no parallel in Britain. In France, for instance, and in some other countries, there are separate unions for Communists and their allies, for Catholics and for those who reject both creeds. But, all in all, there is no other trade union movement with so complex a structure as that of the British movement. There is no other country with craft traditions as

[1] The development of these principles is described in Shirley W. Lerner, *Breakaway Unions and the Small Trade Union*, 1961, Chapter 2.

[2] John Hughes, *Trade Union Structure and Government*, Royal Commission Research Paper No. 5, Part I, p. 29.

[3] Trades Union Congress, *Annual Report*, 1963, pp. 163–4.

strong as they are in Britain. Several other countries, including Australia and Denmark, have a large general union, but only Britain has two of them. Some of the reasons for the contrast between Britain and other countries are clear. West Germany has the most streamlined union structure of all with its sixteen great industrial unions, but this is the result of the completely new start in German trade unionism after the second world war. Sweden and Norway both possess structures which are more simple than Britain's, but their central trade union federations have greater authority than does the Trades Union Congress and have used it to press for rationalisation. With the longest history of continuous development Britain has not had the opportunities for wholesale reconstruction which wars and revolutions have created in some other countries. Moreover, because it has not acquired authority to reconstruct existing unions, the national centre has not been in a position to direct the course of new developments. In 1943 the General Council of the Trades Union Congress was called in to assist the unions organising at the Ford works in Dagenham to secure recognition. The Council agreed and succeeded, but the recognition which they secured had to be for the eleven unions then claiming membership.[1] The number has now risen to about twenty. Similarly the General Council has been in no position to control the rapid post-war development of white collar unions in private manufacturing industry, which has given white collar trade unionists a union structure almost as complicated as that of manual workers.

THE DISTRIBUTION OF TRADE UNION MEMBERSHIP

Table II, which sets out the distribution of trade union membership by industrial groups, does not reveal much about the relative effectiveness of different types of unions. The highest degree of organisation is found in an industrial union, the Mineworkers, but another industrial union, the Tailors and Garment Workers, comes near the bottom. The second industrial group in terms of organisation, national government service, is covered by a bewildering variety of separate unions, whereas the distributive trades, near the bottom of the list, have only one union, the Shop,

[1] Trades Union Congress, *Annual Report*, 1944, pp. 35–7.

TABLE II

DISTRIBUTION OF BRITISH TRADE UNION MEMBERS BY
INDUSTRIAL GROUP, END 1964[1]

Industrial Group	Employees	Trade Union Membership (thousands)	Proportion of Employees in Trade Unions (per cent)
Coalmining	596	576	95
National Government Service	550	480	87
Local Government Service	776	632	82
Gas, Electricity and Water	413	335	81
Transport and Communications (excluding railways)	1312	1000	76
Railways	396	289	73
Footwear	116	73	63
Paper, printing and publishing	632	375	59
Metal manufacture, engineering and electrical goods, shipbuilding and marine engineering, vehicles and metal goods not elsewhere specified	4537	2513	55
Cotton, flax and man-made fibres	276 }		
All other textiles	564 }	350	42
Educational services	1094	453	41
Cinema, theatre, radio, sport, betting etc.	251	103	41
Timber, furniture etc.	296	111	37
Bricks, pottery, glass, cement etc.	359	132	37
Chemicals and allied industries	515	186	36

[1] Royal Commission, *Selected Written Evidence*, p. 23. The figures of trade union membership are the result of a special inquiry carried out by the Ministry of Labour into the industrial distribution of the membership of all unions with more than 25,000 members. The information was of limited statistical accuracy, especially concerning union numbers employed on maintenance work in industries other than those in which the workers in the occupation concerned were normally employed; and it proved impossible to break down the Metals etc. group of industries. Retired members have been excluded so that the figures for some industries, and the overall total, are smaller than those normally used. Numbers of employees (employed and unemployed) in each group are given as at June 1964.

TABLE II (*contd.*)

Industrial Group	Employees	Trade Union Membership (*thousands*)	Proportion of Employees in Trade Unions (*per cent*)
Insurance, banking and finance	637	224	35
Other mining and quarrying	70	24	34
Agriculture, forestry and fishing	551	167	30
Leather, leather goods and fur	64	19	30
Construction	1708	476	28
Clothing other than footwear	453	123	27
Food, drink and tobacco	842	227	27
Professional and technical services not elsewhere specified	1268	341	27
Other manufacturing industries	326	86	26
Distributive trades	3026	386	12
Catering and hotels	633		
Motor repairs etc.	423		
Private domestic service	237	62	3
All other miscellaneous services	686		
Ex-service personnel not classified	2		
Total	23616	9743	41

Distributive and Allied Workers. One industrial group in which craft unions still figure strongly, paper and printing, comes fairly near the top of the list, whereas another, construction, comes surprisingly near the bottom. The two general unions are the most important unions in the fourth and fifth groups on the list —gas, electricity and water, and transport and communications (excluding railways)—but they are equally important in the food, drink and tobacco group near the bottom of the table.

Type of trade union is not the only factor likely to affect the degree of organisation. Occupation is also important, but Table II does not reveal much about the relative strength of trade unionism among skilled and less-skilled male manual workers. Elsewhere, however, there is a good deal of scattered evidence to show that in engineering such highly skilled groups as patternmakers, tool-room fitters and electricians are more fully organised than other groups; that generally in manufacturing industry skilled main-tenance workers are more highly organised than production workers and labourers; and that in the badly organised con-struction industry skilled workers are comparatively well or-ganised.

It is possible to make more accurate comparisons between manual workers of all grades and white collar employees. Table II contains several predominantly white collar groups. One, national government service, comes second only to coalmining in degree of organisation; two others, educational services and the cinema, theatre, radio, sports etc. group, are in the top half of the table; and several come near the bottom. Further informa-tion is provided by G. S. Bain's detailed studies of white collar trade unionism. He shows that in 1964 just over half of Britain's manual workers were trade unionists, whereas the proportion among white collar workers was 29 per cent. But there is a sharp contrast between public employment and private manufacturing industry. "The vast majority of white collar union membership is concentrated in the public sector of the economy. While roughly eight out of ten white collar employees in public em-ployment belong to a trade union, only one out of ten are union members in private manufacturing employment."[1]

Women are not so well organised as men. About half of male employees in Britain are in unions, but rather less than one female employee in four.[2] This helps to explain the poor per-formance of distribution, catering and domestic service, all of which are predominantly women's industries. But this is not the only influence at work, for small-scale units predominate in all three industries, and organisation generally increases with the size of the undertaking.

[1] G. S. Bain, *Trade Union Growth and Recognition*, Royal Commission Research Paper No. 6, pp. 19, 29.

[2] The sex contrast is greater among manual workers than among white collar em-ployees. Just over 60 per cent of male manual workers are trade unionists, compared with 28 per cent among women manual workers. Among white collar employees the figures are 35 per cent for men and 23 per cent for women. (*Ibid.*, p. 19.)

The extent of the closed shop might be expected to be one of the most important factors determining the degree of organisation. Among the industries which McCarthy describes as "comprehensively closed", coalmining heads the list and comes at the top of Table II. Next comes printing whose high degree of unionisation is disguised in the table by inclusion in the paper and printing group. However, the closed shop has less effect on industrial distribution than might be supposed. Although McCarthy regards workers in the engineering industry as constituting a "mainly closed trade", and process workers and skilled maintenance workers in steel as a "comprehensively closed" group,[1] the metals group scores no more than moderately well in Table II. This must be due in part to lack of organisation among white collar workers. Moreover, McCarthy draws attention to several industries which have achieved a high degree of organisation without the aid of the closed shop. They include national government service, white collar employees of local authorities, footplate and white collar employees on the railways, electricity supply and footwear.[2] Five of these industries figure among the seven groups at the top of Table II.

For an industry with a very large number of small scattered units, agriculture is reasonably well organised. The National Union of Agricultural Workers argues that its performance is even better than the figures suggest since an important part of the labour force consists of members of farmers' families who are not potential union members. Their achievement may be contrasted with that of the Shop, Distributive and Allied Workers with their secure basis in the closed co-operative societies and an extremely low proportion of distributive workers organised outside. The Agricultural Workers could not survive without effective organisation on a voluntary basis. The Shop, Distributive and Allied Workers can. This contrast might be taken to suggest that in some circumstances the closed shop can inhibit the drive to expand.

Perhaps the most important factor in explaining the distribution of trade union membership among white collar workers is recognition by employers. Having reviewed other explanations of the relative strength of white collar trade unionism in different industries and services, G. S. Bain emphasises the extent to which

[1] *The Closed Shop in Britain*, pp. 30-1.   [2] *Ibid.*, p. 161.

employers resist the demand for recognition and pursue policies designed to discourage or prohibit their staff employees from joining unions;[1] he also develops a powerful case for the view that the crucial factor in securing recognition among white collar workers has not been the industrial strength of the unions, but government policy, especially in war-time;[2] and he suggests that recognition may now be the key also among groups of manual workers who are still not well organised. He divides the labour force into groups where there is no problem over recognition, those where there is general reluctance to recognise, those in which recognition is a problem in some instances and those in which it would be a problem if the unions tried to organise. The list of areas with no problems includes national and local government; nearly all nationalised industries and public services; manual workers in manufacturing firms with over 25 employees; and white collar workers in a minority of manufacturing industries. Areas with a problem are: catering and similar services; manual workers in small manufacturing firms; distribution; insurance, banking and finance; and white collar workers in most manufacturing industries. Among the areas in which there would be a problem if the unions tried to organise are: other professional and scientific services; the remaining areas of white collar employment in private manufacturing industry; and a further group of services including motor repair and private domestic service. Construction and agriculture are listed as having a "partial" recognition problem.[3]

What does this account of trade union distribution foreshadow for the future? Although total trade union membership in Britain is now, at 10,065,000, almost as high as it has ever been, growth has been insufficient to keep pace with the size of the labour force since 1948. In 1948 between 43 and 44 per cent[4] of the labour force were in trade unions. By 1964 the figure had fallen to 41 per cent. The best way to explain this decline, and to make projections into the future, would be to work out the trends in trade union organisation in each industry, and the trends in employment in each industry. Unfortunately the Ministry of Labour has no figures for other years to parallel those in Table II.

---

[1] *Trade Union Growth and Recognition*, p. 98. [2] *Ibid.*, Chapter IV. [3] *Ibid.*, p. 73.
[4] The official figure was 45·1 per cent, but this includes retired members in total trade union membership.

There are, however, two earlier estimates of trade union membership by industry based on less comprehensive inquiries.[1] They suggest that between 1948 and 1960 there was growth in the proportion of workers organised mainly in declining industries, coalmining, national government and agriculture, or in relatively slow-growing industries such as local government, and that trade unions were losing ground in some of the most rapidly growing industries such as education and professional and business services. If these trends continue, trade unionism will decline. Equally important for the future is the growth in white collar employment at the expense of manual employment in manufacturing industry, where manual workers are far better organised than white collar workers.

The trends are therefore against the trade unions. It would, however, be wrong to give this too much emphasis. The very heavy losses in membership in some of the former strongholds of trade unionism has been largely set off by growth elsewhere. Over the last few years most of Britain's major unions have been growing vigorously, as Table III reveals. Some of this growth is due to the absorption of smaller unions, but most of it is net growth. Membership of white collar unions in private manufacturing has more than kept pace with the very rapid increase in white collar employment, growing by 77 per cent from 1948 to 1964 while employment rose by 58 per cent.[2]

A modest increase in the rate of growth in a few industrial and occupational groups would be sufficient to avoid a further decline in the proportion of workers organised in Britain.

Is there any prospect of such an increase? Trade union strength varies widely from country to country. The British position compares with a trade union density of less than one-third in the United States and probably less than a quarter in France, but comes far behind Australia and Sweden, both of them with about two-thirds of their employees in trade unions.[3] This suggests that it would not be impossible for British unions to attain a much higher degree of organisation.

Trade unions might attract more members by offering better

[1] Keith Hindell, *Trade Union Membership, Planning,* July 1962, and Guy Routh "Future Trade Union Membership," in *Industrial Relations, Contemporary Problems and Perspectives,* ed. B. C. Roberts, 1962.

[2] *Trade Union Growth and Recognition,* p. 26.

[3] A. M. Ross and P. T. Hartman, *Changing Patterns of Industrial Conflict,* 1960, p. 203.

services. They might find means of developing trade union attitudes of mind among groups of workers who at present have no wish to join. They might recruit more vigorously in some

TABLE III

CHANGES IN MEMBERSHIP IN MAJOR UNIONS 1959–68

Trade Union	Membership end 1959 (thousands)	Membership end 1968 (thousands)	Change (per cent)
Electrical Electronic Tele-CommunicationUnion/Plumbing Trades Union	234	365	+56
National Union of Public Employees	200	283	+42
National and Local Government Officers Association	274	373	+36
National Union of Teachers	225	287	+28
Amalgamated Union of Engineering and Foundry Workers	908	1136	+26
Society of Graphical and Allied Trades	193	229	+19
Transport and General Workers' Union	1241	1476	+19
General and Municipal Workers' Union	769	798	+ 4
Union of Shop, Distributive and Allied Workers	352	311	– 12
National Union of Railwaymen	334	199	– 40
National Union of Mineworkers	639	344	– 46

areas where they appear to make little effort, and where their present structure offers no great spur to effort. Above all, however, a higher degree of trade union organisation could be encouraged by union recognition from employers who at present refuse recognition and discourage unionisation among some or all classes of their employees; and this in turn is most likely to happen if the government applies pressure upon employers.

If recognition by employers can be such a powerful influence upon union growth, then it must also be capable of influencing union structure by channelling the growth of a particular union into the plants and industries where it is recognised. In dealing with manual unions in the past employers have usually granted recognition only to unions strong enough to insist upon it, and the acceptance of a *fait accompli* of this kind has not given them much influence over structure, since that has already been established. Even in dealing with white collar unions many employers have insisted upon proof of substantial membership, thus ensuring the structure will be settled before recognition. But employers could, if they chose, exercise a good deal more influence over union structure in industries and services where membership is at present weak and recognition has not yet been granted. To take an extreme example, if the Confederation of British Industry was able and willing to enter into general discussions with the unions, through the Trades Union Congress, about which unions employers would recognise to represent classes of employees at present unorganised in each industry or company, and agreement was reached, the agreement could determine union structure for those employees. Trade unions would gain in membership, and employers would have some assurance of a union structure which suited them.

THE INDUSTRIAL CONSEQUENCES OF UNION STRUCTURE

In recent years British trade union structure has been criticised as a hindrance to the efficient conduct of industry in at least four ways. Firstly, strikes can be caused by disputes between unions which might not have arisen under a different structure. These disputes are of two kinds: demarcation disputes in which two unions differ as to whose members should have the right to perform a given task, or group of tasks; and jurisdictional disputes in which two unions differ as to which of them should organise a given worker, or group of workers. Secondly, whether or not differences between unions caused demarcation and jurisdictional disputes, they can constitute an important background factor in disputes over pay or other issues because one union is anxious to score off another, whereas if only one union were concerned in negotiations in each industry, jealousy could not arise. Thirdly, plant relations are complicated where several unions organise in a single plant. Fourthly, efficient operation can be impeded by union structure where work has to be allocated according to demarcation lines between unions, and not according to the needs of the job. Most British industries can provide instances of one or more of these obstacles to efficiency arising out of union structure. The steel industry is one of those that offers examples of all four of them.

In 1966 there was a strike at a steelworks in Corby over a demarcation issue. The work in dispute was the machining of what are called "hollows". The Engineers claimed that machining was engineers' work and should be performed by their members. The British Iron, Steel and Kindred Trades' Association argued that custom and practice at Corby restricted the Engineers to maintenance work, whereas production work fell within their province; and since the machining of "hollows" was production work, not maintenance, their members should man the machines. As is often the case in disputes of this kind, the company had exacerbated the problem in its attempt to find a solution. At a meeting with the Engineers in the previous year, the company had undertaken to try to reach a new agreement which would share the work between the two unions. The Court of Inquiry set up to investigate the dispute held that this arrangement would have perpetuated friction and that since the work was not maintenance, the machines should be manned by members of the steel union.[1]

During the following year there developed a jurisdictional dispute which involved the whole steel industry. The British Iron, Steel and Kindred Trades' Association is not only the main union for production workers in steel, but also the major union for white collar workers. However, the Clerical and Administrative Workers has had members among white collar employees in the industry at least as long as the steel union and the Association of Scientific, Technical and Managerial Staffs has also organised among them for some years. During the preparations for the second nationalisation of the industry in the course of 1967 the British Steel Corporation decided that recognition should be limited to the unions which were already accepted as representing manual workers. In addition to the steel union, this included the Blastfurnacemen, two general unions and the several unions

---

[1] *Report of a Court of Inquiry into the causes and circumstances of a dispute at Stewart and Lloyds Limited at Corby*, Cmnd. 3260, 1967.

organising maintenance craftsmen. The decision was mainly to the benefit of the steel union, but the Transport and General Workers' white collar section has members in the industry and the craft unions are anxious to retain those of their members who are promoted to supervisory posts. In addition the Draughtsmen benefited from the decision since they were affiliated to the Craftsmen's Co-ordinating Committee. The two unions which suffered were the Clerical and Administrative Workers and the Scientific, Technical and Managerial Staffs.

These two unions objected to the decision, and drew attention to their opinions in the summer of 1968 by a strike at a car plant which was an important customer of the steel industry. The strike was called off when the Department of Employment and Productivity appointed a court of inquiry. The court concluded that these two unions had strong grounds for being included in the national negotiating machinery for white collar employees, so long as the steel union's predominant position was recognised in the distribution of places on the union side of the machinery.[1]

Rather reluctantly the Corporation accepted the decision to the extent of agreeing to grant local recognition to the two unions, a decision which was generally held to imply subsequent inclusion in the national machinery. At this stage the steel union, supported by the other unions already recognised, prepared to direct its members not to accept instructions from supervisors who were members of the two unions. The General Council of the Trades Union Congress persuaded them to postpone the date at which the direction was to operate, but finally decided that recognition should not be extended to the two white collar unions.[2] Early in 1969 the Corporation decided to allow the two white collar unions to retain local recognition where they already had it, and to grant them additional local recognition where the nationally recognised unions were not locally recognised for white collar employees and where the two unions could prove they had a

[1] *Report of a Court of Inquiry under Lord Pearson into the Disputes between the British Steel Corporation and Certain of their Employees*, Cmnd. 3754, 1968.

[2] The Council was in some difficulty in dealing with the issue, which had been before them for some time. They had set up a Steel Industry Trade Union Consultative Committee to handle problems arising out of steel nationalisation. This committee was a firm supporter of the claims of the unions already recognised by the Corporation to retain exclusive recognition. The Council's Organisation Committee, however, showed itself a good deal more sympathetic towards the two excluded unions. (Trades Union Congress, *Annual Report*, 1968, pp. 396–403.)

majority in the relevant grades. But few supposed this could be a final solution.

This instance may appear to contradict the conclusion of the previous section that employers can exercise considerable influence over the representation and organisation of white collar employees. The Corporation recognised some unions, and then found itself under pressure to extend recognition to others. But employers cannot expect their decision on recognition to be effective regardless of the character of the union which they select. Between the two world wars the steel union had a close arrangement with the Clerical and Administrative Workers. But its leaders then realised "that the employers were more prepared to recognise it for staff workers than the C.A.W.U.",[1] presumably because of the cordial relations which had developed between the employers and the steel union. The union therefore terminated its agreement with the Clerical and Administrative Workers. Subsequently, in 1943, the Iron and Steel Trades Employers' Association decided that only unions already established in the industry were to be recognised as representatives of white collar employees, and made an agreement with the steel union on procedural arrangements for clerical staff, laboratory staff and foremen which were to apply where employers chose to recognise it. The agreements "provided a shield behind which an employer could take refuge if approached for recognition for staff grades by an 'outside' union",[2] without being forced to recognise one of the "inside" unions as their representative. The excluded unions took the view that the agreements also acted as a shield for the steel union, which was protected against competition and therefore did not need to exert itself too much over the problems and grievances of white collar employees in steel. Their success in recruitment provides some support for their accusation.[3] The influence which employers can exercise over union organisation may therefore be

---

[1] *Trade Union Growth and Recognition*, p. 52.   [2] *Ibid.*, p. 54.

[3] An irony of the situation in 1967–8 was the position of the general secretary of the British Iron, Steel and Kindred Trades Association, Dai Davies. As assistant general secretary he had for years argued that the union should pay more attention to the problems of white collar members, who must be expected to form a growing section of the union. At that time his arguments had achieved little. When he succeeded to the general secretaryship it seemed that he would be in a position to act on his views, but the conflicts arising out of nationalisation were upon him before he had a chance to convince white collar employees in steel that the union's policies had changed. In 1969 his union appointed a separate full-time officer to handle the problems of the white collar branches.

described in this way: by granting recognition where employees are ill-organised the employer can exercise considerable influence over their initial choice of trade union. However, he cannot be confident that this will settle the problem of recognition for the future unless the selected union or unions show competence and drive in protecting the interests of their new members.

In steel as in other industries the most important cause of strikes is neither demarcation nor jurisdiction, but pay. There was a national strike of maintenance workers in the summer of 1956, and a prolonged strike of maintenance craftsmen at Port Talbot from December 1963 to February 1964 cost the country more working days than any other strike between 1962 and 1966. The most consistent grievance of the craft unions has been the higher levels of pay which some groups of production workers are able to attain. This is a direct consequence of the industry's pay structure, but it has been magnified by the effects of technological change since mechanisation and automation have increased the numbers of maintenance workers and the importance of their jobs. But the problem might have been easier to handle if the maintenance workers had not been in different unions from the production workers, with separate negotiating machinery.

During the post-war years an increasing proportion of the pay of steel employees has been settled in the plant, and the divisions between the unions and the negotiating arrangements has complicated plant pay negotiations. But they have also aggravated other plant problems. J. E. T. Eldridge has described the redundancy negotiations at the Consett Iron Company in 1961, where there was a difference as to whether the principle of "last in first out" should be applied throughout the plant or on a departmental basis. The conflict on this issue between different branches of the steel union was resolved within the union, but the difference between the Blastfurnacemen and the other unions could not be settled within the plant and had to go to arbitration.[1]

Finally, where demarcation lines between jobs are also the boundaries between unions, multi-unionism may be linked with inefficient use of manpower. The Steel Company of Wales informed the Royal Commission that the productivity agreement they were then negotiating would "enable fewer total manhours

[1] *Industrial Disputes*, 1968, Chapter 6.

to be expended on maintenance. This will mean in the short term that the existing direct labour force can take over work now done by contractors, and in the longer term that the total direct labour maintenance force will reduce in numbers." However, the groups of craftsmen between which the company hoped to arrange flexible working belonged to different unions, and their negotiators were finding difficulty in securing the agreement of the unions, especially of the Engineers and Boilermakers.[1] Subsequently the Blastfurnacemen became the main stumbling-block.[2]

REMEDIES AND PALLIATIVES

If the effects of existing trade union structure can be so damaging, it is not surprising that a good deal of effort has been spent on attempts at reconstruction. Many reformers have tried to achieve their aim by amalgamation. The legal requirements for amalgamation, originally laid down in 1876, have twice been rendered less restrictive by Acts of 1917 and 1964. In addition trade unions have found ingenious ways round organisational obstacles to mergers. In several instances in recent years two unions have united as two separate sections, so that all existing offices and interests are protected, leaving rationalisation for the future. In more than one instance the amalgamated union has begun life with two general secretaries. And there have been many amalgamations. The total number of British unions has fallen from 1323 in 1900 to 534 in 1968, mainly through amalgamation. The outcome, however, has not been a great simplification of union structure. Instead amalgamation has helped to produce the several major unions which straddle industrial boundaries and render a wholesale reconstruction of British trade unionism virtually impossible. The Transport and General Workers, the Engineering and Foundry Workers, the General and Municipal Workers, the Electrical Electronic Telecommunication Union/Plumbing Trade Union and the Shop, Distributive and Allied Workers are all products of amalgamation.

This does not mean that amalgamation has accomplished no

[1] *Productivity Bargaining and Restrictive Labour Practices*, Royal Commission Research Paper No. 4, p. 15.
[2] *Report of a Court of Inquiry under Professor D. J. Robertson into a dispute at the Port Talbot Works of the British Steel Corporation*, Cmnd. 4147, 1969.

rationalisation, nor that amalgamation could not achieve more rationalisation in the future. The formation of the Society of Graphical and Allied Trades, for instance, represented an important simplification of trade union organisation in the paper and printing industries, or will do so when the consequences of amalgamation are fully absorbed. So did the merger of the compositors' unions, the London Typographical Society and the Typographical Association in the provinces. It is not difficult to imagine the resulting craft union, the National Graphical Association, absorbing some of the minor craft unions, or perhaps all of them. Thereafter an amalgamation between the new craft union and the Society of Graphical Trades is not impossible. Successive public inquiries have advocated action on these lines.[1] If it was achieved the paper and printing group would have something close to an industrial union.

What it does mean, however, is that similar opportunities are not available in many other industries. The craft unions, or predominantly craft unions, in the building industry could merge into a smaller number of unions or even into one union, but the outcome would not be a tidy organisation. It would be a body with considerable blocks of members in steel, shipbuilding and various sections of engineering, and small sections scattered over a number of other industries. Even then it would exclude the majority of less-skilled workers in construction, most of whom belong to the Transport and General Workers or to the General and Municipal Workers, if they belong to a union at all. A merger of unions in engineering would bring the majority of British trade union members into a single union with some members in every industry.

It also means that amalgamation in Britain can lead to further complications as readily as to simplification. The recent merger of the Electricians and the Plumbers has produced a single union straddling more industrial boundaries than did either of them separately. Similarly the Association of Scientific, Technical and Managerial Staffs covers a bigger range of industries than did either of its constituent unions.

The example of engineering suggests that it is possible to envisage

[1] The National Board of Prices and Incomes, *Wages, Costs and Prices in the Printing Industry*, Report No. 2, Cmnd 2750, 1965; *Report of a Court of Inquiry into the problems caused by the introduction of web-offset machines into the printing industry*, Cmnd. 3184, 1967.

an amalgamation on so great a scale that the new union would include the majority of trade union members in many industries. Internal reconstruction on the lines of the existing structure of the Transport and General Workers could then produce separate trade groups for each industry with their own officers and elected committees exercising considerable autonomy over their own affairs. H. A. Turner has suggested that discussions between the Engineers, the Transport and General Workers and the General and Municipal Workers could ultimately lead to such an amalgamation. It would "unchallengeably provide that massive single influence at all levels of British trade unionism's operation that its present context requires" and "would give an enormous stimulus to the regrouping of trade unions in general".[1] Supposing such a merger were attainable, many of these advantages would follow; but not all. Apart from the clerical and supervisory section of the Transport and General Workers the three unions have little strength in the white collar field, which is the most rapidly expanding area of employment.

If the imagination can travel so far, it can also extend to a scheme in which all unions affiliated to the Trades Union Congress should grant the General Council a free hand to reconstruct the whole movement, dismembering most of our major trade unions to produce new independent unions industry by industry. This would, of course, entail these unions voting for their own dismemberment. In dealing with the future one can only assess probabilities. An amalgamation of our three largest unions is more probable than complete reconstruction through the Trades Union Congress. But neither is likely, and realistic proposals for reform must be more modest.

Where they fail to amalgamate or where amalgamations do not put an end to multi-unionism, unions usually find some means of co-operation. In many instances this is achieved by the "workers' side" of a Joint Industrial Council. When Joint Industrial Councils were first set up the unions agreed among themselves on the allocation of seats, roughly according to membership. The representatives then chosen formed the habit of meeting together before full sessions of the Council in order to decide their line of action. They chose a chairman and secretary

[1] H. A. Turner, "British Trade Union Structure: A New Approach?" *British Journal of Industrial Relations*, July 1964.

from among their own number. Gradually precedents were built up to distinguish the kind of issues which could be decided by the workers' side, and those which had to be referred to the executives of the constituent unions. Where subordinate regional joint councils were established the same procedure was followed and the regional secretaries maintained contact with the national secretary. In the civil service each department has its own Whitley Council, but there is also a National Whitley Council to deal with issues common to the whole service, and its "staff side" has a full-time secretary with an office and staff.

In some industries working arrangements between unions have been formalised by means of federations, many of them ante-dating the Joint Industrial Councils. One or two famous federations have been superseded by amalgamations, as the National Transport Workers' Federation was superseded by the Transport and General Workers' Union, but there are still forty-five in existence.[1] The three most important are the Confederation of Shipbuilding and Engineering Unions, the National Federation of Building Trades Operatives and the Printing and Kindred Trades Federation.

One of the differences between them and workers' sides is that they can handle negotiations in several industries. Constititionally they are distinguished from most workers' sides by providing for a regular annual conference of delegations from the unions to discuss policy; by formal rules for deciding on such matters as calling strikes affecting more than one of their members; and by having their own headquarters, officers and staff. The most important constitutional issue which any of them have had to settle is the position of the Engineers in the Confederation of Shipbuilding and Engineering Unions. By far the largest union in the engineering industry, the Engineers could not allow themselves to be overborne by the others, and these in turn could not agree to domination by the Engineers. This issue was never resolved by the Confederation's predecessor, the Federation of Engineering and Shipbuilding Trades,[2] but in 1948 an arrangement was made with the Confederation whereby the Engineers obtained the largest single share of votes at the conference and on committees, but not an absolute majority. In addition the Engineers' president acts as spokesman for the Confederation in

[1] *Employment and Productivity Gazette*, November 1968.   [2] Founded in 1890.

negotiations with the engineering employers. Thus the Engineers could not dominate the Confederation by themselves, but they did not need to win much support outside their own ranks to have their way.

There is nothing to prevent a workers' side conducting a strike. This has been done for example in docks and in the bus industry, although both of these are so dominated by the Transport and General Workers that the decision of its executive settled the matter. In 1964 the workers' side of the Joint Industrial Council for the electricity supply industry, which is not controlled by any single union, conducted a national ban on overtime. But in an industry in which the strike is likely to be used, a federation with formal rules can perhaps inspire more confidence. This is not so much a matter of the rules themselves. When the Confederation called national shipbuilding and engineering strikes in 1957 they found their rules for conducting a strike ballot were unusable.[1] It is rather that a federation implies a greater commitment on the part of the constituent unions than does a workers' side.

This greater commitment is probably the main asset which the three federations bring to their staple business—the conduct of industry-wide collective bargaining. The results which they achieve are not necessarily better than those of many workers' sides, but they are achieved in more difficult circumstances, and in the face of traditional feuds and demarcation problems. The Confederation has to co-ordinate nearly thirty unions.

In contrast to the Confederation, the National Federation of Building Trades Operatives has clear powers to deal with inter-union disputes, and in 1964 the building unions strengthened its constitution further by providing for quarterly meetings of a central council consisting of the executives of the affiliated unions to take binding decisions and to issue instructions to the federation's executive without further reference to the individual unions.

[1] There are two rules on stoppages. One (Rule VI, paragraph 3) prescribes "a ballot vote of affiliated membership," and the other (Rule VII, paragraph 3) refers to "a decision . . . taken in accordance with the rules governing the societies affiliated to the Confederation." Neither procedure was used, partly because of the delay which would have been involved in taking ballots, and partly because the leaders did not want to run the risk of one union returning an adverse decision. Consequently the union executives took upon themselves the responsibility of calling the strike, whether their rules empowered them to do so or not. (H. A. Clegg and Rex Adams, *The Employers' Challenge*, 1957, pp. 98–102.)

The main criticism of the federations is that they have done little to overcome the difficulties caused by the complex structure of British trade unionism in the plant. In the printing industry it is still the general rule for each union's chapel to go its own way with little regard to the others. The district committees of the Confederation have not brought order into plant relations in the engineering industry. A system of "Confederation stewards" was intended to co-ordinate the stewards of separate unions, but the employers have not recognised it, and it has made no impact. Such arrangements as exist for joint action between stewards in engineering firms with several factories are "unofficial" and unrecognised by the unions and the Confederation.

The Federation of Building Trade Operatives makes a bolder attempt to operate on the local level. It has its own full-time regional officers, federal branches and federal stewards to co-ordinate work on building sites. To assist recruiting there is a "composite section" of the Federation which recruits members in areas which cannot sustain separate branches of the individual unions. For all that, however, the Federation has been unable to help the unions to make any real headway in dealing with their three greatest problems: weak and declining membership in an expanding industry, labour-only sub-contracting, and lack of control over industrial relations on the site.

The remaining device for overcoming the consequences of Britain's complex trade union structure is the "working arrangement" between two or more unions, encouraged by the Trades Union Congress in the preamble to the Bridlington principles. These recommend agreements dealing with spheres of influence, with the recognition of the membership cards of other unions and with the conditions of transfers from one union to another. Working arrangements constitute "a large and important hinterland of multilateral and bilateral union agreements" which is "largely unmapped territory; the agreements are not widely known, publicly available, and freely discussed as are collective bargaining agreements. Their progress is not reported and widely circulated as is much federal activity." Yet they "are of the greatest importance for analysis of trade union structure and its problems".[1] In the past these agreements, along with countless informal understandings between local union officers, have helped

---

[1] *Trade Union Structure and Government*, Part I, p. 30.

to avoid and minimise conflict between unions. The most important of all is the agreement between the Transport and General Workers and the General and Municipal Workers which provides for the transfer of members without loss of their accumulated rights. In 1964 the same two unions set up a joint committee of senior officers to review spheres of influence in the hope that they could eliminate overlapping, where necessary by exchanging members. In some industries in which both have members the two unions had already arranged that only one of them should recruit in each plant, but they hoped to make more arrangements of this kind, and to explore the possibility of extending them to cover companies or even whole industries. One topic which has been discussed, for example, is the possibility of leaving municipal passenger transport entirely to the Transport and General Workers in return for their withdrawal from the gas industry in favour of the General and Municipal Workers.

The scale of potential rationalisation was increased in 1965, when it was announced that the two unions were to open discussions with the Engineers. These talks were to explore the possibility of a co-ordination of services such as research, education "mechanised and computerised office methods" and legal aid; "to discuss the differing rules, constitutions, contributions and benefits which may form obstacles to closer unity"; and to seek to remove friction which might "create membership problems". For this last purpose it was hoped to develop "joint relation committees ... to settle inter-union membership issues, examine the possibility of establishing agreed spheres of influence and generally to avoid inter-union difficulties".[1] These are cautious words, and the talks have proceeded slowly.

There are obstacles. Besides the vested interests of individuals and groups, the courts have ruled that unions have no right to transfer members compulsorily to another union (which amounts to expulsion) even if this is done to comply with a decision of the Trades Union Congress Disputes Committee, unless their rules expressly provide for it. Following the leading decision, the *Spring* case of 1956, the General Council requested unions to give themselves this power. Most have not done so, still less provided themselves with authority to transfer members following an agreement with another union. But where there is goodwill

[1] *Transport and General Workers' Record*, June 1966, quoted *ibid.*, p. 33.

it is usually sufficient to provide that one union will relinquish its negotiating rights in a certain establishment, will cease to recruit there and will advise its members to transfer to another union, in return for a reciprocal arrangement elsewhere. If obstinate minorities refuse to budge, time will solve the problem.

CHAPTER 3

TRADE UNION GOVERNMENT

A Simple Theory of Trade Union Government

All trade unions have an executive committee or council which is generally called "the executive". Almost all of them have some kind of representative conference, in most instances meeting annually, but in a few cases biennially. The major exception is the British Iron, Steel and Kindred Trades' Association. All trade unions have general secretaries who, except in the smallest unions, are full-time officers. Several large unions also have full-time presidents whose authority may equal or even exceed that of the general secretary. In larger unions there are also staffs of subordinate full-time officers, specialists and clerical employees.

In most unions the conference is directly elected by the members, voting in their branches. In the Amalgamated Engineering Union, however, representatives to conference, which was called the National Committee, were elected by the divisional committees, which in turn were elected by district committees chosen from the branches and the local shops stewards. This arrangement has been carried over into the dominant engineering section of the Amalgamated Union of Engineering and Foundry Workers. In some unions, mainly white collar organisations, conference elects the executive. In most of them, however, the executive is periodically elected directly by the members. In a few unions the general secretary is appointed by the executive, in some others he is chosen by conference, but in most unions he is directly elected by the members. Some general secretaries are elected for life. Others are subject to periodic re-election, as are most of the full-time presidents. In most major unions the remaining full-time officers are appointed by the executive. But there remains a considerable number of unions which elect all their full-time officers. In some of them, such as the Mineworkers and the Railwaymen, the election is once-for-all, but in others, including most of the unions which consist or once consisted of apprenticed craftsmen, the rules require periodic elections at which other qualified members of the union can challenge the incumbent. Thus the majority of unions appear to give their members, either directly or indirectly, great authority over their central decision-making process. A simple theory of trade union government accepted by many trade unionists is that an elected conference decides the constitution and policy of the union on behalf of the members; an elected executive has responsibility for administering the union's affairs between conferences in accordance with the constitution and policies laid down by conference, and for giving directions to the general secretary; and he, in most unions also an elected representative of the members, is responsible to the executive for the day-to-day running of business and for supervising the work of the other full-time officers. Where there is a full-time president the task is shared between the two of them. How closely does this theory fit the facts?

ELECTIONS

One criticism goes to the roots by attacking the electoral process itself. In most unions, it is argued, participation in elections is so low that the bulk of the members exclude themselves from any influence over the central decision-making process; and, in addition, the chance of defeating the incumbent at an election is so small as to make the process of election almost a farce.

There are a few unions which can take advantage of unusual circumstances to achieve high polls. The Mineworkers vote at the pit-head as they enter or leave the colliery, and polling is said to be around 60 per cent.[1] Many other unions vote at the branch meeting. This is the practice of the Engineers, who have an unusually large number of elective offices. Excluding the less important of these posts, they achieve "a rate of participation of only 7 per cent in elections to major office".[2] Still other unions disguise the size of the branch poll by allowing the majority decision of those attending the branch meeting to cast the block vote of the whole membership of the branch. This method is

[1] John Hughes, *Trade Union Structure and Government* Royal Commission Research Paper No. 5 (Part 2), p. 47.
[2] *Ibid.*, p. 46.

used by the General and Municipal Workers and the Shop, Distributive and Allied Workers. Since the branch attendances of the General and Municipal Workers are known to be lower than those of the Engineers,[1] it is reasonable to suppose that the proportion of those voting in their elections is at least no higher than in those of the Engineers. Other unions conduct postal ballots. But this does not yield very much higher polls than branch voting. The last election for the Electricians' general secretaryship, where this method is used, "produced a poll of about 15 per cent".[2]

This evidence might suggest that most unions are not controlled by the members, but by small cliques of members who run the branches or take the trouble to vote in elections. There is, however, another and more persuasive explanation. Those who frequently attend branch meetings are not necessarily a "clique". They are the relatively small proportion of union members who are active in union affairs, including most shop stewards. Attendance at branch meetings among shop stewards is very much higher than among other branch members.[3] Moreover, however limited the electoral process by which they are chosen, shop stewards generally are seen and see themselves as the representatives of groups of their fellow members at work. It is also reasonable to suppose that shop stewards and other active members provide a disproportionately large proportion of those who vote in postal ballots. Because they are brought into contact with the union's full-time officers and with the members of district or regional committees who will provide many of the candidates for office, they are in a position to make an intelligent choice among the candidates. By contrast in most union elections most union members are unlikely to know even the names of those who are standing. If the members were to use their votes, they would have to make a random selection or ask their shop stewards or other knowledgeable members for advice. Consequently most

---

[1] See p. 17.   [2] *Trade Union Structure and Government* (Part 2), p. 47.
[3] In the Royal Commission's surveys, only just over half of the sample of members 56 per cent) ever attended branch meetings, and only 7 per cent claimed to have attended ten branch meetings or more in the previous twelve months. By contrast 28 per cent of the stewards said they had attended every branch meeting in the previous twelve months, and another 31 per cent that they had attended more than half. The average attendance claimed by the stewards was 13 meetings during the previous year. (*Workplace Industrial Relations*, pp. 25, 121.)

trade union elections can be represented as a form of indirect election. Shop stewards are the representatives of the members and they exercise a disproportionate, even possibly predominant, influence in the elections at which the majority of the ordinary members fail to vote. A great deal more evidence would be required to confirm this interpretation, but it is consistent with such evidence as we possess.

In unions which require their full-time officers to stand for periodic re-election, the defeat of the incumbent is a relatively rare event.[1] But it would be surprising if it were otherwise. To defeat the incumbent is to sack him from his job, perhaps to rob him of his pension. Trade union members would be acting unfairly and unwisely if they took this step without very strong reasons. In addition the incumbent has a much better chance to make himself known to his electorate than has any of his potential rivals. But it does not follow that the process of re-election is without effect. On the contrary, there is a widespread view among managers that the conduct of many full-time officers of the Engineers is noticeably influenced by the approach of election day.

The democratic process necessarily becomes a farce where the ballot is rigged. The famous case of Communist ballot-rigging among the Electricians established that a whole union can be controlled in this way, at least for a time.[2] In other unions there are plenty of technical infringements of the rules governing elections, and there is sometimes suspicion of chicanery in local elections, such as the casting of the whole branch vote by the branch secretary, although there is some evidence that serious fraud may be rare.[3] But apart from the Electricians, there is no

[1] A survey of the records of nineteen major unions up to 1958 showed that in the four which required periodic re-election, defeat in an election accounted for 12 per cent of the instances of termination of office. Normal retirement was the most frequent cause, and the remaining instances were due to death, resignation, ill-health and dismissal. Dismissal is less common in unions which provide for periodic re-election than in other unions. (*Trade Union Officers*, pp. 79–80.)

[2] The case of *Byrne and Chappell v. Foulkes, Haxell and Others* established fraud in the election of the general secretary, and was the first of a series of court cases which brought about the deposition of the union's Communist leadership. (C. H. Rolph, *All Those in Favour*, 1962.) This first case was extremely expensive. Total costs were estimated at £80,000. The Royal Commission proposed that simpler and cheaper remedies should be made available. (*Report*, pp. 172–4.)

[3] In the survey conducted among a sample of 494 trade union members for the Royal Commission only four claimed knowledge of instances of elections "not fairly carried out" in their unions. All four instances were branch elections. (*Report*, p. 172.)

evidence of ballot-rigging being used to maintain control of the central machinery of government of a major union. In recent years a number of unions have tried to protect themselves against corrupt electoral practices by transferring responsibility for the counting of votes to the Electoral Reform Society. They include the Mineworkers and the Railwaymen. The Electricians have gone further by having the Society supervise a system of postal voting direct to and from the individual members as the strongest possible safeguard against a reintroduction of malpractices.

The simple theory of trade union democracy must be considerably modified if it is to take account of the realities of trade union electoral practices, but, at least on present evidence, it is a question of modification, not rejection. Through elections trade union members can exercise some control over their representatives even if for most of them the control is usually indirect. Criticism of the electoral process, however, is only the first of several that the theory has to meet. The second is that union conferences do not in fact determine the constitutions and policies of their unions.

CONFERENCES

At all union conferences there is a "platform". Its central figure is in most instances the general secretary, but in a few unions the president. In some unions he is supported by a phalanx of executive members and senior officers. Other unions, including the Engineers and Railwaymen, severely limit the number of such office-holders who can attend. Whether the chairman of conference is a full-time president or a "lay" officer,[1] he is likely to be a member of the leading group. Most of the important proposals before the conference come from the executive. Resolutions from the branches and districts are often "composited" by a standing orders committee so that there is only one, or perhaps two, resolutions on any one topic. The wording of a composite resolution can influence its chance of success, and in many unions the standing orders committee works closely with the platform. The committee also arranges the order and conduct of debates. With all these advantages the "platform" has considerable influence in all union conferences, and very considerable

[1] All trade union members except full-time officers are "lay" members.

influence in some of them. But this is not necessarily undemocratic. A union conference might easily become anarchic without leadership from the platform. Although delegates may give considerable attention to the platform's opinions in deciding how to cast their votes, the platform is unlikely to be able to hoodwink or stampede them into a decision which has not the support of a majority, so long as the issue is one on which delegates are knowledgeable.

Constitutional matters are issues of this kind. Representatives at conference, most of them branch secretaries, members of branch committees or district committees, or senior shop stewards, with a fair sprinkling of full-time officers in some unions, are affected closely by an amalgamation, a reconstruction of regional boundaries, a new system of branch administration or new rates of contribution. They can therefore speak with experience as well as feeling on issues such as these, and record an informed and responsible vote. Debates on these topics show conferences at their most business-like. One example was the debate at the 1963 conference of the General and Municipal Workers over a proposal for an increase from 1s. 3d. to 2s. in weekly contributions, coupled with additional benefits. After months of discussion in the districts and the branches it was passed by a small majority.

Because they arouse the opposition of vested interests, constitutional proposals can also reveal union conferences as petty-minded gatherings. When the same union was formed by amalgamation of three separate organisations in 1924, the crucial issue was the rate of commission to be paid to branch secretaries and collecting stewards, who were well represented at the conference. But mean-mindedness is not undemocratic.

Policies, however, can be another matter. Many resolutions before union conferences on so-called policy issues are political matters to be submitted to the Labour Party conference. Others are proposals for labour legislation or expressions of opinion on general topics concerning trade unions. Many of these resolutions concern subjects in which there is no real controversy in the movement, and even when they are controversial the vote in a particular union can often be predicted with accuracy from a knowledge of the alignments of the platform. There are rare occasions, however, when the predicted results are not obtained, as in the series of trade union conferences in the spring and summer of 1961 which for a brief period committed the Labour movement to nuclear disarmament. A comparable defeat of the leadership on an industrial issue was the succession of conference decisions to reject the policy of wage-restraint during the latter months of 1949 and the first half of 1950.

The notion of policy becomes confused when it is applied to collective bargaining. On the one hand negotiations and settlements are executive matters which should be handled by the union's professional negotiators responsible to the executive, and within the limits of conference policy. On the other, it is almost impossible for conference to frame industrial policies which do not leave the negotiators considerable room for manoeuvre, to determine the exact figure at which to settle, or even to decide the question of whether there is to be a strike or not. These may appear to most union members as the most important decisions their unions have to take. If they cannot control these decisions, in what sense can they be said to control union policy?

Moreover, in dealing with collective bargaining issues, many union conferences face special limitations. On constitutional or political resolutions the opinion of each delegate may reasonably be held to be as good as another's. His vote may be guided by the advice of a wiser or more persuasive delegate, but it is his to cast because the members who elected him have the same right to share in the decision as any other group of members. At a conference of the Transport and General Workers, however, or the General and Municipal Workers or the Electricians, any question concerning one industry can directly affect only a minority of delegates and their constituents. The majority has no direct knowledge of the issues and will not gain or lose by the decision. Consequently these three unions exclude resolutions on the affairs of particular industries from their conference agenda. There are, however, many other unions with members drawn from several industries in which conference is allowed to debate such issues, and a disinterested and ignorant majority can decide the issue for those directly concerned.

One way out of this is the "trade group" solution. In the Transport and General Workers' Union, for example, there are thirteen trade groups, each of which covers an industry or group of kindred industries and holds its own conferences to debate

D

issues concerning them.[1] The Electricians have recently introduced regular industrial conferences to serve the same purpose. The General and Municipal Workers' Union, on the other hand, has until recently regarded its regions as the major sub-divisions within the union, and has left industrial issues to the executive. Trade groups, moreover, do not solve all difficulties. A trade group cannot be entirely independent without breaking up the union. In the last resort, therefore, its decisions must be subject to the executive, which in these unions will contain only a minority of members directly concerned with any one industry.

Multi-unionism is an equally important obstacle to effective conference control over collective bargaining. In most major industries no single union is in a position to determine what the union side as a whole shall do. Its conference may pass a resolution proposing demands on pay and conditions, but what is actually put to the employers must be decided jointly with the other unions concerned at a meeting of a federal body or a "workers' side". This process gives a great deal of power to the full-time officers or executive members who almost invariably lead union delegates at meetings of this kind and frequently comprise the whole delegation.

A third obstacle arises from the process of collective bargaining itself. Trade union conferences are expensive and meet only for short periods. There is little likelihood that conference will be in session when a particular negotiation reaches the critical stage. Special conferences may be called to consider proposed settlements but these are sparingly used. In any case, the final proposal is the result of bargaining with employers and the actual negotiators must be allowed considerable leeway in the conduct of negotiations. Even if the settlement comes before a conference it must usually be on a "take-it or leave-it" basis.

The effectiveness of conference is also affected by the number of delegates who attend. A small conference can give closer attention to business, and, because it is cheaper, can remain in session longer. At the other extreme a very large conference is difficult to organise. For this reason the conference of the Shop, Distributive and Allied Workers, with each of more than a thousand branches entitled to its representative, is erratic and unpredictable during the three days of its session. On the other

[1] Within some of the trade groups there are also subordinate trade sections.

hand the Engineers' conference[1] and the Railwaymen's conference of fifty-two and seventy-seven delegates respectively, each meeting for two or three weeks, are both highly organised, and attempt to exercise close scrutiny over the work of their executives. With only one major industry to consider the Railwaymen's conference can extend this scrutiny to collective bargaining and in the summer of 1968 it took over the conduct of railway negotiations and reached a settlement with the British Railways Board. This, however, is a rare event. More often the attempts of these conferences to carry supervision to the extent of doing the work of their executives has led to friction and confusion.

All this means that, with rare exceptions, the authority of trade union conferences over industrial issues is severely limited in many British unions. Union executives, however, are in a much better position to exercise control and even to watch over the process of negotiation. They meet more frequently, they can be called together quickly and their members have more acquaintance with the details of agreements and the art of negotiation. Trade union members might, therefore, be thought to exercise their influence over industrial decisions through their representatives on their trade union executives.

EXECUTIVES

This leads to the third criticism which the simple theory of trade union democracy has to meet. In many major unions the executive is not a group of men "working at the trade" chosen by their fellows to direct the business of the union and control its full-time officers. The seven members of the executive of the Amalgamated Engineering Union are themselves full-time officers. Their posts are regarded as next in importance to those of the president and general secretary. Junior officers of the union see election to the executive as progress in their trade union careers. Besides attending meetings of the executive, its members carry out a great deal of the administrative and negotiating business of the union. The Electricians now follow the same practice. In the National Union of Mineworkers the members

---

[1] This is the conference of the Amalgamated Engineering Union. The fifty-two delegates meet with nine representatives of the foundry section to constitute the conference of the Amalgamated Union of Engineering and Foundry Workers.

of the executive are elected to represent their areas. Both lay members and full-time officers can stand for the executive, but in fact nearly all its members are full-time officers, generally the secretaries or presidents of their areas. The twenty-odd members usually include a few laymen but even these may be full-time branch secretaries, who in some areas are not constitutionally regarded as full-time officers. The General and Municipal Workers have a two-tier administrative body: a general council of twenty-four members including all the ten regional secretaries, and an executive consisting of five regional secretaries chosen by the general council and one lay member from each of the five remaining regions. As among the Mineworkers, these laymen may be full-time branch secretaries. There have always been several full-time branch secretaries on the general council, and at least one or two on the executive.[1] In these unions, and in the smaller unions which select their executives on similar lines, the body which governs the union between conferences appears at first sight to be an oligarchy of senior administrators rather than a committee representing the members of the union.

Other unions, however, have different arrangements. The members of the Railwaymen's executive are all laymen, but in practice they have for many years extended the work of the executive through the year. They serve for three years, and are supported throughout that period by the daily allowance to which they are entitled while on union business. At the end of the three years they are not eligible for re-election. This arrangement helps to keep them "in touch with the members" to whose ranks they know they must return. It also gives them great authority over the administration of the union. The twenty-four members of the executive outnumber the full-time officers of the union, and for the considerable part of each week that they are not dealing with union business outside London they are available in head office to supervise what is done. In these circumstances it is not surprising that the Railwaymen's executive frequently seems to be trying to run the union and to conduct negotiations itself rather than supervising the work of others.

---

[1] In 1964 the union introduced a new grade of branch administrative officer, salaried instead of dependent on a commission on membership. These new officers are recognised as part of the official hierarchy of the union and therefore ineligible for membership of the executive. They will gradually replace the old full-time branch secretaries.

The National and Local Government Officers' Association is another union in which a lay executive exercises unusual control over the conduct of union business. In local government, which was for many years its sole field of operation and still provides the majority of its members, the union has from the start included all grades of white collar employees. Consequently its executive and other leading committees have always included a number of senior local government officers. Their method of conducting the union's business seems to reflect the vexations which they suffer in local government where committees of laymen subordinate senior professional officers to close supervision. Until recently the general secretary was not the spokesman for the platform at conference and negotiations with employers were in most instances conducted by a lay chairman of a negotiating committee and not by the full-time officer of the union responsible for that industry. Local government officers appeared to be determined that, if they could not be the masters in local government affairs, then at least they should be masters in their own organisation.

The lay executives of the Railwaymen and the National and Local Government Officers are exceptional in the authority which they wield and in the control which they can exercise over the chief officers of their unions. A more typical example of the relationship between a general secretary and a lay executive is found in the Transport and General Workers' Union. To some extent this executive is a two-tier body since its main committee, the Finance and General Purposes Committee, transacts much of its business and meets much more frequently than the full executive with its forty-odd members. But all the executive members are bound to be away from their industrial jobs a good deal. The representative which each trade group sends to the executive is bound to be occupied with trade group business as well as executive business. The remaining representatives elected by the regions are likely to serve on a number of regional committees. In addition the members of the executive may have duties as branch secretaries and senior shop stewards, and may serve on regional or industry-wide negotiating bodies. Union business is almost certain to be more interesting to them than their industrial jobs, and the time spent on union business can be extended by nomination to serve on additional committees and negotiating bodies, and by selection for delegations, including delegations making visits overseas. These prerequisites are necessarily subject to the influence of the general secretary. In addition, each of the past general secretaries of the union, Ernest Bevin, Arthur Deakin and Frank Cousins, has been perhaps the most influential and best-known figure in the British trade union movement of his day, and there is little doubt that their successor, Jack Jones, will achieve a comparable status. By contrast the executive members are unknown outside the union and probably also to the great majority within the union. Consequently the Transport and General Workers' general secretary is in a position to exert considerable ascendancy over his executive, and it appears that the successive holders of the office have usually been able to persuade the executive to accept their advice. Perhaps the most dramatic instance of this was the switch in the union's policies from right to the left both in the Labour Party and at the Trades Union Congress when Cousins, after a short interregnum,[1] succeeded Deakin.

CHIEF OFFICERS

The fourth criticism of the simple theory of trade union democracy, therefore, is the very considerable powers that can be accumulated in the hands of the chief officer. Instances of the authority exercised by chief officers can be found in other unions besides the Transport and General Workers. Much to the surprise of the delegates, the leaders and the newspapers, the 1959 conference of the General and Municipal Workers voted 150–126 in favour of a resolution supporting unilateral nuclear disarmament by Britain. Their general secretary, Sir Thomas Williamson, took the view that the union should not permit its long-standing support of the official foreign policies of the Labour Party to be reversed in this way. He persuaded the executive to recall conference two months later for the sole purpose of debating the issue again and reconsidering its decision. The delegates changed their minds by 194 votes to 139. During his last two or three years as president of the Engineers, Lord Carron developed a practice which came to be known as "Carron's law". He cast the block

---

[1] For a brief period in 1955 the post was held by A. E. Tiffin, who died in December of that year.

vote of his union at meetings of the Labour Party conference and the Trades Union Congress as he thought was right rather than with close regard for the decisions of his own conference or the preferences of the majority of his union's delegates at the meeting.

In the Engineers and the Electricians the rule requiring the chief officers to submit to periodic re-election provides an opportunity for opponents to challenge the chief officer of the union. But although chief officers have been dismissed, defeat in an election is virtually unknown in major British unions.[1] Where the chief officer is appointed by the executive, they might be expected to have greater authority over him than in other unions. But there is no evidence of this. Two of the three largest unions which follow this practice are the Public Employees and the British Iron, Steel and Kindred Trades' Association. Bryn Roberts, the secretary of the Public Employees from 1934 to 1962, established an almost autocratic sway over their affairs, and all the general secretaries of the steel union have wielded great authority.

There exists one form of control by which the vote of the members can decide an issue over the heads of conference, the executive and the chief officer. This is the submission of issues to the members in a referendum, or as it is more commonly called by trade unionists, a ballot. Ballots are required by statute to sanction amalgamations and to establish political funds, and in the nineteenth century trade union members were asked to vote on a considerable variety of issues. The ballot continued in widespread use as a method of sanctioning proposed collective agreements or strikes until 1926, but since then it has been employed only rarely. In the years of unrest from 1919 to 1926 many strikes were called against the leaders' judgement as a result of ballot votes; further ballots rejected proposed settlements so that stoppages were prolonged. After almost nine months of a national coal stoppage in 1926, with a drift back to work in many coalfields, the conflict was only terminated by the leaders' resolve to decide the issue at a delegate conference and not by a ballot.

The change in practice is not due to formal revision of rules, for

---

[1] In 1913 Jenkin Jones, the incumbent, was defeated in the election for the post of general secretary of the Amalgamated Society of Engineers by Robert Young, the assistant general secretary.

there has been little change in rules on ballots. Already in 1926 some unions, such as the Railwaymen, gave complete authority to the executive to call strikes and ratify agreements. In other unions, the leaders have avoided ballots by minimising the occasions for them and employing a broad interpretation of their own authority. In fact the most important post-war strike ballots have been arranged by moderate leaders to demonstrate to their left-wing opponents that the members did not want a stoppage.[1]

THE THEORY RECONSIDERED

Where does the simple theory of trade union democracy—control of the union's affairs by the votes of the members—stand after these criticisms have been examined? The influence of the members' votes in the affairs of a union varies according to the method of voting, the type and number of offices subject to election, the structure of the union and the relationship between the various bodies which constitute the central decision-making machinery. There is no union in which votes are without importance, and some in which they are of great importance. On the other hand there are almost insurmountable obstacles in many unions to the members taking a share either directly or indirectly in those decisions which may be supposed to concern them most—the negotiation of pay and conditions in their industries; the structure of their executives in many major unions, together with the position of the platform at conference, provides an opportunity for an oligarchy of senior officers to dominate the affairs of the union; and the chief officer can accumulate so much influence that he can exercise a dominant role in the union either as the leader of an oligarchy, or as its unchallenged ruler.

If the description of trade union government was left at this point it would be reasonable to suppose that power in most British unions is highly centralised in the hands of an oligarchy of leaders, or even of a single autocrat. In fact this inference is so wide of the mark, so inconsistent with the facts of trade union life, as to be laughable. The error lies in supposing that there is

[1] In 1950 and 1962 ballots held by the Confederation of Shipbuilding and Engineering Unions rejected proposals for strikes in support of engineering claims. In 1964 a settlement recommended by the Mineworkers' executive was rejected by their conference but supported decisively by the members in a ballot.

nothing else to restrain trade union leaders in the exercise of power but the votes of the members. In fact leaders are subject to many other checks.

CHECKS ON UNION LEADERSHIP

(i) *Loss of Members*

In a book published in 1954 V. L. Allen argued that there was "only one effective and continuously operative method of making" democracy "work" in trade unions.

"So long as trade union members have the right to 'contract out' of membership if they are dissatisfied with the union they belong to, then a continuous impulse will operate to impel trade union leaders to retain them. Obviously in a free organisation of this nature workers would retain their membership only if they were satisfied with the work their organisation was doing. Dissatisfaction would be reflected in a declining membership, and in the interests of self-preservation union leaders would be compelled to stem the tide. . . . In a voluntary organisation there exists the continual fear that membership may decline and all the time steps must be taken to prevent this happening. Always, therefore, leadership must walk in step with the rank and file."[1]

This attempt to base trade union democracy on "voting with the feet" fails for two reasons. Firstly it implies that the closed shop turns a trade union into what Allen described as a "compulsory society".[2] At the time at which he wrote Allen could not be aware of the extent of the closed shop in Britain. We now know that it applies to about two-fifths of British trade union members, including almost all printing workers, shipbuilding workers and miners, and to most groups of apprenticed craftsmen in the engineering industry. According to Allen's theory the unions which organise these workers must be among the most undemocratic in the country. In fact they have always given every sign of being among the most democratic of unions. Interest in the union and participation in its affairs seem to be high among the members and the concern of the leaders to meet the wishes of the members is more evident than in many other unions. It is true, however, that the existence of a closed shop can provide autocratic leaders with a weapon against members who

---

[1] *Power in Trade Unions*, p. 28. [2] *Ibid.*, pp. 63–4.

choose to oppose them. This was the position in the Seamen's union for many years; but with the majority of its members always at sea the Seamen's union present a unique opportunity to a would-be autocrat.

Secondly, the proportion of workers organised by trade unions in Britain has been stable in most industries for many years past. The main changes in the distribution of union membership, including the heavy losses of the cotton, mining and railway trade unions, are manifestly due to shifts in the distribution of the working population. There have been few sizeable changes in union membership which can be attributed to satisfaction or dissatisfaction with the conduct of union business.[1] On Allen's view this would suggest that all trade union leaders have been equally in step with their members, an inference which does not carry much conviction; or alternatively that trade unionists do not use the powerful instrument with which, according to Allen, they could control their leaders.[2]

These criticisms of Allen's elevation of "voting with the feet" into the central principle of trade union democracy do not show that trade union leaders are unconcerned with gaining members and avoiding losses. They are concerned, and their concern prompts them, other things being equal, to pursue objectives which are popular with workers they are anxious to recruit or with members they fear they may lose. But by itself this check on leadership fails to explain the facts of trade union government. It is therefore necessary to look for others.

(ii) Parties and Factions

In 1956 Martin Lipset and two colleagues published a fascinating study of the social structure and government of the International Typographical Union,[3] the main union in the printing industry in the United States. It is probably the only trade union in the world in which office-holders and candidates for office are organised into two recognised rival groups which compete openly at elections, and in which the minority group has a fair chance of ousting the majority, thus becoming the "administra-

[1] An important exception is the large-scale recruiting in 1954 by the National Amalgamated Stevedores and Dockers in the northern ports which had previously been monopolised by the Transport and General Workers. (See p. 114.)

[2] For further criticisms of Allen's argument see *The Closed Shop in Britain*, pp. 271–3

[3] S. M. Lipset, M. Trow and J. Coleman, *Union Democracy*.

tion" and forcing their rivals into opposition. On the basis of
their findings they set out a general theory of trade union
democracy.

Large-scale organisation, they say, gives leaders great advantages
"over the rank and file or even an organised opposition" including
"control over financial resources and internal communications, a
large, permanently organised political machine, a claim to
legitimacy, and a near monopoly of political skills". Most
members, on the other hand, will not "ordinarily be actively
interested in the affairs of the union". For a union to be democratic, a change of leadership through election must be possible,
and this "means that the leader must be willing to move from a
position of high status, power and income to a much lower one
if he is still to remain within the union. . . . Given the great
emphasis placed by the social structure on achieving and maintaining high status, it is clear that the norms of democracy in
trade unions and those of achievement in the larger society are
often in sharp conflict."[1]

This theory is too pessimistic and narrow. It suggests that there
is only one democratic trade union in the world, and it fails to
provide a means of recognising and explaining different degrees
of democracy in unions which fall short of that ideal.

There is no parallel to the International Typographical Union
in Britain. Generally speaking the atmosphere of trade unionism
does not welcome organised opposition. This is partly due to the
general acceptance by most trade unions in the nineteenth
century of a theory of "primitive democracy". According to this
view the members of a trade union were men carrying out the
same job in the same relationship with their employer, and with
the same objectives. Their interests were therefore identical, and
so long as decisions were taken by the members they could be
assumed to represent a "general will". In a trade union of any
size, however, the members could not take all the decisions, and
there was a danger that a conference, an executive or a full-time
officer would not represent the general will. Steps could be taken
to guard against the danger. So long as conferences and executives
consisted of men genuinely working at the trade, and office
rotated fairly rapidly, the risk was small. Objectives and interests
which were the same for all members could be represented just

[1] *Ibid.*, pp. 403–4.

as well by any group of members so long as they shared the common experience. Indeed elections might be thought unnecessary. Any branch committee could serve as an executive for the whole union, and lay officers could be chosen by lot. Full-time officers were more of a problem, for they could not share the common experience. But things need not go far wrong so long as they were subject to periodic election and were paid the same wage as the members of the union, so that they must live in the same environment.

This doctrine had an especially strong hold on craft unions which sought to operate as extended work groups by imposing their rules and customs upon their trades. All members had the same interests in preserving the power of the union by insisting on the observance of the rules and customs which ensured uniform treatment and protection for every member. There was no room here for organised opposition, and no need for it. The marks of this primitive theory are still visible in many of the institutions and habits of our present unions of apprenticed craftsmen, or which once were unions of apprenticed craftsmen.

Even when organised groups began to play a part in the government of trade unions, like the "new unionists" of the last decade of the nineteenth century, the industrial unionists and syndicalists before and during the first world war, and the Communists with their "Minority Movement" after the war— they did not aim to secure recognition of the legitimacy of organised opposition in trade union affairs. On the contrary they represented themselves as the champions of the will of the members which was being thwarted by leaders now "divorced" from the rank and file. It was their aim to reassert the will of the members, and to devise institutions which would subordinate the leaders to it once more. After that there would be no further need for opposition. For their part, the leaders might remain tolerant of the activities of such "ginger groups' so long as the groups did not begin to sway decisions at conference or on the executive, or put forward candidates who might capture their posts. When their opponents seemed likely to become dangerous, however, the leaders began to accuse them of being the promoters of disharmony and disruption. Where the opponents were members of an outside organisation like the Communist Party and there was evidence that this organisation was influencing their aims and methods the leaders could add charges of disloyalty and take disciplinary proceedings under the rules. A number of unions now prohibit Communists (and Fascists) from holding office.

Consequently there is little encouragement for organised opposition in trade union government, and trade union rules make no provision for it.[1] On the other hand voting in sizeable electorates offers a considerable temptation to organise the vote; and where an assembly has to decide on a number of varied issues on which some of its members are ill-informed and without strong views, as do most union conferences, voting demands organisation. Otherwise the results are likely to be erratic and contradictory. Consequently there is a tendency for opposition to emerge even without encouragement.

Where two organised groups compete for power in British trade unions, they are almost invariably an orthodox Labour Party group on the one hand, and on the other, the Communists along with anyone who is prepared to vote with them. In many unions this includes left-wing Labour Party supporters. Thus for thirteen years up to 1967 Lord Carron led a group of orthodox Labour supporters who were usually in control of a majority at the Engineers' conference and on their executive. When he retired, the election for his successor was won by a left-winger, Hugh Scanlon, with Communist support. It is not yet clear how far he can carry conference or the executive.

The most common situation in most trade unions for many years past has been for an orthodox Labour leadership which controls most offices, the executive, and the platform and most of the votes at conference, to face a left-wing alliance with some representation at conference, probably a place or two on the executive and perhaps including a few full-time officers. This has been the situation in the Shop, Distributive and Allied Workers, the Woodworkers, the Building Trade Workers and many smaller unions. There is a much smaller number of instances of continuous control by a left-wing alliance, including the Draughtsmen, among whom such an alliance has held power for nearly twenty years.

[1] There are, however, instances in which the organisation of opposition is openly tolerated. For many years the Draughtsmen have permitted the preparation of "slates" and canvassing in voting at their conference. (Graham Wootton, "Parties in Union Government, the Association of Shipbuilding and Engineering Draughtsmen", *Political Studies*, June 1961.)

In other unions the position is not so clear-cut. In the Mine-workers the orthodox Labour group has maintained control of the executive and conference since 1926, although sometimes in the post-war period by a slender majority, but the general secretaryship has been held by a left-winger since the war.[1] For much of the post-war period there have been left-wing majorities on the Railwaymen's executive and at their conferences, although rapid turnover on both bodies sometimes makes it difficult to be sure where the balance of power lies. But since 1957 the general secretary has been a right-winger, Sidney Greene.

Then there are unions in which organised opposition, if it exists at all, appears to have little influence in elections or in conference decisions. The orthodox Labour group in the Post Office Engineering Union have been so successful in ridding themselves of the Communists and their allies that they now constitute virtually a one-party union. Under Bevin and Deakin there was a minority left-wing opposition in the Transport and General Workers, although after 1950, when the union excluded Communists from office, Communists could not play a prominent part in the alliance. But after Cousins took over, there were few signs of organised opposition at conference to the left-wing Labour group which he led. This group contrasted with left-wing alliances in many other unions by excluding Communists until 1968 when the ban was removed. The General and Municipal Workers, who also exclude Communists from office, have supported an orthodox Labour leadership throughout their existence. Generally left-wing opposition within the union has been feeble, but there have been occasions, such as the 1959 conference, when the opposition has been able to make something of a challenge.

Accordingly, although British unions lack fully developed party systems, it is evident that organised opposition plays a considerable part in the government of many trade unions. It has recently been argued that this is a sufficient guarantee of democracy, that, so long as an opposition faction is tolerated within a union, the danger of defeat in elections or a reversal of policy is sufficient to ensure that the leaders discover and fulfil the

---

[1] It does not follow that the union leadership is always at loggerheads. Will Paynter, the Communist general secretary, was able to co-operate closely with Sir Sidney Ford, the right-wing president, on a number of issues.

members' wishes.[1] It cannot be denied that organised opposition is a check on leadership, and can change the leadership and policies of a union. Without organisation Leslie Cannon and his colleagues could not have defeated the Electricians' Communist leadership. Without organisation Hugh Scanlon would not have succeeded Lord Carron. But by itself, organised opposition is not a guarantee of democracy. At most times and in most unions organised oppositions, even if they exist, have no expectation of achieving a change of leaders or policies, and the leaders do not therefore need to curry favour with the members for fear that they or their policies will be overthrown. Besides this, a not uncommon consequence of a strong opposition is the capture of some but not all offices in the union, leading to a confusion of policy rather than respect for the wishes of the members. This has frequently been the state of affairs among the Railwaymen, and at several periods in the history of the Engineers.

(iii) Separation of Powers

A method of restraining political power long familiar to students of government is the separation of powers. The most famous example of its application is the constitution of the United States of America which divides formal authority between a legislature, Congress, a president in whom is vested the "executive power", and a Supreme Court which can decide that Acts of Congress are unconstitutional and that actions of the president are *ultra vires*. By itself this arrangement does not guarantee restraint, for it would be possible for the president to achieve effective control of the legislature by means of a party system (as the cabinet does in Britain) so as to exercise both legislative and executive powers. What is required in addition is a method of selecting the separate powers which is likely to keep them independent of each other; and in the United States the president is chosen by what amounts to a vote of the whole electorate and the members of the two houses of Congress are chosen by constituencies. Even this would not necessarily ensure their independence, if it were not that the members of one house, the Senate, are elected as the

---

[1] "Union democracy exists when union Executives are unable to prevent opposition factions distributing propaganda and mobilising electoral support. . . . The survival of faction limits Executive ability to disregard rank-and-file opinion by providing the *potential* means for its overthrow." (Roderick Martin, "Union Democracy: An Explanatory Framework," *Sociology*, May 1968.)

representatives of the separate states within the union, and these states are divided into constituencies to elect the members of the other house. The United States has a federal system of government which grants very considerable independent authority to each state. Consequently Congressmen, and especially Senators, are the representatives of powerful and independent institutions with their own interests and objectives which may well not be same as those of the United States as a whole whose representative is the president. This arrangement helps Congress to act as a powerful check on the president.

One British trade union has constitutional arrangements which resemble those of the United States in a number of ways. This is the engineering section of the Amalgamated Union of Engineering and Foundry Workers. Its two hundred and fifty or so districts are grouped together into twenty-six divisions whose committees elect two members each to constitute the union conference. The seven executive members are elected by the members grouped into seven constituencies for the purpose, and the president and general secretary are elected by the whole membership. District committees have inherited very considerable powers from the period before 1917 when they were responsible for determining the customs of the trade and for negotiations with employers. Thus they have power to "regulate rates of wages, hours of labour, terms of overtime, piecework, and general conditions affecting the interests of the trades in their respective districts".[1] Today their authority rests on their close links with shop stewards in their districts. There is provision for the direct representation of shop stewards on the committees, and many of the remaining members are in fact leading shop stewards. Consequently the districts represented at conference are powerful bodies in their own right and often have interests and objectives separate from those of the union as a whole, which are represented by the president and the executive. Moreover, to continue the analogy with the United States, there is a Final Appeal Court, separately elected by the members, with power to hear and decide appeals against decisions of the executive, and decisions of the executive are not infrequently set aside.

With these arrangements it is not surprising that the Engineers' executive and chief officers appear to be more restricted and to

[1] Rule 13, Section 11.

possess less authority over their union than their counterparts in any other major British union, for no other British union embodies the principle of the separation of powers to anything like the same degree. However, once the principle is properly understood it is evident that any scheme for decentralisation of power within a union may provide a check on central authority on somewhat similar lines. For the separation of powers depends on decentralisation of authority to independent institutions with separate representation in the central decision-making bodies; and this can be found in many unions besides the Engineers.

(iv) Decentralisation: Regions, Districts and Trade Groups

The General and Municipal Workers' Union is divided into ten regions whose regional secretaries are the senior officers of the union after the general secretary. The words "regional autonomy" are frequently heard within the union. They mean three things: firstly that communications on both industrial and administrative matters from head office should pass through the regional secretary; secondly that the head office is dependent on the goodwill of the regions for information, other than returns required by the rules; and thirdly that a great many decisions, particularly on administrative matters, are reserved for the regions. For example, the union has pioneered some developments in trade union education, and has its own training school. Courses are arranged by the education officer at head office. Places are then divided between the regions which can decide for themselves who shall fill them, or indeed whether they shall be filled.

The regions are also strongly represented in the governing bodies of the union. The ten regional secretaries sit on its general council, and five of them constitute the executive along with five lay representatives from the remaining regions. The representatives elected by the branches to conference go there as "regional delegations" and sit as groups in the conference hall along with their regional secretaries. They meet with him to discuss items on the agenda and often, but by no means always, decide to cast a regional vote on a particular issue. Consequently the regions play a part in organising the work of conference which is not unlike that of parties in a political assembly.

These arrangements limit the national leaders of the union in two ways. In many matters they depend on the co-operation of the regions to achieve results; because these are matters within the scope of regional autonomy. But even in dealing with matters which are recognised as of national concern and outside the control of the regions, the national leaders must have the support of the executive or of conference or of both, and the regions are directly represented on both bodies by representatives whose right to take an independent line is recognised and sanctioned by tradition. At conference a delegate who disagrees with the platform has only to convince the majority of one regional delegation to support him to have the backing of a recognised opposition group within the conference, whose right to speak and vote against the platform no one will challenge. Over the post-war years the General and Municipal Workers have been the most consistent supporters of official Labour policies among major trade unions, but these policies have been challenged at conference by spokesmen of regional delegations which stand to the left of the leaders. For some years the London and Birmingham regions vied with each other for the leadership of radical opinion within the union, but they were supplanted by Lancashire, the largest region of all.

The union's constitution is not an example of the separation of powers, for the position of the regional secretaries binds conference and the executive close together. Nor is the restraining influence which the regions can exercise over the national leaders necessarily a democratic check, for in the past some regional secretaries built for themselves such a dominating position within their regions that there has appeared to be very little control over them. But it *can* be a democratic check, for if any considerable number of members differ from the national leaders, the regional delegations at conference offer them a recognised and constitutional channel through which to try to express their views and to win support for them.

The Mineworkers' constitution has many resemblances to that of the General and Municipal Workers. As the Miners' Federation of Great Britain it was until 1946 a federation of independent district unions, and even now, as the "areas" of the National Union of Mineworkers, the old districts retain very considerable powers. To a considerable extent the constitution under which each of them works is a matter for itself so long as it does not violate the relatively restricted national rules. Its full-time officers are officers of the national union, but most of them are also presidents, secretaries or treasurers of the area. Some areas possess considerable financial resources.

Without any constitutional provision binding them to do so, nearly all the areas send their senior officers to represent them on the executive of the national union, and these officers also lead area delegations to its conferences. As in the General and Municipal Workers it is the accepted and traditional right of area representatives to take an independent stand if they choose to do so. Although they have rivalled the General and Municipal Workers in their consistent backing for orthodox Labour policies through the post-war period, the Mineworkers have on a number of occasions given their support by only a small majority, and since its foundation the Communist Party has always had a disproportionate following among the miners. The rivalry between the orthodox Labour supporters and the Communists and their allies has been a contest for control of the areas. Since the war Durham and Nottingham, along with most of the smaller areas, have stood for orthodox labour views. South Wales and Scotland have been consistent in their opposition. Yorkshire has been more volatile.

Area autonomy and representation within the Mineworkers is an even more powerful check on national leaders than regional autonomy and representation within the General and Municipal Workers. It can also be argued that it is a more democratic check, for it is a normal practice in the Mineworkers for important decisions within the areas to be taken by area councils to which each branch sends its own colliery representative, often with branch guidance on how he shall exercise his vote. By contrast the regional councils of the General and Municipal Workers are relatively unimportant. They meet only twice a year, and most decisions are taken by a regional committee of seven members elected by the council, in which the regional secretary can usually establish a dominant position.

The importance of these arrangements can be appreciated by comparing them with those of the Transport and General Workers' constitution. Here, as in other major unions, there is inevitably a good deal of decentralisation. Many administrative matters are devolved on the regions with their regional secretaries, and industrial matters are handled by national trade group conferences and committees with their national trade group secretaries. This is a greater degree of decentralisation than in either the General and Municipal Workers or the Mineworkers, for the national industrial officers who handle industrial matters in the General and Municipal Workers are directly under the control of the executive and the general secretary, and the Mineworkers' dealings with the National Coal Board are handled directly by the executive and chief officers of the union. On the other hand the Transport and General Workers' regional and trade group secretaries do not attend conference and cannot be members of the executive. There are no regional delegations at conference to match the district and area delegations of the other two unions, and the regional and trade group representatives on the executive are lay members of the union. Consequently neither the regions nor the trade groups provide a constitutional channel for organised opposition within the unions to anything like the same degree as the General and Municipal Workers' regions and the Mineworkers' areas. The domination normally exercised by the Transport and General Workers' secretary both at conference and in the executive has therefore not been due only to the powerful personality of the holders of the office but also to the provisions of the union's constitution.

However, these constitutional provisions do not reduce the regional and trade group secretaries to a negligible position in the union. Even if he wishes to interfere in the conduct of industry-wide negotiations, the general secretary can at any one time concern himself with only a fraction of the hundred and more industry negotiating bodies on which the union is represented. Consequently this important aspect of the union's business must be largely in the hands of the trade group secretaries. The secretary of a major region also occupies an important position, which is all the more important because he cannot in fact be confined to administrative matters. In many industries domestic bargaining has a decisive influence on pay and conditions. Constitutionally this is the business of regional trade groups and trade group secretaries responsible to their national counterparts. In fact the national trade groups cannot exercise much control over domestic bargaining, whereas the regional secretary can keep in contact with the chief shop stewards and managers of the major undertakings in his region. Moreover in many areas the union's branches are grouped into districts whose district secretaries play an important part in domestic negotiations and are responsible to the regional secretaries rather than to any individual trade group. As secretary of region No. 5, centred in the West Midlands in which domestic bargaining flourishes even more than in other parts of Britain, Jack Jones was able to build for himself a position of great power within the union. But his influence, and that of the other regional and trade group secretaries, had no formal channel of expression in the union's central decision-making bodies.

A quite different example of unofficial decentralisation can be found in the National Union of Railwaymen. Formally this body is highly centralised. Branches are directly responsible to head office and the work of the full-time officers is directed from head office. The functions of the district council are primarily propagandist. They have no industrial responsibilities, few administrative duties and no full-time district officers. From the start, however, they have assumed the right to debate major issues of union policy and to discuss the conduct of negotiations. On a number of occasions a council has backed its opinions by the threat of an unofficial strike, and indeed on several occasions a district council has actually brought its members out on strike. There was more than one instance during the first world war, and early in 1961 an unofficial one-day stoppage on the Underground called by the London council brought London's traffic almost to a halt. Consequently the district councils, with virtually no powers and no direct representation at conference, or on the executive, can nevertheless put pressure on the union's leaders over issues on which the members can be aroused.

(v) Decentralisation: The Branch

These exists a formidable body of evidence that the union branch is a body of relatively small and declining importance. With industrial business either concentrated on industry negotiations or in the hands of shop stewards, most branches have few important decisions to take. They remain administrative units, and most branch secretaries are burdened with a heavy weight of routine clerical business.[1] However, it would be a mistake to ignore the branch as a factor in union government. In a number

[1] See p. 16.

of industries it still has industrial responsibilities. Among the Mineworkers, for example, the branch is based on the colliery, and the branch officers are responsible for negotiations with the colliery management. Branch meetings may therefore have to decide upon matters closely affecting their members' pay and conditions. The branch is directly represented on the district council, which has considerable authority. Many branches raise additional subscriptions to support a full-time secretary who has the time and opportunity to become an important figure in local union affairs.

Full-time branch secretaries are to be found in large branches in a number of other unions, including the Seamen, the Boot and Shoe Operatives, the Electricians, the General and Municipal Workers and the printing unions. There are also a few in the Transport and General Workers, but they are appointed as full-time branch secretaries in the same way as other full-time officers and equally subordinate to the higher authorities in the union. The General and Municipal Workers are now gradually switching to a similar arrangement. However, where the full-time secretary is the choice of the branch, and even more where he is regarded as a lay member entitled to sit on district committees and councils, to attend conference and even to be elected to the executive, he can be an independent figure of considerable importance. His status can be reinforced by his influence over domestic negotiations affecting the members of his branch. Among the Miners, the Seamen, the Boot and Shoe Operatives and in some other unions his status as a negotiator is officially recognised, and elsewhere he is in a position to build up influence over the shop stewards in his branch and with local employers. It is significant that when the General and Municipal Workers' platform was defeated at the 1959 conference the spokesman for the opposition was Len Macnamee, a full-time branch secretary from Lancashire and one of the Lancashire representatives on the union's general council.

(vi) Decentralisation: The Workshop

It is already evident that decentralisation of power within a union is not entirely determined by its constitution; factors outside the constitution can also affect the distribution of power. One of these is domestic bargaining. Where employers and managers are willing to enter into arrangements and understandings with local officers and shop stewards, power is decentralised, whatever the union rules may say.

Domestic bargaining can leave a wide range of issues to be determined by the work group without close trade union control, and the authority which it confers on the work group assists the group to exercise an influence on union decisions. To some extent this second influence can work through constitutional channels. Shop stewards provide a very considerable proportion of those who attend conferences and sit on district, regional and national committees and councils, and even on trade union executives. Because of the considerable responsibility which usually rests upon a senior shop steward, and the substantial experience in negotiations which is likely to come his way, he can play his part in these conferences and committees with more confidence and authority than would otherwise be possible. In addition, if there is an issue of deep concern to a number of work groups, feelings will be communicated to their shop stewards and from them to the conferences, committees and councils of their unions.

Work groups can also exercise their influence informally, especially when they co-operate to do so. Groups from different unions can come together as shop stewards' committees, or link a number of plants together in combine committees, or form liaison committees on the docks, vigilance committees on the railways, rank-and-file movements among busmen, reform committees among miners and seamen, in order to press un- officially for a change in union policies, for the presentation of additional demands to employers, or for the rejection of offers and settlements. To some extent the power of these bodies may rest on the votes which they can influence in elections and at conference. But it also rests upon the willingness of work groups to follow their unofficial leaders in defiance of their unions, by striking for what the unions will not demand, or against what the unions will accept. In some unions and industries such strikes are not uncommon, and they may be feared more frequently than they occur.

(vii) Trade Union Officers as Pressure Groups
It is not often recognised that a union's full-time officers as a body can exert some pressure upon their leaders. On reflection,

however, it is easy to understand that they might do so. The conduct of union business depends upon them; they almost inevitably form views about issues of union policy; in most unions there is recognised machinery for them to confer in order to put forward proposals on their pay and conditions to the executive; and there are many other opportunities for them to meet and to talk about union affairs if they want. On the other hand, a full-time officer does not generally enjoy the same freedom as other union members to take part in unofficial activities and to bring pressure to bear upon the executive which he serves. In a union like the Engineers where all officers are elected and subject to re-election, and where power is fairly evenly divided between two opposed factions, officers have considerable freedom to voice the views of the faction which they favour even if it does not for the time being control conference or the executive. An almost equivalent licence exists among the Mineworkers. But in a union where one faction is in undisputed control, open support by a full-time officer for an opposing faction can be seen as indiscipline.

In 1944 an officer of the General and Municipal Workers established a National Trade Union Organisers' Mutual Association. The desirability of a trade union for trade union officers may be a matter for argument, but unquestionably its general secretary could hold a position of great power in the trade union movement. In this instance leaders of the General and Municipal Workers feared that the intention of the founder of the new organisation, whose opinions were well to the left of their own, was to create an organisation throughout the union (although he also recruited in other unions) from which he could challenge them. He was summoned to appear before the general council of the union and, when he declined, he was dismissed from office.[1]

However, where union officers are content to let their weight take effect without positive action, they do not lay themselves open to charges of indiscipline. After his election as general secretary of the Transport and General Workers, Cousins quickly swung the union's policy from the right-wing to the left-wing both in political and in industrial matters. Full-time officers who represented the union on Labour Party committees had to speak and a vote in a different sense from the one to which they

---

[1] H. A. Clegg, *General Union*, 1954, p. 82.

had become accustomed. But the extent to which the new policies were effective throughout the affairs of the union was dependent upon the conduct of business by its officers. This was not always subject to control in the same way as a vote, and many of the officers retained a sympathy for the industrial policies of Arthur Deakin.

A somewhat similar state of affairs has existed among the Electricians since Leslie Cannon and Frank Chapple took over as chief officers after the defeat of their Communist predecessors. They and their supporters reversed the policies of the union through decisions of its conference and executive, and were able to debar members of the Communist Party from office, but a considerable number of full-time officers retained a good deal of sympathy for the views which had formerly held sway in the union. They could not give public expression to their opinions, but the degree to which the new policies moulded their conduct of business depended upon their attitudes.

DISCIPLINE AS AN INSTRUMENT OF GOVERNMENT

Disciplinary powers can be used to silence or dismiss full-time officers or union members who challenge union leaders outside the constitutional channels provided by the rules. Most unions possess wide disciplinary powers. Quite apart from specific rules, the majority of unions arm themselves with a general power to suspend, expel or otherwise penalise a member who acts detrimentally to the interests of the union as seen by the appropriate disciplinary body.[1] Opposition to the leadership is commonly expressed through unofficial movements, and not infrequently by means of unofficial strikes, which in some unions are expressly forbidden by the rules and, even where this is not so, can easily be seen as detrimental to the union's interests.

The powers are used. The Transport and General Workers have used them against unofficial movements among busmen[2] and dockers.[3] On several occasions the Engineers have disciplined members of district committees for their part in unofficial

[1] In an unpublished study F. P. Graham found that among eighty unions covering 94 per cent of the membership of the Trades Union Congress, 66 had such rules (quoted in *The Closed Shop in Britain*, p. 100).

[2] H. A. Clegg, *Labour Relations in London Transport*, 1950, pp. 126–30.

[3] V. L. Allen, *Trade Union Leadership*, 1957, pp. 209–10.

stoppages.[1] The General and Municipal Workers have not only acted against the leaders of unofficial strikes, but have on more than one occasion disciplined the whole body of members engaged in such a strike.[2] But it is a common complaint of employers and the press in Britain that unions use their disciplinary powers far too infrequently in unofficial disputes, and there are obvious limits on what most unions can do. Action against members is likely to be ineffective for several reasons. Suspension from office can be used against office-holders. Ordinary members can only be fined or expelled. If they fail to pay the fine the union can only expel them. For most unions this would not be a practical course where considerable numbers are involved. The union would lose members, perhaps to become non-unionists, perhaps to join a rival union, and there would be no guarantee that their expulsion would serve as a deterrent to others. Even a closed shop may not ensure the enforcement of discipline when large numbers disagree with their leaders. In 1962 the Transport and General Workers tried to enforce once again the "one union closed shop" they had formerly enjoyed in Liverpool against non-members and members of the "blue" union. "The attempt failed through lack of support by the T & G membership."[3] Usually, therefore, unions take disciplinary action only against leaders of unofficial strikes, and only when there has been a series of strikes in which the leaders are thought to be exploiting discontent for other purposes, for example to strengthen their own position within the union or to advance the cause of the Communist Party or some other organisation. After a series of unofficial dock strikes, the Transport and General Workers inquired into the activities of seventy-seven members, expelled three and cautioned some of the remainder or debarred them from office for a period. Even this may have its dangers, for it may appear to create "martyrs", whose chances of

---

[1] One example followed a strike at the Swindon works of the Pressed Steel Company (as it then was) in the spring of 1961 (Turner, Clack and Roberts, *Labour Relations in the Motor Industry*, pp. 283-4).

[2] A major instance of the use of disciplinary powers was the dismissal of a full-time officer and the suspension or exclusion from office of a number of lay officers after a strike at the Savoy Hotel in 1947 (H. A. Clegg, *General Union*, 1954, pp. 124-30). Three years earlier there was an instance of disciplining members when "the Northern district replied to an unofficial strike of Newcastle dockers by closing its docks branch and expelling all the strikers. A new branch was formed and the chastened strikers were re-admitted on condition they signed a document promising in future to abide by the constitution of the union" (p. 132).   [3] Devlin Committee, *Final Report*, p. 37.

success at subsequent union elections will be enhanced. A. F. Papworth and J. W. Jones, two of the busmen's leaders who were disciplined for unofficial activities following the London "coronation" bus strike in 1937, were subsequently elected to the union's executive, and figured among the few lay members of a trade union ever to sit on the General Council of the Trade Union Congress.

In any case the use of disciplinary powers in instances of this kind would be relevant to a discussion of trade union democracy only if the prime motive of the leaders had been to silence or remove opponents within the union, and the breach of rule had been used merely as a pretext. An examination of the cases quoted, and such other evidence as is available concerning the three largest unions, suggests that the prime object of the bodies within them concerned with administering discipline has been to establish whether the accused committed the offence with which they were charged and to assess the seriousness of their guilt. On the other hand according to the Royal Commission, "some members of the Electrical Trades Union in the recent past before its change of leadership faced expulsion and possible loss of their jobs for protesting against union malpractices".[1] The Royal Commission also asked a sample of 494 trade union members about the use of discipline and punishment in trade unions. Forty-five of them were able to give details of the most recent cases known to them. The most common offence was a lapsed subscription, and there were also cases of strike-breaking, of defying a ban on overtime or a prescribed limit to overtime, of "misconduct", of theft, and five cases of "disobeying union rules". In four cases the respondent thought that the punishment was unfair, but none of these were cases of expulsion, nor did the account suggest that the motive for the accusation was to injure a political opponent. Most of the forty-five cases appear to have been dealt with originally by branch meetings or by shop-floor meetings. Seven appeals were reported and in all but one of the six instances in which the respondent commented on the appeal, the hearing was said to have been fair. In three cases the decision was varied on appeal.[2] Although the Royal Commission held that too much should not be read into this, they went on to draw the general conclusion that "it is unlikely that abuse of power by trade unions is widespread". Next

[1] *Report*, pp. 166–7.   [2] *Workplace Industrial Relations*, pp. 123–5.

they referred to particular cases which had been brought to their attention "by Members of Parliament, and by others", in which the account supplied to them by the unions "invariably conflicted sharply with the complainant's account", and finally offered the opinion that in a trade union movement of ten million members which relies heavily upon voluntary part-time labour it was "almost inevitable that from time to time instances will occur where members have grounds for complaint of their treatment".[1]

Altogether therefore, there is very little evidence to suggest that the use of disciplinary powers to silence or remove opponents is generally an important factor in union government, and most of the evidence we have, inadequate though it is, points in the opposite direction.

OBSTACLES TO EFFECTIVE LEADERSHIP

To sum up, it is clear that British trade unions are not autocracies, and that trade union members have available to them a number of channels, varying from union to union, through which they can exert influence over their leaders. As in other large organisations, there is a tendency in trade unions for power to concentrate at the top, but there are also a number of checks upon leaders. Elections are held in all unions, and frequent elections in some. There are instances of rigged elections, but they seem to be relatively rare; and the low polls of most unions do not prove that votes are unrepresentative of the views of the members. Factions exist openly in almost all major unions, and in some unions they have wide liberty of action. Division of power between two or more central decision-making bodies can act as a check especially where it is strengthened by decentralisation to regions, districts, trade groups or branches. Workplace organisation often has considerable autonomy in practice, and work groups can use this both to settle their affairs for themselves, and also to protest against decisions which national union leaders have taken or propose to take. The body of full-time officers may also exercise some restraint over the national leaders of a major trade union. To determine the extent to which any one union is democratically governed would require an examination of the working of all these formal and informal arrangements, and probably others, in

[1] *Report*, pp. 168–9.

its decision-making processes. Consequently there can be no simple test of whether a union is democratic.

The degree to which it is democratic, however, is by no means the only important issue concerning trade union government. It is important to know what decisions trade unions take, as well as how they take them. The existence of a number of checks on a decision-making body may do more than hinder the development of oligarchy or autocracy. It may also hinder the taking of decisions. British trade unions have often been accused of conservatism, excessive caution and a failure to adapt themselves to developments around them; and there is substance in the charges. The forms of organisation and government of our three largest unions have remained unchanged for nearly fifty years or even longer. The Transport and General Workers' constitution was given to them in 1921 by their founder, Ernest Bevin, and in all essentials it is the same today. The constitution of the Amalgamated Engineering Union, drawn up at the time of the amalgamation of 1919, was in most respects copied from the rules of its major predecessor, the Amalgamated Society of Engineers, and has been taken over into the dominant engineering section of the Amalgamated Union of Engineering and Foundry Workers. The General and Municipal Workers went through a reorganisation in 1935-7, but this was no more than a rationalisation of the constitution drawn up for the amalgamation of 1924, and in turn closely copied from the rules of its major predecessor, the National Union of General Workers (formerly the Gasworkers). The environment in which these three unions work and the problems confronting them have changed radically since their rules were framed, but their systems of government have altered little. Moreover, each contains within itself ponderous obstacles to change.

One such obstacle among the Transport and General Workers is their trade group structure. The national trade group secretaries have no direct access to the executive or to conference. Although they are the administrative chiefs of their trade groups, responsible for collective bargaining within them, they are formally excluded from the making of "policy". Consequently each is naturally jealous of any interference by the general secretary with administration and negotiation within his own trade group, and as a body they resent intervention in the affairs of any trade

group, for each fears it may be his turn next. For years before the
Devlin Committee was appointed the need for new policies and
new methods in the docks group was proclaimed by frequent
unrest in the ports, by the power won and maintained by unofficial groups in the London docks, and by the failure of the
union to regain control in Liverpool and Hull after the incur-
sion of the "blue" union in 1954, although this rival union
was denied recognition by the employers. Within the trade
group nothing was done. New policies were not its task. From
time to time the general secretary was brought into the final
stages of pay negotiations, and in 1961 he joined with the employers in a declaration announcing a new approach to decasualisation; but this made no difference to the running of the trade
group. The Devlin Committee's final report contained one of
the most outspoken criticisms of a major trade union to be found
in a public document in Britain. It went on to suggest that the
union "must re-establish its power and authority in the three
major ports" by means of "a great campaign in which the Union
concentrates all its available resources. . . . Traditional arrangements and administrative procedures within the Union must not
be allowed to obstruct decisive action . . . The direction of the
campaign must be in the hands of the Union's senior officers."[1]
Following the publication of the report there was a reorganisation
of the staffing and administration of the union in the smallest of
the three ports, Hull, but little or nothing was done in London
and Liverpool. The massive and protracted unofficial strikes in the
autumn of 1967, which followed the introduction of the decasualisation arrangements negotiated by the union for those two
ports, tragically demonstrated its continued weakness and the
disaffection of the dockers there.

The district committees of the Engineers "have considerable
authority over local negotiations within their jurisdiction, and
may regard themselves as the guardians of their craft members'
rights and privileges".[2] Their close contacts with the plants make
it easy for them to obstruct the application of national policies
if they choose to do so. One example concerns the acceptance of
adult trainees to perform skilled work. The Royal Commission
heard evidence that in Manchester and on the Tyne the Engineers
refused "to allow such persons to be employed as skilled men even

[1] *Final Report*, pp. 43–6, 105–6.   [2] *Productivity Agreements*, p. 28.

if registered as dilutees" according to the national agreement on dilution of labour.[1] The influence of the district committees at the union's conference explains the long-standing opposition of conference to redundancy agreements, for many powerful district committees regard the acceptance of redundancy as an admission of weakness. They prefer to insist on work-sharing. Conference decisions, however, do not prevent some officers and stewards from entering into agreements with employers to protect their members from the effects of redundancy, which, at least in the case of closures, the union is powerless to prevent. Effectively, therefore, the union has no policy on redundancy. The district committees may also use their power to obstruct agreements between national union officers and individual companies. This was the response of some of the districts to the productivity agreement negotiated between the I.C.I. and the national officers of the major unions with which it deals.[2] Nevertheless, district powers have not been curtailed.

In contrast to these two unions, the General and Municipal Workers have for a number of years faced a problem of slowly falling membership. From a peak of 824,000 in 1947 it has gradually declined to 798,000 in 1968. One reason for the contrast between these figures and the sustained growth of the Transport and General Workers is that the latter is predominantly a union of the midlands and the south, whereas Lancashire and the north are the main centres of strength for the General and Municipal Workers, and population is shifting from the north to the south. However, the union's leaders have made considerable efforts to reverse the trend. A national recruiting drive was launched in 1961. Consultants were employed, a national recruiting team was put on the job and considerable sums of money were spent, but the results were negligible. One explanation put forward within the union is that the campaign was hindered by regional autonomy. Previously recruitment and retention of members had been regarded as within the scope of the regions, and even now the efforts of a national negotiating team could have a permanent effect only if they received the wholehearted co-operation and support of the districts. This, it is suggested, was not universally granted.

Another view which has some support within the union is that

---

[1] *Report*, p. 89.   [2] *Productivity Agreements*, pp. 28, 62–5.

the enthusiasm of existing members would be more easily aroused, and new members could be recruited more readily, if it offered more scope for them to discuss and settle their industrial problems industry by industry. Whether the matter in question is subject to industry bargaining or domestic bargaining, members in the chemical industry have more in common with each other than with members in local government, the car industry or electrical engineering, and this is true of each industrial group. But any arrangement which gave effective expression to this common interest would inevitably enhance the position of the national industrial officers at the expense of that of the regional secretaries who dominate the executive and lead their regional delegations to conference. There have been attempts to reform. Several years ago a proposal for a chemicals section with its own conference and staff formed part of an arrangement for amalgamation with the Chemical Workers' Union, but the amalgamation was rejected by the Chemical Workers' conference.[1] In 1969 the General and Municipal Workers' conference approved a report proposing seven industrial groups with regional and national industrial conferences. But these conferences are only advisory, and it remains to be seen whether the regional secretaries will permit them to play an effective part in the government of the union.

Despite the experience of these three unions, it would be a mistake to conclude that the checks on authority in British trade unions are so powerful that they constitute an insuperable obstacle to effective leadership. Two recent instances prove that this is not so.

The Electrical Trades Union carried through a radical reconstruction of its organisation and methods of government at its Rules Revision Conferences in 1962 and 1965. Besides the introduction of electoral safeguards and guarantees of members' rights as precautions against a Communist come-back, the part-time executive was transformed into a full-time body. To improve communications with members and shop stewards and to give them more effective service, many small branches in industrial concentrations were merged into larger branches served by a new grade of full-time branch official. At one time the union's area committees played a role within the union somewhat akin to that of the district committees among the Engineers. They

[1] *Trade Union Structure and Government* (Part I), p. 22.

have now been abolished. Area and national industrial conferences have been established as more effective means for
members to participate in the decisions which affect them.[1]
Meanwhile there have been radical changes in the industrial
policies of the union in electricity supply and electrical contracting
leading to industry-wide productivity agreements.[2]

Many of these reforms were directly intended to weaken the
influence of the Communist sympathisers who continued to hold
positions within the union even after the expulsion of the Communist leadership. Moreover, it was in the battle for the control
of the union that the new leaders developed the drive, knowledge
and resourcefulness which enabled them to follow through with
a major reconstruction of the union. But their success shows that
bold and effective leadership is possible in British trade unions.

The second example was not the consequence of a violent
political swing within a union. It was the outcome of slow shifts
of power and technical development, and the leader who was
able to make use of these changes was a Communist, Will
Paynter, the general secretary of the Mineworkers. More than
anyone else he was the author of the 1966 agreement with the
Coal Board, substituting time rates for payment by results as the
method of paying faceworkers using power-loading machinery,
which now accounts for more than 90 per cent of the industry's
output.

This was a startling achievement because the faceworkers
traditionally preferred payment by results on the ground that it
gave them a good deal of control over their own jobs and their
own pay-packets. They were able to push up their own earnings
whereas the majority of wage-earners in the industry, the day-
wagemen who work on the surface and provide support services
underground, were dependent on industry negotiations with the
Coal Board for increases. Although a minority in the union as a
whole, the pieceworkers were traditionally the aristocrats of the
union. They dominated its meetings from branch to conference,
and held most of its offices.

The main argument against payment by results was that
increasing mechanisation had reduced the control which miners
at the face could exercise over their output. Their work has

---

[1] An account of these changes is contained in the Union's written evidence to the
Royal Commission, *Minutes of Evidence*, pp. 2449–54, 2472–4.   [2] See pp. 309–10, 424–5.

E

become largely machine-paced. But the union leaders had for long looked forward to a rational pay structure for the whole industry to complete the daywage structure negotiated in 1955, and they were therefore ready to take advantage of the opportunity provided by mechanisation. They argued that the gap between the earnings of pieceworkers and those of dayworkers was too wide and that there was no possibility of a more equitable pay structure so long as payment by results persisted. This argument naturally appealed to the daywagemen. Although the Coal Board had also looked forward to a rational pay structure there was in 1964 and 1965 a division of opinion among the Board and its experts as to whether the time was ripe for a change. The voice of those in favour was strengthened in February 1966 by the publication of a report of the National Board of Prices and Incomes on *Coal Prices* which gave outspoken support to Paynter's case.[1]

In negotiation with the Coal Board the day rates for power-loading teams were settled on the basis of current average earnings district by district, except that the lowest rate was put at 75s. a shift, which was above the current average earnings of the six lowest-paid areas. This, together with the support of the day-wagemen, was enough to win the support of these areas for the new agreement. They included South Wales, Scotland and Durham. In addition to the geographical areas of the union, the crafts-men (mainly engaged in maintenance work) and the clerical and supervisory groups are organised in separate "functional" areas. Mechanisation has increased their numbers in proportion to those of the rest of the labour force. They are also timeworkers, and Paynter's arguments appealed to them. Together with the low-paid areas they were able to outvote the predictable opposition of nearly all of the higher-paid areas by 269,000 votes to 226,000. Thus Paynter and his colleagues had achieved not only a revolution in the methods of payment and the wage structure of the industry, but also a revolution in the distribution of power within the union.

It is possible to put too much emphasis on the obstacles which British methods of trade union government place in the path of effective leadership. Given leaders of vision and audacity, who understand how to make use of their opportunities, trade unions can be led effectively.

[1] National Board for Prices and Incomes, Report No. 12, Cmnd. 2919, 1966, pp. 13–14.

CHAPTER 4

EMPLOYERS' ASSOCIATIONS

There is no satisfactory term to describe the employers' counterpart of trade unions—"the bosses' unions". Legally many of them are trade unions,[1] but they are manifestly not covered by the normal usage of the term. In some industries the central organisation is a "federation", which uses the word "association" to describe its constituent local bodies. Both could be brought under the heading "employers' organisations", but this term is too general. It could be taken to cover also commercial "trade associations" where these are separate from the organisations dealing with industrial relations. Consequently, for want of a better term the words "employers' associations" are generally used to describe all employers' organisations dealing with industrial relations, whether they are federations or associations and whether they also deal with commercial matters or not.

BEFORE 1914

The history of British employers' associations has not been written. This is partly because employers have generally been more secretive about their business than trade unions. Not being mass organisations, they can generally keep their internal business to themselves if they wish to do so. But this is not the whole story. At least before 1914 much of the material which is used for writing trade union history is also relevant to employers' associations. Many associations have preserved their records and some of these have been made available to students. One or two associations have published individual official histories.[2] The Social Science Association's Report on *Trade Societies and Strikes* is

---

[1] See p. 350.
[2] For instance, L. H. Powell, *The Shipping Federation 1890–1950*, London 1950; and Ellic Howe, *The British Federation of Master Printers 1900–1950*, London 1950.

almost as useful a source for the early history of employers' associations as for that of trade unions.[1] The 1867 Royal Commission on the Organisation and Rules of Trade Unions and Other Associations,[2] and the 1891 Royal Commission on Labour,[3] took evidence from almost as many representatives of employers' associations as trade union officers. For the early years of the present century there is the evidence offered to the 1903 Royal Commission on Trade Disputes and Trade Combinations,[4] and to the Inquiry into Industrial Agreements[5] conducted by the Industrial Council in 1912.

Thus the history of employers' associations awaits the scholar who will undertake the task. In the meantime, a survey of these sources can reveal the broad outlines of their developments, and these outlines must be sketched out if the present behaviour and attitudes of employers' associations is to be understood. They have a long history. Adam Smith asserted that understandings between employers were common in his day[6] and associations of master printers can be traced back into the eighteenth century.[7] The Liverpool Master Shipwrights "reorganised their association" in 1823, after which it remained in existence at least for several decades.[8] Cotton employers were organised equally early in several Lancashire towns and in Glasgow.[9]

In some instances organisation was formal, and in others it consisted of no more than *ad hoc* meetings and verbal understandings. The Royal Commission on Trade Unions was told that for many years "there was no real West Riding Masters' Association . . . but they met when there was any special action taken on the part of the men, or when it was thought necessary to have a reduction or any advance in the price of coals".[10] Some associations were called into existence to deal with strikes. The

[1] Presented to the fourth annual meeting of the association in Glasgow in 1860 and published in the same year.

[2] Henceforth the Royal Commission on Trade Unions. *Minutes of Evidence*, published in several volumes 1867–9.

[3] *Minutes of Evidence*, published in numerous volumes 1892–4.

[4] Henceforth the Royal Commission on Trade Disputes. *Minutes of Evidence*, Cd. 2826, 1906.   [5] *Report* and *Minutes of Evidence*, Cd. 6952 and Cd. 6953, 1913.

[6] "Masters are always and everywhere in a sort of tacit, but constant and uniform combination, not to raise wages of labour above their actual rate." *The Wealth of Nations*, Everyman's Library Edition, p. 59.

[7] Ellic Howe, *The London Compositor, 1785–1900*, 1947, p. 10.

[8] *Report on Trade Societies and Strikes*, p. 482.   [9] *Ibid.*, pp. 393, 396, 433.   [10] Q. 12521.

Preston Master Spinners' Association, for example, "took cognisance of disputes having reference to wages up to the year 1846, after which it is said to have been inactive up to 1853" when it had to deal with a prolonged stoppage. In the interval "it was never finally dissolved".[1]

Some associations did not deal with industrial relations, at least formally. The London Master Builders was formed in "March, 1834 by 15 builders, who met and resolved 'That the parties now present do form themselves into an association . . . the object of which is to promote a friendly feeling and an interchange of useful information' ".[2] But it was not easy to keep within these limits when there was a strike. The London Master Builders "never dealt with any question of that kind but they have convened a public meeting of the trade",[3] and during the London building lockout of 1859–60 there was formed "another association, entirely distinct, called the Central Association of Master Builders, which went through the matter and was dissolved at its close"[4]—only to be called back to life to deal with later disputes.

The Mining Association of Great Britain, formed in 1854, took the view that industrial relations were the exclusive concern of the coalfield associations. Even so "it is impossible to overlook the opportunities which it must afford the coal-owners, by simply bringing them together from all parts of the kingdom, for preparing and concerting their measures towards the men".[5]

Until the last quarter of the nineteenth century most employers' associations were limited to a single town or region. Times of crisis, however, led to action on a national scale. The attack on the trade unions in 1833–4 saw the use of the "document"—an undertaking binding employees to desert their trade unions—in London, throughout the midlands, and in Lancashire and Yorkshire. In December 1864, the ironmasters "of North and South Staffordshire, Sheffield, Derbyshire and the North of England met together and decided to give simultaneous notice of a reduction of wages, equal to 10 per cent".[6] About the same time there was also an attempt to form a permanent General Builders'

---

[1] *Report on Trade Societies and Strikes*, p. 209.
[2] Royal Commission on Trade Unions, Q. 2580.
[3] *Ibid.*, Q. 2583.
[4] *Ibid.*, Q. 2626.
[5] *Report on Trade Societies and Strikes*, p. 20.
[6] Royal Commission on Trade Unions, *Fifth Report*, p. 55.

Association. Its secretary told the 1867 Royal Commission that "the general association is formed of an aggregate of local associations that are scattered all over the country . . ., principally in the west and north of England, and three or four towns in Scotland".[1]

It has often been assumed that employers were generally hostile to trade unions throughout most of the nineteenth century, and there is evidence of antagonism. The "document" was used to destroy trade unions in 1833–4. It was used again in the engineering lockout of 1852 and the London building lockout of 1859–60, although the Engineers continued to support their union despite their signatures to the document, and the withdrawal of the document was one of the conditions on which the building dispute was terminated. The Secretary of the General Builders' Association told the Royal Commission on Trade Unions that: "As an association I may say that we object to trades unions . . . under three general heads; first, that many of their objects are improper and contrary to public policy; in the second place, that those objects that may not be improper or contrary to public policy are pursued by them by improper means; and thirdly, . . . they exercise coercion over both masters and men and tend to separate masters and men."[2]

The excuse offered for their own associations was that these were the employers' only means of defence against the trade unions. One witness admitted to the Commission that his own association was as guilty as the unions of interfering with "the action of those natural laws of supply and demand", and went on to say "I am for having them all abolished, I should be glad if this were the result of this Commission".[3]

However, employers' associations must accept a greater share of responsibility than this for the development of collective regulation of industrial relations. In the first place many associations interfered with the laws of supply and demand on their own, even undertaking to regulate wages without any pressure from unions. This was true of both coal and iron. In coalmining the regulation of prices and wages on a county basis by the coal-owners was the general practice long before stable unions were established. In iron, so the 1867 Royal Commission on Trade Unions was informed, the South Staffordshire association already

[1] *Ibid.*, Q. 2959.   [2] *Ibid.*, Q. 2971.   [3] *Ibid.*, Qs. 3489–3490.

dated back some forty or fifty years.[1] It had held quarterly meetings for many years. At these "the selling prices of iron for the district have been fixed, and wages were invariably regulated by these prices until recently . . ."[2] The first stable union, the Ironworkers' Association, was founded only in 1863. Before 1879, when an agreement was made with the unions, the Cleveland Iron Masters "met together and agreed as to whether they could ask for a reduction of wages or not, and then each works negotiated with its own men separately".[3]

Nor did employers generally object to dealing with trade unions. The practice of collective bargaining can be traced back into the eighteenth century. In the London bookbinding trade a reduction in the working day from eleven hours to ten "was obtained . . ., by mutual agreement, after considerable negotiation. . . . It would appear that it was arranged with a combination of employers, and given by them before it was given by the employers generally throughout the trade."[4] By the middle of the nineteenth century the London printing trade had a long history of joint if intermittent regulation of pay based on "decisions on a scale made in 1810 with additions, definitions and explanations arranged at a Conference of Master Printers and Compositors in 1847".[5]

About the middle of the century the building trade developed the practice of drawing up "town rules" at meetings of building employers and representatives of the building craft unions. Even the General Builders' Association assisted in this development, for all its objections in principle to trade unionism. Its committee met a deputation from the Birmingham unions and arranged for "a public meeting of masters and operatives connected with the building trades for the purposes of appointing delegates on both sides to draw up trade rules".[6]

A rule adopted by the North of England Ironmasters in 1865 may serve to sum up the attitude of many employers at that time. They included among their functions "the holding of free and friendly communication with the representatives of the ironworkers with a view to the avoidance of strikes, and at the same

[1] *Ibid.*, Q. 9829.   [2] *Ibid., Fifth Report*, p. 57.
[3] *Inquiry into Industrial Agreements*, Q. 9035.
[4] *Report on Trade Societies and Strikes*, pp. 95–8.
[5] *Ibid.*, p. 86.   [6] Royal Commission on Trade Unions, Q. 3074.

time the prompt and united resistance of any attempt on the part of the men to enforce unreasonable demands . . ."[1] The strikes and lockouts of the period which have attracted the attention of historians occurred when the employers had decided to oppose what they considered to be "unreasonable demands". In between, particularly in the craft trades, there were long periods of "peaceful co-existence" with "free and friendly communications" as required.

In some instances employers took the lead in establishing collective bargaining. Under the inspiration of a leading Quaker employer, Sir David Dale, the North of England Ironmasters joined with the union to set up a Conciliation Board in 1869. Within a few years it had established a sliding-scale system of regulating wages in accordance with price fluctuations. The regulation of wages by price movements had always seemed to the employers a condition of industrial peace in their industry, and now they had achieved it by agreement with the union.

Dale's board was to some extent copied from the Hosiery Conciliation Board established in Nottingham in 1860 under the leadership of a local employer, A. J. Mundella. The trade had already experienced three strikes during the course of the year, one of them lasting for eleven weeks, and he and some of his colleagues thought "we might devise some better way of settling the thing".[2] The board was therefore set up to regulate the piece prices which governed payment for the thousands of operations included in the industry, and a Hosiery Association formed to supply the employers' representatives.

In 1881 the Cotton Spinners' and Manufacturers' Association, which mainly organised weaving employers, joined with the local weavers' unions to lay down a county-wide procedure for dealing with disputes which could not be settled locally. This was followed in 1884 by the establishment of the Amalgamated Weavers' Association, the first central organisation on the workers' side to cover the majority of the local weavers' associations.

The "new unionism" of 1889 was responsible for new developments among employers including the foundation of some of Britain's major employers' federations. This movement had two aspects: it extended trade unionism to industries previously unorganised or ill-organised; and it created militant groups

---

[1] *Ibid., Fifth Report*, p. 57.   [2] *Ibid.*, Q. 19345.

within some of the existing unions. A consequence of the upsurge of trade unionism on the waterfront, now remembered chiefly for the London dock strike of 1889, was the formation of the Shipping Federation in 1890 with the purpose of defeating the closed-shop policy of the Sailors' and Firemen's union. Conflict with the seamen also brought the Federation up against the dockers' unions. Within three years, by a series of strikes and lockouts, it had reduced the seamen's union and the dockers' unions to feeble remnants. Thereafter it prevented their recovery for almost twenty years. This it achieved by the organisation of strike-breaking on an unparalleled scale. The Federation maintained three vessels to transport and house workers to replace striking seamen and dockers, as well as motor launches on the Mersey and Tyne.[1] Large sums were spent on this and on guarding feeding and providing "beer tokens" for these men while they did the work of the strikers.[2]

Elsewhere the outcome was not the destruction of trade unions, but the hastening of new developments in collective bargaining. In the boot and shoe industry, where the new unionism affected particularly the London and Northampton branches of the powerful National Union of Boot and Shoe Operatives, it lent its support to a policy of meeting new technical developments by the imposition of restrictive practices. It was partly in response to this that a Manufacturers' Federation was formed in 1891. Although its original aim was to maintain hostile action against the union[3] the outcome of a seven-week lockout in 1895 was an industry-wide agreement, accepted by the union, with monetary penalties against a breach of it by either side.

A similar conflict developed in the engineering industry, where the central issues were the "machine question" and the new unionist demand for the eight-hour day. The Amalgamated Society of Engineers, encouraged by the new unionists among its ranks, insisted that new machines for jobs previously performed by skilled men should be operated by craftsmen at craft

[1] *The Shipping Federation, 1890–1950*, p. 8.

[2] "Since 1890 the Federation has paid out to its members by way of strike indemnity £467,120. Other strike expenditure amounted to £201,483" (*ibid.*, p. 144). As there have been very few strikes since 1914, almost all this expenditure must have been incurred in the first twenty-four years of the Federation's existence.

[3] *Footwear Organiser*, August 1923, quoted in Alan Fox, *A History of the National Union of Boot and Shoe Operatives*, 1958, p. 130.

rates. The employers replied by forming an Employers' Federation of Engineering Associations which enforced a lockout in 1897 over the question of a union claim for an eight-hour day in London. As the dispute continued through the autumn the employers spread their organisation throughout the country, shutting down one centre after another. Eventually the exhausting conflict was brought to an end in February 1898 on terms which limited the union in several directions, giving the employers freedom "to appoint the men they consider suitable to work" the machines "and to determine the conditions under which such machine tools shall be worked". In addition a new procedure was agreed whereby unresolved local disputes would be referred to a Central Conference before either side enforced a stoppage.

Meanwhile similar developments had occurred in other industries which were little affected by the new unionism. The Shipbuilding Employers' Federation had been formed in 1889 to counter the rapidly growing strength of the Boilermakers' Society; although it was not until 1908 that they were able to force the Boilermakers and the other shipbuilding unions into a national agreement for processing disputes which had many similarities to the engineering agreement. After several attempts the spinning employers finally succeeded in 1891 in forming the Federation of Master Cotton Spinners' Associations to offset the solidly organised and exceptionally rich Spinners' Amalgamation. After massive lockouts in 1892–3 the two bodies came together to sign the Brooklands Agreement, which also set up a system of processing local disputes to a central meeting.

The nineties was a period of unusual activity in the building industry, and the building unions took full advantage of it. As a result the National Federation of Building Trades Employers, which had been formed in 1878,[1] locked out the plasterers in 1899. The solution was a central disputes procedure for the plastering section of the trade, followed in 1904 by a similar agreement in the whole building industry.

A central disputes procedure is one half of an industry-wide system of collective bargaining, the other is the practice of

---

[1] This successor to the General Builders' Association had among its objects to formulate a common policy on labour matters and to resist the efforts of the unions "to impose restrictive conditions on the building trades". (National Association of Master Builders, *Minutes*, 9 and 23, January 1878.)

negotiating industry-wide agreements on pay and conditions of work. Up to 1914 most industries, even those with central disputes procedures, continued to regulate pay and conditions on a district basis, the national bodies on either side intervening only when no agreement could be reached within the district. But there were exceptions. The cotton weaving industry agreed a "uniform list" of piece prices for weaving standard grey cloth as early as 1892. Henceforth the whole list was adjusted upwards or downwards by additions or subtractions. A uniform list had been an objective of the employers' association ever since its foundation in 1866 at a meeting of the Blackburn and Preston employers to discuss the possibility of a uniform list for their two districts,[1] although the industry-wide list was finally achieved only under considerable union pressure. When in 1908 the shipbuilding industry instituted a system of "national wage fluctuations"— general percentage alterations to existing local rates—the shipbuilding employers achieved an objective which they had included among the aims of their federation at its foundation.

Up to 1914, then, employers' associations had played a vigorous and creative part in building the system of industrial relations as it then was. In some industries they had introduced methods of collective pay regulation before stable unions were formed; in some industries they had taken the initiative in developing collective bargaining; in a number of industries they were responsible for setting up central disputes procedures, even forcing the unions to accept them; and the rare instances of industry-wide wage regulation before 1914 owed more to the employers than to the unions.

SINCE 1914

With the war, however, initiative passed to the government. In most of the many and important changes experienced by the system of industrial relations during the next few years, the employers followed the lead of the state, sometimes readily and sometimes most unwillingly. The government needed the co-operation of the unions in increasing the output of munitions and in improving the efficiency of industries and services which

[1] Roland Smith, *A History of the Lancashire Cotton Industry between the Years 1873 and 1896* (Ph.D. thesis, Birmingham, 1954).

might contribute to victory. In order to win their goodwill, and to provide means of settling disputes without interrupting production, government departments enforced widespread extensions in collective bargaining. Under state control the railway companies and the shipowners, who had until then kept the unions at arms' length, met the unions and entered into agreements with them. The introduction of compulsory arbitration enabled unions to force unwilling employers to appear before a tribunal and to accept as awards changes in wages and conditions which they refused to negotiate with the unions. Towards the end of the war the Whitley Reports led to widespread and generally successful efforts on the part of the government to embody temporary war-time arrangements for collective bargaining into permanent Joint Industrial Councils. Wage-fixing machinery by means of Trade Boards was extended to cover industries where the organisations of employers and the unions were too weak to sustain a system of collective bargaining. By 1920 the great majority of wage-earners and large sections of salary-earners were covered by some form of collective bargaining or statutory wage-fixation.

The first national agreements in the chemicals industry, for instance, were the result of awards issued by the Committee on Production, as the main arbitration tribunal was called. In 1919 a Joint Industrial Council was established as a permanent negotiating body with the recently formed Chemical and Allied Employers' Association as the employers' side. Similarly the Federation of Gas Employers came into existence in 1918, after the Committee on Production had begun issuing national awards covering the gas industry, and took part in establishing the Joint Council for the Gas Industry in the following year. In 1920 the Minister of Labour set up a court of inquiry into the claims of the dockers' unions which recommended, among other things, the establishment of a Joint Industrial Council for the docks. As a result the National Joint Council for Port Transport was set up, and local employers' associations joined together with national organisations of users of dock facilities, such as the Shipping Federation, to constitute the National Association of Port Employers to serve as the employers' side. The National Confederation of Employers' Organisations (subsequently the British Employers' Confederation) also came into being shortly after the war as a consequence of government action.

The effect of government war-time intervention was not confined to organisation. It also gave a new impetus to the introduction of industry-wide pay settlements. The new coalition formed by Lloyd George at the end of 1916 depended heavily upon Labour support, and he was anxious to meet the trade union objections to the conduct of affairs on the home front. One of the main grievances was over wages. In their desire to avoid inflation the Asquith government had used arbitration to restrain wage increases, especially in the engineering industry, and the unions complained that much time and energy was involved in negotiating what was essentially a single claim—for an advance due to war circumstances—through dozens of different district negotiating bodies. In order to expedite matters it was agreed early in 1917 that henceforth engineering and shipbuilding wages would be dealt with every four months and the standard increases would apply throughout each industry. Over the next two years a large number of other industries followed engineering.

Although government intervention in industry was cut back rapidly during the two or three years after the war, employers' associations did not recover the initiative they had lost. Since then important innovations in the industry-wide conduct of industrial relations, when they have occurred, have been inspired by the government. The holidays-with-pay movement of the nineteen-thirties was encouraged by a government committee and supported by granting new powers to statutory wage-fixing bodies. The most important extension of some form of collective regulation of pay and conditions of work in previously unorganised industries has been by widening the scope of statutory wage-fixing, notably to road haulage, to retail distribution and to catering. The conclusion of industry-wide agreements providing work-place consultation over production, welfare, safety and other matters was the consequence of government exhortation in war time, renewed by the post-war Labour government in 1948. During the second world war compulsory arbitration was reintroduced and Essential Work Orders were used by the Ministry of Labour to insist that wages and conditions of work should be settled by voluntary machinery in industries to which direction of labour was applied. Both these devices enabled government pressure to fill in many of the interstices still left in the system of industry-wide collective regulation.

Dramatic proof that employers' associations did not wish to regain the initiative in developing the system of industrial relations came out of the so-called Mond-Turner talks which followed the General Strike of 1926.

In September 1927 George Hicks, that year's president of the Trades Union Congress, threw out a hint at the meeting of Congress that "much fuller use can be made . . . of the machinery for joint consultation and negotiation between employers and employed . . . and practically nothing has yet been done to establish effective machinery of joint conference between representative organisations entitled to speak for industry as a whole".[1] The British Employers' Confederation and the Federation of British Industries (which dealt with commercial matters) made no response, but Sir Alfred Mond, chairman of the newly founded I.C.I., brought together a group of leading industrialists drawn from the country's major industries—including engineering, shipbuilding, cotton textiles and railways—to meet the General Council of the Trades Union Congress, whose chairman was now Ben Turner.

There emerged a set of recommendations which fall under three headings. The first dealt with improvements in the machinery for collective bargaining, together with a proposal for a National Industrial Council of representatives of Congress, of the Federation of British Industries and of the National Confederation of Employers' Organisations. The second covered issues of government economic policy and made proposals for expansion which were in advance of anything the current Conservative government or the subsequent Labour government were prepared to adopt. The third dealt with what was then called "rationalisation". The unions recognised the need for industrial reorganisation and for new machinery and methods of production; and the employers agreed that consultation was necessary, and that there must be protection for the interests of workers who might be displaced as a result.[2]

This was an enlightened programme, but the participants in the talks could not initiate action themselves. Their second set of proposals consisted of recommendations to the government, and the third could only be applied throughout industry if it was

[1] Trades Union Congress, *Annual Report*, 1927, pp. 66–7.
[2] *Ibid.*, 1928, pp. 209–30 and 1929, pp. 188–204.

accepted by some such joint body as was proposed under the first. That depended on the reactions of the Federation of British Industries and the British Employers' Confederation, to whom the Mond-Turner Report was submitted in July 1928.

The Federation responded warmly. On 11 July its Council agreed that the Federation was "wholeheartedly at one with the conference in its prime objects".[1] The constitution of the Federation favoured Mond (now Lord Melchett) and his colleagues. Its affiliates included not only trade associations (some of which were at the same time employers' associations) but also individual firms. Representatives of big firms therefore figured prominently in its councils and committees, and many of the employers' group in the discussions were or had been Federation office-holders.

The Confederation was constructed to a different pattern. Only associations could affiliate, and the lead was taken by the chief officers of the associations, Gregorson of the Iron and Steel Trades Employers' Association, Cuthbert Laws of the Shipping Federation and, above all, Sir Allan Smith of the Engineering Employers' Federation. Although they constituted only about one-tenth of the total strength of the Federation, the Engineering Employers had dominated its activities from the start. They had called the meeting to consider its formation, with Smith in the chair. They had provided it with an office and, in the early days, even with notepaper. And as the Engineering Employers dominated the Confederation, so Smith dominated the Engineering Employers.

The attitudes of Smith and his colleagues towards the unions had been shaped by their experience of the shop stewards' movement during the war, and by the 1922 engineering lockout. In their eyes the engineering workers had been responsible for "a policy of interference, urged on by the unions and encouraged by war conditions ... with a view to shifting the frontier into management's territory. ... Complaints of obstacles placed in the way of executing orders poured into the Employers' Federation from all quarters".[2] During the lockout—which concerned "managerial rights" in general and in particular management's right to decide when overtime was to be worked—one of their number, J. C. Gould, told the House of Commons that its

---

[1] Federation of British Industries, *Grand Council Minutes*, 11 July 1928.
[2] A. Shadwell, *The Engineering Industry and the Crisis of 1922*, 1922, p. 63. Shadwell was the Federation's apologist.

Members did not appreciate "the intolerable conditions imposed upon us in our daily work. Lines of demarcation, disputes as to how many men shall be put upon a machine, overtime conditions, and all these things are being brought up to us from day to day and we . . . are being met by every particle of opposition which it is possible to put against us, . . . because of the wild men who are assuming control of the trade unions."[1] Smith himself wrote to the Amalgamated Engineering Union to tell them that: "My committee . . . have been forced to this conclusion that the difficulty they have to face . . . is one in which political issues have been the motive and in which outside and even international policy have been the real cause of the present unfortunate state of affairs."[2]

Consequently in the summer of 1928 the Confederation's General Purposes Committee acted more cautiously than their colleagues in the Federation. Keeping their own counsel, they decided to ask all the constituent associations to comment on the proposals. As the autumn passed the replies began to come in. Influenced by Mond and his friend Sir David Milne-Watson, doyen of the gas employers, the associations in chemicals and gas took a favourable view. Others were for a middle course, many being hostile to the proposals for new bargaining machinery but ready to accept some form of consultation with the Trades Union Congress. At the end of November the Engineering Employers gave their verdict. They condemned the proposals as a whole, emphasising the links between the Trades Union Congress and the Labour Party, which sought "the abolition of capital". There was, they said, "as little justification for discussion with a political Trades Union Congress as with a political Conservative, Liberal or even Communist Party".[3] When all the replies were in, the Confederation prepared its own report. Closely following the Engineering Employers, it warned that "if the T.U.C. were to be constituted the Workers' side of a National Industrial Council, it might well mean the entire handing over of industrial problems to politicians".[4]

By this time the New Year was past, the press was agitating

---

[1] *Hansard*, 20 March, 1922, cols. 89 and 95.   [2] Letter dated 25 April 1922.
[3] Reply of the Engineering and Allied Employers' National Federation (the full title at that time), National Confederation of Employers' Organisations, *Industrial Peace Files*, 30 November 1928.   [4] *Ibid.*, 28 January 1929.

for an answer and the Federation was chafing. Somehow the employers must agree on a joint response. Accordingly, the Confederation braced themselves to accept at least consultation with the Trades Union Congress, "not", in Cuthbert Laws' words, "in the interests of the Mond-Turner Reports, but in the interests of the unity of employers".[1]

At last, on 23 April 1929, the three organisations met, but only for the Trades Union Congress representatives to hear that the totally different responsibilities of the two employers' bodies forbade them entering into a single National Industrial Council. Instead the employers proposed a permissive arrangement whereby, in matters in which the Federation was competent, either its Council or the General Council of the Trades Union Congress could propose consultations which might or might not be accepted by the other party; and similarly with the Confederation. But these consultations must not "invade the province and trespass on the function of the individual constituents" of any of the three organisations.[2] This cumbersome and impotent machinery was accepted and employed on two or three occasions to issue joint statements on current issues, but soon fell into disuse.

On this occasion Britain missed an opportunity to reconstruct its system of industrial relations to meet the requirements of the future; the cause was the attitude which the majority of the employers' associations had now taken up. Any change, they had come to believe, might be exploited by the unions, and their overriding concern was to resist further union encroachments, even after the defeats which the unions had sustained in 1926. The Confederation had clearly indicated to individual employers that the path to reform in industrial relations did not lie through employers' associations. If they wanted reform they must pursue it in their own companies through their own personnel policies.

PRESENT AIMS AND FUNCTIONS

There are no precise figures for the overall membership of employers' associations. The Confederation of British Industry told the Royal Commission that "in many major industries

[1] National Confederation of Employers' Organisations, *General Purposes Committee Minutes*, 8 February 1929.
[2] Trades Union Congress, *Annual Reports*, 1929, 1930.

federated companies employ 80 per cent or more of the industry's labour force, and in few industries is the proportion below 50 per cent".[1] This is not at variance with the findings of the Royal Commission's survey of national associations and federations which showed that only a minority (over a third of the associations and 17 per cent of the federations) laid claim to as much as 75 per cent of firms eligible for membership, for most of them also said that the non-members were for the most part relatively small firms.[2]

More precise figures are available for some industries. In engineering, with over 18,000 establishments employing more than ten workers, the Federation has 4600 establishments in membership. These employ about two million out of 3·5 million workers in the industry. The National Federation of Building Trades Employers estimates that "between 700,000 and 750,000 are employed in those parts of the industry organised by the Federation and of these approximately 60 per cent are employed in member firms . . . The Federation states that its membership covers nearly all the large contractors employing more than 250 men, 60 per cent of the medium-sized firms employing between 100 and 250, and a diminishing percentage with each smaller size group." In civil engineering most firms are relatively large and it is the opinion of the Federation of Civil Engineering Contractors that its 710 members cover "almost all workers who are employed on civil engineering operations other than by labour-only contractors since actual membership is said to be 98 per cent of potential".[3]

Imprecise though most of them are, these estimates make it evident that employers' associations cover a substantially greater proportion of the labour force than do trade unions with just over 40 per cent of employees in membership. But this contrast is an inevitable consequence of the nature of the two organisations. Apart from the multi-product firm which may pay dues to several associations in respect of different sections of its labour force, employers cannot normally join associations by halves. They must be either in or out, so that when the employer of a thousand workers joins the association he increases its coverage by a

---

[1] *Selected Written Evidence*, p. 259.
[2] V. G. Munns and W. E. J. McCarthy, *Employers' Associations*, Royal Commission *Research Paper No. 7*, 1967, p. 90.   [3] *Ibid.*, pp. 19–23.

thousand. By contrast the unions may think they are reasonably well organised if they have 60 or 70 per cent of those workers in membership.

Figures for the coverage of employers' associations in the past are a good deal less precise even than current estimates. In 1938 J. H. Richardson suggested that "as a rough approximation . . . about one half of British workers are employed in organised firms".[1] If this approximation is anywhere near the truth it seems that over the last thirty years in which their regulative affect has been declining, the associations have substantially increased their coverage.

Why do most sizeable firms join their federations and remain in membership? The surveys of the Royal Commission indicate some of the advantages of membership as seen by managers and association officials. In the first place it must be remembered that the majority of employers' associations are also trade associations, and firms may be as interested in the commercial advantages of membership as in the assistance they receive in labour matters. V. G. Munns found that some national associations and federations "tended to stress the importance of protecting members' interests in the relation with Government, public authorities, professional bodies, suppliers of materials, and 'customers' (that is to say large users of the service or commodity supplied, frequently public bodies or main contractors)".[2] The survey of association officials found that "the great majority of national and local officials thought that their most time-consuming functions lay in the areas of 'technical, commercial and educational' activities. . . . Most of those interviewed thought that the time spent on such trading functions had increased in recent years. Virtually nobody thought it had decreased." The officials were also asked to list the advantages of membership. One of the two most frequent answers was "uniformity of collective action", but the other was "the chance to participate in liaison activities in respect of Government". These activities may be concerned with labour legislation and regulations, but they are as likely to cover commercial matters.[3]

---

[1] *Industrial Relations in Great Britain*, p. 83. In his first edition (1933) he suggested a reduction of 20 per cent to allow for unemployment. The statistical basis for these estimates is unknown.

[2] Munns and McCarthy, p. 26.   [3] *Ibid.*, pp. 91–2.

The opinions reported by the Commission's survey of works managers and personnel officers are set out in Table IV. They show that works managers attach as much importance to technical information as to collective action, and that personnel officers value collective action less than several other association services. Besides organising lobbies on current labour legislation and statutory orders, and advising members on the meaning and application of Acts and regulations which have taken effect, the associations have in recent years considerably expanded their training and technical services.

TABLE IV

REPORTED ADVANTAGES OF MEMBERSHIP OF EMPLOYERS' ASSOCIATIONS[1]

Benefit	Works Managers (per cent)	Personnel Officers (per cent)
Collective action/uniform decisions	28	24
Technical information	28	15
Advice on trade union matters	25	28
Representation/liaison with government and trade unions	24	35
Advice on wage rates	19	19
Advice and information on government or local authority regulations/price policy	16	27
Advice on training schemes etc.	5	8
Advice on holiday arrangements	2	3
Other answers	12	7

Munns found that all the associations which he visited were to some extent concerned with training and that a number of them had appointed training specialists.[2] Some had opened their own training establishments, especially for the training of supervisors. The National Federation of Building Trades Employers offers

[1] *Workplace Industrial Relations*, pp. 93–4. Of the 319 plants covered, 258 were federated. In these plants, 82 per cent of works managers and 92 per cent of the personnel officers said that they derived some practical benefit from membership, but 11 per cent of the works managers and 12 per cent of the personnel officers could not or did not say what the benefits were. The table sets out the replies of the remainder, as a percentage of those claiming some practical benefit.

[2] Munns and McCarthy, pp. 60–1.

"management advisory services" to its members, as do the major textile associations, the Engineering Employers and several local associations in engineering. Among other things they offer assistance in work study or over productivity agreements.

However, even when allowance has been made for all this, collective action remains an important function of employers' associations in the eyes of their members. Munn's findings confirmed the general view that in dealing with conditions of work, such as the length of the normal working week, the number of days' holiday each year, and premium payments for shift work and overtime, "the national agreements . . . are regarded as standard and not subject to improvement at the local level".[1] With rates of pay it is a different matter. In this respect he found that, with the exception of electrical contracting, industry wage agreements do not "produce a national wage structure for the industries they serve. . . . In general, the most that the central negotiations can achieve in this direction is to indicate a pattern of relationships which individual employers may follow in the establishment of their own structure if they wish to, and if they are able to in the prevailing labour supply situation or other circumstances affecting their business."[2] The survey of associations confirmed his finding. Of the twenty-four national associations and federations which negotiated industry pay agreements, twenty settled "basic rates only, allowing management at local level to agree to higher or supplementary rates". Four said that they settled "effective rates, with very little freedom to negotiate other rates at local level". These four organisations were than asked how they prevented members paying above the agreed rates if they wished to do so. One official said that there was no attempt to control, another abandoned the opinion that his organisation settled effective rates and agreed only minimum rates were in fact negotiated. The methods used by the two remaining bodies were "diplomatic letters" or "purely persuasion". Both national and local officials were asked to what extent workers paid by results received "more than the nationally agreed minimum level of earnings", and to what extent time workers were paid more than "the national rate for the job". The majority answered that all but a few workers were paid more than the nationally agreed figures. The major exception was the building industry in which a

[1] *Ibid.*, p. 36.   [2] *Ibid.*, p. 32.

quarter of the local association officials "thought that most time workers in member firms were paid no more than national rates".[1]

In the electrical contracting industry the National Federated Electrical Association maintains that "rates are standard rates and may not be increased by bonuses of any kind or by abnormal conditions money or by any other addition, except in the case of workers of special ability or responsibility or long service", although the association has occasionally had to agree to special site payments,[2] and overtime earnings are often high. So unusual is this degree of uniformity that Munns explained it by the industry's special circumstances. Much of the work is undertaken on subcontract with tendering on a fixed-price basis, and the proportion of labour costs is high, usually about 50 per cent. There is thus a considerable advantage in known fixed labour costs. The work does not lend itself to payment by results. Most of the firms are small and therefore more dependent on their association than larger firms would be.[3] He might have added that the industry is organised by a single powerful union, the Electricians, who have for many years been supporters of standard rates in this industry.

Consequently the general rule in private industry in Britain today is that collective action over pay does not mean the settlement of a pay structure for the industry by means of industry negotiations. It means instead that from time to time an industry agreement adds to the levels of pay, themselves largely or partly determined in the plants.

The Royal Commission quoted as evidence of the "decline in the extent to which industry-wide agreements determine actual pay" the rates and earnings of certain grades of adult male wage-earners in 1938 and 1967.[4] The figures for engineering and building, brought up to date, are given in Table V. They are fairly typical of most private industries and services.

The divergence between these two sets of figures can, of course, be explained by the high level of employment since the early years of the war. But its consequence is that industry agreements signed by employers' associations exercise much less control over the

[1] *Ibid.*, pp. 92–4.
[2] National Incomes Commission, *Report on the Agreements of February–March 1963 in Electrical Contracting, etc.*, Cmnd. 2098, 1963, pp. 20–1.
[3] Munns and McCarthy, p. 33.   [4] *Report*, p. 14.

contents of wage packets than they did at the beginning of the period, and that decisions taken in individual companies and plants determine a much larger share, by means which will be explored in the next chapter.

TABLE V

EARNINGS AND TIME RATES OF MEN IN OCTOBER 1938
AND OCTOBER 1968

Industry	1938		1968	
	Time rates for a normal working week	*Average earnings of adult male wage-earners in last pay week in October 1938*	*Time rates for a normal working week*	*Average earnings of adult male wage-earners in second pay week in October 1968*
Engineering	Fitters £3.7.2½d	£3.13.8d	Fitters £12.17.8d	£23.1.6d (engineering and electrical goods) £28.8.11d (vehicles)
	Labourers £2.10.4d (average rate in 14 towns)	(general engineering and iron and steel founding)	Labourers £10.17.4d	
Building	Bricklayers £3.13.2d	£3.6.6	Craftsmen £15.8.4d	£22.17.5d
	Labourers £2.15.0½d (average rate in 38 towns)	(building, decorating)	Labourers £13.3.4d (outside London)	(construction)

Even so it does not follow that the associations exercise no influence over the amounts actually paid. Federation officials were asked if their local associations tried to control payments above the level laid down in the industry agreement. Half said they did not and half of the remainder said that the only means of control was informal persuasion. But in the remaining quarter there was some machinery for trying to exercise control.[1] In practice what seems to happen quite commonly is that local associations arrange for exchange of information between members about the actual levels of pay in the plants, and this may lead to discussion between members about how to handle claims for domestic increases.

Arthur Marsh has described the kind of circumstances in which the local engineering associations might try to promote uniform action. They would not prevent members changing their "domestic wages structures", although they would expect to be kept informed of important changes. They would, however, "tend to rally their members if they thought that trade unions themselves were attempting locally to regulate wage or earnings levels, or to leapfrog claims systematically from one local firm to another. The prime cause of a tightening of members' attitudes in associations is usually the suspicion that some explicit or implicit trade union policy is emerging locally which would affect their interests." So long as the unions and shop stewards are content to deal with matters plant by plant, the association stands back.[2]

Another aspect of collective action is handling disputes. Where industry agreements lay down standards, the function of the disputes procedure is to settle disputes about the application of the standards. Where members are free to exceed the provisions of the industry agreement the procedure provides a means of conciliation in domestic disputes which members are unable to solve for themselves. Consequently a disputes procedure does not lose its value to its members as the regulative effect of industry pay agreements declines. On the contrary, it may become more important. Of the twenty-four national officials questioned in the Royal Commission survey, eight reported an increase in the number of cases handled through the procedure, and only one of them a decrease. The rapid increase in the number of cases handled by the engineering procedure in recent years is almost entirely due to a growing number of domestic disputes.[3]

Some associations offer a financial indemnity to members

[1] Munns and McCarthy, p. 93.
[2] A. Marsh, *Industrial Relations in Engineering*, 1965, p. 69.   [3] See pp. 239–40.

involved in stoppages, provided that they have followed the association's guidance. The Engineering Employers' Federation pays compensation on the basis of £10 a week for each adult male employee. But this practice seems to be a relic of the nineteenth century, for it is almost unknown in associations formed in the present century. Even where it exists it is not now thought to be an important incentive to firms to join assocations or to maintain their membership. Today the moral support of the association is probably more important in a strike; and this is guaranteed so long as the disputes procedure is used. The settlement provided by the procedure may not be entirely to the taste of the firm's managers, and the stoppage may not be averted, but so long as they have followed the association's advice they can rely on the support of their fellow managers throughout the industry.

The importance attached to collective action by employers has declined over the years. The Royal Commission survey revealed that today 75 per cent of national officials and 67 per cent of local officials thought it would make little or no difference to their association if all eligible firms were to join.[1] At one time some associations used pressure to recruit members. During the engineering lockout of 1897 it was observed that "the organisers of the Employers' Federation have exercised pressure of the most extraordinary kind upon employers who did not wish to join them".[2] In 1867 the Bury branch of the General Builders' Associations forbade the sub-letting of "the whole or any portion of any work or works to any employer of labour who is not a properly affiliated member of this society".[3] And in 1912 the secretary of the National Federation of Building Trades Employers said that the Federation used "inter-trading rules . . . as a method of organisation",[4] although the practice does not appear to have been universally successful.[5] On occasions of crisis members sometimes bound themselves to follow a common line by means of a "bond", or monetary guarantee, to be forfeited in the event of disloyalty.[6]

There are still occasions on which discipline is used. The Royal

---

[1] Munns and McCarthy, pp. 90–1.
[2] F. W. Hirst, "The Policy of the Engineers", *Economic Journal*, March 1898.
[3] Royal Commission on Trade Unions, Q. 3397.
[4] *Inquiry into Industrial Agreements*, Q. 5100.   [5] *Ibid.*, Qs. 5042–3.
[6] Examples are the Preston cotton strikes of 1853 (*Report on Trade Societies and Strikes*, p. 215) and the Scottish tailors' strike of 1903 (Royal Com. on Trade Disputes, Q. 5191).

Commission survey discovered two instances in which members were expelled for refusing to apply national agreements, and one in which expulsion followed a refusal to close down all the firm's plants during a national dispute.[1] Possibly there would be more instances of this if large-scale strikes were now as common as they were before 1927. In 1959 more than two hundred firms left the British Federation of Master Printers "because of independent action in accepting the demand for a 40-hour week during the printing strike".[2] But as it is discipline is rare. In the survey of works managers and personnel officers the respondents were asked if they had ever wished to make concessions which were not approved by the association. In about 12 per cent of the firms covered they had, mostly on pay or overtime issues. Most of the firms affected went ahead with the concessions, and in most instances their associations did nothing. Three firms, however, either resigned or were expelled.[3]

A decline in the regulative authority of the associations is consistent with the survey's findings that the most common specific criticism voiced by managers was that their associations were too weak and could not enforce their decisions, and that a quarter of the respondents thought their associations had no power at all, compared with 54 per cent who thought their associations had a fair amount of power and only 11 per cent who thought they had a lot of power. It is also significant that when the 80 per cent who thought their associations had no power or only a fair amount were asked whether they thought they should have more power, only about a quarter thought they should.[4] Perhaps the reasons why declining authority has not caused members to leave their associations is that most of them are not anxious to belong to powerful associations. As the Royal Commission put it: "The readiness of employers to federate does not . . . arise from a desire for strong organisation."[5]

It would be a mistake, however, to conduct a discussion of the reasons for joining associations and the benefits of membership as though companies conduct a precise calculation of benefits and costs to determine whether to join or whether to remain affiliated. Associations are not seen only as agencies to be hired for the monetary value of their services, but also as "clubs". It is

---

[1] Munns and McCarthy, pp. 97–8.   [2] *Ibid.*, p. 21.
[3] *Workplace Industrial Relations.* p. 94.   [4] *Ibid.*, pp. 94–6.   [5] *Report*, p. 22.

remarkable how often the word "club" is used by officers and members when talking about their associations. The Engineering Employers' Federation told the Royal Commission in their written evidence that "the advantages" of federation "are such as would accrue from membership of any 'club' ".[1] In his description of the local engineering associations, Arthur Marsh emphasises that "some aspects of the 'club' tradition still colour all associations, whether large or small".[2]

The typical process of admission emphasises the analogy. "The intention is to secure that members will not bring discredit on the Association by their conduct of business, and the method of vetting applications is normally similar to that of a club. Applications are dealt with at a local level . . . and commonly require a proposer and a seconder who should satisfy themselves on . . . the applicant's business standing."[3] Quite apart from the quantifiable advantages of association, British employers like to be federated.

STRUCTURE AND GOVERNMENT

The Royal Commission reported that "some 1350 employers' associations" were listed by the Department of Employment and Productivity. Of these 81 were registered as trade unions, 118 were registered under the Companies Act and therefore could not be trade unions, and there were approximately 1150 unincorporated associations of employers, some of which might be unregistered trade unions.[4] There are therefore far more employers' organisations in existence than employees' trade unions. But the majority of them are small local bodies, and for most purposes it is reasonable to neglect the associations not affiliated to the Confederation of British Industry, which has more than a hundred "national employers' organisations" in membership.

Employers themselves are fond of contrasting the simple structure of their organisation with the complexity of British trade unionism. The contrast is unquestionably there, but it is not quite so strong as employers sometimes claim. Engineering employers point to a single Engineering Employers' Federation dealing with thirty national unions, loosely bound together in the

---

[1] *Selected Written Evidence*, p. 403. [2] *Industrial Relations in Engineering*, p. 65.
[3] Munns and McCarthy, p. 25. [4] *Report*, pp. 7, 210-11.

Confederation of Engineering and Shipbuilding Unions. They often neglect to add that the engineering unions also negotiate with the Shipbuilders' and Repairers' National Association which is quite separate from their own federation, with several small associations within the engineering field such as the National Light Castings Ironfounders' Federation and the National Federation of Vehicle Trade Employers (who manufacture specialist car bodies) and with a considerable number of non-federated engineering firms. If the engineering unions were able to force all the engineering and shipbuilding organisations with which they deal to come together in a single national negotiating body, the structure of the employers' side would not be simple.

Accordingly, while it is true that the structure of employers' associations appears to be more simple that that of the unions, part of this apparent simplicity derives from the ability of employers to determine the coverage of collective bargaining arrangements. If the engineering and shipbuilding employers choose to sustain two separate organisations, the unions have no choice but to negotiate separately with each of them. If Ford chooses to stay outside the Engineering Employers' Federation, the unions have to deal separately with Ford or have no say in the negotiation of the pay and conditions of Ford employees.

Moreover the internal structure of some of the large employers' organisations is far from simple. The National Federation of Building Trades Employers "comprises 10 Regional Federations and over 260 Local Associations, together with a number of bodies which are affiliated under formal agreements, viz. the Federation of Registered House-Builders and the National Federation of Plastering Contractors, which are in full membership; the Joinery and Woodwork Employers' Federation and the National Association of Shopfitters, which are affiliated for labour matters only; and the Scottish National Building Trades Federation (Employers) which retains full freedom of action in regard to those matters on which Scottish law and building practice differ from English law and practice. The Federation has a special section for members who design and erect industrial buildings".[1] The Wool (and Allied) Employers' Council is a federation of six

---

[1] Written Evidence of the Confederation of British Industry, *Selected Written Evidence* p. 327. Pp. 326–61 give a useful account of the structure of some of the main employers' associations.

specialist organisations ranging from raw materials to the final stages of manufacture. Three of these organisations are in their turn federations of associations, one consisting of smaller specialist associations and two of local associations.[1]

If employers' associations have less of an advantage over the unions in structural simplicity than might appear at first sight, they unquestionably face far fewer difficulties in communicating with their members, because their membership is much smaller. There are more firms in membership with the National Federation of Building Trades Employers than any other association, but the total is no more than 16,000. The Engineering Employers' Federation covers 4600 establishments, but a considerable number of these are part of multi-plant companies, so that the total of firms in membership is considerably less. The British Federation of Master Printers has 4000 members. At the other extreme the Newspaper Publishers' Association comprises a dozen producers of national newspapers.

Apart from correspondence, the normal method of communicating with members and ascertaining their views is by meetings. In a small association the whole body of members can be invited to send one or more managers to regular meetings. The larger organisations deal with their members through meetings of local or specialist associations. In some instances three stages are required. "The district associations of the London Master Printers' Association hold monthly meetings of members timed to precede the meetings of the Council of the Association and this Council meeting similarly precedes the meetings of the Federation Council; in this way a continuous process of consultation can be achieved."[2] In some of the largest organisations there is a regional stage between the local associations and the national federation. In building the regional federations have considerable authority. Local organisations are now administrative units receiving specialist services from the full-time staff employed by the regions.[3] Outside London the local printing associations are grouped into regional "alliances". The main purpose of the eleven regions of the Engineering Employers' Federation, however, is to group the small associations to elect representatives to

---

[1] *Ibid.*, p. 352.   [2] Munns and McCarthy, pp. 65–6.
[3] The regions appoint full-time secretaries to serve a number of associations grouped together in an "area" (*ibid.*, p. 67).

the Management Board, and they are not an important element in the system of communication.

Generally associations aim "to obtain a consensus of opinion rather than to take a vote".[1] The story is told of one association whose general meeting decided to vote only to find that there was no one present who could remember the rule covering the voting procedure. But voting is sometimes used. "The National Federated Electrical Association arranged a series of Regional Conferences of members before the crucial decision was taken to adopt a policy of uniform wage rates and took a vote on the issue. In the engineering associations voting by membership is resorted to on national wage claims. Members' votes are weighted in relation to their wage roll so that the result reflects the importance of the decision to each member. . . . The result of the voting is reported to the Federation Management Board which takes the decision in the light of the support or opposition to the action proposed."[2] The Engineering Employers' Federation also consults its local associations by means of questionnaires, leaving it to the associations to consider the answers at a meeting or to ask their members to fill in the answers individually.

The governing body of a major employers' organisation is generally a committee or council of elected local or sectional representatives, together with a number of office-holders—presidents, vice-presidents, past presidents and so on. In most instances this body is too large to meet more than once a quarter so that its main function is to appoint committees to carry on the business of the association and to review and ratify their work. There is normally an executive committee, with perhaps a separate committee to deal with finance; and a negotiating (or wages and conditions) committee to deal with the unions, perhaps with separate committees to cover training, accident prevention and such matters. There may also be separate committees to deal with specialist sections of the industry, and where the association deals also with commercial matters there is a set of committees to cover these.

The General Council of the Engineering Employers' Federation consists of elected representatives of the local associations and federation office-holders, about 120 members in all. This council normally meets once a year, and the conduct of business is mainly

---

[1] *Ibid.*, p. 66.   [2] *Ibid.*, p. 66.

in the hands of a Management Board drawn from three sources: members elected on a regional basis, federation office-holders and members co-opted by the board itself. The board meets monthly and appoints the standing committees of the federation. General issues are dealt with by a finance committee, a policy committee and an administrative committee. There are three separate committees for dealing with the unions: a conference committee which handles disputes at the monthly Central Conference held at York; a negotiating committee which deals with the pay and conditions of manual workers; and a staff committee which deals with the salaries and conditions of white collar workers. In addition separate technical committees handle negotiations affecting sections of the industry such as constructional engineering and lift erection, and there is an apprentices committee.

It is not always easy to man association committees. V. G. Munns found that "not all members are ready to accept the duties of office, and those who show themselves ready to do so are frequently re-elected. Difficulties are experienced in persuading both small employers and the chief executives of large firms to spare the time for association work, and some associations have found it necessary to stipulate that the representatives of firms should be actively concerned with the management of the business."[1] Where the governing body of the organisation is elected from local associations there may be a special difficulty in securing adequate representation of the head offices of large multi-plant firms and several associations have found it necessary to make special provision to ensure that they are brought in. The Management Board of the Engineering Employers' Federation can use its power to co-opt "persons who, from their wide industrial experience, can make a valuable contribution to the deliberations and discussions of the Management Board".[2] However, even this has not provided a complete solution to the problem for, according to the Royal Commission, the majority of those co-opted "are senior directors of major firms", most of them lacking "specialist knowledge in personnel matters. To meet this deficiency the officers of the Federation have had to devise means of consultation outside the formal constitution."[3]

The National Federation of Building Trades Employers has a similar problem. Almost all the national building contractors

[1] *Ibid.,* p. 65.   [2] *Selected Written Evidence,* p. 399.   [3] *Report,* p. 21.

have London head offices, and therefore affiliate to the federation through the London Master Builders' Association. To meet their needs the association has formed a special group for them, about eighty strong. Even so their influence within the official federation machinery is limited to the weight given to London. The federation therefore formed a consultative committee of the twenty-odd biggest firms which meets twice a year, and some of the big firms consider that they should be directly represented on the Council of Federation.

When the British Spinners' and Doublers' Association was formed by amalgamating the Federation of Master Cotton Spinners with certain other textile associations, it was decided to give direct representation on the Committee of Management to the major firms in the industry. The Federation of Master Cotton Spinners had restricted membership of its main committees to the representatives of the local associations. The change was said to have improved the quality of membership on the governing committee.

There is an additional problem in filling places on committees in those industries where separate associations deal with commercial matters, for the number of places is greater. Moreover it is a widely held view that in these circumstances the more able men are likely to be found in the trade associations; for the path to the top in most firms has, at least in the past, been more open to managers who have established their reputation in this field than to those who have specialised in personnel work.

There is no available estimate for the number of full-time officers of employers' associations. Many small associations have no full-time staff and rely on a solicitor or accountant to conduct their business.[1] The Royal Commission's survey showed that "9 out of 35 national organisations (together with a large number of local associations) have no full-time employees at all".[2] In the inquiry which he conducted for the Royal Commission, V. G Munns included seven small associations which had appointed a firm of accountants to provide all their secretarial services. They had "the services of several employees of the firm either full-time or part-time. . . . Some of these officials spend all their time on the

---

[1] "Many small associations lack the resources to provide effective services to their members. Some are virtually run by firms of solicitors and chartered accountants." (Royal Commission *Report*, p. 200.)   [2] Munns and McCarthy, p. 98.

work of one association, some work for two or three different associations, and some spend only part of their time on association work of any kind."[1] The officers of the Soap, Candle and Edible Fats Employers' Federation and the National Seed Crushers' Association are employees of Unilever, their largest constituent. On the other hand the major national federations and associations employ a considerable staff of full-time officers, headed by a director,[2] and including specialists in training, work study and other fields. In addition major local associations such as the West Midlands Engineering Employers, the London Master Builders and the London Master Printers also employ sizeable staffs.

The Royal Commission's survey showed that relatively few chief officers had previously held industrial relations posts. A far larger proportion had qualified as solicitors or accountants.[3] Nor have they or their staff in the past received formal training for association work, although there have been some recent changes. The Coventry Engineering Employers have a cadet trainee on their staff and the Engineering Employers' Federation has developed a scheme for training new entrants.[4]

There are those who hold that the full-time officers of associations have too much power. In his evidence to the Royal Commission, D. F. Hutchinson of Philips Industries spoke of his experience as a chairman of local engineering conferences dealing with disputes between members of the local association and the trade unions.

"You sit with all the shop stewards and district officers, and here you have the panel of the employers and here you have the official representative of the association who does the talking; and although you, as chairman, are in charge theoretically, you dare not open your mouth, because what everybody is concerned with is not the issue but what goes on the verbatim notes, because the next stage is York, so that anything once on the notes becomes a precedent; so that the official who is conscious of all the traps

---

[1] *Ibid.*, p. 69.

[2] The Engineering Employers' Federation has a director-general supported by there directors.

[3] In national associations 11 per cent had previously held industrial relations posts and 11 per cent were accountants or solicitors, but in the national federations 17 per cent were accountants and solicitors whereas none had held industrial relations jobs, and in the local engineering associations a third were accountants or solicitors compared with 14 per cent who had held industrial relations jobs. (Munns and McCarthy, p. 99.)

[4] *Ibid.*, p. 70.

F

that lie in agreements and procedure does all the talking and you can see him manoeuvring that he gets the right thing on the notes, never mind the issue; and then pressure is brought to bear on the individual company to settle somehow or other and not let it go any further."[1]

It is impossible to say how commonly this opinion of officers is held in employers' associations. It is, however, clear that the relationship between the director of a major association (and his staff) and the committees of the association differs considerably from the relationship between the general secretary or president of a union (and his senior officers) and the union executive. Both inside and outside the union its chief officer is far better known than the members of the executive. He may be a national figure, frequently reported in the newspapers and interviewed on television. They are not. Many of the senior committee members of an employers' association, by contrast, are directors of important firms whose standing equals or exceeds the officials whom they appoint and who serve their committees. Their position and reputation does not depend only on their prominence in the organisation, as with the members of union executives, but also on the standing of their firms. V. G. Munns draws an analogy between the officers of an association and the civil service. "While actual decisions on policy are taken by the elected representatives, the formulation of alternatives, the examination of implications, and to some extent the selection of matters to be considered are the responsibility of the senior officials."[2] Civil servants can wield great power, but in a trade union the chief official is the senior elected representative as well as the head of the civil service.

The previous chapter argued that some major trade unions are held back by their structure and methods of government. Employers' associations also have their organisational problems, but they do not provide the main reason for the sluggishness of British employers' associations from before the second world war until recent years. D. F. Hutchinson complained that his association was "a horrifyingly deadening, heartbreaking, reactionary organisation 25 years ago".[3] If so, it was not because defective organisation or inadequate means of communication prevented him and those who thought likewise from accomplishing change.

---

[1] *Minutes of Evidence*, Q. 4198.   [2] Munns and McCarthy, p. 69.
[3] Royal Commission, *Minutes of Evidence*, Q. 4190.

It was primarily because most of the members of his and other associations were content to leave things are they were. The proof of this is the considerable changes in policy which have occurred during the 'sixties with few major alterations in structure.

SIGNS OF CHANGE

There have been some changes in structure. Contraction in the cotton industry has brought a succession of mergers. In 1961 the Federation of Master Cotton Spinners amalgamated with the Yarn Spinners' Association (a trade association) and the Cotton Yarn Doublers' Association to form the British Spinners' and Doublers' Association. In 1969 this new association joined forces with the Textile Manufacturers' Association (itself an amalgamation of cotton weaving and man-made fibre organisations) and the Textile Finishing Trades' Association to form the British Textiles Association. The merger of the Federation of British Industries, the British Employers' Confederation and the National Association of British Manufacturers in 1965[1] was accompanied by several amalgamations between employers' associations and trade associations in individual industries, including chemicals, shipbuilding and rubber. The Shipbuilding Employers' Federation joined with the Shipbuilding Conference and the Repairers' Central Council to form the Shipbuilders' and Repairers' National Association, and the Chemical and Allied Employers' Association merged with a number of trade associations to become the Chemical Industries Association.

These reconstructed associations have pioneered new methods of collective bargaining with the unions, but there have also been changes in collective bargaining in associations whose structure and government have remained unaltered. The most outstanding of them have concerned "productivity bargaining".[2] Where a company plans adjustments in pay and conditions to fit a number of related changes in working practices and performance, these adjustments must of necessity clash with a strict enforcement of industry-wide rates and conditions. The first and most famous of productivity agreements signed in 1960 at the non-federated refinery of Esso at Fawley, near Southampton, was viewed with

[1] See p. 410.   [2] See p. 305.

little enthusiasm by employers' associations. In 1964 Esso, followed by other oil companies, withdrew from the Employers' Panel of the Oil Companies' Conciliation Committee, an association which insisted on a strict application of its pay agreements, in order to introduce a productivity agreement in its distribution operations.[1] Even where withdrawal from an association is not "a necessary pre-condition of a productivity agreement ... the proposals of a particular company may demand an agreement so different from those prevailing in the rest of the industry as to render continued membership of the association a serious embarrassment. It was on such grounds that Alcan decided to withdraw from the South Wales and Monmouthshire Iron and Steel Manufacturers' Association, and for similar reasons the Milford Haven refinery left the Welsh Engineers and Founders' Association whose agreement had previously applied to their maintenance craftsmen."[2]

In 1965, however, opinion was changing rapidly. In that year the Confederation of British Industry stated that it recognised "the benefits created by many plant productivity bargains but considers it essential that they should be closely related to the national collective bargains in the industry".[3] In the autumn of the same year Shell was discussing with the National Union of Seamen the introduction of "general-purpose crews" on its oil tankers by means of a productivity agreement. Negotiations were halted when the Shipping Federation, another association which at that time required uniform acceptance of industry pay agreements, told Shell that concessions would "prejudice arrangements for the introduction of general-purpose crews on other types of ship".[4] In 1967 the *Final Report* of the Pearson Court of Inquiry on the Shipping Industry was published. The Court held that "any attempt to produce a cut-and-dried solution on the way that seamen might be deployed and rewarded for more flexible working in the near future would invite disaster. Companies need to explore the full range of possibilities in the course of carefully planned and supervised experiments in their ships."[5] Soon afterwards productivity agreements were signed by Shell

---

[1] In 1968 the defunct Employers' Panel was replaced by the Petroleum Industry Employers' Committee on Employee Relations.
[2] *Productivity Agreements*, p. 36.   [3] *Selected Written Evidence*, p. 269.
[4] Royal Commission, *Report*, p. 197.   [5] Cmnd. 3211, p. 34.

and several other shipping companies. In 1968 the Engineering Employers' Federation issued a Research Paper on *Productivity Bargaining and the Engineering Industry* written by its research director, E. J. Robertson, which commended productivity agreements to its members so long as they were properly negotiated and applied.

In most instances the change in approach required no alteration in rules or structure. It was the consequence of a new demand by the members which could have been met years before if the members had asked for it then. A second quotation from the Pearson Report supports this point. "Centralisation", says the report, "seems to have been accepted as the natural order of things. The major oil tanker companies have told us that they now take the view that the National Maritime Board [the industry's negotiating body] has not paid enough attention to their special problems. We think there is substance in this complaint and welcome the decision of the Shipping Federation to establish a tanker section. But the neglect of special tanker interests is nothing new, and the Federation responded as soon as the companies demanded attention. It would seem that for many years the needs of the tanker companies went unrecognised because it did not occur to them that the prevailing centralisation could be challenged."[1]

In a few instances industry-wide agreements have been modified to suit current conditions. They include the rubber and chemicals industries. In July 1967 the rubber industry agreed to replace its existing basic rates by a "minimum basic wage" of £13 for men and £9.15.0d for women. There were to be no "consequential increases to workers whose present earnings are above the new minimum weekly wage, in order to maintain existing differentials and/or traditional relativities, or for any other reason . . . Earnings for skill, responsibility and incentives will be determined at local level by local negotiation." The intention was to leave the settlement of actual pay structures to individual plants, where it was hoped that productivity agreements could be negotiated.

A more elaborate agreement was negotiated by the Chemical Industries Association later that year. It covered both the process unions and the craft unions which had previously negotiated entirely separate agreements. The parties accepted that "the

[1] *Ibid.*, pp. 2–3.

wage rates in national agreements are minima". They decided that productivity bargaining was to be encouraged, but accepted that "it cannot be done by a national negotiating committee, remote from the wages structure involved, the work practices involved and the attitudes existing. . . . While in certain cases relating to a company framework, it must . . . take place for the most part at works level". They established a national Joint Standing Committee to encourage and guide productivity bargaining. It was to establish an advisory service, to receive notification from managers and unions intending to enter into productivity discussions, and to authorise departures from national agreements other than wage agreements (where no authorisation was required).[1] By March 1969 the committee had received 39 notifications of discussions and thirteen draft proposals. Nine final agreements had been signed and four agreements which were to be negotiated in stages had reached the first stage.

One of the most notable features of both these agreements, and of the changes in the Shipping Federation, is that employers' associations have made progress by recognising their own limitations. For many years they refused to recognise that their pay agreements were losing their regulative effect. Many associations still do not wish to recognise this loss of control. But with few exceptions, of which electrical contracting is the most important, acknowledging it seems to be the precondition of exercising influence over the reality of collective bargaining.

[1] The length of the normal working week and of annual holidays was not subject to variation.

CHAPTER 5

MANAGEMENT

THE FIRM IN INDUSTRIAL RELATIONS

Before 1914 relatively little was heard about the firm in industrial relations. The Royal Commission on Labour which was appointed in 1891 and reported in 1894 conducted by far the most exhaustive enquiry into British industrial relations prior to the appointment of the Royal Commission on Trade Unions and Employers' Associations in 1965. It sat in three committees to hear 583 witnesses in 151 sittings; it circulated questionnaires to trade unions, employers' associations, trades councils and public employers; it appointed a staff of assistant commissioners to conduct special inquiries; and it issued its evidence and reports in 65 blue books. For all that the Commissioners paid almost no attention to the firm, and hardly mentioned its existence in the 113 foolscap pages in which they summarised the evidence and set out their recommendations.[1] These dealt with the improvement of relations between trade unions and employers' associations, and the advisability of further legislation to control wages, hours of work, "sanitary conditions" and the closed shop. The minority report signed by four trade union Commissioners and the numerous observations and memoranda appended by other groups and individuals serve only to record different or supplementary views on the same points.

The exception was a paragraph entitled: "Trade unions and single establishments". This concluded that "there seems to be no sufficient reason why the conversion of separate establishments into independent industrial polities consolidated on a footing of partnership, should not exist side by side with trade unionism as a means to solving the problems which the relations of capital and labour present".[2] But only one means of attaining this object

---

[1] Royal Commission on Labour, *Fifth and Final Report*, C-7421, 1894.
[2] *Ibid.*, p. 38.

was mentioned—profit-sharing—and the paragraph was clearly a concession to one member, Sir George Livesey, a lifelong champion of profit-sharing who added a memorandum on the subject as an appendix to the report.

At the time this omission surprised no one, for industrial relations were generally regarded as external to the firm. There were even then, however, other exceptions besides profit-sharing. Firstly, there were firms which dealt direct with trade unions without the intermediary of an employers' association. Most "non-federated firms" were also non-union firms, but not all. Secondly, there were firms whose very operation demanded a complex set of rules governing internal relations between workers, supervisors and managers. Because of their size and complexity the railway companies were in this class. At the time of the Royal Commission nearly all major railway companies except the North Eastern insisted that their rules were "domestic", for they refused to recognise the unions, but when the first system of railway conciliation boards were established in 1907 they were set up *within* the companies to establish—by a process at least closely akin to collective bargaining—a set of rules to operate *within* each company.[1]

The Commission's neglect of the firm reflected the government's overriding concern with preservation of industrial peace. In the middle of the nineteenth century the government's duty in industrial disputes had been to see that the law was kept, but towards the end of the century pressure began to mount for a more positive approach. A "Labour Correspondent" was appointed to the Board of Trade, a network of local correspondents was developed and there began the collection of large volumes of statistics on trade unions, stoppages, wages and hours of work. The government began to admit to a duty to try to avoid, minimise and settle industrial disputes, which was dramatically acknowledged in 1893 by the first cabinet intervention in a strike. Gladstone sent his foreign secretary, Lord Rosebery, to

---

[1] "The principal feature of the first Railway Conciliation Scheme was the establishment of two types of Board of Conciliation on each railway company. Sectional boards were to deal with problems arising in the principal grade groupings. . . . The Central Conciliation Board in each company . . . was to endeavour to reach a settlement if there was no positive outcome at the Sectional Board level." Only if neither board could reach a settlement could there be reference outside the company—to arbitration. (P. S. Bagwell, *The Railwaymen*, 1963, pp. 270-1.)

try to bring about a settlement in the great coal lockout of that year.

This concern was reflected in the terms of reference of the Royal Commission on Labour. They were to investigate "questions affecting the relationship between employer and employed, the combination of employers and employed, and the conditions of labour, which have been raised during the recent trade disputes in the United Kingdom".[1] Most of the stoppages which caused concern to the government, especially at a time when firms themselves were relatively small, were those which affected groups of employers. Had unofficial strikes been as common as they are today, or had the government then regarded itself as directly concerned with the productive efficiency of industry, the terms of reference of the Commission, its investigations and its findings would necessarily have paid closer attention to the firm.

Employers' associations also saw industrial relations as external to the firm. Many of them would have agreed with the Engineering Employers' Federation that their job was to limit trade union "encroachments" intended to subject "the employers' business to management at the dictation of trade union officials".[2] This they would do by dealing collectively with the unions over those issues which should properly be subject to joint regulation, leaving individual firms to deal with other matters as they saw fit. "The Federated Employers," declared the 1898 settlement, "while disavowing any intention of interfering with the proper functions of the Trade Unions, will admit no interference with the management of their business." For their part, the trade union officials who appeared before the Commission might have differed with the employers about the range of issues appropriate to joint regulation, but they also saw their jobs as external to the firm. The Commission did not look into the opinions of the shop stewards and other workshop representatives who were already playing some part in industrial relations at that time.

Today it is impossible to ignore the part of the firm in industrial relations, and the rest of this chapter sets out the main trends which have brought about an increase in the importance of the

---

[1] *Fifth and Final Report*, p. 8.

[2] Quoted from the manifesto of the Engineering Employers' Federation, signed by the president, Colonel H. C. S. Dyer, and issued on 4 August 1897. (*Notes on the Engineering Trade Lockout 1897-8*, published by the Amalgamated Society of Engineers, n.d., p. 21.)

firm in the regulation of employment, and some of their consequences for management.

SIZE OF UNIT AND SOCIAL CHANGE

The most obvious of these trends is an increase in the size of plants and firms. This growth has probably been fairly continuous since the industrial revolution but no measures were available until quite recently. Excluding establishments with less than ten employees, establishments with more than 500 employees in 1935 accounted for 35·3 per cent of the labour force in manufacturing industry and establishments with more than 1000 employees for 21·4 per cent. In 1961 the comparable figures were 48·6 per cent and 34·5 per cent.[1] But size of establishment is not the same as size of firm, for most large firms control a number of establishments. The names of many of them are literally household words—I.C.I., Unilever, British Leyland, Courtauld, G.E.C., Shell and so on—and all of these have come into existence since 1900. The 1963 census of production showed that 3·5 million out of 8·5 million employees in mining, manufacturing and construction worked for companies or groups of companies with 5000 or more employees. In 1935 the number employed in companies or groups of this size was less than a million.[2]

Size of unit affects industrial relations through the process which sociologists call bureaucratisation, the elaboration of impersonal rules. The manager of a small undertaking can run his business without many rules. He can deal personally with each of his employees and decide issues as they arise. If there is to be collective bargaining it can be between his association and the union to which his employees belong so that the rules which are collectively agreed are external to his undertaking, and outside of them he can continue with personal dealings. But a large undertaking cannot be run by personal dealings alone. In order to handle a staff of hundreds or thousands the employees must be divided into grades and assigned to departments. Rates of pay must be

---

[1] *Annual Abstract of Statistics*, 1935–46 and 1968.

[2] Royal Commission, *Report*, p. 47. The Commission commented: "The census of production does not cover such industries as agriculture, transport, distribution, banking and insurance; but in some of these also, particularly the last two named, individual companies employing very large numbers of employees are to be found."

regulated by rules. Procedures have to be set up to deal with selection, promotion, discipline and dismissal. There must be standard arrangements for drawing stores, for recording work and for making complaints.

It is possible to meet some of the needs of larger undertakings by increasingly complex collective agreements covering a wider range of issues, and collective agreements have generally become more elaborate over the years. But this is only effective where standard arrangements can be applied to all the undertakings covered by the agreement. Where products, processes and forms of organisation vary there cannot be standard rules governing work. Consequently growth in size of unit brings with it an increase in the number of rules governing employment which are made within the firm. Since these rules are the subject-matter of industrial relations, the firm has become more important in industrial relations.

However, growth in size has not been the only influence at work. It has been reinforced by other changes. "The number of managers possessing a university degree has been increasing, whilst the number with elementary education only has been decreasing. Great emphasis is being laid on the importance of professional qualifications. . . . Recently there has been a considerable increase in the number of managers who have been to a Public School."[1] Where the manager is promoted from the shop floor the tendency to rely on personal dealings is likely to be reinforced, whether these dealings are permissive or autocratic. Where the manager is separated from those he manages by his school background, a university education and professional qualifications there is far less foundation for personal dealing and a system of impersonal rules may be a welcome alternative.

Size, of course, is not unrelated to the educational standards of managers. At some point in the growth of his undertaking the most able and versatile employer must devolve responsibilities, and this most naturally done by handing over specific functions —sales, accounts or purchasing, for example—to subordinates who thereby become specialists. To advance their position specialists naturally turn to professionalisation. They organise training and tests leading to qualifications. Those who use the services of

[1] I. C. McGivering, D. G. J. Matthews and W. H. Scott, *Management in Britain*, 1960, pp. 65-6.

specialists encourage the process because professional standards help to guarantee the service they receive. Among the separate managerial functions which have emerged in the present century is personnel management, and this is of such importance to industrial relations that it requires a section on its own.

With increasing complexity of organisation, educational standards and professionalisation it was to be expected that the tools of analysis and measurement should be turned upon the processes of industrial organisation in the attempt to develop a science of management, or a group of management sciences. This further encouraged the making of rules within the firm. For if the managerial processes of the firm were to be conducted according to the findings of these new studies, precepts had to be laid down to guide them in the right direction.

So far the main impact of management science upon industrial relations has been through its influence on pay systems, and this chapter therefore treats the contributions of management science to the development of industrial relations in Britian together with the effects of pay systems. However, changes in pay systems have also been an independent influence upon the importance of the firm in industrial relations. More complicated pay systems have in many instances proved to be beyond the control of external collective agreements, and more decisions on pay have had to be taken within the firm.

Ever since the industrial revolution there have been managers who have philosophised about the relationships between management and men, seeking for ethical principles which would jusify this relationship or show how it should be changed. One of these principles has been that of workers' participation in management. From Robert Owen onwards some managers have tried to associate their workers more closely with the conduct of the firm. In Britain during the present century the most popular form of workers' participation has been joint consultation. The process of rule-making in many firms has been considerably affected by the doctrines of joint consultation, and consequently these doctrines and their effects also receive a section of their own.

Over the years there has been a widening of the area of industrial relations which is regarded as appropriate for joint regulation. This is partly because subjects once considered as matters for management alone to decide, such as redundancy, are now thought to be appropriate for collective bargaining; and partly because new types of benefit have emerged, new at least for manual workers, such as sick pay and pensions. Both these trends have extended the scope of job-regulation within the firm because, generally speaking, they have not been covered by external collective agreements. Accordingly this topic also has its own section.

Besides their effect on the rules governing employment and the way in which these rules are made, these several influences on the position of the firm in industrial relations have also had considerable consequences for relationships within management. As important as any of these has been the change in the position of the supervisor or foreman, the "first line of management". This topic is therefore covered in a final section.

PERSONNEL MANAGEMENT

Personnel work was slower to emerge as a separate branch of management than some other specialisms, but its origin as a profession can perhaps be traced back to the beginnings of the Institute of Personnel Management. The institute started its life in 1913 as the Welfare Workers' Association. Its first secretary was Miss Mary Wood, who had been employed as a welfare worker in Rowntrees since 1896, and many of the original members came from Quaker firms.[1]

The war brought big changes. In December 1915 a welfare section was created in the Ministry of Munitions with Seebohm Rowntree as its director. Its aim was "to raise the well-being of workers to as high a point as possible in all factories engaged in the manufacture of munitions of war".[2] Its staff inspected munitions factories to advise on protective clothing, first aid, the installation of seats in workshops, washing and rest facilities and provision for recreation facilities. They recommended the appointment of welfare supervisors, and arranged for their selection and training. About a thousand lady supervisors and nearly three hundred boys' supervisors were known to be at work in munitions factories by the end of the war;[3] and with the appointment of

[1] M. M. Niven, *Personnel Management 1913–63*, 1967, pp. 21–37.
[2] *Official History of the Ministry of Munitions*, Vol. V, part III, p. 6.
[3] *Ibid.*, pp. 37, 42.

boys' supervisors men as well as women were brought into industrial welfare work. Besides accepted welfare work their duties included supervision of discipline, absenteeism and bad time-keeping, inquiry into dismissals and the preliminary sifting of applicants for jobs (or in some instances actual selection).[1]

The association, rechristened the Central Association of Welfare Workers in 1917, now consciously aimed to be a professional body. With a total of seven hundred members, including some male welfare workers, and increased subscriptions, a full-time secretary was appointed and a journal founded. The association was recognised by government departments and a two-year training course was introduced at University level.[2]

Shortly after the war a new trend was set up by the appointment of C. H. Northcott to work on the structure of wages at Rowntrees. Soon afterwards Major Urwick joined him to work on problems of organisation and an industrial psychology department was added in 1922. Next came the appointment of R. Lloyd Roberts as "labour manager" for Brunner Mond. He continued in the post for I.C.I. after the merger in 1926.

For some time this development made little difference to the Association, but in 1931 there was another change of name to the Institute of Labour Management and a year later Northcott and Lloyd Roberts became members, bringing other "labour managers" with them. Lloyd Roberts forced the Association to face a new issue by insisting that every firm should have a labour policy approved by the board, which should govern the work of the labour manager. This bold affirmation of the importance of the firm in industrial relations disturbed some of the older welfare workers. They thought of their jobs as a form of social work directed by a set of ethical standards different widely from the standards governing the successful conduct of the firm as a business undertaking. But Lloyd Roberts carried the day, and a document embodying his views was accepted by the Institute in 1936.

Meanwhile a new branch of personnel work appeared with the development of "staff management" in major stores and large offices. A separate association was formed as an affiliated group. A further extension came when London Transport was brought into public ownership in 1934 by the appointment of the former

---

[1] *Ibid.*, pp. 31-2.   [2] M. M. Niven, *Personnel Management*, pp. 59-64.

assistant general secretary of the Transport and General Workers' Union, John Cliff, as a part-time member of the board with "special executive duties in staff matters". After the London bus strike of 1937 the board decided to make a further appointment as chief welfare officer, and subsequently Mr. Cliff became full-time deputy chairman with responsibility for a Staff and Welfare Department.

These developments brought little increase in the total membership of the Institute, whose 759 members in 1939 barely exceeded the 1920 figure, although the proportion of men had risen over this period. The second world war, however, brought an almost four-fold expansion in membership to nearly 3000. By 1944 over three thousand factories employed personnel or welfare officers, and the total number so employed was almost 5500.[1]

Among the reasons for this was the reservation from military service of labour and welfare officers, which led firms to use these designations liberally, and the creation of new disciplinary problems by the imposition of Essential Work Orders which ultimately applied to over eight million workers. Wage structures were rendered more complex by the "application in the various departments of a factory of basic wage increases, cost-of-living and war bonus advances, the speeding up of piece-rate jobs, interpretation of overtime awards [and] relaxation of existing agreements to permit women to replace men".[2] The trend from welfare work to labour management was confirmed by the wide responsibilities accorded to labour officers in the factories managed by the Ministry of Supply, which at one time employed 300,000 workers. All questions of employment and industrial relations within each factory were handled by a department under the control of a senior labour manager who reported direct to the superintendent of the factory.[3]

As before, continued growth brought further heart-searching over the nature of the profession. In 1940 the Institute appointed a committee to "consider what type of association [it] should aim at becoming". The committee drafted a definition, approved at a general meeting in 1943, which took Northcott's doctrine a

[1] Ministry of Labour and National Service, *Report for the Years 1939–1946*, Cmnd. 7225, 1947, p. 115.
[2] G. R. Moxon, *The Growth of Personnel Management in Great Britain during the War, 1939–1944*, 1945, pp. 18–19.   [3] *Ibid.*, pp. 23–4.

stage further by insisting that personnel management could not be separated from management generally. It was "that part of management which is primarily concerned with human relationships within an organisation. Its objective is the maintenance of these relationships on a basis which, by consideration of the well-being of the individual, enables all those engaged in the undertaking to make their maximum personal contribution to the effective work of the undertaking."[1]

The profession was given additional recognition by the publication of a Ministry of Labour careers pamphlet on personnel management. The Ministry had made special wartime arrangements for the training of personnel officers and in 1945 a permanent Personnel Management Advisory Service was established "to assist in the improvement of relationships and manpower efficiency in industry by providing advice and information to employers on personnel management".[2]

Continued full employment after the war prevented a decline in the profession such as followed the first world war. Practising members of the Institute, now entitled the Institute of Personnel Management, numbered 2500 in 1950 and 3000 in 1960. As for the total numbers of personnel officers, by 1960 "various estimates from 10,000 upwards have been made by management associations but these are guesses only . . . nor does the Ministry of Labour know the exact position".[3] By 1970 estimates were ranging well above 20,000.

Changes in composition have been as marked as the increase in total numbers. In 1939 it was "estimated that the number [of personnel officers] did not exceed 1800, 60 per cent of whom were women".[4] Miss Crichton's samples of Institute membership in 1950 and 1960 put the proportion of women at 47·7 per cent in 1950 and 30·5 per cent in 1960. Personnel management is now a man's job. Her samples also show that the proportion of members in the over-forty age group increased considerably between 1950

---

[1] Quoted *ibid.*, p. 32. During the same year G. R. Moxon was appointed director of personnel advisory services at the Institute and wrote a pamphlet on the *Functions of a Personnel Department*, in which he set out the work of a department in six "divisions": employment, wages, joint consultation, health and safety, welfare (employee services), education and training.

[2] Ministry of Labour, *Industrial Relations Handbook*, 1961, p. 129.

[3] Anne Crichton "The I.P.M. in 1950 and 1960" *Personnel Management*, December, 1961.

[4] *The Growth of Personnel Management in Great Britain during the War, 1939–1944*, p. 28.

and 1960 and that the proportion of members with University education rose from 40·5 per cent to 48·0 per cent. Members of the Institute, however, are not typical of personnel managers as a whole. Miss Crichton suggests that personnel work can "be done by two groups of people, the one specialising in human relations aspects of management all their lives and getting their experience by moving from one personnel management specialist post to another; and the other kind staying with one company and learning to take responsibility in many aspects of management, personnel management being only one in a series of these experiences. The Institute would seem to cater mainly for the first type of personnel officer." But men probably predominate among both types and the increasing seniority of the profession generally is also borne out by the salary figures quoted in advertisements for personnel officers, and in appointments of career personnel officers to the boards of major companies.

These developments have been accompanied by further extensions of the scope of personnel management. During the post-war years there has been a boom in training courses for managers, and, following war-time experiments in the selection of candidates for officer training in the services, more attention has been paid to the selection of managers, and to investigating the suitability of candidates for various managerial posts. Together training and selection have been the basis of "management development", a planned career to develop the potential of each manager through appropriate stages of training and experience. This responsibility has usually been given to the personnel manager, and in some instances his duties extend also to the study of the organisation for which he works. As early as 1957 a group consisting mainly of senior personnel officers argued that their profession had a special responsibility in this area. "Confusion, uncertainty or secrecy about the organisation chart can have dire effects on morale, and especially in the middle and higher levels of management. The personnel officer has, or should have, special knowledge and experience about working groups, viable relationships, and causes of friction in this field, and he should be familiar with the growing volume of research—however tentative its conclusions—which is being devoted to the subject."[1] More recently "manpower planning" has become popular. It covers the

[1] Guy Hunter, *The Role of the Personnel Officer, A Group Review*, 1957, p. 13.

study of trends in the supply of and demand for various grades of labour not only in the whole economy, or industry by industry, but also within the firm. At this level the study of trends can be associated with planning improvements in the performance and stability of the labour force by training, by redevelopment and by changes in organisation. In a number of instances manpower planning has been used to develop a productivity agreement. Thus manpower planning can be regarded as covering many aspects of personnel management, and might lead perhaps to the construction of a "personnel system" suitable for computer processing. But there are very few British firms in which manpower planning has progressed beyond its early infancy.

The story of British personnel management is an impressive record of growth, which could easily give an exaggerated impression of the part which personnel officers have played in developing the system of industrial relations in this country. In fact until recently their effect has been narrowly limited.

Before the war their numbers were too small for them to have widespread influence, and many of them were still little more than welfare officers. It is true that by that time the profession accepted that they were part of management and ought to be the agents of a labour policy approved by the boards of their undertakings. But this was the practice of only a few firms such as Cadbury and Rowntree, Courtauld and I.C.I., which were in this respect as in many others untypical of British industry, even of large undertakings. The expansion of the second world war brought a rapid growth in numbers and functions, but a good deal of this was in government organisations disbanded or sharply cut back at the end of the war. It is only in the last twenty years that the appointment of personnel officers with responsibility and authority has become widespread in Britain.

Even now it is relatively rare to find a firm with a clear and accepted personnel policy in the sense of a coherent set of principles governing the employment and performance of staff, based where possible on tested evidence and with checks to see that it is applied. According to the Royal Commission, "many firms have no such policy, and perhaps no conception of it".[1] Many personnel officers would not be capable of devising and applying a personnel policy. The status and standards of personnel manage-

---

[1] *Report*, p. 25.

ment are rising, but the average is still not high. It is significant that personnel management has not yet established itself as a profession to anything like the same extent as, say, accountancy or engineering. Although a considerable number of personnel officers now take the examinations of the Institute of Personnel Management there is no general agreement on the training required for the job, whether because no training is thought to be necessary or because it is thought that no adequate training has yet been devised. There are also other obstacles to the development of a personnel policy.

"Many of the older generation of personnel managers see themselves simply as professional negotiators. Even if a personnel manager has the ability to devise an effective personnel policy, the director responsible for personnel (if there is one), or the board as a whole, may not want to listen to him. Many firms had acquired disorderly pay structures and unco-ordinated personnel practices before they appointed a personnel manager, and the burden of dealing with disputes and problems as they arise has absorbed his whole time and energy."[1]

There is, moreover, a particular problem about the status and function of the personnel officer within the firm. Managers and supervisors are dealing with employees all the time, and a personnel policy will exist only if it governs these dealings. How can the personnel manager see that it does? If his function is to deal with specific tasks, such as selection, training and negotiation, and the rest of the business is not his concern, then he cannot be responsible for a personnel policy. The customary solution to this problem is the principle of "line and staff". The personnel officer, it is said, should be part of the "staff". Consequently he has no direct responsibilities except for his own immediate staff and perhaps personnel records. The "line" management is the direct chain of command from supervisor to board, and the line managers must be responsible for decisions on personnel matters, although they should be taken within a personnel policy and with expert advice from the personnel officer and his staff. But to whatever theoretical principles of organisation firms pay lip-service, in practice personnel officers do not find it easy to avoid responsibilities which line managers are eager to pass to them. The consequence of confusions about line and staff, writes Urwick,

[1] *Ibid.*

"have been disastrous" and have allowed line managers to shuffle off to a specialist the "vital function which in all modern armies is regarded as the inalienable responsibility of the 'line commander' at all levels".[1] In Britain, "unresolved confusion over the role of personnel management can produce a compromise that gets the worst of all worlds. In major areas of labour relations policy— such as employment, negotiations, communication and training —line management may shed all the details of administration, while retaining ultimate authority and an illusion of responsibility."[2]

Nowhere is this confusion more obvious than in negotiation with trade unions. Line managers, lacking intimate knowledge of agreements and customs, are only too happy to leave it to personnel officers, who may be glad to undertake the job in order to extend their authority in a direction in which they feel especially fitted. Many of them feel "strongly that the personnel officer not only can, but should undertake this job. He must not try to keep out of places where hard decisions, unpopular decisions have to be made."[3] On the other hand if the personnel officer does succeed in restricting himself to staff activities, his effectiveness depends almost entirely on the willingness of line managers to call him in, not for occasional meetings, not as a "fireman" to help deal with crises, but as a continuing participant in decision-making so that he can interpret personnel policy and suggest applications as these are required. Not many British firms have reached a sufficient degree of sophistication in their managerial practices to see that such an arrangement works smoothly and satisfactorily.

PAYMENT BY RESULTS

Long before the widespread appointment of personnel officers with responsibility for the pay structures of their firms, the methods of payment now in use in British industry were developing and affecting the position of the firm in industrial relations. This is true, for example, of payment by results in which there were big changes from the turn of the century onwards.

---

[1] L. Urwick, *Personnel Management in Perspective*, 1958, pp. 6, 10.
[2] *The Fawley Productivity Agreements*, p. 254.
[3] *The Role of the Personnel Officer, a Group Review*, p. 14.

In the nineteenth century both employers' associations and trade unions tried where they could to regulate piecework by drawing up "lists" of piecework prices to apply throughout the area of their jurisdiction. There were town or district lists in printing, in clothing, in iron and steel, in hosiery and lace, and in shipbuilding. From 1892 the cotton weaving industry had a single "uniform list" for its standard product, and two district lists for Bolton and Oldham between them determined the pay of mule spinners throughout Lancashire. In coalmining a price might be settled for a given seam throughout the district in which it was worked, although varying geological conditions might lead to a good deal of bargaining over special allowances pit by pit.

Geological conditions, however, are not the only features in the situation which vary. The assumption of the standard piece-price list is that production methods and machinery are also standardised. The great success of the Lancashire lists lay in the gradual perfection of the "mule" as a spinning machine and of the Lancashire loom as a weaving machine during the course of the nineteenth century, and in the reluctance of the British cotton industry to experiment with newer methods of production, such as ring spinning and automatic looms, even when they were proving successful abroad. Ring-spinning acquired its own uniform list in time, but payment on automatic looms has always been regarded as a matter for settlement mill by mill as they were gradually introduced into the industry.

The widespread introduction of piecework into the engineering industry towards the end of the century was not, however, the consequence of standardisation of machinery and production methods. The new mass-production machinery was not standardised and methods of production changed frequently. Consequently piece-prices, or, as new methods of assessing work were introduced, the "times allowed" to complete jobs,[1] were fixed for each job and each plant. The Amalgamated Society of Engineers and other craft unions were hostile to piecework and it was first formally recognised in the settlement following their defeat in the 1897–8 lockout. This left the price to be agreed between the manager and the worker or workers concerned, an

---

[1] "Time allowed" is a method of relating piecework payment to a time rate, by fixing a period of time to produce a given output and paying the "pieceworker" who exceeds this output a bonus related to the "time saved".

arrangement which fostered the growth of the shop steward's authority.[1] Subsequent agreements laid down minimum conditions, for instance a provision that the price or time should be such as to allow a worker "of average ability" to earn a certain minimum level of pay; but so long as these conditions were satisfied, the pieceworker's actual earnings depended, and still depend, upon decisions taken within his own firm.

Accordingly the spread of piecework in the industry involved a transfer of control over payment from the local engineering employers' associations and the district committees of the unions, which then settled time rates of pay, to managers and workers, or their shop stewards, in individual firms. The extent of the change can be traced with fair accuracy since 1886. The proportion of men employed on piece work (for 1886 and 1906 men *and* boys) has grown as follows:

> 1886   5 per cent (Board of Trade Figures)[2]
> 1906 27·5 per cent (Board of Trade figures)[2]
> 1927 49·6 per cent (Employers' Federation Figures)[3]

Since 1927 the periodic censuses of the Ministry of Labour suggest that there has been relatively little change. However, they probably understate the extent of the change since a higher proportion of women than men are paid by results, and the share of women in total engineering employment has increased very considerably during this century.

Since the first world war part of the pay of engineering pieceworkers has been a fixed sum laid down in industry-wide agreements and known as the piece-workers' "bonus" or "supplement". Consequently pieceworkers are in fact paid partly by the "piece" and partly by time. It does not necessarily follow that these two elements in pay correspond exactly to payments settled within the firm and payments settled by the industry, for some pieceworkers also receive time payments which are settled within the firm, for example "merit money".

The growth of payment by results in other industries cannot be traced with the same certainty as in engineering, but the general trends are fairly clear. "The spread of mass production methods

---

[1] See p. 268.
[2] *Report of an Enquiry by the Board of Trade into Earnings and Hours, 1906*, Vol. VI.
[3] Quoted in M. L. Yates, *Wages and Labour Conditions in British Engineering*, 1937, p. 118.

to other industries including chemicals, rubber, food manufacture and light metals led to systems of payment by results akin to those of engineering."[1] Where payment by the "piece" formed only a part of total pay these industries often used the terms "incentive bonus" or "payment by results" rather than "piece-work", although this continued to be the common term in engineering. At the same time new methods of production in long-established industries gradually undermined the standard piece-price lists inherited from the nineteenth century. Some of these continue to apply to diminishing sections of their industries, as firm after firm shifts to factory bonus incentive systems; others have quietly dropped into oblivion.

For a number of years the Ministry of Labour conducted a periodic census of the extent of "payment by results"—now the generic term. The last occasion was in 1961 when 33 per cent of wage-earners were paid by results, 30 per cent of the men and 44 per cent of the women. The proportion of women paid by results was much the same as in 1938, but the proportion of men had increased from 18 per cent to 30 per cent. The figures are considerably higher in manufacturing industry than in mining, construction, transport and public services, for both men and women. The Ministry has conducted no further enquiries since 1961 on the grounds that it cannot find an adequate working definition of payment by results. There is not only the difficulty of distinguishing "lieu" payments from "incentive" payments in industries such as engineering,[2] but also the possibility of disguising time payments as payment by results. Building provides an example. Up to 1947 the building industry's agreement made no provision for payment by results and its time rates were laid down as standard payments to be applied throughout the industry. In that year a new clause permitted the introduction of incentive bonuses which have since become relatively common among larger firms. On some sites these are related closely to output by careful measurement of work; on others no effective standards of measurement are in use; and frequently a "bonus" is no more than a flat addition to the time rate of every worker on the site, or to every worker in a given grade on the site.[3]

---

[1] Royal Commission *Report*, p. 23.   [2] See pp. 273-4.

[3] In 1961 the Ministry of Labour recorded 14 per cent of construction workers as paid by results, whereas in 1968 the National Board for Prices and Incomes conducted a survey

Even where piece rates and times allowed are fixed in each plant, industry-wide agreements normally attempt to exercise some control. Most of them provide that the pieceworker's earnings over a standard week should exceed the timeworker's pay by a given margin, sometimes a fifth or a quarter, often a third. The justification for the margin is that the pieceworker works harder than the timeworker, and it is intended to match this greater effort. Accordingly a pieceworker is being paid, not for his output, but for his effort. This conclusion is supported by the almost universal provision in agreements covering payment by results that prices or times shall be revised when new methods, machinery or materials are introduced, since these may change the effort required to produce a piece. If the firm chooses to introduce a harder material, which takes longer to cut or to machine, it is generally held to be unfair that the pieceworkers' earnings should fall. Equally where the firm introduces a labour-saving machine the assumption is that the pieceworker should not thereby receive an additional differential over the time-worker. The time or piece should be revised so that for the same effort he continues to receive the same payment as before.

Individual capacity also varies, and a price or time which allows an inefficient worker to earn the required margin over the time-worker would allow others to earn more. On the other hand to fix the price or time for an outstandingly able worker would make it difficult for the general run of pieceworkers to reach the margin. So the agreements require the standard to be set for the worker "of average ability" or the "qualified" worker. If the job can be performed in several ways, it is important that the method used for timing or pricing is also the method used in production. If not the earnings of the worker even of average ability may diverge from the intended level.

Traditionally the setting of the time or price was the responsibility of the foreman or of a specialist "ratefixer" who relied "only on his own knowledge and past experience", and even now this arrangement is not uncommon. The National Board for Prices and Incomes found that "this method of work measurement

of building pay which returned nearly 33 per cent of craftsmen and about 47 per cent of labourers as receiving a variable bonus related in some way to output. (*Pay and Conditions in the Building Industry*, Report No. 92, Cmnd. 3837, 1968, p. 31.)

is usually unsatisfactory".[1] It is subjective and erratic, leading to "tight" and "loose" prices which make for inequities between one worker and another, and involve the employer in paying high earnings to some workers for relatively low effort. The remedy generally recommended for these shortcomings is "work study".

WORK STUDY

Work study is defined by the British Standards Institute as consisting of a number of techniques, particularly method study and work measurement. Work measurement is "the application of techniques designed to establish the time for a *qualified worker* to carry out a specified *job* at a defined level of performance". Method study is "the systematic recording and critical examination of existing and proposed ways of doing work, as a means of developing and applying easier and more effective methods and reducing costs".[2] Method study can, therefore, help to make sure that the method of work chosen for timing is an effective method and that it can be carefully specified.

This set of techniques had its origin in the work of an American, F. W. Taylor, "the father of scientific management". The strength and weakness of his methods were evident in the famous experiment in the handling of pig-iron in which he claimed to have discovered "the law governing the tiring effect of heavy labour on a first-class man".[3] By careful analysis of the job and by training in new methods suggested by the analysis, the average number of tons shifted per man went up by over 250 per cent.

The simplification which made Taylor's work possible was the assumption that workers could be studied as if they were machines. The danger in such an assumption is that its limitations will be forgotten. Since Taylor went on to claim that "every single act of every workman can be reduced to a science"[4] his theories of management often seemed to be based on the gross error that workers could and indeed should be treated as if they were machines.

[1] *Payment by Results Systems*, p. 49.
[2] *Glossary of Terms in Work Study*, 1959, p. 6.
[3] F. W. Taylor, *The Principles of Scientific Management*, 1947 ed., p. 57.
[4] *Ibid.*, p. 64.

This error was widely recognised in Taylor's own day[1] and led many of his opponents to throw out the baby with the bath water. That there was a baby was proved by the immense developments in production engineering since Taylor's day; and this development shows that work study does not depend on Taylor's intolerably narrow view of human nature. Subsequent exponents of work study both developed Taylor's techniques of empirical research and became more modest in the claims which they made for them. His notable contemporary, Frank Gilbreth, conducted his work on the unsound assumption that a "one best way" could be developed for the performance of every task; but this is also unnecessary and has subsequently been abandoned.

Taylor's work began to attract attention in Britain during the early years of the present century, and interest increased sharply with the outbreak of war. In September 1915 the new Ministry of Munitions established the Health of Munition Workers Committee to advise on "industrial fatigue, hours of labour, and other matters affecting the personal and physical efficiency" of the munition worker.[2] Studies were made into the relationship between output and hours of work and shift systems, into the effect of rest periods, into the factors affecting "lost time", as absenteeism was then called, and into effect on output of factory conditions, especially lighting, heating and ventilation.[3] By the end of the war industrial psychology had become an established discipline. With government support the Industrial Fatigue Research Board (subsequently Industrial Health Research Board) was established in 1918 to take over the work, and the National Institute of Industrial Psychology was established on a voluntary basis in 1921. Its scope also included the adaptation of psychological tests to examine aptitudes for particular tasks and types of work. When C. S. Myers, the principal of the Institute, brought out his *Industrial Psychology in Great Britain* in 1926, he made use of three main divisions in expounding his subject: Industrial Fatigue, Movement Study, and Vocational Guidance and Selection. He forcefully dissociated himself from the errors of Taylor and Gilbreth. The "intuitive opposition" of British workers to

---

[1] A full account of the criticism of Taylor's work is given in Georges Friedmann *Industrial Society*, 1955, Chapter 1, "Taylorism and the Human Sciences".

[2] *Official History of the Ministry of Munitions*, Vol. V, Part III, p. 1.

[3] The best summary of this work is H. M. Vernon, *Industrial Fatigue and Efficiency*, 1921 Vernon was an investigator for the Industrial Fatigue Research Board.

their ideas, had, he said, "a sound psychological basis". By contrast the Institute's research workers had "gained the confidence of the worker" by aiming "to ease the difficulties which may confront him".[1]

The connection between work study and payment by results was, however, re-established by the industrial consultants. The firm of Bedaux (now Associated Industrial Consultants) brought its techniques of work measurement and incentive payments across the Atlantic about 1930 and caused a number of strikes which led to an investigation by the Trades Union Congress,[2] but Bedaux's business continued to expand. A year or so later Colonel Urwick set up the consultancy firm of Urwick Orr. Others followed, and the production needs of the second world war greatly increased the demand for their services, which continued to grow after the war. Although industrial consultants may advise firms on many topics in addition to wages, and on other aspects of wages besides payment by results, nevertheless for nearly forty years the staple business of the major firms has been the installation of systems of payment by results on the basis of work study.[3]

Consequently, although work study is now widely used as a means for planning and controlling work in timeworking as well as in pieceworking firms, payment by results is still its main usage; and it is used for settling pay *within* the firm. Admittedly there have been attempts to exercise some control over the outcome at industry level. In cotton-spinning, for instance, work study was the main instrument in shifting mills from the industry-wide uniform piece-price lists to payment assessed within the firm. As new machinery was introduced into both the spinning and preparatory departments, "redeployment" was needed for its effective use, and this was generally carried out on the basis of work study. By 1964 the process had gone so far that the two sides of the industry signed a new agreement—the Manchester agreement—to give guidance on payment in re-equipped mills. Six grades of job were identified. The tasks to be performed by the members of each grade were to be settled by mill negotiations on

---

[1] 1933 edition, pp. 28-9.   [2] Trades Union Congress, *Bedaux*, 1933.
[3] In 1968 The National Board for Prices and Incomes found that "about three-quarters of the payment systems" which consultancy firms "had installed involved conventional P.B.R." (*Payment by Results Systems*, p. 20).

the basis of work study within the mill. The agreement gave guidance on the levels of pay which should emerge by laying down a wage "band" for each grade within which its average earnings at each mill should fall. About half the industry now operates under this agreement. But few other industries have tried to exercise any control at industry level apart from the prescribed minimum earnings levels for the "qualified" or "average" worker, and these are commonly exceeded by wide margins. The National Board for Prices and Incomes, for example, quoted the case of an engineering firm with a bonus level of 350 per cent above the pieceworker's standard at a time when the minimum level prescribed in the industry agreement was 45 per cent;[1] and even higher levels are common in engineering.

Although work study is an improvement on traditional rate-fixing as a means for settling consistent times and prices for payment by results, it cannot achieve complete precision. There are bound to be small margins of error with any timing device, including a stop watch, and allowances for rest periods or pauses are bound to be somewhat arbitrary. Of greater importance is the need for "effort-rating"—judging whether the individual under study is a qualified worker of average ability working at an acceptable piecework pace, and making an appropriate adjustment upwards or downwards for any deviation from that standard. It is possible to achieve and maintain a fair degree of consistency in effort-rating where time-studies are made by men and women trained in the same methods and subject to frequent cross-checking, but even here small differences occur, and differences will tend to be larger where controls are less rigorous. Another means of achieving a high level of consistency is the use of "synthetic" times, which are "records of times for tasks and job-elements which have been established and accepted by workers in the past. A work study department which has built up a library of such times is . . . often able to construct acceptable standards for new jobs from elements that have already been studied."[2]

A further difficulty is the "learning curve".[3] There is a good deal of evidence to show that workers employed on repetitive

---

[1] *Ibid.*, p. 22.   [2] *Ibid.*, pp. 50–1.

[3] National Board for Prices and Incomes, *Payment by Results Systems* (Supplement) Cmnd. 3627-1, Paper 3, "The 'Learning Curve' Theory".

jobs improve their performance not only from the first month
to the second and from the first year to the second, but also from
the tenth year to the eleventh, if the job continues unchanged for
so long. In these circumstances the notion of a qualified worker
of average ability loses precision; and to achieve equivalent levels
of earnings for equivalent effort, times and prices would have
to be adjusted not only when methods of production change, but
also where they do not change for a considerable period.

PAYMENT BY RESULTS IN PRACTICE

The investigations of the National Board for Prices and Incomes
have enabled them to present a fuller account of the working of
payment by results systems in Britain than has ever been available
before.

They found instances of payment by results under close control
providing an undoubted incentive to high effort and based on a
careful use of work study.[1] But there were other instances in
which work study was not used at all, and still others in which
careful studies of the methods and times had almost no effect
on the values actually set to determine earnings. Often this
discrepancy was the consequence of bargaining with workers
and shop stewards, a matter which is examined further in
Chapter 7.

Bargaining can lead to two "conversion factors", or factors by
which the standard time should be multiplied to give the acceptable level of earnings. The lower factor is the figure laid down
by management to guide work study engineers and rate-fixers
on the values they should settle. The higher factor is the average
percentage above standard actually being earned in the shop or
department for which workers and shop stewards may be expected to haggle before they will accept a value. Successful
bargaining can lead to an ever-widening divergence between the
two figures.

Such a divergence can also be the consequence of failure to
readjust values as production processes change. Where a minor
change in specification is a frequent occurrence there is a temptation to neglect the revision of values on the ground that the effect
of any one change is marginal. But a series of changes is likely to

[1] *Ibid.*, Paper 6, "A Payment by Results System Under Control"

have a cumulative effect and "earnings will tend to rise unequally and without any increase in workers' effort".[1]

It also happens that "managements may deliberately allow P.B.R. standards to slip for some workers so as to yield attractive earnings to a scarce grade of labour".[2]

Under these influences a system of payment by results "degenerates" or becomes "demoralised". The Board quoted cases. "At one engineering firm we studied, the price of its main product has remained constant over the past few years while increased earnings have absorbed all the productivity gains derived from an expensive programme of technological change." At another firm "average wage earnings must have risen by 75 per cent between 1963 and 1967, much faster than the most optimistic estimate of a real increase in output, an increase which was in any case brought about by increased capital investment".[3]

Another consequence is "wide discrepancies in pay . . . between individuals doing much the same kind of work: at one factory the spread of skilled pieceworkers' earnings was from £14.15.0d to £50 a week, with the highest and lowest earners in the same section. . . . Once a P.B.R. system gets out of effective management control, its takes on a life of its own as individuals and groups seize on any chance of raising their earnings to the level that they think is 'fair'."[4]

In their investigation of the building industry the Board studied payment systems on twenty-six sites. They classified incentive payment schemes as "good", "bad", and "indifferent". There were six "good" schemes, "distinguished by relatively high efficiency and a payment system at least fairly well under control. The 9 'bad' sites, conversely, were all notable for a payment system out of control and relative inefficiency. On the 'indifferent' remainder, bonus earnings were not particularly high and neither was efficiency."[5]

The Board's view is that the "demoralisation" of a payment-by-results scheme "is not usually the consequence of a poor work study or ratefixing department . . . It usually arises because too low a priority is given to the integrity of an establishment's payment system by top management itself".[6] Consequently the shift from negotiated piecework lists to factory piecework systems

[1] *Payments by Results Systems*, p. 55.   [2] *Ibid.*, p. 54.   [3] *Ibid.*, p. 34.   [4] *Ibid.*, pp. 28–9.
[5] *Pay and Conditions in the Building Industry*, p. 32.   [6] *Payment by Results Systems*, p. 55.

has not necessarily been a transfer of control over pay from employers' associations to the managers of individual companies and plants. In many instances it has been a loss of control over pay which techniques of work study and personnel management have been unable to prevent.

The defects evident in some schemes of payment by results have led to experiments with methods of payment which are intended to offer an inducement to maintain a high level of effort without variable earnings. The most common of these is "measured day work" under which the employee receives a time rate far higher than those commonly specified in industry agreements in return for an understanding that he shall sustain a specified level of performance, often based on work study. Variations include a "premium pay plan" under which a worker can choose one of several graduated levels of performance and be paid accordingly so long as he maintains the appropriate level of performance. There are also schemes such as the "Scanlon" and "Rucker" plans which vary the whole pay structure of the plant upwards or downwards according to a measure of labour performance throughout the plant.[1] The most striking example of a shift away from payment by results is the coal industry's national powerloading agreement.[2] There is, however, "no clear evidence of any overall movement to, or away from, P.B.R. since the Ministry of Labour's 1961 enquiry". By means of an enquiry among employers' associations and similar bodies, the National Board for Prices and Incomes discovered that shifts away from payment by results in some industries were matched by an increased use of payment by results in other industries, notably papermaking and food manufacture.[3] The Board concluded that the findings of the 1961 enquiry were probably "still approximately valid" for 1968 with one-third of wage-earners paid by results over all, and rather more than two-fifths in manufacturing.

These figures, however, do not reveal the number of workers whose pay is affected by payment by results. Where plants employ both pieceworkers and timeworkers it is common for the pay changes of the timeworkers to be linked either formally or in practice with the pay of pieceworkers. The most common method

---

[1] There is a useful discussion of these alternatives to payment by results in *Payment by Results Systems*, Chapter 6, "Some Alternative Systems".
[2] See p. 117.　　　　　　　　　　[3] *Payment by Results Systems*, p. 8.

according to the Board, is a "lieu" bonus which is "often calculated according to the average bonus of the direct workers,
on the theory that if production increases, the indirect workers
must have contributed and should benefit in the same way as the
direct workers".[1] In other cases there is a variety of links with
pieceworkers' pay or with plant or departmental output for
different groups of timeworkers. In some plants it is left to these
groups to put in claims for increases in pay as the earnings of the
pieceworkers rise.[2] Payment-by-results systems directly affect
over four million workers, but "probably about eight or nine
million workers are employed in undertakings where they are
used".[3] It is likely that payment by results has some effect on the
pay of the great majority of those eight or nine million workers.

PAY STRUCTURES AND JOB EVALUATION

Even where payment by results has little or no influence it does
not follow that the design and maintenance of a pay structure is a
simple matter. In engineering the technical developments which
encouraged the growth of payment by results also rendered
obsolete the assumption that the industry employed only two
classes of wage-earner, the craftsman and the labourer. New
machinery brought a variety of semi-skilled jobs, but it was left
to the individual firms to arrange for their payment by making
additions to the labourers' rate, and this is still broadly true. Many
other private industries also leave individual firms to settle
detailed pay structures on the basis of a small number of rates
agreed at industry level.

Besides this it is possible for firms to make additional payments
above the time rates. The printing industry makes relatively little
use of payment by results, but this does not mean that most
printing workers are paid only their time rates. In addition the
National Board for Prices and Incomes drew attention to "shift
extra, overtime . . . 'machine extras', 'merit money' and 'house
rate' ".[4] This is by no means an exhaustive list, and the additions
in many instances constitute a considerable part of the pay-packet.
Consequently even in a timeworking plant the development and
control of a wage structure can be a complicated business.

[1] *Ibid.*, pp. 5–6.   [2] *Ibid.*, p. 30.   [3] *Ibid.*, p. 9.
[4] *Wages, Costs and Prices in the Printing Industry*, p. 5.

The techniques designed to help in this task are known as "job evaluation", succinctly defined by the Trades Union Congress as a device used "to determine the relationship between jobs and to establish a systematic structure of wage rates for them".[1] Several methods are in use, from the simple process of ranking jobs to the points rating system. This lists the characteristics of jobs which are held to deserve payment, such as skill, responsibility, working conditions and so on; weights these according to their relative importance in the eyes of those making the judgement; and awards points to each job under each heading. The total of points for each job establishes its relative claim to pay.

In countries abroad one or other of these methods has been used to settle relative rates of pay for whole industries. The Dutch have even tried to develop a nation-wide system of job-evaluation. But in Britain, apart from coalmining and one or two small industries such as tobacco and jute, job evaluation has been used within companies and plants. There is a reason for this. Job evaluation tries to rationalise attitudes to differentials in pay. It does not and cannot create the attitudes themselves. So that if attitudes differ from place to place and from industry to industry, a rank order or a points-rating which gives satisfaction in one establishment will clash with values held in another. Among process workers in steel, for instance, responsibility is valued more highly in relation to skill than among engineering workers; in the north dirty work is held to have less claim to additional compensation than in the south; and it has proved difficult to apply a single system of evaluation to both manual and white collar workers. Consequently, whatever happens elsewhere, in Britain job evaluation has been another force pushing control in pay decisions away from employers' associations towards individual firms.

Sometimes job evaluation is used in harness with payment by results. There are firms which establish a structure of basic rates by means of evaluated job rates and add a work-studied incentive system providing variable earnings above the rates. Where this is done the original pay structure can be maintained only if the incentive pay system is carefully controlled. Otherwise a degeneration of the incentive scheme can bring differentials in earnings widely different from those laid down by the evaluation. An

[1] Trades Union Congress, *An Outline of Job Evaluation and Merit Rating*, 1964, p. 1.

G

evaluation may also be undermined by pressure from a particular group for a sectional increase, or by a shortage of labour in a particular grade. "There are often pressures from managers and supervisors, too, since a job-evaluated pay structure reduces their freedom of discretion."[1] Periodic regradings may be used to give disguised increases in pay not justified by any change in the jobs themselves.

However, where job evaluation is properly used it should help to provide a company or plant with an acceptable and controlled pay structure. If many British firms do not possess pay structure of this kind it is not because they have misused job evaluation, but because they have not used it at all. In 1967 the National Board for Prices and Incomes conducted a survey to find the extent of its usage. They found the highest coverage among white collar employees, with 30 per cent of managerial jobs evaluated and 27 per cent of "staff" jobs. Non-craft manual employees came close behind with 26 per cent, but only 11 per cent of craftsmen were covered.[2] This is a serious limitation on the effectiveness of job evaluation, for where, as is common, craft and non-craft workers are employed in the same firm, adjustments to craft pay may set up pressures which disturb the evaluated pay structure for other workers.

OVERTIME

There has been a rapid growth in the volume of overtime worked by men in Britain over the post-war years. In 1938 the difference between the weighted average of "normal hours" laid down in industry agreements and the average hours worked by men was half an hour a week. It rose sharply over the war but fell back to an hour in 1947. Thereafter there was a fairly steady increase to over six hours a week in 1965, and the latest figures show very little change since then. The growth in overtime is not caused by men working longer, for average hours worked now are much the same as in 1947. Over that period collective bargaining has reduced average "normal hours" from 45·3 to 40·4.[3] However,

---

[1] National Board for Prices and Incomes, *Job Evaluation*, Report No. 83, Cmnd. 3772, 1968, p. 24.   [2] *Ibid.*, p. 10.

[3] A much fuller study of these developments is given in E. G. Whybrew, *Overtime Working in Britain*, Royal Commission Research Paper No. 9, 1968.

the difference between normal hours and hours worked under-
states the volume of overtime. At any one time figures for average
hours worked cover some workers on short-time, and others
who have missed working time during the week, from a few
minutes up to four days. Some of the latter may work overtime,
so long as this is on a daily basis, even though they have missed
part of the normal working week. Consequently the average of
46·4 hours a week worked by men in April 1969 probably
indicates average overtime of between seven and eight hours.
The average of 56·6 hours returned for men in road haulage
indicates overtime approaching twenty hours a week.

Overtime working is a male habit. Average hours for women
have come down in step with the agreed working week, and are
now 38·3 hours a week. This does not mean that no women
work overtime. In transport (average hours 43·1) women work a
good deal of overtime, and some bus conductresses work exceedingly long hours. But in most industries women's overtime is
comparatively rare.

There are grounds for thinking that overtime earnings are an
alternative to earnings from payment by results. The leading
industry group of any size in the official figures is Transport and
Communications (except railways and sea transport) with average
working hours 50·5 for men; the last returns showed only 7 per
cent of men paid by results in this group. There is a good deal of
evidence of the same thing within individual plants.[1]

Why is overtime worked? The obvious answer is to meet the
needs of production, together with the continuous shortage of
labour of the post-war period. The bus industry, for example,
has been desperately short of labour in the post-war years, with
some undertakings 25 per cent below establishment. If anything
like full services are to be provided, heavy overtime must be
worked. But over recent years a series of studies have thrown
doubt on this simple explanation. Summing up their findings,
Whybrew concludes that:

"There is considerable evidence that actual patterns of overtime
working are considerably influenced by relative pay factors.
Overtime is highest in those industries with low average hourly

[1] "The fact that payment-by-results workers tend to work less overtime than timeworkers has been noted by almost all those who have examined hours of work questions."
(*Ibid.*, p. 61.)

earnings. It grows fastest in those industries with below-average increases in earnings. Within industries overtime is highest in the lowest-paid occupations and among those workers not on incentive schemes which would enable them to increase their earnings in normal hours. Practically every interpretation of the relationship between pay and overtime would suggest that overtime is not being used in a way that would be reflected in the production figures. Indeed some interpretations supported by specific evidence would suggest that overtime encourages people to waste time at work."[1] Among the evidence now available are the Devlin Committee's findings concerning the practice of "welting" in the Liverpool docks and other ports,[2] and many of the investigations of the National Board for Prices and Incomes.[3] Whybrew also discounts the view that overtime is a necessary consequence of full employment by showing that other countries under the same pressure, except for France, have not used overtime to anything like the same extent as Britain, and that Holland in particular has been able to keep overtime under close control.[4] The strongest evidence of all that overtime in Britain is not always used to get work done, but to produce a weekly wage packet which is regarded as tolerable by both parties, comes from those industries in which hours paid are not necessarily hours worked. The National Board for Prices and Incomes wrote of hours recorded as worked in road haulage that they "mostly represent units of payment rather than hours strictly worked; the size of the pay packet is determined not so much by the hours actually worked as by the number of hours for which the employer is prepared to pay".[5] The newspaper industry also uses overtime in this way.

The premium rates provided for overtime in most collective agreements on pay are usually held to be a deterrent intended to prevent managers using overtime except when it is urgently necessary. Where these premium rates are used to inflate earnings the collective agreement loses much of its regulative effect, and the rapid growth of overtime in post-war Britain is therefore a further shift of decision-making in industrial relations from the

---

[1] *Ibid.*, p. 63.   [2] See p. 8.
[3] See, for example, *Productivity Agreements*, pp. 6–7.
[4] *Overtime Working in Britain*, pp. 32, 64–6.
[5] *Charges, Costs and Wages in the Road Haulage Industry*, Report No. 48, Cmnd. 3482 1967, p. 13.

employers' associations which negotiate the agreements to individual plants. But, as with many schemes of payment by results, so with overtime the decisions taken in the plant are not necessarily part of a planned pay structure. If there is a planned pay structure, overtime earnings are likely to distort it.

JOINT CONSULTATION

There is another reason besides payment by results, additional time payments and overtime for the failure of many British firms to replace the declining authority of industry agreements by effective plant agreements governing pay. This is the doctrine of joint consultation which has been a central element in the ideas accepted and taught by British personnel managers since the first world war.

In its proposals for the post-war reconstruction of industrial relations the Whitley Committee recommended that the functions of the joint industrial councils which they wanted to see established in all well-organised industries should include not only the settlement of pay and conditions of employment, but also "the better utilisation of the practical knowledge and experience of the workpeople" and "improvements of processes, machinery and organisation and appropriate questions relating to management and the examination of industrial experiments, with special reference to co-operation in carrying new ideas into effect and full consideration of the workpeople's point of view in relation to them". Moreover, "it is not enough to secure co-operation at the centre between the national organisations; it is equally important to enlist the activity and support of employers and employed in the districts and in individual establishments".[1] Consequently the committee recommended that district joint councils and works committees should also be set up. The works committees "should not be allowed to interfere" with "questions, such as rates of wages and hours of work, which should be settled by District or National Agreement . . .; but there are also many questions closely affecting daily life and comfort in, and the success of, the business, and affecting in no small degree efficiency of working, which are peculiar to the individual workshop and factory. The purpose of a Works Committee is to establish and

[1] *Interim Report on Joint Standing Industrial Councils*, Cd. 8606, 1917, pp. 4–5.

maintain a system of co-operation in all these workshop matters."[1] The Whitley Committee thus established three important principles of joint consultation as it subsequently developed in Britain: that there are many topics of concern to employers and trade unions, and to managers and men, which are not suitable for settlement by negotiation and collective agreement; that these topics should be handled by co-operation; and that relations within the plant should be predominantly or entirely confined to co-operation over issues outside the scope of collective agreements.

Although they were represented as an extension of industrial democracy, these principles were in fact a retreat from the position which many war-time works committees and shop stewards' committees had established. In its survey of works committees published in the same year as the Whitley Committee's *Supplementary Report on Works Committees*, the Ministry of Labour distinguished between "industrial committees" and "welfare committees". The industrial committee, "the first and main variety . . . generally constituted on a Trade Union basis, deals with particular questions affecting the conditions and remuneration of labour in a given works—questions of principle being reserved for the district and national organisations concerned". The welfare committee "deals with what may be termed works amenities".[2] The Ministry went on to show how far a works committee might venture into the field of negotiation. "A tool-room bonus, for instance, may be arranged in a works between a committee and the works manager, and they may agree in regarding it as a works affair, while the local branch (or district committee) of the Union concerned may consider that it is a question of wages which demands their sanction."[3] It is probable that the Whitley Committee's views on the function of works committees were influenced by the anxiety of its trade union members to see a restoration of trade union authority over workplace negotiations after their experience of the war-time shop stewards' movement.

As it happened post-war unemployment accomplished the task for them (where it did not destroy the influence of trade

[1] *Supplementary Report on Works Committees*, Cd. 9001, 1918.
[2] Ministry of Labour, *Report on Works Committees*, 1918, pp 8–9, 39.
[3] *Ibid.*, p. 39.

unionism altogether) and at the same time diminished interest on both sides of industry in works committees of all types. As a result of government acceptance of the Whitley reports as applying to the civil service, local joint committees were set up in government offices and establishments, and at the instance of the unions the Railways Act of 1921 gave statutory sanction to the railway negotiating procedures, which included Local Departmental Committees; but in private industry the majority of works committees established during and after the war were swept away.[1] Nevertheless the inter-war period saw important developments in joint consultation. A number of the major firms which led the field in personnel management established consultative works councils on the Whitley model, or maintained those they had already established. Among them were Rowntree and Cadbury, and in 1927 they were joined by the new industrial giant, I.C.I., which proposed to set up works committees in all its plants without reference to the unions. Under union pressure the firm agreed to complete its structure of works committees by a Central Advisory Labour Council in which its managers met trade union representatives, but shop stewards were not recognised and the workers' resperesentatives on the works committees were elected by the whole body of workers, not by trade unionists alone.[2]

This model was generally adopted when the second world war brought a new upsurge of workshop democracy. On this occasion the mood in the workshop was far less rebellious than in 1914–18. At least after the German invasion of Russia there was fairly general support for the war effort and for expanding output. The first Joint Production Committees appear to have originated spontaneously in late 1940. By the following summer the engineering unions were demanding that joint production committees should be set up throughout their industry, and the Trades Union Congress had given its blessing to the movement. In February 1942 the Director General of Ordnance Factories made an agreement with the unions to set up Joint Production Consultative Committees in all factories operated by the Ministry of Supply, and in the following month an agreement between the

---

[1] Committee on Industry and Trade (Balfour Committee), *Survey of Industrial Relations*, 1926, p. 305.
[2] H. A. Clegg, *General Union in a Changing Society*, 1964, p. 130.

engineering employers and unions provided for Joint Production Consultative and Advisory Committees in federated firms. The Ministry of Supply reported that by July 1943 there were 4169 "joint production committees or similar bodies" operating in private firms in the engineering and allied industries, covering two and a half million workers.[1] In addition there were yard committees in shipbuilding, pit production committees in coal-mining, site committees in shipbuilding and similar developments in many other industries.

By the end of the war the movement had received ideological support from two very different quarters. Following on the Hawthorne experiment,[2] Elton Mayo and his colleagues in the United States had developed a philosophy of "human relations in industry". They contrasted restriction of output in the "bank wiring room" with rising output in the "relay assembly rest room" which they explained by the involvement of the girls in the experiment, and the good relations among the girls themselves and with their supervisor.[3] Mayo argued that "a small society lives in an ordered manner such that the interests of its members are subordinated to the interests of the group". But with in-dustrialisation this condition had been destroyed, and a "planlessness . . . is becoming characteristic both of individual lives and of communities".[4] The danger was that informal groups in industry would try to create their own defences against planlessness and in doing so work against the aims of management. The social challenge was therefore to recreate in industry a situation in which work groups could serve as means of effective, purposeful and satisfying collaboration. Joint consultation seemed an ideal in-strument for the purpose.

It is easy to see why Mayo's theories appeal to managers, par-ticularly to managers whose frame of reference for thinking about industrial relations is what Alan Fox has described as a "unitary structure", a structure with "one source of authority and one focus of loyalty", likened to a team whose members "strive jointly towards a common objective, each pulling his weight to

[1] International Labour Office, *British Joint Production Machinery*, 1944, p. 88.
[2] See p. 7.
[3] Recent re-examination of the Hawthorne experiment has shown that in fact its evidence does not support these conclusions. (See Alex Carey, "The Hawthorne Studies: a Radical Criticism", *American Sociological Review*, 1967.)
[4] Elton Mayo, *The Human Problems of an Industrial Civilisation*, 1946 edition, pp. 124–5.

the best of his ability". Managers of this kind, says Fox, "can be found deploring any reference to 'the two sides of industry', in the belief that such talk encourages the wrong attitudes".[1]

It is more difficult to say why Mayo's ideas should win sympathy among trade unionists. Mayo himself was no friend of trade unionism. He wrote of the "developed misunderstanding between employers and workers in every civilised country" as one of the symptoms of planlessness,[2] and considered that "militant tactics" were "invariably the sign of . . . imperfect understanding of the principles of organisation".[3] American unions had little time for his teachings' which they dismissed as "moo-cow sociology"— the study of the social conditions most conducive to increased output from the worker. In Britain, however, there was a difference. Not only did his teachings become accepted doctrine among British personnel managers for many years, but trade unionists were also influenced by them.

During and after the first world war British trade unions were for the most part converted to doctrines of workers' control or joint control which held that in a socialist society industry should be run by the unions or by a joint board half chosen by the unions and half by the government. Only if workers ran industry through their own organisations, held the proponents of these doctrines, could "wage-slavery" be ended. Their proposals were effectively killed by the arguments over Herbert Morrison's London Passenger Transport Bill of 1930, which proposed that board members should be selected on their merits, and not as representatives.[4] However, the burial was delayed until 1944 when the General Council of the Trades Union Congress brought out their *Interim Report on Post-War Reconstruction*. They accepted Morrison's position, although they suggested that "experience gained in the collective organisation of Labour is a strong qualification" for board membership. Trade union officers appointed to the boards of nationalised industries should, however, "surrender any position held in, or formal responsibility to the Trade Union". At this point the General Council faced a difficulty. They had to admit that this proposal would not by itself satisfy the aim of

[1] Alan Fox, *Industrial Sociology and Industrial Relations*, Royal Commission Research Paper No. 3, 1966, pp. 3, 12.
[2] *The Human Problems of an Industrial Civilisation*, p. 170.
[3] *The Social Problems of an Industrial Civilisation*, 1949 edition, p. 128.
[4] Herbert Morrison, *Socialisation and Transport*, 1933.

extending "the influence of workpeople over the policies and purposes of industry", which rested "primarily on the simple democratic right of workpeople to have a voice in their industrial destinies". How could this right now be established? The Council's answer was by joint consultation. They pointed to the war-time joint production committees whose value had "been recognised on all sides". Consultation should be "retained as a permanent feature of our industrial organisation". This was to apply to both public and private employment, but "in socialised industries there would, of course, be no difficulty in ensuring that such Works Councils were set up and consulted".[1]

In 1946 the Coal Industry Nationalisation Act placed an obligation upon the National Coal Board to agree with the unions upon joint machinery for consultation on questions of safety, health and welfare, on the organisation and conduct of the industry and other matters of mutual interest.[2] Subsequent nationalisation Acts contained similar provisions, and systems of consultative committees were established at workplace, regional and national levels.

Elsewhere there had been a considerable decline in the number of joint production committees as war-time enthusiasm evaporated. But soon the post-war Labour government found its economic difficulties made the need for increased production as urgent as in war-time, and in 1947 the National Joint Advisory Council to the Minister of Labour recommended that joint consultative machinery should be set up wherever it did not exist "for the regular exchange of views between employers and workers on production matters".[3] In 1948 a survey conducted by the Ministry of 54 industry bargaining bodies showed that 26 had agreed to recommend the establishment of joint committees to their members, 8 had decided that existing machinery was enough, 17 wished to leave the matter to local action and 3 had failed to reach a decision.[4]

By this time the Whitley principles had undergone some revision. It was no longer possible to pretend that bargaining by shop stewards did not play an important part in the industrial

---

[1] pp. 7, 21–3.   [2] Section 46.
[3] *Industrial Relations Handbook*, 1944 edition, Supplement No. 3, 1948, p. 4.
[4] Ministry of Labour and National Service, *Annual Report*, 1949, Cmd. 8017, 1950, p. 110.

relations of many industries. Consequently two systems of work-shop representation were widely recongised: one, generally through shop stewards, for collective bargaining; a second, usually through elections in which all employees could vote regardless of union membership, for consultation. Most nationalised industries had these dual systems, and in 1947 I.C.I. recognised shop stewards in addition to its consultative works committees. Theorists of consultation[1] put forward the view that separate forms of rep-resentation were required by the nature of the two functions. Bargaining needed tough representatives who would press for the best possible deal for their members. Consultation required part-nership in a continuous process for informing the workers of the facts and of conveying the attitudes of the workers to management so that the decisions of the firm would become an expression of a common view of everyone from the directors to the labourers. By denying the existence of workplace bargaining the original Whitley doctrine had obviously inhibited the development of effective machinery for workplace bargaining. But even now that workplace bargaining was recognised the revised doctrine still had an inhibiting effect. Consultation was emphasised at the expense of bargaining. Treatises were written on the proper functions and correct constitutions for consultative committees, while methods of workshop bargaining were left to develop as best they could. It was held that consultation required a unified plant committee representing all grades of worker, whereas each grade might be left to bargain on its own if its members chose. The range of subjects appropriate to agreement was kept as narrow as possible so that matters such as the volume and distribution of overtime, the manning of machines, employment and dismissal, and the pace of work were generally regarded as consultative matters. Consequently if shop stewards exercised control over them, as they often did, they controlled by custom and practice and not by recognised bargaining procedures. Influenced as they were by a doctrine such as this, it is understandable that British personnel managers did not generally recognise the consequences of the growth of workplace bargaining.

There are links between this aspect of the doctrine of joint consultation and the "unitary frame of reference". "Most em-ployers and managers", says Fox, "have been obliged to accept

[1] For example, G. S. Walpole, *Management and Men*, 1944.

trade unionism", but those who hold the unitary frame of reference sometimes express distrust of collective bargaining "because it is said to encourage the 'two-sides' mentality". It is therefore to be expected that they should wish to limit the scope of collective bargaining and to extend the scope of the co-operative relationships which are thought to be appropriate to joint consultation. Such employers and managers "have difficulty in accepting the validity of work-group ... control. ... This means that managerial and work-group control systems may co-exist without ever coming to terms with each other. ... Management averts its eyes, and work-group control systems grow unchecked without ever being called upon to relate themselves to a rational, consistent managerial policy."[1]

Since the fall of the first post-war Labour government, joint consultation has been on the decline. Marsh and Coker estimated that the number of joint production committees fell by a third in federated engineering establishments between 1955 and 1961, when fewer than one in ten federated establishments still retained a functioning committee.[2] This decline coincided with an increase in the number and influence of shop stewards. McCarthy held that "few consequences of workplace bargaining have been so well investigated as its effect on joint consultative committees. ... Either they must change their character and become essentially negotiating committees carrying out functions indistinguishable from ... shop-floor bargaining, or they are boycotted by shop stewards and, as the influence of the latter grows, fall into disuse." He backed this conclusion with a survey of the findings of a wide range of published and unpublished research.[3]

With the decline of joint consultation there has begun to develop a new view that consultation and negotiation are part of a single process of involvement of workers and their representatives in decisions affecting their working lives, and that both should be handled by a single committee in which managers meet shop stewards. This development has been hastened by productivity bargaining. According to the 1961 edition of the *Industrial Relations Handbook:* "While matters discussed by joint

[1] *Industrial Sociology and Industrial Relations*, pp. 10–14.
[2] "Shop Steward Organisation in the Engineering Industry", *British Journal of Industrial Relations*, June 1963, p. 183.
[3] *The Role of Shop Stewards in British Industrial Relations*, pp. 33–6.

consultative committees . . . are, in general, quite different from those dealt with by negotiating machinery, the two sets of subject-matter may, of course, be closely related. For example, an employer who plans to introduce a new process or new materials may well discuss the matter with his employees through consultative machinery, but if the changes in process or material are to be followed by changes in wage-rates, that would be a matter for negotiation."[1] It would be wearisome and frustrating to handle a complex series of proposals for changes in performance and in pay through dual machinery of this kind. Consequently many productivity agreements have led to a change in plant machinery. In oil distribution, for example, there already existed Joint Consultative Committees which had "acquired powers to negotiate locally on a number of issues by 'custom and practice'." During 1965–6, "the need for the wholesale replanning of drivers' schedules and the reorganisation of work within the plant arising out of Esso's Distribution Agreement involved formal recognition of plant negotiations and substantial increase in their volume".[2]

This view of plant relationships implies a "pluralistic frame of reference" which Fox contrasts with the unitary framework. Pluralism recognises not only "the legitimacy and justification of trade unions in our society" but also "the reality of work-group interests which conflict quite legitimately" with those of management, and provide a rational basis for "restrictive practices and resistance to change. . . . This leads on directly to the necessity of the pluralistic frame of reference for the development of more sophisticated bargaining techniques designed to reconcile management and work-group interests at a higher level of mutual advantage. Such techniques are now emerging under the name of 'productivity bargaining'."[3]

FRINGE BENEFITS

There is no agreed list of the items which go under the heading of "fringe benefits". They include provision for payments to employees which do not form part of their normal wage or salary, such as pensions and sick pay. Provision for holidays with pay is often included, but because in Britain this is the one fringe

[1] p. 126. [2] *Productivity Agreements*, p. 37.
[3] *Industrial Sociology and Industrial Relations*, pp. 7, 12.

benefit which is generally included in industry agreements, it is left over to the next chapter. Redundancy pay is another fringe benefit, but provision for redundancy may include a procedure for selecting and warning those to be made redundant, or may set up such a procedure without provision for payment. This procedure may also be regarded as beneficial to the workers affected and therefore a fringe benefit. Similarly workers might be regarded as "better off" for the existence of a disciplinary procedure and such a procedure could be included among fringe benefits. Then there are those fringe benefits such as the provision of canteens and the subsidisation of meals, or the provision of sports facilities, which are a cost to the employer but can only be regarded as a form of additional payment to those employees who make use of them.

However they are defined, fringe benefits, apart from holidays with pay, have played a relatively unimportant part in formal collective bargaining in British private industry. "Such matters as the period of notice of dismissal, arrangements for dealing with possible redundancies, sick pay, pension schemes and circumstances justifying individual dismissal have not been the subject of collective bargaining for workers generally"[1] outside the public sector. This contrasts with the United States where fringe benefits have formed a prominent issue in collective bargaining in the post-war years. One reason for the contrast is that British unions "believe that National Insurance benefits should be sufficient to maintain standards of living without supplementation from private or industrial schemes, and union attempts to achieve income-security for their members have been directed mainly towards lobbying for increased social security benefits rather than towards bargaining for industrial schemes".[2] But, at least until the introduction of earnings-related benefits during the course of the sixties, this strategy did not meet with great success. While comparing favourably with those in the United States, British social security benefits fell far behind those of most other Western European countries.

Perhaps for this reason there has been a considerable growth of fringe benefits in post-war Britain outside the scope of formal

[1] Royal Commission, *Written Evidence of the Ministry of Labour*, p. 33.
[2] G. L. Reid and D. J. Robertson, *Fringe Benefits, Labour Costs and Social Security*, 1965, p. 30.

collective bargaining. It has been estimated that the coverage of private occupational pension schemes rose from 1·6 million employees in 1936 to between 6·5 and 7 million in 1964. By that time schemes in the public sector accounted for nearly 4 million employees.[1] By June 1961, according to a survey conducted by the Ministry of Pensions, 57 per cent of men employees, 62 per cent of single women and 53 per cent of married women were covered by provision for payments from their employer during sickness. The proportions were higher in the public services and the nationalised industries where schemes covering a whole industry are found, and lower in private industries and services; as between different classes of worker they were highest among professional workers and lowest among unskilled.[2] It is not uncommon for the management of a private firm introducing a sick pay scheme to discuss it beforehand with representatives of the unions. The comments of the unions may lead to amendments to the scheme, and if the firm were to make changes later on it would consult with the unions again. However, such a firm would insist that the scheme was *ex gratia* and not negotiated. Some pension schemes have been introduced in a similar manner.

The public services and nationalised industries are also well provided with redundancy schemes, but in private industry the most recent survey, for 1962, showed only 1·25 million workers covered by negotiated industry-wide schemes. A larger number, 1·75 million, was employed by the 371 companies which were then known to have their own explicit redundancy policies, about half of them drawn up after consultation with the unions and a few embodied in formal agreements; and the number of these companies was rising rapidly. In every one of the 54 actual cases of redundancy noted by the Ministry of Labour in 1962, which affected 74,000 workers, a "procedure was devised specially to cover the specific circumstances". In about half of these cases the procedure was drawn up after consultation with the unions, and in some of the remainder there was a consultation in the application of a procedure drawn up by the firm alone.[3] Minimum provision for payments to redundant workers are now laid down in the

[1] J. Wiseman, "Occupational Pension Schemes" in G. L. Reid and D. J. Robertson, *op. cit.*, p. 170.

[2] *Report of an Enquiry into the Incidence of Incapacity for Work*, Part I, *Scope and Characteristics of Employers' Sick Pay Schemes*, summarised in the *Ministry of Labour Gazette*, July 1964. [3] *Ministry of Labour Gazette*, February 1963.

Redundancy Payments Acts 1965, but redundancy agreements or policies may provide additional benefits, and retain their importance in providing for consultation procedures and the choice of workers to go.

Formal procedures for dealing with the dismissal of individual employees, and appeals against dismissal, are "general in the public sector of employment and fairly widespread in large firms, especially those employing 2000 or more".[1] As with redundancy procedures these arrangements are in some instances agreed with the union, in other instances introduced after discussion with the union and in others established by management acting alone. It is arguable that industry procedures also cover dismissals. In most industries the union can object to a particular dismissal by taking it through the industry's disputes procedure. Most of these procedures, however, were not designed to handle dismissal disputes, which generally require speedy handling and some accepted criteria on what kind of action can justify a disciplinary dismissal. Most of them deal with few cases of dismissal. In practice, therefore, the benefits enjoyed by the worker in this respect depend, as with other fringe benefits, upon the arrangements which apply in his own firm.

THE FOREMAN

Although boards of directors, line managers or personnel managers may shape the industrial relations policies of their firms, most of their dealings with their employees are handled by intermediaries, the foremen or supervisors. Foremen are therefore of considerable importance in industrial relations. Despite this there is surprisingly little information about the part they play, although one or two surveys have provided evidence and some general trends can be discerned.

Changes in the size of the firm have affected the foreman's position. In an undertaking with only one foreman, or with two or three, the foreman is likely to be an important person with considerable scope in the running of his section. If he chooses he can rely on personal dealings, whether permissive or authoritarian. If there are to be rules he may be able to make some of them himself. But the large concern places the foreman near the

---

[1] Ministry of Labour, *Dismissal Procedures*, 1967, p. 19.

bottom of the hierarchy of management, and subjects him to a body of rules handed down from above.

The changing educational standards of management have increased the gap between supervisors and higher management which the taller hierarchy of the large firm has opened up. Supervisors are still promoted, but a smaller proportion of senior managerial posts is filled by ex-foremen. A study of the Acton Society Trust picked our seventeen characteristics in the background of managers' educational and industrial experience, and found that service as a foreman seemed to be the most disadvantageous to prospects of promotion.[1] This suggests that the tone of middle and higher management is set more and more by men who have not "come from the factory floor".

The growth of specialisation reduces the foreman's scope because decisions formerly left to him are now taken by the specialists. Decisions about the time allowed for a job, for example, may be taken by a work-study department, or on the basis of studies carried out by the department. A job evaluation scheme may leave a foreman with no influence over the pay of the members of his section, at least within normal working hours. The personnel department may take over responsibility for selection and dismissal.

Joint consultation can undercut the foremen by opening up a direct line of communication between higher managers and workers' representatives which excludes the foremen. In fact this may happen wherever shop stewards are powerful enough to have direct dealings with higher management, whether there are consultative committees or not, and the foreman will then learn of managerial decisions through the shop steward.

These changes have led to the popular image of the foreman as the "forgotten man of industry". Most of them were already described in a study of foremen conducted in 1948–50 by the National Institute of Industrial Psychology. They discussed the effect of the increase in the number of functional departments, of the growth of joint consultation and of the increasing influence of shop stewards, and added two more developments adverse to the foreman. The first was the effect of full employment on industrial discipline and on selection. The foreman had "far less opportunity of building up a team of his own choice". The

[1] Acton Society Trust, *Management Succession*, 1956, pp. 28–9.

second was that "increasing wages have benefited hourly-paid workers relatively more than their supervisors", harming the foreman's pocket and prestige.[1] The study concluded: "It has been said again and again that the supervisor holds a key position in industry. At the moment he is holding it against considerable odds."[2]

The Royal Commission surveys offer a check on the present position. In a sample of 598 foremen 70 per cent were interested in promotion, and about half of these thought there was a reasonable hope of it. This suggests that channels of promotion are fairly open, although not necessarily to the top. The survey also suggests a sizeable differential between most supervisors and those they supervise. The average *net* income of the sample was £20 10s 0d compared with £16 10s 0d for trade union members and £15 for non-members. On the other hand complaints about the by-passing of foremen appear to be fully substantiated. One-third said that stewards were under no obligation to raise issues with them before going to higher management, and 70 per cent of the remainder said that stewards could in practice by-pass them.

However, many foremen seemed to retain considerable authority. Seventeen per cent of those who dealt with shop stewards could settle piecework prices, 19 per cent could settle questions of grading and 38 per cent could deal with the distribution of overtime. Half of them were personally responsible for engaging workers and could dismiss on their own responsibility. Half of them also had authority to impose disciplinary penalities.[3] This suggests that it is dangerous to generalise about the position of foremen in Britain. The trends have had an effect, but they have not completely eroded the powers of many foremen.

The National Institute found that 40 per cent of the supervisors they interviewed claimed to have had formal supervisory training.[4] More than fifteen years later the Royal Commission came up with almost exactly the same proportion in their sample, suggesting that there had been little improvement. The National Institute emphasised that "supervisory training can be fully effective only if managers themselves are appropriately trained

---

[1] National Institute of Industrial Psychology, *The Foreman*, 1951, pp. 78–9.
[2] *Ibid.*, p. 104.   [3] *Workplace Industrial Relations*, Chapter 5.
[4] *The Foreman*, p. 54.

and are in general sympathy with the aims and content of the courses attended by their supervisors".[1] It is still possible to find firms which have not learned this lesson.

Another finding of the Royal Commission survey was that foremen generally did not seem to be dissatisfied with their position in industrial relations. Three-quarters of them disliked being by-passed by shop stewards, but only a small minority were dissatisfied either with the working of the negotiating procedures in their plants or with the authority given them to deal with shop stewards.

This might suggest that the effect of industrial change on the position of the foreman has been exaggerated. But other interpretations are also possible. Foremen may claw back some of the authority which they seem to have lost. By distributing overtime they can recover some control over earnings, and perhaps a method of discipline. By disregarding the rules of the work-study department they can continue to settle times and prices under payment by results. Alternatively, even where such issues are controlled by custom and practice rather than the foreman, he may join with those he supervises in accepting, applying and protecting the customs developed in the shop, so that his relations with his men are easy and comfortable. In either situation the position of the foreman may seem to him to be not unsatisfactory; although it may not recommend itself to higher management, where they were aware of it.

Productivity bargaining has provided some evidence on this score. The National Board of Prices and Incomes found that productivity agreements could subject foremen to "considerable strains. In the past the supervisors were involved in a good deal of pretence. They were supposed to be in control of overtime and the pace of work, but practices tolerated by management prevented their control being effective, and protected them from criticism. Now they are directly responsible for seeing that improved performance is achieved, and cannot plead the old excuses."[2] It is a common experience of firms preparing productivity agreements to find that they have to reorganise the job of the foreman, to replace a number of supervisors and to devise a training programme for the remainder before they can hope to apply the agreement successfully.

[1] *Ibid.*, p. 76.   [2] *Productivity Agreements*, p. 25.

CHAPTER 6

INDUSTRY BARGAINING

THE DEVELOPMENT OF INDUSTRY BARGAINING

Since the first world war the system of collective bargaining in Britain has generally been described as a system of national bargaining, or, more precisely, of "industry-wide" or "industry" bargaining. As the Ministry of Labour put it in its evidence to the Royal Commission: "The main feature of the British system of industrial relations is the voluntary machinery which has grown up over a wide area of employment for industry-wide collective bargaining and discussion between employers' associations and trade unions over terms and conditions of employment."[1] The process of growth is described in the latest edition of the Ministry's *Handbook of Industrial Relations*. "In the early days of collective bargaining, negotiation was generally confined to localities, but in most industries the scope of the machinery has continually extended until national negotiations have largely replaced local interchanges on industrial questions."[2]

Collective bargaining is aimed at reaching agreements, which are, as Chapter 1 explained, classified into two types: *substantive* agreements which regulate "terms and conditions of employment"; and *procedural* agreements which establish a constitutional method of reaching substantive agreement and of resolving disputes about them. Most of the early agreements at industry level were procedure agreements only. The regulation of pay, hours of work and conditions of employment was left to the local branches or district organisations of unions and employers. If they could not reach agreement, however, the dispute was to be referred to a meeting between the national employers' organisation and the union head office. Generally it was agreed or understood that there should be no strike or lockout unless the

---

[1] Royal Commission, *Written Evidence of the Ministry of Labour*, 1965, p. 11.
[2] p. 22.

central bodies had met and failed to find a settlement. It made no difference whether the question at issue was a claim from the union branches for some new concession from the local employers or a difference over the interpretation of an existing agreement. So long as there was a local dispute the central bodies were to be given a chance to settle it.

Probably the first of these industry procedure agreements was the joint committee set up to deal with disputes throughout the cotton weaving industry in 1881. Cotton spinning came next with the famous Brooklands agreement in 1893. During the next twenty years they were followed by the boot and shoe trade, the building industry, the shipbuilding industry and, most important of all, the engineering industry in 1898. Meanwhile the practice of holding *ad hoc* conferences between the two sides at industry level to deal with disputed questions developed in other industries including printing and steel.

It was shown in Chapter 4 that the initiative came in nearly every instance from a recently formed employers' federation, more often than not after a national lockout. Some national employers' federations were founded expressly for the purpose of giving assistance to local associations in conflict with the unions; others, formed for different purposes, found themselves called in by their constituents. It was natural for them to try to stipulate that the unions should not call a strike without first giving them an opportunity to intervene. For the most part the national leaders of the unions were sympathetic to the proposal. Perhaps their most difficult task was to hold their more unruly branches in check. By pressing a local claim a hotheaded branch or district committee could provoke a stoppage in which they would expect the support of the whole union. Head office would be expected to find the money without control over the course of the dispute. In many unions the rules on local autonomy were generous or ambiguous, and in any case it was not easy for the national executive to enforce rules against powerful sections of their unions even when these sections were clearly in the wrong. Consequently the leaders were not averse to the additional authority of a procedure agreement which gave them a clear mandate to intervene along with the employers' federation in any local dispute before a stoppage began.

Even this was not a final guarantee that the branches and

districts would not take the law into their own hands. They might be pushed into voting for the procedure, especially after a prolonged lockout, but it did not follow that they would honour it when their tempers were raised—because the employers refused what seemed to them an amply justified claim, or demanded a wage cut, or challenged some craft privilege. In fact some of the bitterest stoppages of the first quarter of the century arose out of action by powerful districts in defiance both of their national leaders and their industry disputes procedure. They include the engineering strikes on the Clyde and the north-east coast in 1902–3, the London building lockout of 1914 and the national building lockout of 1924. The hostility of the members led the Boilermakers' Society to withdraw from the shipbuilding procedure in 1912, and the Amalgamated Society of Engineers from the engineering procedure a year later. Nevertheless the trend was clear. The national organisations on both sides of industry were convinced of the advantages of disputes procedures; the employers' federations were supported by their members; and the weaker union branches and districts might also see that the procedure could work to their advantage.

Gradually the national leaders began to venture into substantive agreements at industry level on issues of general concern. In one or two instances these agreements preceded the conclusion of a permanent procedure agreement. In 1893 the Shipbuilding Employers' Federation and the Boilermakers' Society agreed on a ratio of apprentices to craftsmen and next year all the ship-repairing unions entered into an agreement to regulate work in oil-tankers. A few years later the first industry agreement in printing dealt with rates of pay on the new linotype machinery which was then being introduced. In 1902, four years after signing their industry-wide procedure agreement, the leaders of the Amalgamated Society of Engineers joined with the employers in drawing up the Carlisle Memorandum to control the Premium Bonus system, a method of payment by results then growing in popularity with engineering employers. It was not popular with the members of the union. The executive did not dare to put the agreement to them for ratification, and it was terminated ten years later.

The practice of industry-wide pay adjustment was a later and more reluctant development than the introduction of procedure agreements, and here again the initiative was taken by employers' associations as in cotton weaving and shipbuilding.[1] But support for industry-wide pay regulation was not confined to employers' organisations. On the union side there was growing propaganda for the idea of a minimum wage, especially among the miners. In 1912 the Miners' Federation launched the biggest strike the world had seen in support of their claim for a national minimum wage throughout the industry. The federation, however, had only recently established its sway over the country as a whole, with the affiliation of Northumberland in 1907 and Durham in 1908. South Wales was another relatively recent convert to the federation's policies. There was therefore need for a national programme which would unite all the coalfields. The coal-owners for their part had no interest in industry-wide pay regulation. In the exporting districts, especially South Wales and Scotland, they considered that widely fluctuating prices demanded flexible wages. In the end the dispute was settled by parliament, which established statutory machinery for settling minimum wages, but district by district.

Before the war, therefore, it was difficult to discern a definite trend towards industry-wide pay settlement. The war made the difference. The cost of living rose rapidly throughout, so that wages had to be adjusted upwards repeatedly. In these circumstances the settlement of rates of pay separately town by town and district by district seemed cumbersome and dilatory. At the same time the extension of state control throughout the munitions industries and into coal, transport and elsewhere meant that the government had assumed final financial responsibility for much of the economy and had in the last resort to take decisions about increases in pay. Consequently in many instances the unions were able to by-pass local groups of employers with their separate attitudes and interests and take their case to a government department capable of reaching a decision for the whole industry. The railways were taken over at the outbreak of war and early in 1915 came the first "war bonus" applying to all the railway companies. Government control of the coal mines at the end of 1916 led to a national war bonus for miners in 1917. The engineering industry also had to wait until 1917 for an agreement between the Engineering Employers' Federation and the many unions concerned that "general alterations in wages" should apply in "all districts".

[1] See p. 127.

When it came this decision was of overriding importance not only because of the large numbers of workers directly affected, but also because some of the decisions on engineering pay were extended to other industries. By the end of the war the practice of industry-wide pay adjustments had spread to other munitions industries, most sections of transport, and a number of other manufacturing and service industries.

Although almost all these arrangements were made for the period of the war only, the great majority of them were retained afterwards. The cost of living continued to rise rapidly until well into 1920. Government control of industry was only gradually relaxed over the three years after the armistice. Some unions, notably the railway unions and the Miners' Federation, were firmly attached to their new systems of pay settlement, although the miners were forced to revert to district settlement in the subsequent depression. A number of employers' associations also appreciated the advantages of industry-wide pay settlement. The system which had allowed the unions to obtain advances for all their members in one settlement while prices were rising permitted the employers to secure pay cuts for all their members during the deflation of 1921-3. Even when the tide turned again they could still see advantage in it. In the past a wage increase in a prosperous district had been followed by a series of demands in other districts which the local employers' associations could not easily ignore. With industry-wide settlements the employers could insist on taking into account the conditions of the industry as a whole. The Engineering Employers' Federation, for example, resisted union demands for advances in the districts where car manufacture and electrical engineering predominated, because the marine and heavy engineering districts could not afford them.

In addition the new system had government support. Looking forward to the post-war reconstruction of industrial relations in 1917 the Whitley Committee had recommended "the establishment for each industry of an organisation, representative of employers and workpeople, to have as its object the regular consideration of matters affecting the progress and well-being of the trade. . . ."[1] The government accepted this along with the Committee's other proposals, and during 1918 and 1919 the new Ministry of Labour called meetings of the two sides of almost

[1] *Interim Report on Joint Standing Industrial Councils.*

every industry which lacked an industry-wide procedure agreement in order to promote the establishment of joint industrial
councils. By 1921 seventy-three had been set up, and although
the depression swept a number of them away, there were still
forty-seven in being in 1926. It is clear from the Whitley reports
and from the Ministry's model constitution for a joint industrial
council that it was left to each council to choose for itself whether
conditions of employment should be regulated by industry-wide
agreements or local agreements. In fact, however, most of them
opted to continue the industry-wide system of pay regulation
which they inherited from war-time. Many of them had little
experience of organised industrial relations before the war. Such
collective dealings as there had been in chemicals, the food
industries, the gas and electricity supply industries, and tramways,
for example, had generally been between the individual undertaking and the unions. The war had brought industry-wide pay
adjustment and had called into being industry-wide associations
of employers to handle their side of it. These were the associations
which formed the employers' sides of the new councils and it
was natural that they should take over the agreements which had
created them, and establish disputes procedures through which to
handle the problems arising from the application of the agreements
in individual undertakings. Since these industry-wide arrangements were the central features of most of the joint industrial
councils which survived, and the government had assisted in the
creation of the councils and given them its blessing, it appeared
the industry-wide bargaining, including industry-wide pay settlement, had the approval of the state.

In its early years industry-wide pay adjustment fell far short
of industry-wide regulation of pay by means of a uniform pay
structure. In engineering, for example, the adjustments were to a
war bonus, subsequently a "national" bonus, paid in addition to
the district rates, most of which remained at the level they had
reached before 1917. All the districts settled a rate for skilled
workers and another for labourers, but there was a good deal of
variation between them in the extent to which they collectively
regulated the rates of semi-skilled workers, many of which were
settled factory by factory. After the war the employers resisted
demands for increases in district rates in the more prosperous
areas, so that district rates could be regarded as "frozen". Some

industries graded their districts, each grade having a slightly different level of pay. It was open to the unions to attack these differences as anomalous, and gradually the process of upgrading reduced their number until many industries came to have a single national rate of pay for all areas, with the exception of a "London rate" or a "London addition". At the same time some industries took over the regulation of actual rates of pay for the various grades of workers, and of special rates of pay for special jobs and abnormal conditions of work. In some instances these various rates of pay together with industry agreements on overtime, night-work, weekend work and shift payments came near to constituting an industry-wide pay structure, a complete code capable of determining every element in the pay-packet of every manual worker throughout the industry except those paid by results. As this process continued it came to be accepted more and more widely that an industry pay structure should be the ultimate objective of unions and employers in every industry.

Because of the widespread acceptance of the Whitley reports' recommendations, and the developments which followed from them, the second world war and its aftermath brought no such upheaval in industrial relations as the first. There was no doubt as to what constituted a satisfactory system of industrial relations. The return of full employment and government control was therefore used to extend this system to industries which had not yet achieved it or had slipped back between the wars. Between 1939 and 1946 another fifty-six joint industrial councils or similar bodies were set up or revived, and industry-wide pay settlements were reintroduced into the mining industry. The trend towards industry-wide pay structures continued both during and after the war. It appeared that Britain was well on the way to a system of industry-wide regulation of all aspects of industrial relations, in which the job of joint district bodies, individual firms and local union officers would be limited to the interpretation and administration of agreements reached on their behalf by the national unions and employers' federations.

INDUSTRY NEGOTIATING BODIES

So far it has been assumed that industry bargaining is a matter of reaching agreements which regulate industrial relations throughout the industry concerned. In fact it is rarely as simple as that, sometimes far from it. In describing collective bargaining in the steel industry as it was in 1961 the *Industrial Relations Handbook* outlined the systems of national negotiations which applied to production workers in blastfurnaces in "integrated" plants in England and Wales, to production workers in the heavy steel sections of the industry, and to maintenance craftsmen in both blastfurnaces and steel works. Then it went on to set out the sections of the industry which were not covered by these arrangements. In heavy steel there were separate negotiations through the following joint bodies: "Midland Iron and Steel Wages Board, South Wales Siemens Steel Trade Conciliation Board, Welsh Tinplate and Sheet Trades Joint Industrial Council, the Sheet Trade Board and Galvanizing Conciliation Board. There were also *ad hoc* negotiations between the South Wales and Monmouthshire Iron and Steel Manufacturers' Association and the Iron and Steel Trades Confederation, Transport and General Workers' Union, and the National Union of Enginemen, Firemen, Mechanics and Electrical Workers. Special arrangements also exist in Sheffield to cover workers engaged in the production of special steels—here the Iron and Steel Trades Confederation negotiates with the following employers' associations: Sheffield and District Engineering Trades Employers' Association, Sheffield and District Rollers, Tilters and Forgers' Employers' Association and the Crucible Steel Makers' Association." There were almost as many local exceptions in the blast-furnace section, and both sectional and local arrangements for dealing with certain groups of maintenance craftsmen.[1] The *Handbook* does not mention negotiations for white collar employees in steel. There was provision for this in a number of companies, but quite separate from the machinery for negotiating on behalf of manual workers.

Enclaves of local bargaining are not found to this extent in many other industries, but the sectionalisation of industry negotiations in steel has many parallels elsewhere. This is true of both kinds of sectionalisation, into sub-industries such as blastfurnaces and steel production, and into occupational groups such as production workers, maintenance craftsmen and white collar employees.

Discussion of separate negotiations for sub-industries raises the difficult question of the definition of an industry. In Britain we

[1] pp. 43–6.

regard engineering as a single industry for the purposes of industrial relations, although vehicles, electrical engineering, aircraft, agricultural machinery, and marine engineering might all be regarded as separate industries without straining the term in any way. Shipbuilding, however, has always negotiated as a separate industry; so have government ordnance factories, and the government dockyards have never been regarded as part of the shipbuilding industry. Railway workshops, even those engaged in the manufacture of rolling-stock, have been treated as part of the railways although their negotiating machinery has been separate from that for the grades engaged in operating the railways and maintaining the permanent way.

The quarrying industries have a unified disputes procedure but leave the negotition of pay and conditions to four separate sectional councils for freestone, roadstone, chalk and slate. These could have been four separate industries; alternatively there might have been a single agreement on pay and conditions covering all sections. In chemicals there is a Joint Council for Heavy Chemicals, Fertilisers and Plastics. This settles minimum rates of pay, but leaves the negotiation of other rates and conditions to group councils for each of the three sections. Drugs and Fine Chemicals, however, has its own council, as do Gelatine and Glue, Paint, Varnish and Lacquer, and Soap Candles, and Edible Fats.

Some of these arrangements may be attributed to union structure. There might, for example, be a single industry negotiating body for production workers in steel but for the existence of separate unions for blastfurnacemen and steelworkers. But in most instances the major influence has been the structure of the employers' organisations. In quarrying and chemicals the same unions operate in almost every section. It is the employers who are divided. Much the same unions operate in shipbuilding as in engineering, but the Shipbuilding Employers' Federation is distinct from the Engineering Employers' Federation. If there existed separate employers' associations for vehicle manufacture and electrical engineering, for aircraft and agricultural machinery, then there would almost certainly be distinct negotiating machiery for each of them without any modification of union structure. Ownership divides the railway workshops and the government ordnance factories from the engineering industry, and the government shipyards from shipbuilding.

Occupational sub-division owes more to the unions. In many industries there are separate negotiations for maintenance workers and for production or process workers because the former are represented by craft unions and the latter by process workers' unions, or more commonly by general workers' unions. In engineering and shipbuilding there is no such distinction because a number of unions which organise craftsmen also organise production workers, including the Amalgamated Union of Engineering and Foundry Workers, which is by far the largest in the industry. Where there are separate negotiations for production workers and for maintenance workers, there is generally a single unified arrangement covering all the production workers' unions, but craft negotiations are in many instances fragmented. In steel the Amalagamated Union of Building Trade Workers negotiates apart from the other craft unions on behalf of men engated in the construction and maintenance of furnaces and chimneys; in chemicals the engineering unions and the National Federation of Building Trades Operatives negotiate separately; and in flour milling the Electrical Trades Union and the Amalgamated Union of Engineering and Foundry workers negotiate respectively for electricians and for mechanics.

Where white collar unions are recognised they almost invariably negotiate separately from the manual workers' unions. The one important exception to this is the railways, in which there is a single procedure covering salaried and "conciliation" (roughly manual) grades. However, at local and regional level the salaried employees have their own Local Departmental Committees and Regional Councils, and it is possible for the Transport Salaried Staffs' Association to negotiate on its own at national level if it chooses to do so. Consequently this is no more than a partial exception to the general rule. In addition there are separate negotiating arrangements for professional and technical staffs and for senior salaried staff. The great majority of private manufacturing industries, however, have no national machinery covering white collar workers. Where they exist, collective arrangements on their behalf are between their unions and individual plants or companies. The major exceptions to this generalisation are printing and engineering. In engineering there are six industry procedures for white collar employees: one with the Draughtsmen, two with the Association of Scientific,

Technical and Managerial Staffs (deriving from the two separate unions which amalgamated under this title in 1968) and three with the clerical unions.

In some of the public services the sectionalisation of industry bargaining is taken to extremes. There is a General Council representing the unions and the employing authorities in the National Health Service. Its functions, however, are extremely limited, and the conduct of negotiations on pay and on most conditions of employment is left to functional councils of which there are no less than nine. They cover (a) administrative and clerical staffs (b) ancillary (or manual) staff, (c) dental staff, (d) medical staff, (e) nurses and midwives, (f) optical staff, (g) pharmaceutical staff, with two further councils for the remaining groups of professional and technical staffs. Several pages would be required to set out the number and variety of separate negotiating bodies in the civil service.

Occupational sub-division helps to reduce the number of unions involved in any one set of industry-wide negotiations but even so it is rare for a single union to constitute the workers' side of any industry negotiating body. In most industries and many services the main body of manual workers are represented by both the great general unions, and often one or two smaller unions besides. The maintenance workers normally belong to more than one union. There are no less than seven unions on the National Craftsmen's Co-ordinating Committee in steel. Some of the functional councils in the Health Service have as many as a dozen organisations on the staff side. In engineering and shipbuilding negotiations the unions are represented through the Confederation of Shipbuilding and Engineering Unions, with thirty affiliates, and in building by the National Federation of Building Trades Operatives with fifteen.

It might be supposed that such diverse and fragmented arrangements would have come in for a good deal of criticism. In fact they have not. Multi-unionism has of course long been under attack, but the attack has been directed against its tendency to promote demarcation disputes and an inflexible labour force, not generally at any failure of the unions to work together in industry negotiations. Occasionally the existence of separate agreements for production workers and craftsmen has been criticised, but most of the criticism of the structure of negotiating machinery has concentrated on four industries: engineering, printing, railways and buses.

There has for many years been a body of opinion in favour of breaking down engineering negotiations into separate sub-industries. The argument is that car firms, aircraft manufacturers, electrical engineering firms, and so on, have different levels of profitability, different problems and also different levels of pay (despite their common minimum wage rates). Consequently, it is suggested, each section could negotiate more efficiently on its own. Since the structure of negotiations in engineering derives from the structure of the Engineering Employers' Federation this amounts to a criticism of the federation.

On several occasions in the post-war years the printing employers complained of "leapfrogging" tactics in wage negotiations with the London craft unions trying to increase their lead over the provinces and the provincial unions striving to catch up. The amalgamation of the London unions with the provincial craft union to form the National Graphical Association in 1964 has put an end to this. Since then the remaining inter-union divisions have been blamed for supporting obstacles to the efficient use of manpower, rather than provoking conflict in industry negotiations on pay and conditions.

The railway unions have also been accused of leap-frogging tactics. The old conflict between the National Union of Railwaymen's boast that it is an industrial union and the Locomotive Engineers' and Firemen's insistence on the need for separate organisation for footplate staff is easily fanned into flames. But since the railwaymen covered by the main railway negotiating procedure are represented by only three unions, fewer than are found in most other major industries, this conflict cannot be a consequence of multi-unionism alone. Its causes must also lie in the system of industrial relations on the railways, including the extreme sectionalisation of management which has not yet been eradicated.

The leapfrog process on the buses is akin to that which the printing industry used to experience. The London busmen have retained a considerable differential over the provinces since before the first world war. Over the last thirty years it has narrowed and widened again more than once. There is also a further complication. Not only does London Transport negotiate separately from the provinces, but there are two negotiating bodies in the provinces, one for the municipal bus undertakings, and the other for the so-called "company" undertakings. This increases the possibility of rivalry. However, this rivalry has nothing to do with multi-unionism. The General and Municipal Workers and the National Union of Railwaymen organise groups of busmen in the provinces, but the Transport and General Workers' Union is the only union for London busmen and is the dominant union in both provincial negotiating bodies.

Procedure agreements which provide methods of dealing with disputes arising in the plants will be discussed in a subsequent section; but there is also the procedure whereby the two sides meet to make or revise industry agreements. In some industries this is still an informal arrangement. It is understood that a meeting will be arranged to discuss a proposal coming from either side. In joint industrial councils, on the other hand, the negotiation and revision of agreements is normally a formal function of the council itself. In fact this makes no difference. So long as it is understood that the two sides meet on the initiative of either, negotiations can be started. All the joint industrial council offers is regular meetings, which can be used for the purpose. Thereafter in both types of procedure there can be a reply, with perhaps an offer, and successive meetings to close the gap, or reference to a sub-committee or to informal discussions.

Perhaps the only important variation in these arrangements lies in the use that is made of arbitration. There is no constitutional obstacle to prevent the two sides in any negotiating body from referring their differences to arbitration if they choose to. They can find their own arbitrator, or ask the Department of Employment and Productivity to provide them with an arbitrator or a Board of Arbitration, or they can make use of the Industrial Court. Some negotiating bodies, however, expressly provide for arbitration. Most of them are in the public service. Differences in civil service negotiations are referred to the Civil Service Arbitration Tribunal; the police and the teachers have their own arbitral bodies. Other public services and nationalised industries agree to refer their differences to the Industrial Court. Generally it is stated or understood that the award of these tribunals should be accepted. The two sides of the coalmining industry can choose whether or not to submit an unresolved dispute to their National

Reference Tribunal, but if it is referred the award is binding. The British Railways Board and the railway unions, on the other hand, agree to refer their differences to the Railway Staff National Tribunal, but do not bind themselves to abide by the award.

Special arrangements for arbitration are much less common in private industries and services. Cotton weaving is one of the exceptions. Unresolved differences must be referred to a conciliation committee with three independent members, one of whom is chairman. However, there is an escape route. If the conciliation committee does not reach a settlement, the chairman can issue an award, but only if both sides invite him to do so. Otherwise he issues a recommendation which is not binding. In any case this machinery has not been used for many years. The "company" section of the bus industry formerly provided for arbitration but the arrangement was terminated in 1957. The Industrial Court is not often asked to settle a major dispute at industry level outside the public sector. Things were different in the first world war, and from 1940 to 1951, when strikes and lockouts were prohibited and binding arbitration was available, and even between 1951 and 1959 when binding arbitration was available without the prohibition. Arbitration was then a major element in our system of industrial relations in both public and private industry.

THE SUBSTANCE OF AGREEMENTS

There is great variety in substantive agreements at industry level, but also some uniformities. Virtually all of them specify a "normal" working week. For manual workers this is 40 hours in most major industries, although instances of 42 hours, 44 hours and 45 hours are still to be found. For white collar employees 38 hours is common. The gap between the two groups has narrowed in the period since the war. Holidays are also prescribed almost universally. Two weeks' annual holiday with pay in addition to statutory holidays is now rapidly being replaced by agreements providing for three weeks' holiday for manual workers, and many white collar workers, especially those in senior grades, are entitled to more than three weeks.

Quite apart from shift work, an industry agreement may
H

allow the normal week to be worked on some other basis than five days of eight hours each, for example four days of ten hours each or less than eight hours on weekdays with Saturday morning included in the normal week. Overtime begins, according to most agreements, when work continues beyond the normal daily period of work. For manual workers overtime hours are almost invariably paid at a rate in excess of the normal hourly rate. A common arrangement is to pay an additional 25 per cent above the hourly rate (time-and-a-quarter) for the first two hours of overtime, 50 per cent (time-and-a-half) thereafter, except for week-end overtime, which generally receives a premium of 100 per cent (or double time). But there is a good deal of variety in detail. White collar workers are less generously treated in this respect. Some of them are expected to work a margin of overtime, when required, without additional payment. Beyond the margin, if there is one, payment is in many instances at the standard hourly rate. Where there is a premium it is usually less than the premium for manual workers. Since a common explanation for the existence of premium overtime rates is that they are to discourage employers from using overtime work by raising its cost, it is worth noting that manual workers, with the higher premium, almost universally average more overtime than do white collar workers. It appears that the incentive to the employee outweighs the disincentive to the employer.

Many industry agreements covering manual workers make provision for shift working, and, with the development of electronic data processing, shift arrangements for white collar workers are becoming more common. Shift work may be day and night, double day, continuous night, three shift or continuous shift, and agreements may make separate arrangements for each of them and for some of the many variations upon them. Almost invariably the shift worker enjoys a higher hourly rate than the day worker, yielding either more pay for the same number of hours, or the same weekly pay for a shorter working week. The amount of the differential is intended to reflect the inconvenience of working that particular type of shift.

White collar workers are usually paid by the week or by the month. Most manual workers are still "hourly paid", even though their contracts of employment may require up to four weeks' notice of termination under the Contracts of Employment

Act. This means they are entitled to pay only for the hours during which they are available for work and work is available for them, except in so far as they are protected by a Guaranteed Week agreement. These agreements, which succeeded temporary arrangements made under emergency legislation during the last world war, provide that a worker available for work shall be entitled to so many hours' pay at the end of the week even if he has not worked. The guarantee is generally hedged with qualifications, especially a suspension of the obligation to pay if the lack of work is due to a strike in the same undertaking.

In industries which employ numbers of apprenticed craftsmen there is likely to be an agreement on apprenticeship, laying down the period of apprenticeship, the age of entry into apprenticeship and rates of pay for apprentices. In addition there may be quite elaborate provisions for training and for the establishment of joint bodies to supervise training. The types of skilled work reserved for craftsmen are not usually defined, but nevertheless there are in a number of industries "dilution" or "relaxation" agreements which permit workers who have not served an apprenticeship to perform "skilled" work under certain conditions and safeguards usually including reversion to less skilled work whenever sufficient apprenticed craftsmen are available.

Nearly all industry agreements set out rates of pay for various groups of workers, but here uniformity is at an end. The number of rates and the rates themselves are endlessly diverse. In a craft industry the starting points may be a rate for craftsmen and another for labourers, but in most instances these are supplemented by additional rates for other classes of worker, such as "semi-skilled" grades and those with special skills, and "plus" rates for those temporarily or permanently engaged on special types of work, which may be numerous. In addition there will probably be a special rate, or special rates, for women, and age scales for juveniles of both sexes (in addition to rates for apprentices). Process industries may begin their provisions on pay with a set of rates for grades of process workers classified according to skill and experience, or more likely two sets, one for men and one for women, but these may also be supplemented by a variety of additions, and separate rates for maintenance craftsmen. Many industry agreements provide for additional rates of pay for all grades in the London area, which is variously defined. Some also provide two or more sets of rates for the provinces. The engineering industry prescribes separate distinct rates for more than a hundred districts, all of them within a range of a few shillings. Pay agreements for white collar employees commonly provide an age scale for adults as well as for juveniles, and scales for each grade where there is more than one.

Some industry agreements specifically provide that their rates of pay are intended to be minimum rates which can be supplemented in individual companies and plants, as does that of the Joint Industrial Council for Heavy Chemicals. Others, like the "Working Rules" for the building industry, expressly describe their rates as "standard". Many industry agreements make no mention of the matter either way. These differences have little practical effect in most industries.[1]

There are still one or two industries whose pay agreements include lists of piecework prices. Cotton spinning and cotton weaving each have two such lists, but every year they apply to diminishing proportions of the workers in their sectors of the industry, and half or more of the workers in the spinning section are now covered by the Manchester agreement.[2] The footwear industry also attempts direct regulation of earnings under work-studied incentive schemes in an industry agreement. Otherwise industry agreements generally prescribe a minimum percentage by which the earnings of the worker paid by results should exceed the time rate. Among the many special provisions which may be required for workers paid by results are their own overtime arrangements. The most common of these is payment of the normal time rates, plus the prescribed overtime premium, plus incentive earnings on the same basis as at other times. Where this method is followed the proportional increase in earnings for overtime is necessarily less for the worker paid by results than for the timeworker. Few if any industry agreements for white collar employees make any provision for incentive payments.

The bulk of the substantive provisions of almost all industry agreements fall within the range of topics briefly described in the previous few pages. The variety comes mainly in the special provisions for different classes of worker and for different classes of work. Most publicly owned industries, however, cover a wider range. They have agreements on sick pay, and pension

[1] See pp. 137–9.   [2] See pp. 175–6.

schemes drawn up after consultation with the unions if not by agreement. Most of them also have agreed provisions for redundancy. All these matters are rare in industry agreements in private industry.

CHANGES IN THE STANDARD WORKING WEEK, HOLIDAYS AND PAY

Besides administering and interpreting substantive agreements, collective bargaining changes them. The provisions of most industry agreements on pay, on holidays and on the standard working week have undergone considerable alteration in the last twenty years, and some uniformities can be observed in these changes.

Before 1914 there was wide variation in the normal working week. Where its length was governed by agreements these were for the most part district agreements and ranged from 48 hours to 60 hours, or even more widely. Although a number of craft trades, notably in engineering and building, had secured the nine-hour day in the years 1871-4 there does not otherwise appear to have been a marked tendency to coincidence in changes in the length of the normal working week until the first world war introduced widespread industry bargaining and a general demand for post-war improvements in the lot of working men and women. Between 1918 and 1920 most major industries agreed on a normal working week of 47 or 48 hours for manual workers. For another twenty-five years there was no general changes, although one or two industries moved ahead. The building industry introduced an optional 44-hour week shortly after the war and the printing industry made 45 hours their standard in 1937. The miners won a seven-hour day underground by legislation in 1919, raised to eight hours in 1926, and reduced to $7\frac{1}{2}$ in 1930. The second world war brought a demand for general improvement again and in the years 1945-7 the norm became 44 hours with 45 common in many textile trades. More than a decade of stability followed. From 1948 to 1959 the Ministry of Labour's average of normal weekly hours fell from 44·7 to 44·4. Then nearly thirteen million workers gained a reduction within two years and by 1962 the norm was 42 and the average 42·4. But the 42-hour week was not a stable position. Clearly it had no hold on the imagination akin to the 40-hour week and by 1964 industry agreements were again on the move, many of them providing for the introduction of the 40-hour week in two steps of one hour each. By 1967 40 hours was the norm and the average was 40·5.

Before 1938 annual holidays with pay were the exception. A committee under the chairmanship of Lord Amulree estimated that out of 18½ million manual and lower-paid white collar employees less than eight million were entitled to annual holidays. The committee recommended that annual holidays should become universal and their proposal that statutory wage-fixing bodies should be empowered to establish them within their jurisdiction led to the Holidays with Pay Act, 1938. By the end of the war a minimum of one week's holiday was practically universal, and in the early fifties there was a general shift to two weeks' holiday for all workers with one year or more of service. From 1963 onwards a number of industries agreed on longer annual holidays for long-service workers, and the Draughtsmen launched a well-directed campaign to push individual engineering companies into three weeks' holiday for their members. In 1968 a general move towards three weeks' holiday had begun, with demands for four weeks for white collar employees.

No one has yet traced the origins and course of these rapid shifts in provisions on hours of work and holidays with pay. However, it is certain that industry agreements have become much more uniform in both these matters than they once were. This is especially true of manual workers' agreements, but the change has also affected white collar workers and their advantage in holidays and working hours over manual workers has been substantially reduced. In addition changes are uniform and are concentrated in relatively short periods of time. If the starting point cannot be accurately identified, at least the best-organised industries tend to be in the front of the queue, and a tail of poorly organised industries is left to follow behind.

Movements of pay are a good deal more complicated than this, but there is general agreement that, over periods of some years, pay in different occupations and industries moves in step. Pay relationships, says Guy Routh, "seem to have the capacity to regain previous shapes, sometimes after lapses of many years. Thus class relations were similar in 1935 to those of 1913, and, as between managers, foremen, skilled, semi-skilled and unskilled manual workers the structure was not much different in 1960 from what it had been in 1913. Coalminers and agricultural workers suffered relative declines after the first world war, but regained their previous position after the second. The relative pay of railwaymen and Civil Servants was allowed to deteriorate during and after the second world war and was then restored by drastic upward revisions in the middle or late 1950's."[1]

These long-run movements tell us little, however, about the individual decisions on pay in industry bargaining, for over the last thirty years most industries have decided upon an upward revision of pay at intervals of between one and two years; and these short-term decisions have not kept in step. According to Dr. Routh pay structure is "by its nature incapable of reaching a state of rest, because it is made up of a multitude of units (that is units for purposes of determining rates of pay) who have different ideas as to what their relationships to one another should be. Group A may claim parity with Group B, which may claim a differential of x per cent over group A. Both groups cannot then be at rest at the same time."[2]

The most detailed study of short-run changes in industry pay agreements yet published was by K. G. J. C. Knowles and Derek Robinson.[3] They studied movements in the wage rate of the lowest grade of manual worker in 146 "negotiating groups", almost all of them industry negotiating bodies, from 1952 to 1958. Their first object was to discover whether there was anything that could be described as a "wage round" defined as "periods in which wage settlements are relatively concentrated" and determined by the month in which the pay change came into operation. They found six major wage rounds in this period of seven years, but the intervals varied and they could not be seen as annual events. Only one-fifth of their 146 groups appeared in all six of these rounds, and only two-thirds of them in four or more. In addition there was a good deal of variation in the amount of the increase, whether in terms of cash increase or of percentage addition. They concluded that if the definition of

[1] Guy Routh, *Occupation and Pay in Great Britain, 1906–60*, 1965, p. 148.
[2] *Ibid.*, p. 150.
[3] "Wage Rounds and Wage Policy", *Bulletin of the Oxford University Institute of Statistics*, 1962.

uniformity was "fairly rigorous" then "there is little or no uniformity in the short term". However, they were able to observe "certain regular coalitions of groups" in terms of timing, and temporary concentrations or "bunchings" in particular ranges of increase. But neither the coalitions nor the bunchings had regular leaders. As to the longer run, their verdict was not in conflict with Dr. Routh. "The variability of the total increases secured by our groups over the full period was smaller (sometimes considerably smaller) than the variability of increases in shorter periods. In other words, there was more uniformity between the cumulated increases than there was between the increases secured in a 'round' or other short period."

These conclusions seem to be very much at variance with the belief of many professional negotiators on both sides of industry that there is an annual wage round, or an "annual ritual dance", which determines industry pay settlements. But Knowles and Robinson do not destroy the view that there is a strong tendency towards uniformity in time and amount of increase. They prove no more than that this is not the only influence at work.

Their survey, for example, excluded negotiating groups with cost-of-living sliding scales which provide for automatic adjustment of wage rates on some prearranged basis in accordance with changes in the official retail price index. In 1965 some two million workers were covered by arrangements of this kind, the largest single group of them being manual workers in the building industry. Some of their agreements provide for a periodic adjustment according to the movement of the index, for example every six months. Others provided that wages should be adjusted whenever the index shifted by a given number of points. In either case the dates of wage changes are necessarily independent of "wage rounds" determined by other factors. Furthermore the amount of the increase in pay at these dates is determined by the shift in the index. Few of the formulae provide an increase in pay proportionately as great as the increase in the index. Even those that do so cannot maintain the level of rates in step with levels elsewhere, for taking one year with another, wage rates have increased by considerably more than retail prices over the last thirty years. Consequently if these negotiating groups wish to keep their increases in wage rates in line with general increases, they have to negotiate advances over and above those which arise from the sliding scale; and in fact all of them do so. In foot-wear (and in the printing industry before it abandoned its scale in 1967) adjustments outside the scale are settled every two years, leaving the sliding scale to do its work in the interval. Elsewhere adjustments outside the scale come in irregular steps, the timing being influenced by, among other things, the amount of the adjustment arising under the scale and the amount of the general increase in wage rates elsewhere. Consequently the negotiating groups with sliding scales were very properly excluded from the study by Knowles and Robinson. But their influence on other negotiating groups, if there is any, could not be excluded. This influence would press other negotiating groups to diverge from whatever general wage round there may be, to the extent that the sliding scale groups were out of step.

Another factor which can work against short-run uniformity is the intervention of an inquiry or an arbitration award. The Guillebaud Committee[1] provides a good instance. It was appointed by the British Transport Commission (as it then was) and the three railway unions, with government approval, in the autumn of 1958 to enquire into the relationship between railway pay and pay elsewhere, and reported in March 1960. While its investigations were in progress the two sides refrained from negotiating a general advance in pay, although increases were being settled in other industries, until the National Union of Railwaymen demanded an interim increase a few weeks before the report appeared, and a general increase of 5 per cent was promised. In the event the Committee's report established that the pay of all railway grades was below that of comparable occupations by an amount considerably more than this. The consequent settlement gave railwaymen pay increases varying between eight and eighteen per cent, very much more than most other industries had received in the interval since the previous general increase in the railways. Consequently on this occasion the railwaymen were out of step in timing and in the amount of the increase.

The history of bus pay negotiations since 1956 offers a series of similar examples. On 1 April 1957, the London bus driver's differential over his colleagues in the provincial sectors stood at 18–19 per cent. Two months later an award of the Industrial Disputes Tribunal for company busmen (which was followed

[1] Railway Pay Committee of Inquiry, *Report*, 1960.

by the local authorities) cut the differential to about 11 per cent. Discounting short-run fluctuations it crept up to about 13 per cent in 1963. Then as a consequence of the interim and final reports of the Phelps Brown Committee,[1] the differential widened to about 22 per cent. After their claim had been before a Board of Arbitration the municipal busmen secured an advance not very much less than the London increase. On 1 April 1965, therefore, the London differential was 22·6 per cent above the companies and 14·4 above the local authorities. During the next twelve months, the company busmen received a similar increase following on the report of the Wilson Committee,[2] and the London busmen obtained another increase under what had come to be known as the "Phelps Brown formula". On 1 April 1966, therefore, the London differential over both provincial sectors was 23–24 per cent. Shortly afterwards the National Board for Prices and Incomes issued its first report on the *Pay and Conditions of Busmen*,[3] approving a further increase which had already been negotiated in London, and recommending negotiations in the provinces within the terms of the current incomes policy. By 1 April 1967 these negotiations had been completed in the local authority sector but not in the companies. At that date the London differential over the local authorities was 26·7 per cent, and 32·2 per cent over the companies. A whole range of public bodies therefore influenced the timing and amounts of increases in the various sectors of the bus industry, and limited the extent to which they could follow any general wage round.

Another consideration is that the amount of an industry pay increase may be affected by some other change in industry agreements, such as a reduction in the length of the normal working week. It is common to agree upon a smaller pay increase, or no increase at all, in a period in which the working week is shortened. This would not lead to diverse pay movements if all industries adjusted their agreements on working hours at the same time, but they do not do so. The adjustments are spread over two or three years, and during that period pay changes are therefore

[1] *Interim Report* and *Report of a Committee of Inquiry to Review the Pay and Conditions of Employment of the Drivers and Conductors of the London Transport Board's Road Services*, 1963 and 1964.

[2] *Report of a Committee of Inquiry into the Causes and Circumstances of the Difference Existing Between the Two Sides of the National Council for the Omnibus Industry*, 1965.

[3] Report No. 16, Cmnd. 3012, 1966.

more than usually out of step. An extreme example comes from the docks. The reduction from 44 hours to 42 hours came later in the docks than in most other industries, in August 1962, but 42 hours did not prove a convenient arrangement for dock work, and the industry moved to 40 hours in July 1964, on this occasion ahead of most other industries. Over this period the weekly wage rate for dockers remained unaltered,[1] but the national index of wage rates rose by about 10 per cent. At this point the dockers' unions demanded a substantial wage increase to bring them back into line. The port employers argued that the reduction in working hours had led to increased overtime which was equivalent to a pay increase. A strike threat prompted the appointment of the Devlin Committee, whose first report led to an increase of approximately 10 per cent in wage rates.

About ten years ago a number of industries began to sign fixed-period agreements, many of them three-year agreements, providing for three successive annual increases in pay. This arrangement made it impossible for them to follow any trends in timing and amounts which might emerge in other industries. In fact several of them failed to foresee the amount of wage increases elsewhere, and the device lost some of its popularity.

These institutional pressures for short-run diversity in pay movements are sometimes supplemented by personal factors. A new negotiator leading for the trade union side may strain to achieve a settlement more generous than those in other industries in order to establish his reputation. A senior negotiator, under political pressure within his own union, may feel the need to re-establish his reputation in the same way. It may even be that the employers' representatives have some sympathy with these ambitions. If the negotiator is successful he will be able to relax in subsequent years and the marginal advantage he has gained will be eroded. Personal factors on the employers' side are perhaps more likely to affect the date of a settlement than the amount. If the negotiating committee of an employers' association wants to gain a reputation for toughness they may show extreme reluctance to agree on a figure which the unions regard as acceptable. A settlement is thereby delayed and the industry may lag behind its

[1] Hourly rates had of course been increased to maintain weekly rates when working hours were cut, and the method chosen had caused a marginal increase from £9.8.10 to £9.9.2 in weekly rates.

normal "bunching". A possible consequence of this manoeuvre is a settlement at a higher figure than might have been accepted at an early stage in the negotiations, and therefore a further irregularity.

Another reason for diversity, of rapidly growing importance is recent years, is the divergence between rates of pay and earnings. The long-run uniformities discovered by Routh are, at any rate for manual workers,[1] uniformities in earnings. Knowles and Robinson investigated movements in wage rates. It is not possible for both earnings and rates to keep in step, industry by industry, unless the relationship between rates and earnings is the same in all industries. If the relationship differs from one industry to another, or from one occupation to another, then earnings will move in step only if movements in rates diverge; and uniform changes in rates will cause earnings to move apart. It might be expected that an industry which was lagging in earnings would from time to time settle on an unusually large increase in wage rates to try to restore the balance.

There are many examples of this. The Phelps Brown Committee of Inquiry into London bus pay made comparisons between the pay of London busmen and that of other manual workers in the London area and held that "the London busmen now rank too low in the London wage structure".[2] This verdict, however, did not concern relative wage rates. The rates of London busmen were then, as they have always been, among the highest for manual workers anywhere in the country; but their earnings, which before the war had also stood well above the national average, had slipped behind. Following the committee's reports, London busmen's rates were increased by amounts far larger than the increases in other industries over the same period, and the drivers' weekly earnings rose from 332s. 1d in October 1963 to 400s. 3d a year later, while the national average of men's earnings rose from 334s. 11d to 362s. 2d. For the next three years the pay of London busmen was adjusted by the "Phelps Brown formula" (a formula which the committee certainly did not recommend). One important element was the average earnings of men in the engineering industry in the London area. But since rates constitute a much larger share in earnings for busmen than for

---

[1] Figures for earnings of white collar workers were in many instances not available.
[2] *Interim Report*, p. 14.

engineering workers, parity of earnings could be maintained only by further increases in pay for London busmen larger both in cash and percentage terms than those agreed for engineering workers.

In 1966 the electrical contracting industry signed an agreement providing for three successive increases in pay at intervals of a year. The first of these added about 13 per cent to the industry's standard rates which can be compared with a general increase in wage rates of rather less than 3 per cent during the course of the year. Rates were already far higher than those for electricians in most other industries, but the avowed aim of the negotiators was "to combat the higher wage competition from other industries",[1] and Ministry of Labour figures showed that average earnings of skilled electricians in construction were 419s. 0d compared with a range from 476s. 1d to 514s. 4d. for skilled electricians in engineering, steel, shipbuilding and chemicals. This was the industry's second attempt at improving the relative position of its employees. An earlier three-year agreement signed in 1963 had provided increases in rates which were also intended to have this effect, but they were not big enough. In fact the increase in the earnings of the industry over those three years was rather less than elsewhere. Electrical contracting is one of the few private industries which make a serious attempt to enforce their rates as standard rates, and it does not countenance payment by results. Consequently the earnings of its employees can only keep pace with those of other workers if its rates are increased proportionately more than theirs.

Divergent movements in earnings within industries can also have an effect on industry pay negotiations. The engineering industry has on three occasions, in 1950, in 1963 and in 1968, signed agreements intended to raise the earnings of relatively low-paid engineering workers in relation to others. The details of the agreements are complex, especially those of the second and third, which prescribed a series of adjustments over a period of time, but the principle is simple. The full increase was to be paid only to those workers whose earnings (excluding overtime) were the same as the minimum rates or only a little in excess of them. Other workers were to receive smaller increases or no

---

[1] Quoted in the National Board for Prices and Incomes, *Wages and Conditions in the Electrical Contracting Industry*, Report No. 24, Cmnd. 3172, 1966, p. 14.

increases at all. The intention was to reduce the divergence in earnings but so far none of the agreements appears to have accomplished this objective.[1] The amount of the increase was on each occasion intended to be rather larger than increases in other industries, because it was supposed to have its full effect only on a minority of engineering workers.

A much more effective "consolidation" of earnings was achieved by the electricity supply industry through its "status" agreement of 1964–5. Among other things the agreement was intended to secure a drastic reduction in overtime working without a cut in earnings. Consequently wage rates had to rise sharply. Between 1964 and 1965 the rates of craftsmen in the industry rose by 25 per cent. The reduction in overtime was also achieved, and weekly earnings actually fell by a fraction.

Generally speaking, the salary rates of white collar workers constitute a much larger part of their total pay than the share of the wage rates of manual workers in their total earnings. Consequently the relative pay of white collar workers can be maintained only by larger proportionate increases in salaries than in wage rates. An instance is the increase from £15 to £18 10s in the minimum salary for draughtsmen aged 21 in the engineering industry during 1968. The engineering employers agreed with the Draughtsmen's Association that although the salaries of their members were, as they had always been, comfortably ahead of the rate for skilled craftsmen, their earnings had fallen behind.

The relationship between the salary rates of white collar workers and the wage rates of manual workers is not the only differential which negotiators are called upon to adjust. They have, for example, to consider the differentials between different grades of manual worker. The simplest arrangement is to adjust them all in percentage terms, thus preserving a constant proportional relationship between the different rates. At some periods, however, the fashion has been for standard monetary adjustments which diminish the proportional advantage of the higher-rated worker when wages are rising and increase it when wages are falling. This fashion has been particularly evident during the two world wars when public approval for "equality of sacrifice" has supported the view that the lower-paid have most need for compensation for rising retail prices. In the en-

[1] See p. 427.

gineering industry the labourers' rate, which had been 72 per cent of the skilled rate in 1934, stood at 84 per cent of the skilled rate in 1948 as a consequence of equal cash increases. From that time, however, the negotiators resisted further narrowing of differentials and in 1968 they were widened so that the labourers' rate stood at 80 per cent of the skilled rate. These adjustments have not necessarily been reflected in earnings. From 1934 to 1942 the earnings of engineering labourers remained at about two-thirds of the skilled workers' earnings although the labourer's time rate rose from 72 per cent to 80 per cent of the skilled time rate. The switch back from munitions to peacetime production cut into wartime earnings, and by 1948 the labourer's earnings were almost four-fifths of the skilled man's earnings. But he did not maintain this relationship. By 1969, with his time rate back at 80 per cent of the skilled time rate, the labourer on timework was earning 70 per cent of the skilled timeworker's earnings, and the labourer on piecework was earning 71 per cent of the skilled pieceworker's earnings.[1]

The differential between women's rates and men's rates has also narrowed over the years, and this narrowing has continued during the post-war period. By 1969 the rate for women in engineering stood at 90 per cent of the labourer's rate, and 72 per cent of the skilled rate. This was a notable advance on the pre-war relationships of 60 per cent of the labourer's rate and 45 per cent of the skilled rate. But the victory had been achieved almost entirely in terms of rates without any marked effect on actual earnings. In 1938 women's weekly earnings in engineering were just under half those of men. In April 1969 they stood at a little over 51 per cent of men's earnings in engineering and electrical goods and at a little under that figure in vehicles. In terms of hourly earnings the gap has been closed to some extent since men work a good deal more overtime now than they did before the war, and this boosts their weekly earnings; whereas women have never worked much overtime. Even so the narrowing in hourly earnings is much less than the narrowing in hourly rates. So far as women's pay is concerned it appears that movements in

---

[1] The figures for the years 1934 to 1948 are taken from K. G. J. C. Knowles and D. J. Robertson, "Earnings in Engineering, 1926–1948", *Bulletin of the Oxford University Institute of Statistics*, June 1951; and those for 1969 from *Statistics on Incomes, Prices, Employment and Production*.

earnings are able to frustrate the efforts of industry negotiators almost entirely.

Where payment by results is common, negotiators have also to consider the differential between the timeworker and the worker paid by results. If the system of payment by results provides that a certain performance shall bring a percentage addition over time rates, the adjustment in time rates will automatically provide a proportional increase in the earnings of the worker paid by results. If piecework is in use, the negotiators can preserve the relationship by increasing all piece rates by the same percentage as the increase in time rates. There is, however, a tendency for pieceworkers' earnings to rise in relation to those of timeworkers, and negotiators may seek to compensate for this by setting a lower percentage increase for pieceworkers than for timeworkers. This is the practice of the docks. In 1964 the Devlin Committee found that: "The claim on the Workpeople's Side appears to be based on the view that the hourly rate of remuneration of the piece-worker is on the average more than twice that of the time-worker and accordingly the percentage increase in his case should be less than half that of the time-rate. The employers, on the other hand, appear to base their final offer on the view that the percentage increase for the piece-worker should be rather more than half that of the time-worker." Not surprisingly, the committee decided that "a relationship of two to one for time-work and piece-work respectively does rough justice."[1] The immediate consequence was bound to be a narrowing of differentials. Presumably the assumption was that the upward drift in piecework earnings would restore the original relationship.

In engineering the provisions for the pieceworker's pay are more complicated. For many years he was paid a base rate and a pieceworkers' supplement, with his "piecework" standard related to the base rate. In 1948 the base rate was 66s. for the skilled worker and the supplement was 33s. If he earned "100 per cent bonus" his piecework earnings would have been 66s. and his total earnings 54 per cent over the timeworkers' "consolidated time rate". Industry-wide adjustments in rates generally increased the consolidated time rate and the pieceworker's supplement by

[1] First Report of the Committee of Inquiry into certain matters concerning the Port Transport Industry. Cmnd. 2523, 1964, p. 4.

the same amount, while the pieceworker's base rate remained unchanged. Consequently a constant percentage bonus reduced the pieceworker's differential over the timeworker. By 1963 a bonus of 100 per cent gave him earnings only 23 per cent over the consolidated time rate. The 1964 "package deal", however, provided for an increase of the basic rate to 105s. When this took effect in 1968 the differential of a pieceworker earning a bonus of 100 per cent increased to almost 41 per cent over the consolidated time rate. These relationships are drawn between the earnings of a hypothetical pieceworker and the consolidated time rate. They do not reveal the actual relationship between timeworkers' and pieceworkers' earnings. In fact in June 1968 the average weekly earnings of skilled workers paid by results were less than 4 per cent above those of skilled timeworkers. The agreement of December 1968 set aside minimum piecework standards until a new "comprehensive national agreement on payment by results could be arranged". In the meantime the pieceworker was to be assured the same minimum time rates as the timeworker.

How can the movements of pay in industry negotiations be explained? Are they the consequence of the intentions of the negotiators? These intentions were analysed by Lady Wootton in a book first published in 1955.[1] She found the arguments used for pay claims to be, in order of importance: the cost of living, relativities, undermanning, productivity and profitability. Since then there has almost certainly been some change in fashions. The cost of living has dropped down the list and productivity has climbed up. There has also been a change in the use of the productivity argument; advances in pay are justified less by reference to increases in productivity that have already occurred and more by increases which might be obtained if working practices were changed in return. Otherwise industry wage claims are argued in terms which would have been familiar to negotiators ten, twenty or thirty years ago.

Theorists also advance explanations for pay movements. Among these are the economists' doctrine of the interaction of supply and demand, and the sociologists' theory of social conservatism, advanced by Lady Wootton herself[2] and supported by Routh,

[1] *The Social Foundations of Wage Policy.*
[2] "Conservatism does duty on both sides. On the one side, the unions . . . appeal to precedent, and defend their proposals as necessary to restore the *status quo*—if not literally

which rests on the general acceptance of the established pattern of relativities. There is, however, also the theory of relative bargaining power.

This is not the place for a detailed examination of those arguments and theories. So far as relative pay movements are concerned only social conservatism offers a tenable explanation of the long-run stability of the nation's pay structure. Changes in productivity differ widely from one industry to another, both in the long term and in the short term, and can provide no explanation of a stable structure. Shifts in the demand for labour and in bargaining strength do not seem to be reflected in this structure. Indeed such shifts as there have been in relative pay have as often as not run counter to market forces. The narrowing of skill differentials during both world wars did not reflect a relative abundance of skilled workers; they were in desperately short supply. The relative decline in civil service pay during and after the second world war was not due to a decline in the demand for their services, which was expanding; and they regained their position at a time when their numbers were on the decline. Railway pay recovered its pre-war position just as the railways were entering a period of large-scale redundancy. Nor does there seem to be any way in which these shifts can be demonstrated to follow changes in bargaining power.

These issues must be unravelled by economists and sociologists. For the study of industrial relations it is of central importance to observe that whatever the explanation of relative and general pay movements, it is no longer of much value if it is applied only to changes negotiated at industry level. Before 1914 and again in the inter-war years earnings diverged little from rates. Since 1939 they have moved almost continuously apart. Before the war it was reasonable to confine the study of pay movements largely to shifts in rates. Now it would be foolish. Only confusion can result from explaining the busman's advantage over the skilled engineer in rates of pay by relative bargaining strength or relative labour shortage or by anything else, when in fact the average earnings of skilled engineers exceed those of busmen.

ante bellum, at least before some selected date-line; whilst employers, on the other hand, take their stand on the simple rule of 'no change'. The dispute between them turns, not so much on the choice of the direction in which to move, as on rival interpretations of what is meant by standing still."(*Ibid.*, p. 162.)

Movements in rates cannot be explained until the composition and movement of earnings has been understood; and this requires an examination of domestic collective bargaining.

Before turning to this topic, however, there remains one important element in industry agreements which has not yet been examined—the procedure for settling disputes within the industry. It is appropriate that this should be discussed before turning to collective bargaining at the place of work for, at least in some industries, the procedure is intended in part as a means of controlling workplace bargaining.

DISPUTES PROCEDURES

The first industry disputes procedures were properly described as "conciliation" procedures or "procedures for avoiding disputes". They were set up to handle differences which the district organisations could not settle for themselves by seeking an acceptable solution which would avoid a strike or lockout.

Where the two sides entered into a substantive agreement at industry level, such as the premium bonus agreement in engineering, the industry procedure might be called on to determine a local difference which turned upon the meaning of the agreement. In these instances the procedure could be said to be interpreting the agreement. Otherwise disputes had to be settled on their "merits".

As the number and coverage of industry substantive agreements grew, the scope for interpretation disputes increased. On the other hand the authority of district or regional joint bodies to make agreements of their own or to vary industry agreements was universally curtailed and in many industries abolished. There remain some famous district agreements, like the Coventry toolroom agreement in engineering,[1] but they are relatively rare so that industry procedures are hardly ever called upon to settle district or regional disputes. Consequently for practical purposes disputes can be classified into interpretation disputes and domestic disputes, that is disputes which arise in plants about matters not specifically covered by industry substantive agreements.[2]

---

[1] The industry agreement provides that skilled toolroom workers shall be paid the average earnings of skilled production workers in the plant. In Coventry they are paid the weighted average for skilled production workers in the district.

[2] This is the classification used in Munns and McCarthy, p. 45.

What determines the share of each in the business of disputes procedures? Here we lack sufficient information. There exist one or two studies of particular procedures, and one recent comparative study,[1] but they cover only a part of the field and do not answer many important questions. But something can be said about the influences at work. There are industries which refuse to recognise any other kind of dispute but one of interpretation. When the present negotiating machinery for the National Health Service was set up in 1948, the "functional" joint councils covering the various classes of employee drew up agreements on pay and conditions of work at industry level, but did not set up a disputes procedure. Soon afterwards they "found it necessary to appoint sub-committees to deal with appeals against local interpretations of their agreements". Next, Regional Appeal Committees were set up to take over the job of interpretation. Even here, however, "there have been occasions . . . when the decision of Appeals Committees have settled rates for workers not yet specifically covered by Whitley [functional council] agreements, and thus have seemed to negotiate rather than interpret."[2]

This shows that unless industry substantive agreements regulate every aspect of employment, a domestic dispute can arise over some issue which is not included. Issues which are in many instances not covered by such agreements but not infrequently cause disputes include complaints of unfair dismissal, redundancy, manning, the closed shop and demarcation. The engineering industry specifically authorises its procedure to deal with differences over "alterations in recognised working conditions" and redundancy without laying down any substantive rules against which the differences can be judged.

Then there is the extent to which the procedure is authorised to deal with claims to improve upon industry substantive agreements. The building industry is explicit on this point. The parties undertake that "they will not permit, endorse, sanction or otherwise condone any claim or agreement to vary . . . any of the Rules, Regulations or Working Rules hereunder and having for its object the determination of any of those matters on any other than a National basis. . . ." The procedure cannot therefore

---

[1] A. I. Marsh and W E. J. McCarthy, *Disputes Procedures in Britain*, Royal Commission Research Paper No. 2 (Part 2), 1968.

[2] H. A. Clegg and T. E. Chester, *Wage Policy and the Health Service*, 1957, pp. 26–7.

entertain such a claim. So far as the length of the working week, holidays, shift work and similar conditions of work are concerned, this is the normal arrangement, but a number of industries take a different view on rates of pay. The engineering industry, for example, recognises the right of small groups within plants, or of all the manual workers within a plant, to seek payments above those laid down in the industry agreements, and the engineering procedure has to deal with many claims for payments of this kind.

Payment by results presents a special case. Unless it is regulated by a price list for the whole industry, the actual piece-rates or incentive values must be settled domestically. Accordingly differences about their settlement or operation are domestic disputes, unless it is contended that the general standard has not been met. Prior to 1947 the building industry prohibited payment by results. In that year a new national rule allowed any employer to "initiate an incentive system of bonus payments". Thereafter special "incentive panels" were established within the disputes procedure to handle differences arising under the new rule, bringing one type of domestic pay dispute within its scope.

Finally, interpretation disputes tend to be more numerous where there is an industry "grading" scheme. Nearly all industry pay agreements settle more than one rate of pay. Where one rate is for a craftsman and another for a labourer, or where the agreement names the jobs to which the rates apply, there is little room for argument over which rate is appropriate for a given worker. But a grading scheme is an elementary form of job evaluation whereby the agreement sets out several rates of pay and descriptions of type of work which should qualify for each rate. Application of such an agreement usually calls for a good deal of judgement, and therefore allows room for appeal to the procedure for an interpretation where judgements differ.

This list of influences can explain the different incidence of interpretation and domestic disputes from one procedure to another, so far as this is known. In his research for the Royal Commission, V. G. Munns asked a number of employers' associations about their experience in this respect. In engineering, shipbuilding and printing he found that "the proportion of interpretation disputes is very small". In printing the majority of cases were about matters not regulated by the industry agreements "particularly demarcation and manning questions. . . . In engineering and shipbuilding . . . where workplace bargaining has become more important than national negotiations in determining actual earnings, the handling of disputes has become very largely a form of domestic wage negotiation."[1] Engineering has a high proportion of workers paid by results, and does not debar any kind of pay dispute from its procedure. On the other hand, interpretation disputes predominated in building and electrical contracting. Building has a smaller proportion of workers paid by results than engineering and allows no other kind of domestic pay dispute into procedure; and electrical contracting has no payment by results and permits almost no deviations from the rates laid down in its industry agreements.

Grading schemes are common among white collar workers, especially in the public services. Examples are the Local Authorities Administrative, Professional, Technical and Clerical Services and the clerical grades on the railways. As most of these services do not permit local deviations from industry agreements it is understandable that interpretation disputes constitute the staple business of their procedures. However, interpretation does not predominate in all white collar procedures. The industry agreements for the various grades of white collar employee in engineering prescribe minimum rates of pay which can be exceeded domestically, and do not even lay down standard conditions of work; these are also settled by domestic negotiation. Consequently these procedures offer less room for interpretation disputes and more for domestic disputes than almost any other procedure.

Procedures differ not only in the type of business they handle, but also in the way that they handle it. Most of the procedures in major industries consist of three stages in addition to domestic discussions. The first of these brings full-time officers from the union and the employers into discussion of the difference. In engineering this is known as a "works conference". The second is a hearing of the case by a district or regional body, known in engineering as a "local conference"; and the third is a reference to an industry body, known in engineering as a "central conference". But there are variations. In steel the second stage, and in chemicals the first and second stages, are replaced by an "on-

[1] Munns and McCarthy, pp. 45–7.

the-spot" investigation by a joint team drawn from unions and companies not directly concerned in the dispute and appointed by the central body. In chemicals this is known as a "headquarters conference" and in steel as a "neutral committee". Supporters of the arrangement argue that such a committee is better able to acquaint itself with the real facts of the dispute, and to convince the participants in the dispute that their views are fully heard. Its detractors suggest that it may be too vulnerable to the immediate issue so that too little attention is given to the general considerations which ought to be brought to bear on it. These considerations, they feel, can only be properly appreciated in a calmer and more remote atmosphere.

The building industry has two procedures. The first of them has in fact four stages and is intended to handle normal business. In this procedure the meeting of union and association officers on the site is followed, if no settlement is reached, by a local joint committee meeting. From the committee the dispute goes to a regional conciliation panel, and finally to a national conciliation panel. There is also provision for a fifth stage since it is possible to refer a disagreement at the national conciliation panel to arbitration, the method to "be determined in each case by a majority of the Council present and voting". The second procedure is for emergencies. If the union and association officers on the spot cannot settle the difference, and the normal procedure does not seem likely to handle it without a stoppage, the national officers concerned can refer it direct to a "regional joint emergency disputes commission" and thence to a "national joint emergency disputes commission". These bodies are instructed to hold an inquiry without delay, and this is normally held at the place where the dispute occurred. It has been suggested that it was intended to deal with differences over matters not covered by the industry substantive agreements such as "refusal to work with men alleged to be 'objectionable' ",[1] but there is no clear distinction between the types of business handled by the two procedures. At industry level the most common dispute in both procedures is a complaint against dismissal. The distinction is whether or not the issue has caused a stoppage or seems likely to cause a stoppage before the normal procedure could be expected to reach a decision. In other industries the general rule is that the procedure

[1] I. G. Sharp, *Industrial Conciliation and Arbitration in Great Britain*, 1950, p. 199.

cannot operate where a stoppage has already begun. If a stoppage does commence before the procedure has been fully used, it is "unconstitutional" and work must be resumed before the procedure can consider the question at issue—or recommence consideration which has already begun. In building this under-standing applies to the use of the normal procedure but not of the emergency procedure, which can operate after a stoppage has begun although workers are usually persuaded to return to their jobs while waiting for its verdict.[1]

Most procedures consist of joint bodies, with equal numbers from the employers and the union side, and alternating chairmen. At local and central conferences in engineering, however, the arguments of the management and of the union are heard by a committee consisting only of employers. This apparently authoritarian arrangement does not make much difference to the final decision, since the committee's verdict can only lead to an agreement if it is accepted by the union or unions. If not, the result is a failure to agree as it would be in a joint body. But it has been argued that the arrangement makes a difference to the atmosphere of the proceedings, and is less likely than a joint procedure to promote a conciliatory attitude.

Another unusual feature of the engineering procedure is its attempt to secure special privileges for management. The preamble opens with that statement that: "The Employers have the right to manage their establishments and the Trade Unions have the right to exercise their functions".

By itself this means nothing, but subsequently the text of the agreement specifically allows managers to introduce changes in their factories despite objections from the workers, whose redress is to pursue an objection through the procedure. Here again it is possible to exaggerate the practical importance of the agreement, especially in a period of full employment for, in the words of one of the Royal Commission Research Reports "it is evidently a matter of some difficulty to force men to work on conditions which they find unacceptable".[2] However, the effect on trade union attitudes cannot be ignored. Ever since this section was incorporated in the agreement after a national lockout in 1922, the unions have complained of its inequity, sometimes vehemently.

[1] *Disputes Procedures in Britain,* p. 55.
[2] *Ibid.,* p. 17.

There were minor revisions in their favour in 1955. Following the report of the Royal Commission in 1968 the employers initiated discussions on a radical overhaul.

Several other procedures follow building by providing for arbitration as a final stage which, as in building, is rarely used. The agreement between the National Coal Board and the National Union of Mineworkers, however, prescribes arbitration at three stages, at the colliery and at district level as well as at industry level. The assumption is that the subjects of disputes can be divided into domestic pit issues, matters affecting a whole district and problems of concern to the whole industry. Pit issues which cannot be settled at the pit go first to a committee of the District Conciliation Board and thence to an "Umpire" appointed by the Board, and district matters which cannot be agreed at the Board go to a "Referee". As district agreements have declined in importance, so has the work of the Referees, but the prevalence of piecework for many classes of underground work continued to provide business for the Umpires until more recently. Without question this arrangement provided a speedier method of determining pit disputes than the typical industry procedure can offer, but the assumption that domestic disputes could be settled for each pit without affecting other pits proved to be mistaken. A liberal award on piece-rates at one pit could readily lead to demands for concessions at other pits, all the more so because they were all part of the same undertaking. Each district has its own panel of Umpires and the normal arrangement is that they handle cases in rotation. The consequence of this is that decisions tend to be erratic. Another consequence, noted by the Coal Board's spokesman to the Royal Commission, is "the danger—which . . . I suppose is inherent when you have the kind of decision at pit level—a disposition to buy off because if it goes to the umpire you may have something worse".[1]

In 1966 a National Powerloading Agreement provided for the progressive replacement of payment by results by time rates for the great majority of pieceworkers in coalmining. Once the change takes place at a colliery the only matters left for domestic negotiation for the powerloading teams is the task to be performed on a given face and the size of the team, and the agreement takes these issues out of the hands of the Umpires. Instead

[1] *Minutes of Evidence*, Q. 780.

a committee of two a side, whose members must be knowledgeable on "powerloading systems in other parts of the District",
are to visit the face and report their finding to a "meeting of the
parties at District level for decision".

How can the relative merits of different procedures be assessed?
One test is the opinion of those who operate them. For full-time
union officers the Royal Commission surveys provide some
evidence on this point. The number of officers questioned was
sufficient to allow conclusions to be drawn about their opinions
of the procedures in the industries in which they operated, at
least for certain groups of industries dominated by one or two
specific procedures:[1] The results are given in Table VI.

TABLE VI

TRADE UNION OFFICERS' OPINIONS OF PROCEDURE IN
CERTAIN INDUSTRIES

Industry Group	Main Procedure(s)	Per cent saying procedures work well	Per cent saying procedures inadequate	Balance of Opinion
Gas, Electricity and Water	Gas and Elec-tricity Joint Industrial Councils	36	2	+34
Chemical and Allied	Chemicals Joint Industrial Councils	24	7	+17
Construction	Building Joint Industrial Council	16	19	− 3
Metal Manufacture	Steel Procedures	0	8	− 8
Vehicles	Engineering	3	21	−18
Engineering	Engineering	11	51	−40

[1] Only industry groups in which at least twenty of the officers questioned had members
are included in this table. Groups in the original table (*Workplace Industrial Relations*,
p. 63) such as "Other Manufacturing Industries", "Textiles" and "Miscellaneous Services"
are excluded here because they include so many varied procedures that no conclusion
can be drawn about any specific procedure.

This range of opinion cannot be attributed to any one difference in the business handled by procedures or in the methods of handling it. But the strongly adverse view of engineering procedure adds to the evidence that its "employer conciliation" and "managerial prerogative" aspects, whatever their practical effect, are not popular with trade unionists. Substantive agreements in both gas and electricity cover a wider range of subjects than is common in private industry and leave little room for domestic settlement. Consequently it is probable that interpretation disputes predominate in their procedures. The table suggests therefore that trade union officers tend to prefer such procedures to those which, like engineering, deal almost entirely with domestic disputes and offer only limited industry-wide regulation. Finally, the table offers little ground for thinking that the inclusion of on-the-spot investigation by itself makes a procedure popular with trade union officers. Chemicals has such a procedure, but so has steel and building also, at least for emergency disputes.

The opinion of trade union officers is only one test of procedures. Another is the proportion of disputes which they settle, for settling disputes is what they were established to do. Between 1955 and 1966 the proportion of works conferences in engineering which successfully disposed of the issue referred to them fell from rather more than four-fifths to rather less than three-quarters. At local conferences rather more than half of the cases left unsettled by works conferences were resolved, and at central conference the success rate was much the same. However, the word "success" must be qualified. Of 519 cases referred to central conference in 1966, "failure to agree" was registered in just under half, 239. The number of cases "settled" was only 55. No less than 127 were "retained"; 85 were referred back for further domestic negotiation; and the remainder were withdrawn or "not proceeded with". By contrast between 1960 and 1966 only 14 per cent of the disputes referred to "headquarters" conference in the chemical procedure were left unsettled and passed on to a central joint disputes committee. In building the figures for 1966 and 1967 show between two-thirds and four-fifths of the issues referred to regional conciliation panels and disputes commissions being settled there, and the analysis of disputes handled by the National Conciliation Panel in Marsh and McCarthy shows eighteen out of twenty-four cases settled, two "failures to agree" and the remainder deferred or referred back to the locality of the dispute.[1] In general it seems that the joint procedures have a considerably better record for solving disputes than engineering's "employer conciliation". It is, of course, no condemnation of a procedure that it should refer a dispute back for further local discussions or retain it for further evidence or subsequent consideration. Nor is it a fault to fail to agree in some instances. An honest disagreement may be better than a compromise which either side, or both of them, regard as wrong in principle. But it is also evident that it is a sign of ill-health in a procedure if its rate of cases resolved falls below a certain level; and that the engineering procedure's central conference score appears to be well below that level.

The volume of business in engineering has been rising fast in recent years. Between 1957 and 1966 the number of works conferences rose from 1484 to 3854, of local conferences from 320 to 1033 and of central conferences from 80 to 519, with "failures to agree" at central conference up from 40 to 239. The number of central conferences under the white collar procedures rose from 83 in 1963 to 351 in 1966 with "failures to agree" up from 44 to 257. Between 1960 and 1966 the annual number of headquarters conferences in chemicals were more than doubled, but there was no upward trend in central joint disputes hearings. In building the number of disputes brought to regional and national panels and commissions has fluctuated, but shown no trend in either direction. Engineering and chemicals appear to be the exception in this respect, for in their survey of employers' associations for the Royal Commission the Social Survey found that about two-thirds of the officers of both national and local associations reported no change in the number of cases referred to their disputes procedures over the previous ten years.[2]

Another test is speed. Other things being equal, a prompt settlement is better than delay. In 1959 it took on the average thirteen weeks for an issue unresolved by an engineering works conference to reach central conference, and the figure does not appear to have changed much since then. A few issues, however, took less than five weeks and a few others took almost a year. From 1960 to 1965 the average time between headquarters

---

[1] *Disputes Procedures in Britain*, p. 59. The figures in this and the next two paragraphs come from this source.   [2] Munns and McCarthy, p. 94.

conference and central disputes committee in chemicals (with no intervening stage as between works conference and central conference in engineering) was seven weeks, three days. Average times, however, may not be so important as the prompt handling of urgent cases. It is impossible to distinguish these from the remainder in engineering or in chemicals. In building the average time to reach a regional commission under the emergency procedure was sixteen days, and the average time from the region to the centre a further eighteen days, making five weeks in all. It is also believed that the ordinary conciliation procedure in building works more speedily than the engineering procedure. On the other hand the engineering procedure handles many times the volume of disputes experienced in building.

A central aim of industry disputes procedures is to see that the two sides of industry do not enforce a stoppage without first taking their differences through each stage. In this, procedures appear to have been successful. During the last decade the number of official stoppages has been running at about seventy a year, a much lower rate than pre-war, when the total number of strikes was much smaller.[1] However, these relatively few official stoppages have amounted to no more than five per cent of the total number of recorded stoppages, the rest being unofficial. Excluding coalmining, the total of recorded stoppages has been rising fast, from 635 in 1957 to 2157 in 1968, all but a handful of them unofficial, and this increase, notes the Royal Commission "has been fairly general throughout industry". This subject is pursued in Chapter 8.

One common feature of most industry procedures which might be related to the rising number of unofficial strikes is their failure to prescribe a precise and detailed process for the conduct of relations in the plant. In many procedures, including those for white collar workers in engineering, there is no provision at all. Shop stewards were recognised by the building employers only in 1964, and their duties are loosely defined. They are to "approach management . . . as necessary" on "any complaints and difficulties arising" and "to co-operate with management to ensure that the Working Rule Agreement is observed by both parties". Even

[1] Pre-war figures are available only for the year 1936 when 189 strikes out of 818 were known to be official, 435 unofficial, 89 of unorganised workers and information was lacking on the remaining 115 (K. G. J. C. Knowles, *Strikes*, 1952, p. 33).

in the engineering procedure for manual workers which sets out stages for handling domestic problems, most of these stages are optional. A number of public inquiries in recent years have insisted on the need for improved domestic procedures. The Devlin Committee, for example, recommended that the dockers' unions should institute "a system of properly elected and accredited shop stewards" for the first time in the docks.[1] The Cameron Inquiry into the Barbican and Horseferry Road construction disputes proposed that "in all large site contracts prior to commencement of operations, the company and representatives of the unions concerned should negotiate a site procedure agreement supplementary to the provision of the W[orking] R[ule] A[greement] to include details of procedure for processing individual, group or collective claims".[2] In reporting on an inquiry into a dispute at Rootes Motors in Scotland, Professor D. J. Robertson and his colleagues proposed "a standing body . . . of management representatives and representatives of the Unions" to "be the body for detailed consideration of new negotiations and for consultation and communication", and "to which disputes arising out of existing conditions should make their way if they require to go as high in the machinery as to be considered by a group representing the factory as a whole".[3] Finally, the Royal Commission came to the general conclusion that "factory bargaining remains informal and fragmented, with many issues left to custom and practice", and proposed factory or company agreements to provide "effective and orderly bargaining over such issues as the control of incentive schemes, the regulation of hours actually worked, the use of job evaluation, work practices and the linking of changes in pay to changes in performance, facilities for shop stewards and disciplinary rules and appeals".[4]

To judge whether this diagnosis is correct requires an assessment of domestic industrial relations. It therefore seems impossible to understand and evaluate industry procedure agreements, any more than industry agreements on pay, without examining the process of collective bargaining within the plant.

---

[1] *Final Report*, p. 107.

[2] *Report of a Court of Inquiry into trade disputes at the Barbican and Horseferry Road Construction sites in London*, Cmnd. 3396, 1967, p. 76.

[3] *Report of the Court of Inquiry under Professor D. J. Robertson into a dispute at Rootes Motors Ltd., Linwood, Scotland*, Cmnd. 3692, 1968, p. 27.

[4] *Report*, pp. 36, 40.

CHAPTER 7

DOMESTIC BARGAINING

DEFINITIONS

Provided that a fairly liberal use of the word "industry" is allowed, there is no special difficulty about the term "industry bargaining". It means the making and operation of substantive and procedural agreements which cover an industry. By contrast the term "plant" bargaining, which is often used to include all other levels of collective bargaining, is inadequate to indicate the range of bargaining levels below the industry.

Such vestiges of independent district or regional bargaining as remain in Britain have already been mentioned in the last chapter. Leaving them aside, the next level is the company agreement, of which there are two distinct types. Firstly there are the company agreements of "non-federated" firms which negotiate direct with the unions. Where one great corporation covers the whole of an industry its settlements are both industry and company agreements. The National Coal Board and the British Railways Board are two examples. However, most non-federated firms do not monopolise an industry. Their company agreements are independent enclaves within the boundaries of the relevant industry agreements. Among them are such well-known companies as Ford, Vauxhall and I.C.I. Secondly there is company bargaining in federated firms. Some federated firms negotiate formal agreements which supplement industry agreements, and elsewhere understandings or arrangements may be made between company and union spokesmen at informal meetings.

Where a company consists of more than one plant there is a distinction between company and plant bargaining. Some non-federated multi-plant firms prefer to allow each plant to negotiate its own agreements with the unions in place of a single company agreement. The major oil companies provide an interesting variety of practice. Each of them negotiates its own settlements for the employees in its distribution section, covering plants and terminals all over the country. These are company agreements. Refinery employees, however, are for the most part covered by agreements negotiated separately for each refinery. These are plant agreements. In addition the companies belong to the Shipping Federation whose agreements apply to their marine sections. It is also possible for a non-federated multi-plant firm which negotiates company agreements to allow plant managers some latitude to negotiate supplementary plant agreements. Most federated multi-plant firms leave negotiations with the unions to plant managers, so that in many industries plant bargaining supplements industry agreements with little or no formal bargaining intervals at the level of the company.

Finally there is the workshop bargaining which takes place in sections of a plant in both federated and non-federated firms and in both multi-plant and single-plant companies. It can include anything from negotiations covering hundreds or even thousands of workers in a major department of a great undertaking down to a discussion with two or three workers in a company with a total employment of a dozen or so.

In the engineering industry the term "domestic bargaining" is used for the process whereby issues are settled in the plant. This evidently covers matters handled entirely within the workshop as well as those settled for the whole plant. It can readily be extended to include such bargaining as there may be at company level in a multi-plant federated firm, as "domestic" to the company compared with the industry bargaining in which the company takes part through its association. However, if it is stretched to cover company bargaining in non-federated firms, it must be recognised that company agreements between unions and non-federated firms are a special class of domestic agreements, treated separately in this chapter, and that where the company monopolises an industry its company agreements are industry agreements.

The total number of industry agreements runs into hundreds but the great majority of workers within the scope of collective bargaining are covered by a score or so of them. Several of these have been the subject of academic investigation, and in recent years the National Board for Prices and Incomes and other public bodies have issued reports on many of them and also on a number of industry agreements with a smaller coverage. Because of this it is not unreasonable to try to give a general account of industry bargaining in Britain, based mainly on the experience of the major industries.

Domestic bargaining is another matter. By now a number of case studies have accumulated but, even so, they cover only an infinitesimal fraction of the total number of "plants", and only a fraction of the employed population. The personal experience of any individual is likely to be even more limited. The material which is available suggests very wide variations in the structure, operation and effects of domestic bargaining, so that an individual's experience is likely to be unrepresentative. Moreover, many of the case studies describe instances in which bargaining methods were about to be radically revised, for managers are more ready to allow the investigation of arrangements which they have already decided to change. Consequently much of the material is inevitably out of date.

In these circumstances any attempt to describe and analyse domestic bargaining is bound to be tentative.

THE SCOPE OF DOMESTIC BARGAINING

It is possible to make a calculation of the coverage of industry bargaining. In its evidence to the Royal Commission the Ministry of Labour estimated that about 14 million manual workers out of a total of 16 million in employment were covered by "negotiating machinery at the national level (including statutory wage fixing bodies)" and that 4 million out of 7 million non-manual workers were also "covered by such arrangements".[1] But it is quite impossible to put figures upon the coverage of domestic bargaining. The most that can be done is to suggest some indications of its scope among manual workers, mainly from the evidence of the Royal Commission surveys; for white collar workers the evidence is even more scanty. The Royal Commission chose a sample of 400 establishments in manufacturing and construction, in order to interview works managers, personnel officers and foremen. The manufacturing establishments were

[1] *Written Evidence*, p. 19. It is to be noted that the Ministry were not using the same dividing line between manual and non-manual workers as G. S. Bain in his *Trade Union Growth and Recognition* (see p. 61).

I

drawn from those employing more than 150 workers, and the construction sites from those employing more than 50. Of these 400 establishments 57 did not recognise trade unions and were left aside.[1]

The survey established a relationship between size of plant and the existence of domestic bargaining. Personnel officers were found mainly in the larger firms in the sample— those with 250 or more employees. Of the 319 works managers interviewed, 78 per cent negotiated with shop stewards compared with 93 per cent of the 121 personnel officers. The same conclusion emerges from the distribution of shop stewards. It seems reasonable to regard the presence of shop stewards as an indication of domestic bargaining for, although not all shop stewards bargain, the great majority of them do so. In their separate survey of a sample of almost 1200 shop stewards the Royal Commission found that 84 per cent of them regularly discussed and settled at least one type of bargaining issue at their place of work. The survey of managers showed that shop stewards were present in 82 per cent of the establishments in the whole sample but in 97 per cent of those with personnel officers, and in only 34 per cent of the construction sites.[2]

This association between size and domestic bargaining might have been expected. In tens of thousands of small firms in which the employer is not federated and few or none of the workers are organised, it is reasonable to suppose that pay and conditions are settled and adjusted at the discretion of the employer. Any discussion about them is between the employer and the individual employee, or if there is collective action on a common problem it is a matter of two or three workers approaching their employer together. This may be the situation even where there is a higher degree of organisation among the workers. There may be no shop steward, no union officer need ever visit the plant, and if it is federated, there may be no appeals to the industry's disputes procedure and no domestic procedure either formal or informal.

This can happen even in a larger establishment. A building site employing about 150 workers can provide an example. About

---

[1] *Workplace Industrial Relations*, p. 71. This decision may not be justified in all cases. Groups of skilled workers may exercise collective pressures which come close to collective bargaining even where unions are unrecognised and have no members. The chefs in certain large hotels provide one example.   [2] *Ibid.*, pp. 71–81.

half the employees on this site were unionised, the proportion being higher among the craftsmen and lower among the rest. The firm was federated and honoured all the agreements of the National Federation of Building Trades Employers except that it paid a bonus amounting to a shilling an hour for most workers. In addition there was a work-studied incentive scheme. Problems arising under the scheme were not settled by any process of negotiation, but raised with the foremen. Disputes over the time fixed for a particular task were settled by the firm's senior work-study engineer. No shop steward had been elected on the site, and no full-time union officer had visited it. Grievances were handled individually by foremen or managers. Thus collective bargaining affected the site only through the National Working Rules of the industry and their periodic revision.

However, it was also evident that this situation was partly due to special factors, and could not be guaranteed to last. A high proportion of the workers on the site were regular employees of the main contractor, and this helped to foster the personal relations of a family firm. Even so the awkward handling of a grievance, the engagement of two or three forceful trade unionists, or a set-back in bonus earnings might easily have led to "trouble", to visits from union officers, to the appointment of stewards, to negotiation over the incentive scheme and to the development of a considerable volume of site bargaining. The likelihood of some such event would be even greater on a major construction site, or in an industrial undertaking. For domestic bargaining comes to an end when a construction site is closed down and has to be re-established on a new site, whereas most industrial undertakings are more permanent.

If domestic bargaining is rare in small plants, say those with less than fifty employees, and in firms which either do not recognise trade unions or have a low level of trade union organisation; if in addition domestic bargaining has not developed in some larger federated undertakings with a fair level of unionisation; then it is almost certain that domestic bargaining affects only a minority of firms, and it is possible that it affects only a minority of employees, even of manual workers. In manufacturing and construction, however, the Royal Commission has established that domestic bargaining is almost universal among establishments with over 250 employees which recognise trade unions.

It is also probable that the incidence of domestic bargaining has been increasing during the post-war period. Between 1947 and 1961 the number of stewards accredited by the Engineers rose by 56 per cent compared with a 30 per cent rise in membership.[1] McCarthy and Parker estimated that there were probably about 175,000 shop stewards in Britain in 1966 and that this total was about 14 per cent higher than in 1956.[2] The increase in trade union membership over those two years was between two and three per cent. Once more the evidence accords with what might have been expected in a period of full employment in which the average size of establishment has been growing rapidly.

DOMESTIC AGREEMENTS AND PROCEDURES

In industry bargaining, signed agreements are reached through recognised procedures. Even where the procedures are not embodied in an agreed document they are generally well understood and no one is in doubt about the arrangements for calling a joint meeting or for conducting its business. Members of of the two sides may, of course, meet and talk outside the procedure and even come to understandings about how to handle particular issues, but the constitutional procedures and the signed agreements remain the basis of their relationship. It is very different with domestic bargaining. One of its features which helps to account for the difficulty of giving a clear account of its working and importance, and which often puzzles visitors from countries with different systems of industrial relations, is that in domestic bargaining there need be neither signed agreements nor recognised procedures.

This can easily be envisaged in a small plant with only one shop steward representing all the workers. There is no need for a procedure. He can ask to see the manager when he wants to, or the manager can send for him. Let us suppose that he convinces the manager that one group of workers is underpaid in view of the work they are doing, and the manager agrees to pay them an extra 6d. an hour. This may be done by a verbal instruction to the

---

[1] Marsh and Coker, "Shop Steward Organisation in the Engineering Industry", *British Journal of Industrial Relations*, June 1963.

[2] *Shop Stewards and Workshop Relations*, p. 15.

wages clerk, and there need be no explanation of why the payment is made; or perhaps it may be referred to as a merit rate or just a plus rate. Successive decisions of this kind can lead to a separate pay structure for the plant, quite different from the industry agreement. To settle arguments about overtime the manager may ask the steward to keep a rota of men willing to work overtime. Again there need be no record on paper except the list which the steward keeps in his pocket.

There is no clear line between bargaining of this kind and consultation. The decision is an agreement if the manager accepts that he cannot change it without the consent of the steward. The manager may be forced to do so if he finds that the men are prepared to strike or if the steward appeals to his full-time officer and through him to the industry's disputes procedure. But in any particular instance in which it has not been put to the test there may be doubt as to whether a particular managerial decision is an agreement or merely an exercise of managerial prerogatives after consultation with the steward.

Understandings of this kind are commonly called "custom and practice", but custom and practice can also arise without any conscious decision by management. Let us suppose that it is the shop steward himself who decides to keep an overtime rota, asking the foreman henceforth to follow the rota in offering overtime work. The foreman, not concerned with anything else but getting the work done, acquiesces in the arrangement, which thus becomes custom and practice, regarded as binding on the manager even though he has never heard of it. Furthermore in industrial relations as elsewhere custom can emerge without any conscious decision at all. Let us suppose the firm has its own vans to deliver its products. It so happens that the drivers stand by while their vans are loaded. No one can remember why. One day it occurs to the manager that deliveries would be speeded up if the drivers helped to load. He tells them to do so. They demur, saying that the existing arrangement is custom and practice, and if he wants to change it he must negotiate with the steward.

Domestic bargaining may be conducted in this way even in larger undertakings. A manager may deal separately with each of two or more stewards, or leave his departmental managers to do so. If some common issue arises the stewards can ask to see him collectively, or he can send for all of them at once. Their joint dealings may result in nothing more than unwritten understandings. However, as the size of the undertakings increases the demands of administration are likely to bring some formality and written understandings. Where there is a number of stewards it may be convenient for one of them to call the others together from time to time and to arrange for meetings with the manager. It may also be useful to call on this senior steward or convener to deal with issues which cannot be settled between departmental managers and their stewards. The manager may decide to keep a note of his meetings with the stewards. If he asks the senior steward to agree the note then the decisions recorded come close to written agreements.

Even if recognised procedures have not emerged, some joint arrangements are almost bound to be written down. A payment-by-results scheme, for example, is usually too complicated to be carried in the mind. If the manager wishes to introduce such a scheme with the consent of the stewards he must show them a written proposal in order that they can grasp what he intends. If amendments emerge from the discussions these must be entered in the document. At the end of the process it does not matter very much whether or not the stewards or the senior steward sign the scheme. It amounts in practice to an agreement.

It is therefore common for domestic bargaining to regulate industrial relations in a plant by a mixture of written agreements, written understandings, unwritten understandings, informal arrangements and customs and practices (some of which might not be accepted as binding by the management).

THE EFFECT OF INDUSTRY PROCEDURES ON DOMESTIC PROCEDURES

All this assumes that so long as they observe their industry's substantive agreements as minima and submit unresolved disputes to their disputes procedure, managers and shop stewards are free to do as they please in their domestic arrangements. But that is rare. Most industries give some guidance on the handling of grievances within the plant, and many of them provide for setting up plant committees with negotiating rights, or with authority to consult, or both; and some industries require that their substantive agreements be observed as standards, not as minima.

In most private industries the provisions for handling grievances within the plant are regarded merely as guidance. Conflicting practices emerge unhindered, notably the short-circuiting of stages so that stewards raise issues directly with higher management;[1] and if a firm and its stewards decide to draw up a different set of provisions no obstacle is put in their way. It is only if they fail to settle within that procedure that they are obliged to follow the stages external to the plant set out in the industry's disputes procedure. In nationalised industries and public services, on the other hand, it is generally expected that all stages of the industry procedure will be followed.

Some private industries make no formal arrangements for negotiating within the plant, as opposed to handling grievances. Where provision is made it is usually sketchy. In engineering a works committee consists of not more than seven representatives of management and not more than seven shop stewards elected for the purpose by the workpeople and subject to re-election at least every year. Its agenda is to be issued three days before it meets, if possible. It may deal with a question which cannot be settled within a shop or department and with any "question" which affects "more than one branch of trade or more than one department of the works". In fact these arrangements are rarely observed. Many works committees have more than seven shop steward representatives, and these are almost invariably chosen by their fellow stewards, not by the "workpeople". In any event a plant is under no obligation to set up a works committee, and can negotiate domestically by some other means if it chooses. Nationalised industries and public services are again exceptional in setting out their agreements on plant committees more fully and in expecting them to be followed.

Because of the importance traditionally attached to joint consultation in British industrial relations, the industry agreements which provide for the establishment of joint consultative committees in private industry are usually more elaborate and explicit than those on negotiating committees. The engineering agreement, for example, covers the eligibility of candidates and of electors, filling vacancies, co-option, the choice of chairman and joint secretaries, accommodation, payment for attendance, agenda, minutes and sub-committees. It also deals with functions. These

[1] See p. 198.

are "to consult and advise on matters relating to production and increased efficiency". Specific illustrations are given and the agreement firmly debars the committee from discussing "matters which are trade questions such as wages, and like subjects, or which are covered by agreements with trade unions or are normally dealt with by the approved machinery of negotiation." Consequently there is some expectation even in private industry that the constitution of consultative committees will be observed, especially their exclusion from negotiation.

What effect do these various agreements have on domestic bargaining? Two examples illustrate the effects that can follow from attempts at detailed regulation. The first comes from nationalised industry. It is an electricity generating station observed several years ago. The industry agreement provided for two joint bodies in the plant, a works committee and a Local Advisory Committee. The works committee here consisted of seven members elected by the workers of seven different departments meeting with the station's senior managers. Within the narrow limits in which it permits plant bargaining the industry agreement entrusts it to the works committee. All the elected members of this committee are automatically members of the Local Advisory Committee where they meet along with representatives of the station's white collar employees to discuss with management matters of common interest outside the scope of negotiations.

The agreement does not recognise shop stewards. A worker with a grievance is supposed to raise it with his supervisor and can call in his works committee representative if he wishes. Failing satisfaction he can raise it with his trade union. The next stage is a meeting of the works committee at which the trade union "shall have the right to appear". Any formal authority claimed by the stewards rests on construing them as "the union" under the agreement. At this station there were three stewards, each from a different union. Two of them were also elected works committee representatives.

In these circumstances a worker not unnaturally brought his problem either to his works committee member or to his steward (where the two offices were not held by the same man) whichever was more convenient at the time. But there was no doubt of the superior status of the steward. If a committee

member could not settle a matter for himself he would go to his
steward. If there was some general issue to be raised one or more
of the stewards would approach management. The stewards
rarely called in their full-time officers and regarded it as a failure
if an issue had to be put on the agenda of the works committee.
The committee members determined their line on this agenda at
preliminary meetings dominated by the stewards. From time to
time managers met the three stewards outside the works committee.

The industry agreement laid down the rates for each grade of
workers and at that time made no provision for payment by
results. It did, however, allow excess payments up to a limit of
4d. an hour for performing dirty or unpleasant work. It was also
possible for a man to claim that his particular job required more
skill or involved more responsibility than was appropriate to his
grade. If his claim was accepted it could be met either by paying
him a personal excess rate while on the particular job, or by
regrading the job. Managers preferred the first of these alternatives. A regrading required authorisation from senior management and negotiations at district and possibly national level,
whereas a personal rate could be settled with the stewards on the
spot. Occasionally a rate for a particularly unpleasant job went
above the limit laid down in the industry agreement. This too
was settled with the stewards. In addition the stewards discussed
and settled matters of demarcation, protective clothing, arrangements for payment, for holidays, for maintenance shut-downs,
and for interchange of personnel with other stations.

The stewards were also the guardians of certain customs or
unwritten understandings such as the time allowed for men to
clean up after finishing a dirty job. In their own view they did not
negotiate overtime, but they reported to their members management's overtime requirements for overhauls, and informed
management of what the men were prepared to do. There was an
understanding that overtime should be equally distributed among
shift workers, and a rota was kept for the purpose by a man on
each shift who was neither a steward nor a works committee
member.

The staple business of the Local Advisory Committee included
efficiency, training, welfare, the canteen, temperature, washing
facilities and so on, but the stewards were able to make use of it to

expedite negotiating issues. They could bring up a matter under other business and the argument over whether it was appropriate business for the committee could lead to a reference to the works committee for prompt settlement.

The second example is an oil distribution plant observed before the industry agreement was replaced in 1966 by separate productivity agreements for each of the major companies. The industry agreement made no mention of shop stewards or plant negotiations but provided for plant joint consultative committees. Only one union was recognised, the Transport and General Workers' Union. Its shop stewards were in fact all elected to the joint consultative committee. They included the chairman and secretary of the workers' side, who often dealt with the plant manager between meetings.

Besides welfare, accidents and similar topics, the committee dealt with the employment of drivers' mates. There was a general understanding (referred to as an agreement) that mates were to be allowed on journeys involving "hazard" or "undue strain". The workers' side secured an undertaking that mates would also be used on all "initial deliveries".

Another controversial issue was the use of contractors to meet peak demand. It was part of the industry agreement that contractors' men must be paid according to its provisions while working for oil companies, but the workers' side also secured an undertaking that when they were working at this plant contractors' men must observe plant practices, including being union members in good standing.

The men's earnings were sustained by high levels of overtime. The drivers averaged about 55 hours a week and the plant operatives somewhat less. No one doubted that the work could be done in less time than this, but the manager accepted that he could not speed up the schedules. Pay was not normally a matter of negotiation, but on one occasion the earnings of the nightshift drivers came before the committee. Some years before the management had decided that there should be no overtime on this shift. Consequently, despite the nightshift premium, the earnings of these drivers were below the plant average. Their compensation was to be allowed to work "job and finish", so that they could go home as soon as their work was done while receiving full pay for the shift. Most of them finished in six hours or less. Nevertheless, some of them objected to their relatively low earnings and after a short strike it was agreed by the committee that they should be scheduled for eleven-hour shifts, making 55 hours during the week.

These two examples show that industry agreements cannot legislate as they please on procedures in the plant with confidence that their provisions will be followed. Where they make no provision for shop stewards but work group organisation is well developed, shop stewards can secure recognition and either take control of the approved plant procedures or ignore them; where the plant procedure does not allow for collective bargaining, shop stewards can still impose a form of collective bargaining; and where the plant procedure does not provide for collective bargaining over any particular issue of importance to the workers, their stewards may find a means of settling it with management in a manner which amounts to bargaining, or of deciding it for themselves by unilateral action.

Outside nationalised industries and public services, however, most industry agreements on plant procedures are not generally regarded as giving more than guidance which individual plants are free to follow or not much as they please. What happens here?

Some indication is given by two of the Royal Commission surveys, the survey of shop stewards and the survey of managers and personnel officers. In interpreting this evidence, however, it is important to note that the two samples were constructed in different ways. The first was a sample of stewards drawn from six major unions covering distribution and some public services and nationalised industries, as well as manufacturing and construction. The second was based on a sample of firms from manufacturing and construction only, and although it was confined to firms recognising unions, almost one-fifth of the firms said that they had no shop stewards. Given these differences it is not surprising that the answers do not always tally. It is interesting that they agree as closely as they do.[1]

They show that in most sizeable firms bargaining between managers and stewards has developed an institutional structure. Three-quarters of the stewards said that there were senior stewards

[1] The details of the two samples and their answers to questions are given in *Workplace Industrial Relations*, Chapters 2 and 4.

at their workplace and the proportion was 86 per cent in plants with more than five hundred employees. Just over 70 per cent of them said there were joint committees at their plants where stewards met with managers to discuss and settle problems, and almost all of them personally took part in these committees. The proportion of plants with committees increased with the size of the plant. The sample of managers returned rather smaller proportions throughout, but this can be explained by the inclusion of plants with no stewards.[1]

To what extent did these procedures follow the industry agreements? The prevalence of senior stewards suggests that generally they do not do so, for the engineering procedure and many others make no provision for this office. To what extent are they formally embodied in written plant procedures? Among the stewards, 51 per cent said there was no written domestic procedure in addition to a national procedure and 38 per cent said they had such a procedure.[2] Among managers, on the other hand, 59 per cent of those who worked for federated firms said they had their own formal plant procedure in addition to the national procedure, and the proportion was 70 per cent in large plants. In this instance the difference between the two samples cannot easily be explained by their composition. In fact it might have been expected that more shop stewards than managers would have answered that they had their own formal plant procedures, because the managers' sample included firms with no shop stewards. The results therefore suggest that in some plants where stewards think they have no formal joint plant procedure, managers believe that they have.

A possible explanation for the state of affairs is that many managers codify a part of their domestic procedure, mainly for their own guidance and for the benefit of their colleagues. Consequently they can properly answer that they have their own formal domestic procedure. The stewards, on the other hand, may be unaware of the existence of the document, or documents, or if they know of them they may regard them as internal managerial instructions and therefore not agreed procedures binding upon themselves. Even if the documents have been agreed,

---

[1] The figures were 55 per cent with senior stewards (and 78 per cent among plants with over five hundred employees); and 54 per cent with joint committees.

[2] The remainder gave other answers or did not know.

the shop stewards might take the view that, since they covered only one aspect of procedure, they did not really constitute a written domestic procedure agreement. That would require a detailed constitution governing the whole range of their relationships with management.

Unfortunately there has been no general study of plant procedures against which these suggestions could be tested, but it is possible to find a number of instances which fit. We know, for example, that a considerable number of large plants have their own domestic procedures for dealing with discipline, and some of them also for handling redundancy, but that they are rarely ratified by an agreement.[1] It is also common for larger firms to introduce additional stages into the grievance procedure laid down by the industry. Where the steward cannot settle an issue with the foreman, for example, he may be expected to pass it on to the senior departmental steward for discussion with the departmental manager. The next stage could be a discussion between the senior steward of the plant and the personnel manager, with reference to a meeting between the works committee and the general manager as the last resort before calling in the full-time officers and the employers' association. Clearly there is a wide range of possible variants, and the larger the plant the more stages there are likely to be. The managers are almost bound to codify these arrangements, whereas the stewards may regard them as customary variants on the industry procedure. Plants operating schemes of payment by results may codify the conditions under which a worker can seek to have a job re-valued and the way he should go about it. This might be regarded by managers as a formal procedure and by the stewards as custom and practice. Alternatively the stewards in sections paid by results might accept that they operated a written procedure, whereas the timeworkers' stewards might properly take the view that they have no written procedure because this arrangement does not apply to them. Similarly where a job-evaluation system is in use for manual workers, it is usual to have a committee to review claims for revaluation and a procedure for submitting claims to the committee. But it is also not uncommon for such a scheme to apply to process workers and not to craftsmen, or to time-workers and not to workers paid by results. Here again managers

[1] See pp. 195–6.

would take the view that they had a written procedure whereas the stewards might be divided on the question according to the coverage of the procedure.

It follows that it is relatively uncommon to find a comprehensive procedure in the sense that it provides for handling all the issues discussed and settled between management and stewards, and covers all the manual workers in a given plant. But there are variations from one industry to another. In printing it is still the practice for managers to deal entirely separately with each chapel, and for procedures to be regulated by custom, although custom is often highly formalised. In building on the other hand "the drawing up of separate company agreements with the trade unions designed to bring wages and industrial relations under closer joint control" was noted by the Phelps Brown committee as an "important recent development". Most of these agreements are mainly concerned with incentive schemes or other pay arrangements, but the committee noted that the agreement between John Laing Construction and the unions "includes provision for the training of shop stewards, the encouragement of trade union membership, site procedures for handling grievances, and site amenities and welfare arrangements".[1]

There has also been a recent trend among large engineering firms towards the negotiation of comprehensive agreements covering a plant, or in some instances a group of plants owned by a single firm in the same district. One example is a large establishment where there are regular meetings in the company's time of the shop stewards from all departments. Periodically the stewards elect a steward from each department to sit on the works committee which meets regularly with management, and a chairman and a convener who are supplied with an office and secretarial assistance by the firm. The agreements between the firm and the committee include procedures for handling individual grievances and collective disputes within the plant, rates of pay for all classes of manual workers, the details of a payment-by-results system, and a number of other items including shift arrangements, holidays, transfers and so on. These arrangements' are written and formally signed by the company and the officers

---

[1] *Report of the Committee of Inquiry under Professor E. H. Phelps Brown into Certain Matters concerning Labour in Building and Civil Engineering*, Cmnd. 3714, 1968, p. 167.

of the works committee. Apart from the periodic upward adjustments of pay by the agreements of the Engineering Employers'
Federation, and the acceptance that hours of work and certain
other conditions should be governed by those agreements, this
plant therefore has its own set of substantive agreements.

THE PART PLAYED BY FULL-TIME OFFICERS

One interesting feature of this set of agreements is that, in contrast
to the company agreements in building, they are negotiated and
signed by the works committee and the official machinery of the
unions outside the plant has no part in them, although the full-
time district officers of the unions are well aware of their existence.
If this can happen in a major undertaking with a comprehensive
agreement, it is even more likely to happen in the numerous
instances where procedures are fragmentary and only partly
codified. In some engineering plants it is a matter of pride for
both the stewards and the managers that they never call in the
full-time officer; and examples can also be found in other industries. The spokesmen of the International Publishing Corporation told the Royal Commission of the past practice in a major
newspaper office: "The whole thing has been settled without the
union officials knowing anything about it—the management
were running away so fast. Certainly in our own company in
the last six or seven years it was almost an unwritten law—in my
experience as Production Director of the *Daily Mirror* in 1960—
that we never sought the assistance of union officials; it was
considered better to try to settle within the house. . . ."[1]

Industrial relations in the newspaper industry have always
allowed an important position to negotiations between the management and the chapel. Anxiety to exclude the full-time officers of
the unions from domestic arrangements can, however, also be
observed in industries in which, at least formally, pay and
conditions are determined by industry agreements. This was, for
example, true of the oil distribution plant discussed in the previous
section.[2] The overtime arrangements which had such an important effect on earnings were not recognised as a matter for formal
negotiation with union officers. It was also true of the electricity
generating station discussed there. The shop stewards tried to

[1] Royal Commission, *Minutes of Evidence*, Q. 9297.   [2] See p. 254.

settle all the issues which arose within the station for themselves, and regarded it as a defeat if they were obliged to call in their full-time officers.

The exclusion of union full-time officers from domestic bargaining is, however, not a general rule. There are plants in which the full-time officer is more important than the shop steward. A plant within the chemical group of industries provides an example. Industry agreements cover basic rates of pay and conditions of work but do not provide detailed arrangements for the conduct of relations in the plant. At that time there was no works or consultative committee of any kind, and one shop steward represented all the workers. The firm's starting rate exceeded the national minimum and a grading system prescribed higher rates of pay for various grades of job according to skill. These arrangements were agreed with the local full-time officer of the union who also negotiated a group payment-by-results system. Under it bonus earnings for men averaged between £3 and £4 a week over the year with less for women, but in the short run earnings fluctuated widely from week to week and from department to department. In addition considerable overtime was worked at certain periods of the year.

All this would appear to present a generous opportunity for domestic bargaining but, in fact, the opportunity was not used. The shop steward had taken up only one grievance over the inequitable distribution of overtime. He had not been concerned in the negotiation of the payment-by-results system and had not been called on to deal with any complaints about the settlement of job values or over any failure of the scheme to yield adequate earnings. Apparently everyone was satisfied with the scheme.

Consequently the steward had little influence over pay, although he was asked from time to time to take up a question of the appropriate rate of pay for a particular job. Besides this he handled complaints about cloakroom facilities and working conditions in the plant and cases of disciplinary action. He went direct to the personnel manager with any issue brought to him and if the two of them could not settle it they sent for the full-time officer who worked closely with the personnel manager.

The modest level of domestic bargaining owed a good deal to the management's efforts to maintain a contented staff, to the shop steward's willingness to accept a humble part in the plant's affairs and to the chance that no large-scale unpremeditated dispute had blown up to disturb the existing arrangements. But above all it was due to the desire of the personnel manager and the full-time officer to keep domestic industrial relations in their own hands and their willingness to work together to achieve this.

The Royal Commission surveys give a general indication of the part which full-time officers play in domestic negotiations. Almost half the works managers said that full-time officers did not play an important part in industrial relations in their plants; a third said that full-time officers played a fairly important part; and less than one-fifth said that they played an important part. These answers were confirmed by the frequency of their contacts with full-time officers. A third had not contacted a full-time officer for more than a year, and almost half had made contact on between one and four occasions during the year.[1]

There was some difference between shop stewards and full-time officers over the frequency of their contacts with each other,[2] but a majority of both groups took the view, in contrast with the managers, that full-time officers played an important part in negotiation within the firm. Among shop stewards 68 per cent thought that their full-time officer was very important in negotiations with their firm, against 27 per cent who thought that he was not very important. When the officers themselves were asked whether they thought full-time officers should play a more important part in local negotiations, 60 per cent thought they already played an important part.[3]

The explanation for this apparent difference of opinion between trade unionists and managers may be that stewards are reasonably confident that they can rely on the full-time officer in case of need. Over three-quarters of them said that they had no difficulty in contacting the full-time officer when they needed him. For their part the officers think that they can control the shop stewards when they are called upon to intervene; 87 per cent of them thought that full-time officers had sufficient influence over the

---

[1] *Workplace Industrial Relations*, pp. 86–7.

[2] The officers claimed to have met 52 per cent of the stewards for whom they were responsible during the previous four weeks. Among the stewards 54 per cent said they had met their full-time officer only four times over the previous year, or less frequently. (*Ibid.*, 20–1, 58–9.)

[3] *Ibid.*, pp. 21–2, 63.

activities of shop stewards and trade union members in the industries for which they were responsible.[1]

It is evident, however, that this relationship must in most instances be a matter of guidance from the full-time officer on major issues only, for there are not enough officers to service a closer control over domestic bargaining. According to the Royal Commission survey the average number of plants for which a full-time officer was responsible was 102, and the average number of stewards was 172. The officers of the Transport and General Workers had the most modest load, with 68 plants and 120 stewards; among the Engineers the figures were 193 plants and 477 stewards.[2]

It would, however, be going beyond the evidence to conclude that the number of full-time officers that a union is prepared to employ determines their influence on domestic bargaining. Managers' preferences are also important. Of the 82 per cent of works managers in the Royal Commission sample who thought that full-time officers played an unimportant part or only a fairly important part in industrial relations in the plant, no more than 15 per cent said they would like to see them play a more important part. Another influence is the anxiety of the shop stewards to keep matters in their own hands. A number of managers who would have liked full-time officers to have a more important part said that the officers were not welcomed by the shop stewards and were not trusted or wanted by the workers. But this does not seem to be a major influence. When shop stewards were asked whether they would like their full-time officers to play a more important part in negotiations with their firms, 34 per cent said "yes" and only 24 per cent said "no". A larger role for full-time officers in domestic bargaining is thus a considerably more popular proposal with shop stewards than with managers. Among the stewards' reasons for wanting them to play a more important part were that results would be better or quicker, that management would be more responsive, and that the full-time officers could remedy the stewards' deficiencies and make things easier for them.[3]

---

[1] If there was an exception it was the vehicle industry in which 18 per cent of officers thought shop stewards had too much power, and 41 per cent of the shop stewards thought that officers did not play an important part in negotiations with their firm. (*Ibid.*, pp. 21, 65.)   [2] *Ibid.*, pp. 57–8.   [3] *Ibid.*, pp. 21–2, 86–7.

MULTI-UNIONISM AND FRAGMENTED BARGAINING

Another reason sometimes put forward for the limited part played by full-time officers in domestic bargaining is multi-unionism. Where a matter concerns several unions the managers, it is suggested, can relatively easily discuss it with their stewards, but to bring together the full-time officers of all the unions would be a tiresome business and might make it more difficult to reach a settlement. So the full-time officers are not usually called in. This hypothesis is not entirely supported by the Royal Commission evidence, although their surveys confirmed that multi-unionism was the norm. Over four-fifths of the stewards came from plants in which there was more than one union representing manual workers, and nearly a third from plants where more than one union competed for members in the same grade of work. Two-thirds of the joint committees through which they negotiated with managers were multi-union.[1] However, when managers, shop stewards and full-time officers were asked whether it would help if fewer unions were involved, the differences were striking. Only 13 per cent of works managers in plants with more than one union handled multi-union issues very often, or fairly often, compared with 41 per cent of the stewards and 61 per cent of the officers. Of the works managers who dealt with issues affecting more than one union, only 42 per cent said it would help if fewer unions were involved, compared with 50 per cent of the stewards and 80 per cent of the full-time officers.[2] Whatever the explanation for these differences, they do not suggest that multi-union issues are kept from the full-time officers because of their difficulties in handling them. On the contrary they suggest that where multi-union issues occur, and especially where they seem to be intractable, the full-time officers are likely to be involved.

One reason why managers are not involved in multi-union issues more often is the fragmentation of so much domestic bargaining in Britain. In many industries process and maintenance workers negotiate separately at the plant as at industry level. In engineering it is open to an individual or a group of workers belonging to a single union to pursue a grievance through every stage up to central conference, whether or not it affects members of other unions in the plant. In shipbuilding it is

[1] *Ibid.*, pp. 18–20, 26.   [2] *Ibid.*, pp. 19–20, 62, 76.

customary for each trade to put forward its own claims, generally waiting to the stage in construction at which its members' services are most in demand. In the printing industry each chapel negotiates separately. There is no machinery in the plant for co-ordinating the work of the chapels, or even for ensuring communication between them. This is often true even if two chapels belong to the one union.

This point is important, for it shows that fragmentation is not invariably associated with multi-unionism. The steel industry provides another instance. There the process workers organised by the British Iron, Steel and Kindred Trades' Association do not have stewards as such. Negotiations are conducted by branch officers and in a major steel works each department normally has its own branch. Each branch is built around its own promotion ladder, jealously guarded by the members who expect promotion. Since most important industrial relations issues in steel are now settled at the plant, this means that the branches act almost as independent unions.

If fragmented bargaining can exist within a single union, it is also possible for several unions to operate a unified bargaining system within the plant. This is the normal arrangement in several nationalised industries, including the works committees in gas and electricity supply where it is prescribed by the industry agreements. But unified bargaining systems can be achieved in engineering plants despite the right of each union to appeal separately to the industry procedure; and productivity bargaining has also achieved a number of unified procedures in multi-union situations.[1]

THE CONDUCT OF SHOP STEWARD BUSINESS AND COMBINE COMMITTEES

Two aspects of domestic procedure are particularly liable to be settled by custom or by the stewards themselves. The first of these is the range of issues to which the Royal Commission referred when it recommended that companies should aim "to conclude with unions representative of their employees agreements regulating the position of shop stewards in such matters as: facilities for holding elections; numbers and constituencies; recognition

[1] See p. 308.

of credentials; facilities to consult and report back to their members; facilities to meet with other stewards; the responsibilities of the chief shop steward (if any); pay while functioning as steward in working hours; day release with pay for training".[1] It is possible to find domestic agreements which cover some of these matters. The number and constituencies of stewards is sometimes covered by an arrangement. The office of senior steward may be recognised and his position in the plant procedure set out, but, even where this is so, his other duties and responsibilities, his payment and the facilities offered him to carry out his work are usually arranged informally.

The second aspect is "combine committees". Company combine committees, consisting of representatives of shop stewards' committees in the several plants of a multi-plant company, are especially common in the engineering industry. No provision is made for these bodies in union rules, in industry procedures, or in plant procedures, and they are rarely accorded even informal recognition by managers. Their most universal function is the exchange of information about pay and conditions, but sometimes they go beyond this to agitate for equalisation of pay and conditions between factories, or to co-ordinate action over pay claims, or over recruiting campaigns. In recent years they have often been active in redundancies, or in mergers which it is feared might lead to redundancy, co-ordinating the protests of individual plants and agitating for action by the trade unions. Occasionally they have called strikes. Some combine committees keep in touch with each other and there was at one time a Motor Industry Shop Stewards' Combine, but it was mainly concerned with political agitation and had little influence in negotiations at any level.[2]

PAYMENT BY RESULTS

These, then, are the procedures of domestic bargaining. What do they settle? What substantive domestic agreements and arrangements are made and interpreted through them?

Bargaining can occur at several points in systems of payment

---

[1] *Report*, p. 45.
[2] Shirley Lerner and John Bescoby, "Shop Steward Combine Committees in the British Engineering Industry", *British Journal of Industrial Relations*, July 1966.

by results. It must almost inevitably take place over the introduction of the system, and it may occur both on the settling of the original values and on the revision of values. Revision, moreover, may take place in two different circumstances. Where the equipment, the method or the material is changed, the consequence is usually an increase in output per head without an equivalent increase in effort. In these circumstances it is usually to the advantage of the firm to revise values, although on some occasions the change may make the job more difficult so that it is in the workers' interest to amend them. However, there is also the possibility that an unchanged job may continue to yield stable earnings at a time when earnings generally are rising and new values are being set to take account of these higher earnings. If so the workers have a case for the upward revision of the value of this particular job in order to bring it into line. In addition, there may be occasions on which workers are unable to reach their normal earnings because of some temporary circumstance: the machinery breaks down, there is a shortage of material or parts, there is a batch of substandard material, a worker is moved from his normal high-earning job to a low-earning job, or from measured work to an unmeasured job outside the incentive system. In all these and many other circumstances there are grounds for claiming a special allowance to protect the worker from a loss of earnings due to no fault of his own, or to give him partial compensation.

These opportunities for bargaining exist, but they are not always used even where workers are well organised. On the building site and in the chemical plant described earlier in this chapter[1] there was no domestic bargaining on any of these matters, not even over the introduction of the system. Tom Lupton's classic study in the sociology of payment by results covered two plants, in one of which there was no domestic bargaining over job values although the workers were unionised.[2] By far the most extensive survey of payment by results in the country was undertaken by the National Board for Prices and Incomes to provide the basis for their report on *Payment by Results Systems*. As a result of the forty case studies included in the survey the Board concluded that there was a marked difference between men and women in the readiness to haggle over job values, on which "women appear to have accepted the results of

[1] See pp. 246–7, 260.   [2] *On the Shop Floor.*

work measurement as 'correct' and tend not to bargain over times and prices".[1] In all these instances, however, it would have been open to the workers and their stewards to object to values and to seek revision, but they did not do so. They were apparently satisfied with the values established by management.

In other instances values are challenged from time to time so that the job has to be restudied and there may be some bargaining over the results, but these changes are relatively marginal accommodations in a system which is generally accepted and observed. The Board's survey provided a number of instances of this kind, which seems to be the normal arrangements in footwear and cotton spinning.[2]

On the other hand there are many plants where domestic bargaining over payment by results is the central feature of industrial relations. The Board noted "the significant amount of valuable time" that can be spent on it "by workers, shop stewards, foremen and managers". They quoted a division of one plant, with 540 workers paid by results, in which piecework negotiations occupied eight thousand man hours in 1967 and another in which every £100 of incentive earnings cost £45 in administrative expenses. They emphasised the effect on shop stewards of the "stress and friction involved in constant bargaining", and the "constant time-consuming process of shop-floor haggling". They reported that in "the factories we studied where the labour force is predominantly male there has often been a readiness to argue and fight for quite small gains. In one Midlands factory, for example, relationships between ratefixers and the shop floor were described in terms of 'battle' and 'war', and a good shop steward was defined as one who spends 'at least 50 per cent of his time in the ratefixing office, arguing'."[3]

What accounts for these differences? One answer is work study. Where work study is carefully applied, payment by results should yield a fair reward for effort, and the earnings from one job should be reasonably fair in relation to other jobs. Many managers argue that bargaining should be confined to the conversion factor, or the average level of earnings which the system should yield, leaving it entirely to work study to translate the

---

[1] *Payment by Results Systems*, p. 19.
[2] *Payment by Results Systems (Supplement)*, Cmnd. 3627-1, Papers 6, 13, 14.
[3] *Payment by Results Systems*, pp. 19, 24, 29, 40.

conversion factor into job values. However, the absence of work study cannot by itself explain high levels of domestic bargaining over payment by results. The Board observed one company in which "management's original intention . . . was that piecework prices would be determined solely by time study. . . . In subsequent years, however, this system has become so distorted by both shop-floor bargaining pressures and formal negotiation that it functions very differently from the way that was originally intended." The average earnings of the pieceworkers had been rising at an annual rate of 9 per cent over the previous seven years.[1] Moreover, if work study does not guarantee control it is also true that reasonable control can be established by other methods. The Board examined one plant in which the head of the ratefixing department had, without recourse to work study, pursued a policy of agreeing time elements for jobs until about 80 per cent of the total time allowed was covered by these agreed elements.[2] One example of a successful incentive system quoted in their report on building pay depended on "target prices calculated on the bill of quantities from past experience".[3]

Engineering employers often blame the shortcomings of payment by results on the "mutuality" clause in their industry agreement which stipulates that job values "shall be fixed by mutual arrangement between the employer and the workman or workmen who perform the work". The employers' original intention in imposing this clause on the unions in 1898 was "to ensure that the setting of piecework prices, bonuses or basis times was a domestic matter *between the management and each individual worker*, the union or its representatives in the workplace having no part in the process until such an attempt at personal bargaining had broken down".[4] But the clause also puts into the hands of the worker the right to hold up indefinitely the operation of a new value or the revision of an old value. Its introduction was soon followed by a rapid development of shop-steward bargaining over values, and since then the difficulty of securing shop-floor acceptance of values has increased with full employment. However, the mutuality clause cannot by itself explain different levels of bargaining activity. The Board studied two factories belonging

---

[1] *Payment by Results Systems (Supplement)*, pp. 51, 53.   [2] *Ibid.*, p. 68.
[3] *Pay and Conditions in the Building Industry*, p. 33.
[4] *Industrial Relations in Engineering*, p. 169.

to the same engineering company, both subject to this rule. In one factory the value offered was rarely refused by workers, and if it was "the foremen sought acceptance from another operator who was familiar with the operation". Such lack of solidarity on the part of organised workers is probably exceptional. At the second and larger factory there was "strong union representation", and the Board "found more resistance on the part of workers and their shop stewards played a more active role. But still, deadlocks over the agreement of piecework prices were rare."[1] It is also possible to find a good deal of haggling over values in other industries without this rule. The building industry has no mutuality rule for individual workers. According to its agreement, targets should be issued by management and wherever practicable agreed with the accredited representatives of the operatives on the site before an operation is started, and they should be altered only if there is a "material change in circumstances". However at the Barbican site the firm of Myton found that various factors, including "inconsistent and late instructions from the Architects", made it difficult for their employees to earn reasonable bonuses. "As a result, the firm had to relax bonus targets *ad hoc* so as to bring earnings up to a reasonable level. . . . The Company claimed that the Works Committee had sought to create unrest on the site by exploiting the difficulties the firm were experiencing in operating the bonus scheme. . . . In the course of negotiations on labourers' and scaffolders' targets, the Works Committee had shown no sign of wishing to reach an agreement. On each occasion that Myton had prepared a draft solution in response to one request, a fresh demand had been made by the operatives."[2] If it were possible to agree and enforce a rule forbidding appeals against job values, there could be no haggling. But this would be unjust, for work study is not an exact science, and, even if it were, mistakes can occur. Moreover in time, due to changing circumstances, an established value can cease to yield equitable earnings. Such a rule would be unacceptable to trade unions, and, even if they accepted it, its enforcement would be no easy matter where well-organised workers felt a grievance.

[1] *Payment by Results Systems (Supplement)*, pp. 48–9.
[2] *Report of a Court of Inquiry into trade disputes at the Barbican and Horseferry Road construction sites in London*, p. 25.

Moreover, bargaining on payment by results is not confined to the settlement of values. When piecework was the rule for coalmining faceworkers, the central issue in pit bargaining was the settlement of special allowances for variations in geological conditions and for other factors which hindered the men making their normal earnings. In the docks, piecework prices are settled between the employers and the full-time union officers. On ships and quays gangs of dockers bargain for allowances for handling cargoes which are dirty or unpleasant, or awkwardly stowed. In engineering it is common for lost time to be paid at different rates according to the cause of the hold-up. In some instances the choice can be a matter of shop-floor bargaining, and in one case the Board found the records showed "that foremen intended to book their men for the most lucrative compensation, largely irrespective of the cause".[1] There are plants in which the workers have managed to establish an understanding that all time lost through no fault of their own should be paid at their average piecework earnings over some previous period of time.

The suitability of work for payment by results is another factor in explaining different levels of workshop bargaining. In the engineering company in which the Board found effective control over payment by results, the work was standardised, large batches were produced on continuous flow lines with high mechanisation and individual jobs were short and repetitive. All these features, said the Board, "help in the control of the piecework system". On the other hand the Board examined a plant in which batch sizes were small, much time was spent on setting machines, the work was highly skilled and planning was frequently upset by the injection of priority jobs. Here "fragmented bargaining" had "produced a situation in which earnings are determined as much by bargaining skill and strength as by effort". The Board appeared to regard this as an inevitable consequence of the circumstances. "Once bargaining power, a mistake, an inconsistency, or an instance of earnings instability occurs, once in short an injustice is felt to have been done, the system is likely to spiral into constant bargaining and bad industrial relations." By themselves, however, different methods and products cannot be the decisive factors. In the machine tool industry the Board examined three firms, two of them in the same area. In one of these two, "in-

[1] *Payment by Results Systems (Supplement)*, p. 52.

dustrial relations appeared to be largely free of the continual conflict which the Board has found commonly associated with piecework circumstances". At the other, there was an "almost purely bargaining system of setting times". Industrial relations were poor, and "a major source of trouble seemed to be the perceived inconsistencies in the results stemming from the freedom within the barter system".[1]

The Board attached great importance to the "ground rules" established to control payment by results. In the engineering industry these are often matters of custom. Workers may refuse to allow the use of a stop-watch in setting times. They may refuse to allow work-study engineers to practise effort rating, insisting on a custom that bargaining must be based on the times actually recorded.[2] They may assert that each man has an absolute right to demand the restudy of a value if he feels it does not yield sufficient earnings, no matter how recently the value was agreed. Elsewhere it may be accepted that some period must have elapsed, say two years, or that low average earnings must have been established for a period of weeks.[3] The conversion factor may also be a matter of custom, so that, for example, new and revised values should allow a worker to reach the average earnings level for his grade in his department either at once or over a period of weeks or months. The common practice of "cross-booking" allows time actually spent on one job to be recorded against another, thus obscuring the extremely high earnings on a particular job which might, if discovered, lead to a revaluation. Where a worker is paid partly on measured work and partly on unmeasured work, cross-booking can record less time on piecework jobs than they have actually taken. If the time spent on unmeasured work is paid by the hour the pay-packet is thereby inflated. If the rate of pay for unmeasured work is average hourly piecework earnings, the size of the pay-packet is increased further. The practice of storing tickets for completed work "at the back of the book", to be handed in when the worker chooses, serves to cushion him against fluctuations in earnings. Limits on output may have the same effect.

---

[1] *Ibid.*, pp. 45, 59–60, 64–5.   [2] *Ibid*, pp 58–9.

[3] The Board quotes a case in which jobs can be revalued if the "operator has been earning less than the average of the previous six weeks, and . . . if earnings . . . are 'unreasonably low' by comparison with the rest of the section. About a quarter of all piecework prices are adjusted on the basis of low average earnings alone." (*Ibid.*, p. 54.)

The alternative to this dependence on custom is to work out a set of rules and settle them by agreement. The Board made suggestions for the topics that should be covered by ground rules, and recommended industries to negotiate "framework" agreements. As examples they referred to the industry agreements in footwear and cotton spinning, both of which provide for work study stipulate the circumstances in which values are to be reviewed and establish a conversion factor (in the case of cotton spinning this is a range of earnings instead of a single figure). These agreements have not put an end to wage drift. The Board judged that something like 2 per cent a year is the minimum rate of drift to be expected in the best-regulated incentive system. Cotton spinning has experienced 3 per cent drift in recent years. Nor have they prevented the development of supplementary practices and arrangements.[2] But the extent of control is evidently far greater than is common in engineering and building. It is, however, open to doubt how far other industries could now introduce effective control through similar agreements. Both cotton and footwear have long traditions of negotiated piece-price lists in the settlement and interpretation of which full-time union officers played a prominent part. Their present agreements were negotiated with the express intention of carrying over into modern incentive systems the same degree of central control as had been established in the past. Both industries employ more women than men.

The conclusion seems to be that although payment by results does not inevitably lead to domestic bargaining, among well-organised male workers it generally does so. Quite frequently it brings a time-consuming process of constant bartering or battling over job values. Whether or not it does this depends a good deal on managers choosing a suitable payment system, establishing relevant controls, and negotiating a suitable system of rules to deal with disputes over values; and also on the extent to which the industry agreement provides a framework which encourages managers to do these things.

The evidence does not, however, support a conclusion that the pressure of domestic bargaining is the overriding influence in the degeneration of incentive systems. The Board found that "manage-

[1] *Payment by Results Systems*, pp. 55–62.
[2] *Payment by Results Systems (Supplement)*, Papers 13, 14.

ment and foremen generally thought that stewards had a moderating influence on their members in bargaining over P.B.R. values, so that in our case studies of conventional P.B.R. systems, shop stewards usually appear as a force for stability".[1] In their study of 'A Bad Case of Wage Drift" they recorded that "it was usually the individual operator who pushed hardest in negotiations and not the shop stewards. Management said that shop stewards were a great help in restraining unreasonable demands and in preventing negotiations from dragging on. . . . In fact, it appeared that the powerful senior shop stewards were content to preserve the existing range of differentials in piecework earnings".[2] Nor are the workers themselves always in favour of unlimited workshop pressure. In discussing a case in which workers had asked for the introduction of measured day work in place of fluctuating incentive earnings, the Board said that "they had indicated a marked desire for stable earnings. . . . A second factor is that even if the cards were stacked in the bargaining process in favour of the men, there was evidence that many did not enjoy the business of negotiation. It was seen by a good number as time-wasting and some, by their nature, disliked constant haggling of the bazaar type".[3]

TIME PAYMENTS

Domestic bargaining over payment by results has been investigated more thoroughly than other forms of domestic bargaining over pay. It may be more important than any other form in its effect on earnings, and it is almost certainly the richest in complexity. But other forms are also important, and in many industries their effects outweigh those of payment by results.

Some domestic bargaining over time rates is the direct consequence of payment by results. This is often so in plants where the workers directly engaged in production are paid by results and the "indirect workers" are not. Rising piecework earnings prompt these indirect workers to seek methods of increasing their own pay in step. One method is to devise schemes for paying them by results as well, and this is sometimes done. However, there are often difficulties in devising a serviceable scheme,

---

[1] *Payment by Results Systems*, p. 52.
[2] *Payment by Results Systems (Supplement)*, p. 54.　　　[3] *Ibid.*, pp. 69–70.

and the Board noted that in some instances there was "no pretence that bonuses are linked to output, and the result has been a medley of lieu bonuses, special bonuses, dubiously entitled merit payments, and 'out of office' supplements". In other instances the timeworkers negotiated for themselves a bonus related to the average earnings of the pieceworkers. In one plant studied by the Board different groups of workers had their own bonuses or lieu rates. "All these workers watched how the earnings of pieceworkers were moving and periodically applied for increases perhaps on the basis of 'a re-assessment of their responsibilities'. In yet another firm, the various groups of indirect workers periodically submitted separate claims for time rate increases. These claims came in waves: usually the toolroom workers and electricians led, and were then followed by the others."[1] Not infrequently negotiations over time rates provide the main business for factory-wide negotiations even in predominantly pieceworking plants. Pieceworkers can settle their disputes in the departments in which they arise, value by value, but the consequential increases for the time workers may affect several departments and involve a far larger sum of money than any single job value, so that they require factory-wide discussions.

Payment by results may also affect the negotiation of time rates in factories which do not use incentive systems. Few if any engineering time workers are paid no more than the industry's minimum time rates, and their supplementary lieu, merit or other payments are negotiated either sectionally or for the whole plant. Rising piecework earnings in neighbouring plants are often quoted as the main pressure in negotiating increases in these payments.

Although the Board says that the timeworkers' problems "become particularly acute where skilled craftsmen on time rates of pay see the earnings of unskilled and semi-skilled production workers rising above their own",[2] and although reports on other negotiations have displayed many instances of inversion of differentials by piecework, domestic bargaining by timeworkers seems generally to have sustained their earnings fairly successfully. In December 1969 the average weekly earnings of skilled timeworkers in engineering and other metal-using industries were £26 0s. 7d compared with £26 15s. 4d for skilled

[1] *Payment by Results Systems*, p. 30.   [2] *Ibid.*, p. 29.

pieceworkers, £24 2s. 8d for semi-skilled pieceworkers and £18 19s. 11d for unskilled pieceworkers. The comparison between skilled timeworkers and skilled pieceworkers is especially interesting.[1] The difference was less than 3 per cent. Even excluding the extra overtime put in by skilled timeworkers (about two hours a week) it was under 6 per cent. For labourers the difference between timeworkers and pieceworkers was about the same, but for semi-skilled workers it was rather more. These figures are surprising, for every discussion of engineering earnings suggests that the rising earnings of pieceworkers pull the pay of other workers up behind them. It almost seems that domestic negotiators do not believe that pieceworkers expend much more effort than timeworkers, and have set themselves to diminish the differentials which payment-by-results has introduced into the pay system.[2]

Timeworkers, however, do not need to have the inducement of rising piecework earnings among their colleagues in the same plant or neighbouring plants in order to negotiate pay increases for themselves. The main trades engaged in the construction of ships (as opposed to the finishing trades) switched from piece rates to lieu rates decades ago,[3] and the negotiation of lieu rates, yard by yard, ship by ship, and trade by trade, has become the staple form of their domestic bargaining. Similarly in the newspaper industry, where incentive payment is still the exception, the highly developed system of chapel bargaining deals mainly with the negotiation of various kinds of time rates, including merit pay, house money, and special payments for operating particular types of machinery. Another common device is to negotiate reduction in manning, dividing the pay of the "ghosts" among the remaining workers. As a result the average weekly earnings of wage earners in newspapers, at £33 11s. 4d in April 1969, exceed those of every other industry; and some grades of craftsmen on London newspapers were then earning between £90 and £100 a week.

---

[1] At £27 17s. 8d the weekly earnings of skilled timeworking electricians slightly exceeded the £27 17s. 3d of their pieceworking colleagues.

[2] In April 1969 there was a strike of pieceworkers at the B.L.M.C. plant at Longbridge on the grounds that a job evaluation agreement for timeworkers had taken their earnings ahead of the pieceworkers.

[3] The domestically negotiated rates were thus *in lieu* of the piecework earnings that earlier generations had enjoyed, not *in lieu* of piecework earnings enjoyed by their colleagues. (See p. 321.)

Domestic bargaining is fragmented in both shipbuilding and printing. By contrast in many light manufacturing industries it is common for domestic negotiation to establish comprehensive grading systems for process workers, with a hierarchy of rates of pay to match the grades. Increasingly job evaluation is employed to guide the construction of these grading systems, and also to bring order into the negotiation of time rates in plants in which bargaining had previously been fragmented. But job evaluation does not exclude domestic bargaining over pay. The investigations of the National Board for Prices and Incomes show that job evaluation is "normally carried out by a committee . . . containing in many instances shop-floor or union representation".[1] When the evaluation is complete the resulting grades and rates of pay have to be negotiated, and a system of appeal for regrading is normally established. Even so, in some instances it fails to put an end to the pressures of fragmented bargaining. In some case examined by the Board they found that "an operative wishing to enhance his own position was able to appeal for a higher job evaluation. A successful appeal could cause anomalies in the rating for similar jobs in other parts of the plant, since there was no automatic provision for reviewing similar jobs in other parts of the factory." Following re-equipment "management diagnosed that certain job characteristics had changed in relative value . . . and that the contribution of such characteristics as skill and experience had greatly increased".[2]

Table VII, based on the Royal Commission survey of managers,[3] gives some idea of the extent of domestic negotiation over both payment by results and time payment in manufacturing and construction. It establishes beyond doubt that some form of domestic bargaining over pay is normal and that in many plants several different forms exist side by side.

OVERTIME PAYMENT

The growth of overtime work and earnings in post-war Britain has already been noted, with the reasons for suggesting that much of this overtime exists rather to pay workers than to get work done.[4] Where overtime earnings are considerable, it is to be

---

[1] *Job Evaluation*, p. 21.   [2] *Job Evaluation (Supplement)*, p. 51.
[3] *Workplace Industrial Relations*, p. 80.   [4] See pp. 182–5.

expected that organised workers will attempt to acquire some control over it. Industry agreements are not an effective tool for this. Most industry agreements leave an employer free to use overtime as he chooses so long as he pays the agreed rates. A minority, including engineering and building, place restrictions

TABLE VII

WAGE ISSUES DISCUSSED AND SETTLED BETWEEN MANAGERS
AND SHOP STEWARDS

Issue	Proportion of works managers who negotiate with stewards (78 per cent of sample) dicussing and settling this issue with stewards (per cent)	Proportion of personnel officers who negotiate with stewards (93 per cent of sample) dicussing and settling this issue with stewards (per cent)
piecework issues	51	42
other forms of bonus payment	63	62
plus payments for dirty work etc.	47	37
job evaluation	51 } 82	44 } 80
allowances of any other kind	54	57
merit money	49	44
up-grading	57	57

on overtime. But "a close examination of the details of these restrictions reveals two things. First they are so full of exceptions that almost any hours of work could be justified. Secondly, they impose not an absolute limit to the amount of overtime that shall be worked but a limit to that which may be worked *without the local union organisation being consulted.*"[1] According to the survey of building pay made by the National Board for Prices and Incomes, "in the majority of cases the decision to work overtime was made by the site agent. The evidence of our case studies

[1] *Overtime Working in Britain*, p. 33.

K

leads us to doubt whether permission is usually sought from the local joint committee or, if it is, whether the granting of permission is more than a formality."[1] The effect of the engineering agreement, according to the report of a Court of Inquiry in 1922, is only to render overtime in excess of 30 hours a month "open to the suggestion that it is unreasonable".[2]

Some form of domestic bargaining about overtime seems now to be general among well-organised workers. Summarising the results of the inquiry into workplace bargaining by shop stewards conducted by Coker and himself, McCarthy wrote: "In all establishments investigated, some form of domestic bargaining took place over working hours. . . . The most common cause of grievances and claims arising out of hours of work concerned overtime. In all the workplace situations studied, grievances had arisen over the uneven distribution of overtime. In local government, gas, electricity, the docks and confectionery, management had come to accept the need to approach union representatives before introducing major variations in overtime working. . . . In one of the engineering firms studied, a position had been reached in the recent past in which stewards, in effect, were recognised by management as having the right to grant or withhold overtime. In the chemical plant studied, numerous disputes over uneven overtime working led to a seven-months 'unofficial' ban on overtime until a local agreement was negotiated regulating its distribution in more detail."[3]

This finding is confirmed by the Royal Commission surveys. Among the 78 per cent of works managers who negotiated with shop stewards, 62 per cent discussed and settled the level of overtime with them, and 50 per cent its distribution. Among the 93 per cent of personnel officers who negotiated with stewards the proportion discussing and settling the level of overtime was 59 per cent, and 60 per cent dealt with its distribution.[4]

Where a considerable part of earnings derives from overtime, workers may also try to protect their pay by practices designed to make sure that the overtime is there. Before the productivity

---

[1] *Pay and Conditions in the Building Industry*, p. 45.

[2] Quoted in *Industrial Relations in Engineering*, p. 157.

[3] *The Role of Shop Stewards in British Industrial Relations*, p. 12.

[4] *Workplace Industrial Relations*, p. 80. On the other hand works managers dealt with stewards over breaks in working hours (64 per cent) and stopping and starting times (65 per cent) more frequently than personnel officers (45 per cent and 36 per cent respectively).

agreements in oil distribution "in many instances the union branches laid down overall average journey speeds which determined the time for which vehicles must remain outside the plant".[1] In the plant described earlier in this chapter,[2] where drivers averaged a 55-hour week, the branch rule prescribed an average speed of 12 miles an hour for the first hour and 18 miles an hour for the remainder of the journey. The manager said that scheduling on this basis gave an overall plant average of 14 miles an hour whereas he believed that 17–18 miles an hour could be achieved without breaking the law. The stewards held that a plant average of 20 miles an hour would then be possible. It was accepted that drivers spent a good deal of their time in transport cafés in order to keep out of the plant until their scheduled time was up. When work was plentiful and relations amicable the rule was not strictly enforced. When work fell off or the stewards were wrangling with management they insisted on its strict observance. Management and men believed that offenders would be "branched" and fined.

The same purpose is served by the practice of welting or spelling among dockers in Liverpool and other ports, "whereby only half a gang is working at any given time; for each half it is one hour on and one hour off. During his hour off the man does what he likes; he is resting or smoking or having a cup of tea." In Liverpool the men have always relied for their earnings on working a great deal of overtime and the employers have encouraged this by offering a large overtime premium. "On weekdays after five o'clock it is double the time-rate as compared with time-and-a-half in many other ports. . . . There are correspondingly higher rates at weekends." In contrast to oil distribution, however, the union claimed that it was strongly opposed to welting and blamed the employers "for failing to co-operate effectively in stamping out the practice".[3] The similar practice of the "blow" on the London newspapers, whereby men do two hours on and one off or one hour on and one hour off, is intended to inflate the size of the gangs rather than to ensure overtime working.

It is sometimes suggested that the strict enforcement of demarcation lines between crafts, as in the shipyards, is intended to

[1] *Productivity Agreements*, pp. 6–7.   [2] See pp. 254–5.
[3] Devlin Committee, *Final Report*, pp. 16–18.

provide extra overtime, and since the peak demands for each craft occur in successive stages of ship construction, they have this effect. But here overtime is also encouraged by rules requiring, for example, that if overtime is worked at all, it should be worked for a minimum period of two or four hours, that if overtime is worked on Saturday the men must also be offered Sunday work, and that if one member of a trade is offered overtime, all his colleagues must be included in the offer. Somewhat similar rules are found in the ports and in some other industries.

Such a rule can lead to payment for overtime that has not been worked. The Devlin Committee were told that in London "the quays are deserted at 6.15 p.m. although overtime lasts until 7.0 p.m.".[1] In road haulage[2] and in London newspapers the practice of paying for overtime not actually worked has grown to such an extent that overtime hours recorded represent units of payment rather than units of time worked. In these instances negotiation with individual workers or shop stewards over the level of overtime is sometimes indistinguishable from negotiation over an increase in time rates, and sometimes a crude form of piecework bargaining—so many hours overtime paid for the completion of such and such a job.

WORK ARRANGEMENTS

In many instances bargaining over pay is also bargaining over work. This is evident in payment by results, but it is also true of job evaluation and of some types of bargaining about overtime. But bargaining may also take place directly over work. This is formally acknowledge in many systems of measured day work, for example under the Coal Board's national powerloading agreement. This has put an end to colliery bargaining over pay on powerloading faces but has left to the colliery the settlement of the tasks to be performed in return for the time rates of pay now determined by an industry agreement.[3] The manning of the face is also left to colliery bargaining, and manning scales are recognised as a matter for negotiation in the docks, the steel industry and elsewhere. In engineering, changes "in material, means or method" which "may result in one class of workpeople being replaced by another in the establishment" is a matter for consultation in the

---

[1] *Ibid.*, p. 19.   [2] See p. 184.   [3] See pp. 237–8.

plant. After that the change can be introduced subject to appeal by the workers to the industry's disputes procedure. In many other industries methods of work are regarded as a matter for settlement by managers, subject only to such consultation with the workers as they may choose to allow.

Whatever the formal position, the Royal Commission surveys have established that domestic bargaining on many aspects of work is a normal feature of plant relations in manufacturing and construction. Table VIII sets out the figures.

TABLE VIII

DISCUSSION AND SETTLEMENT OF WORK ARRANGEMENTS
BETWEEN MANAGERS AND SHOP STEWARDS[1]

Issue	Proportion of works managers who negotiate with stewards (78 per cent of sample) discussing and settling this issue with stewards (per cent)	Proportion of personnel officers who negotiate with stewards (93 per cent of sample) discussing and settling this issue with stewards (per cent)
distribution of work	46	33
pace of work	53	30
quality of work	62	35
manning of machines	47	38
transfer from one job to another	62	70
introduction of new machinery/jobs	61	43
taking on new labour	46	56
number of apprentices	30	39
acceptance of up-grading	41	43

[1] *Workplace Industrial Relations*, p. 80. The differences between works managers and personnel officers reflect the responsibility of works managers for production and the personnel officers for employment.

The prevalence of domestic bargaining on these issues provides an answer to the question sometime posed by shop stewards in pieceworking plants: what do stewards do where there is no piecework? In his account of the survey conducted by Coker and himself, McCarthy reported that they observed "a broad relationship between the extent to which stewards had managed to secure a measure of influence over members' earnings and their relative standing both with management and workers". But even where "their opportunities for influencing management were largely confined to various non-monetary issues, they could still maintain the elements of a negotiating position and find plenty of things to do. ... Here bargaining largely revolved around such questions as the distribution and pace of work, the provision of clothing, working conditions and the administration and enforcement of discipline".[1]

Where workers withhold consent to changes in work arrangements proposed by managers, and the managers dare not enforce their proposals, the workers' attitude is usually described as a "restrictive practice", or to distinguish it from a commercial restriction, as a restrictive labour practice. The term is also used to cover many of the practices described on previous pages which have developed around overtime arrangements and systems of payment by results. These practices are supposed to be common in Britain and to have a serious effect on the level of labour productivity. The Confederation of British Industry informed the Royal Commission of their view "that in one form or another ... they have seriously retarded economic growth in the past—and that they represent perhaps the greatest obstacle to future growth". They listed as examples: overmanning, demarcation rules, systematic time-wasting, "ceilings" on earnings, resistance to technical innovation and to work study, restrictions on recruitment, reluctance to undertake overtime or shiftwork, and "resistance to the idea of merit being the main criterion for promotion, rather than, say, seniority or union membership".[2] Evidence from individual employers' associations gave detailed examples of particular practices.[3]

---

[1] *The Role of Shop Stewards in British Industrial Relations*, p. 16.

[2] *Selected Written Evidence to the Royal Commission*, pp. 266.

[3] For instance, the *Written Evidence* of the Engineering Employers' Federation, Appendices B–F, *ibid.*, pp. 439–46.

Although their secretariat came to the conclusion that it was impossible to give "any precise picture of the extent and seriousness of restrictive labour practices in Britain today",[1] the Commission came closer to accepting this part of the Confederation's evidence than much of the remainder. Having reviewed all the evidence they could assemble, their verdict on the use of manpower in Britain was that "there is substantial room for improvement" and their discussion of means for achieving improvement implied that restrictive labour practices were an important impediment to it.[2]

Some restrictions, said the Commission, are enforced by the unions. "Sometimes proposals affecting craft demarcations in industries like shipbuilding and printing may run up against deep-rooted trade union resistance because they appear to threaten the whole basis on which a craft union exists."[3] In shipbuilding there has been a good deal of codification of demarcation rules. Besides its general-purpose procedure agreement, the industry has had a special Demarcation Procedure Agreement since 1912. Disputes about the apportionment of work which are not settled in the yard can be referred to a committee of three representatives from each union concerned sitting with three employers from another yard. The committee takes it decisions by majority vote. This arrangement has helped in the development of district "books of apportionment" drawn up between unions and accepted by the employers. These books, however, affect mainly the finishing trades, and are by no means universal even there. Neither the Boilermakers nor the Shipwrights were party to the 1912 agreement, and continued to rely on the direct enforcement of the customs of their trades. Custom and practice also played an important part in the interpretation of books of apportionment,[4] and customs often varied from yard to yard. The amalgamation of the Boilermakers, the Shipwrights and Blacksmiths is likely to have a considerable effect on demarcation in ship construction, and in 1969 a new demarcation agreement was signed by all the unions, but it is too early to judge what its consequences will be.

[1] *Productivity Bargaining and Restrictive Labour Practices*, p. 56.
[2] *Report*, pp. 74–81.
[3] *Ibid.*, p. 78.
[4] Accounts of the demarcation arrangements and their operation are given in J. E. T. Eldridge, *Industrial Disputes*, Chapter 3, and in G. Roberts, *Demarcation Rules in Shipbuilding and Shiprepairing*, 1967.

Another example of a restriction imposed by a union is the decision of the Transport and General Workers' Union, since relaxed, to maintain "a speed limit of 30 miles an hour for heavy good vehicles, even when the legal limit was raised to 40 miles an hour". The union's case for this unilateral limitation was that it was necessary in the interests of safety.[1] Even with a national decision of this kind enforcement necessarily depended upon the vigilance and determination of shop stewards at the depots, just as the application of decisions of district committees of the Engineers concerning, say, the manning of machines depends upon the shop stewards in the factories.

Most restrictive practices, however, according to the Commission, "are not enforced by the unions as such" and "can be understood only in relation to particular circumstances in particular undertakings or plants".[2] Managers are often reluctant to accept this. In their evidence to the Royal Commission the Engineering Employers' Federation wrote of "union insistence on unreasonable manning practices" and "union limitations on earnings" although in some of the cases they quote the restrictions were enforced by the workers themselves or by their stewards.[3] Despite the dictum of the National Board for Prices and Incomes that "methods of work and traditional practices cannot be changed by decision of an industry or a company, but only by the men who do the work",[4] the negotiation of productivity agreements has run into trouble time and time again because managers have supposed that they could settle work practices with full-time union officers.

This remains one of the most obscure areas of British industrial relations. Not only do practices differ from plant to plant and from workshop to workshop, but their determination is a process in which managerial prerogative, worker regulation, collective bargaining and joint consultation seem to be hopelessly entangled. There is urgent need for more study of these practices and how they are settled and modified.

One point is clear, however. Restrictions on the use of manpower are not invariably forced on unwilling managers. Besides those practices which managers wish to change but are prevented from doing so by union or workshop pressure, there are also

[1] *Productivity Agreements*, p. 7.   [2] *Report*, p. 77.
[3] *Selected Written Evidence*, Appendices B–F.   [4] *Productivity Agreements*, p. 38.

practices which "both the parties directly concerned see as justified but which outside observers do not", such as unnecessary overtime working to retain labour, or the hoarding of skilled labour; and "those which amount simply to managerial inefficiency", at least in their origin, such as bad time-keeping and excessive tea-breaks.[1]

WORKING CONDITIONS, DISCIPLINE AND REDUNDANCY

According to the Royal Commission's survey of managers, the remaining items discussed and settled with shop stewards include the most popular of all issues for domestic bargaining.[2] These are set out in Table IX.

TABLE IX

DISCUSSION AND SETTLEMENT OF WORKING CONDITIONS, DISCIPLINE AND REDUNDANCY BETWEEN MANAGERS AND SHOP STEWARDS

Issue	Proportion of works managers who negotiate with stewards (78 per cent of sample) discussing and settling this issue with stewards (per cent)	Proportion of personnel officers who negotiate with stewards (93 per cent of sample) discussing and settling this issue with stewards (per cent)
safety questions	77	73
health questions	63	76
general conditions in the workplace	74	80
reprimands by foremen	64	64
suspensions	58	58
dismissals	71	74
short time	38	28
redundancy questions	50	50

[1] *Productivity Bargaining and Restrictive Labour Practices*, p. 53.
[2] *Workplace Industrial Relations*, p. 80.

The popularity of these items is no cause for surprise. If they are touched upon in industry agreements it can only be in the most general terms, leaving all the particular decisions to the plant: and whereas some plants work no overtime, many of them have no payment by results, and more of them no system of job evaluation, virtually all plants of any size must have some problems of safety, health, general working conditions and discipline.

General conditions, safety and health are perhaps the most obvious issues for co-operation between managers and employees in undertakings of all kinds, and seem to provide much of the staple business of joint consultative committees where these exist. A number of firms have separate joint safety committees to emphasise the common concern in avoiding accidents. This does not mean that matters of this kind are uncontroversial. Ventilation, temperature, dirty conditions, unsafe conditions and the enforcement of the Factories Acts can be matters of bitter controversy, and have been the cause of strikes.

In every establishment which they studied McCarthy and Coker found that managers used shop stewards "to communicate dissatisfaction over the observance of various rules and orders", such as rules on time-keeping, smoking or pilfering, and warnings of tightening up on discipline. Stewards were also asked to provide information on the extent of breaches of discipline. They always refused to name individuals, although it was common to give private warnings to individuals. In every instance the stewards acted as spokesmen for those facing disciplinary charges. In particular their aim was to have the penalty set aside or reduced, but in general they aimed to establish a set of precedents by which particular cases could be judged, and which they themselves were prepared to accept.[1] McCarthy also quotes an unpublished study by M. D. Plumridge to show that although there were wide differences between plants over the appropriate penalties for particular offences, the use of precedent led to consistency within the plants. This "helped to take the uncertainty and arbitrariness out of the most controversial and vague of rules—such as those governing insubordination and intoxication".[2]

Discipline is an area in which unacknowledged custom and practice can hold sway. In the London docks, for example, the

[1] *The Role of Shop Stewards in British Industrial Relations*, pp. 12–13.
[2] *Ibid.*, p. 18.

rule against smoking in holds of ships is widely disregarded by both dockers and supervisors. One supervisor justified this on the ground that the men were bound to smoke, and if he tried to enforce the rule they would be liable to drop burning cigarettes into the cargo when he approached, whereas if he disregarded the rule he could rely on them to stub out their cigarette ends and put them in a box which they carried in their pockets for the purpose. In these circumstances any attempt to enforce the rule by taking steps against an individual would amount to victimisation and would be treated as such by the dockers.

An even more delicate area of unacknowledged custom and practice is the pilfering common in a number of British industries, an aspect of industrial relations which has not yet been the subject of academic study. In this matter the docks again provide an example. It is said that in some ports there is a recognised percentage of certain cargoes which is expected to be lost in transit, and there have been strikes in which the dockers have protested victimisation even where a man has been caught in the act of stealing. On 19 January 1969 the *Sunday Telegraph* carried an article on the extensive pilferage from the Queen Elizabeth 2 while under construction.[1] "Stealing shipfittings", said the author, "is a Clydebank custom going back many years", and he quoted in support the defence offered in one instance of wholesale theft which came to court.[2] No one can say how widespread such customs are in British industry, but docks and shipbuilding are certainly not alone in providing examples. It is worth emphasising that customs of this kind can only persist with the acquiescence, not only of supervisors, but also of managers to quite a distance up the hierarchy of control. An equally delicate and little explored area of custom and practice is racial discrimination.

With the increasing rate of change in industrial organisation redundancy has become a more common issue in British industrial relations. Industry agreement have been negotiated in nationalised industries and public services, although in some instances, such as coalmining, these leave a good deal to be settled on the spot. In private industry a proposal for redundancy is almost invariably

---

[1] The article was entitled: "How to Steal an Ocean Liner—Scandal of Q.E.2 workers' spoils".

[2] "There was in this ship an atmosphere which tended to encourage this kind of conduct and there was a lack of discipline on the ship".

challenged by the stewards, but employers have been reluctant to develop agreed procedures for handling them. A number of firms have drawn up their own managerial policies, but the majority prefer *ad hoc* bargaining when the issue arises.[1] Their reluctance has been shared by many shop stewards, who tend to prefer worksharing to redundancy. There have been cases in which managers have not proceeded with proposals for redundancy in the face of shop-steward resistance. Instead they have tolerated a ban on overtime or even arranged for short-time working. In these circumstances the cut in earnings often achieves the objective of reducing the labour force, although the firm may lose those workers whom it most wished to keep, since the best workers are the most likely to be able to find other jobs.

Over the last few years two factors have altered the climate of redundancy negotiations. The first is the Redundancy Payments Act. By providing considerable payments in compensation to long-service workers dismissed through no fault of their own, the act encourages "voluntary redundancies". The company asks for volunteers to leave, and workers due for these payments may be tempted to step forward. Some firms add to the inducement by offering additional non-statutory compensation. Where this is done the firm may have to sacrifice some key workers, but the shop stewards can have little ground for obstructing the redundancy arrangements.

The second is the growing number of plant closures due to the increasing popularity of takeovers and mergers. In these circumstances the power of workers to obstruct their employers is narrowly limited. They can make difficulties for fulfilment of outstanding orders and the run-down of the plant, but that is all. They can also appeal to combine committees and to their trade unions, but trade union leaders appreciate the extreme difficulty of preventing the closure of a plant which managers have decided to be an economic necessity, and their view may be shared by shop stewards in other plants so long as they are not themselves included in any redundancy proposals. Consequently the interest of union leaders and stewards in other plants is not to obstruct but to negotiate for additional benefits, for transfers to other plants, for arrangements to seek alternative employment, and for supplementary unemployment payments while workers are look-

[1] See p. 195.

ing for new jobs. Closures have therefore led to interesting developments in plant bargaining in which managers have dealt simultaneously with shop stewards, full-time union district officers and national union leaders. An early example was described by Alan Fox.[1] In 1967-8 another example was provided by the closure of the A.E.I. plant at Woolwich, following the takeover by G.E.C., and since then proposals for closures and redundancies in engineering have led to a number of "composite conferences" in which managers have discussed the problem with representatives of all three groups at the same meeting.

THE CHARACTERISTICS OF DOMESTIC BARGAINING

In his evidence to the Royal Commission, Allan Flanders described what he called "intra-plant bargaining" as "largely informal, largely fragmented and largely autonomous".[2] To what extent can this be accepted as a characterisation of British domestic bargaining?

The characteristic on which it is most easy to come to a decision is autonomy. The evidence establishes beyond doubt that, generally speaking, trade union officers and employers' associations in Britain leave their shop stewards and constituent firms free to deal with their own problems so long as they themselves are not asked to intervene.

The extent of fragmentation is not so easily settled. In some industries, such as printing and steel, it is the rule. In some nationalised industries and public services it is the exception. In engineering and other nationalised industries there are forces working both for fragmentation and for unification, although the pressure for fragmentation is probably still the more powerful. One of these pressures is informality. It is possible for fragmentation to be formalised, as it is in steel and printing, and in the agreed engineering procedures. But generally the more informal the arrangements for domestic bargaining the more readily can groups and individuals act on their own if they please, whereas unification usually requires the support of recognised and agreed procedures and sanctions.

Informality is the most difficult of the characteristics to define. Flanders observes that "formal plant agreements, signed on

---

[1] *The Milton Plan*, 1965.   [2] *Selected Written Evidence*, p. 552.

behalf of unions by their full-time officials, have been mainly confined to non-federated firms in this country. Elsewhere, while there may be in fact some jointly agreed or tacitly accepted rules regulating relations between management and workers, they usually remain uncodified, or, if they appear in writing at all, in the minutes of meetings or perhaps in a statement of company policy".[1] Although there is a trend towards more elaborate codification, and signed plant agreements are becoming less rare in federated firms, this comment still remains generally true. But it suggests that unwritten arrangements are necessarily informal, whereas formality implies that an arrangement is explicit, not that it must be written down or signed. Putting in writing and adding signatures assist formality, but they are not essential to it. The procedures for industry bargaining in engineering and some other industries, for example, are not embodied in signed documents, but they are explicit, acknowledged and therefore formal; and this is also true of some of the procedures and arrangements of domestic bargaining. Arrangements are informal if they are not openly acknowledged.

The Royal Commission implied that the formal system of British industrial relations consists mainly of industry agreements, and that domestic bargaining constitutes an informal system. It went on to say that "the formal and informal systems are in conflict".[2] In some instances this is literally true, for instance where a joint consultative committee bargains over pay in breach of the limitations placed upon it in an industry agreement. More commonly, however, the conflict is between the assumptions of industry agreements and the practice of domestic bargaining. In the electricity generating station described on pp. 252–4 the procedures followed by the shop stewards did not seriously infringe the letter of the industry agreement. But in drawing up a constitution for works committees the industry negotiators had envisaged that the committee itself would settle domestic bargaining issues. Whereas in fact the stewards dominated domestic bargaining whether they were members of the works committee or not, and settled many issues outside the committee in direct dealings with management. If the Royal Commission conclusion is to be defended it must be on the ground that, in the past, the formal assumption of most industry bargaining has been that

---

[1] *Ibid.*, p. 552.   [2] *Report*, p. 36.

industry agreements on substantive and procedural matters provide the framework of industrial relations within which domestic bargaining takes place, whereas in practice a good deal of domestic bargaining lies outside this framework. In some industries the bulk of it does so; and in industries like engineering the industry agreements no longer provide even a framework.

Thus it is a formal assumption of industry bargaining that the major problems of overtime are solved by agreements on the length of the working week and on overtime rates of pay, together perhaps with some limit on overtime working. In practice the level and distribution of overtime are of equal or greater importance and are regulated entirely by domestic bargaining. The practice of domestic bargaining therefore conflicts with the assumptions of industry bargaining; and this is so even if the domestic rules on the level and distribution of overtime are entirely formalised. In that case a formal domestic arrangement is in conflict with the assumptions of the formal industry agreement.

Within domestic bargaining there is unquestionably a great deal of informality. Perhaps the best evidence of this is the prevalence and importance of customs and practices which are not openly acknowledged by managers. McCarthy and Coker found the "use of informal arrangements and customs to supplement and extend written agreements" so widespread that they diagnosed a "preference for informality in both the procedural and the substantive aspects of workshop bargaining" and sought to discover the reason for it by questions to managers and shop stewards.

Managers, they found, had four reasons. Concessions which were enjoyed through the grace of management would, if openly acknowledged, become established rights; even if the present stewards would not abuse openly acknowledge privileges, the next generation of stewards might do so; if the present arrangements were formalised, the stewards would seek a further set of informal privileges beyond them; and, "finally, some *de facto* concessions could not be written down because management, particularly at board level, would not be prepared to admit publicly that they had been forced to accept such modifications in their managerial prerogatives and formal chains of command". As examples of these concessions, McCarthy quoted "an understanding that no work change of any kind would be introduced without the prior agreement of shop stewards", and acceptance "that the senior steward could demand to see the works manager whenever he wished, and did not need to discuss matters first with subordinate management. Practices of this kind exist in many firms, but few managements would be prepared to say so in writing."[1]

These excuses confirm Alan Fox's view that many British managers do not fully accept collective bargaining as a means for the joint regulation of industrial relations.[2] They suggest that managers hope to keep the upper hand by avoiding too open a commitment to joint regulation. They also indicate a deep distrust by managers in their own ability to conduct effective collective bargaining with stewards, and to hold firm to any joint decision if the shop stewards wish to go beyond it.

McCarthy and Coker found the position of shop stewards to be more ambivalent. "In general they . . . do not seek to deny that their influence and status would be in some way advanced by a measure of codification" of procedural arrangements, and thus confirm some of the fears expressed by managers. On the other hand they were "by no means certain that they would benefit from the introduction of formalisation in the area of substantive agreements". In contrast to the managers they felt this might limit their scope to secure further concessions; some concessions could only be secured on the understanding that they would not be avowed; and through informality they could achieve understandings on matters which managers "maintain are not suitable for negotiation with shop stewards".[3]

Taken together with the well-established preference of managers for dealing with shop stewards rather than full-time union officers, when they have a choice between them, this evidence suggests that the informality of much domestic bargaining in Britain is primarily due to the attitudes and wishes of managers.

The Importance of Domestic Bargaining

Figures of wage drift are sometimes used to indicate the importance of domestic bargaining. There are a number of measures of drift. The Department of Employment and Productivity

---

[1] *The Role of Shop Stewards in British Industrial Relations*, pp. 27–8.   [2] See pp. 191–2.
[3] *The Role of Shop Stewards in British Industrial Relations*, pp. 28–9.

measures it by comparing the rates of change of average hourly earnings excluding overtime and of average hourly rates from one period to another. For example, between April 1954 and April 1955 average hourly earnings excluding overtime rose by 8·2 per cent and average hourly wage rates by 7·2 per cent. Drift, according to the Department's definition, was therefore 1 per cent.

These figures might suggest that of the increase of 8·2 per cent in earnings during that year, 7·2 per cent came from the upward adjustment of industry rates and only 1 per cent from domestic pay changes. But this would be true only if industry rates and average earnings had been equal at the beginning of the year. Where, as is almost universally the case among male wage-earners, earnings are higher than rates, earnings must show a larger cash increment than rates if earnings are to increase in the same proportion as rates. If earnings increase by a greater percentage than rates the difference in the cash increment must still be greater. Take, for example, an engineering fitter whose industry rate in 1963 was £10 1s. 2d, but whose earnings for a forty-hour week were £20 2s. 4d, by no means an exceptionally high figure. By April 1964 the industry rate was £10 11s. 8d, having increased by 5·2 per cent. If nothing else had changed his earnings would have been up by 2·6 per cent, and drift would, in the economists' jargon, have been negative. For his earnings to go up by 5·2 per cent would have required a cash increment to his earnings of 21s., of which 10s. 6d would have come from the industry increase and the rest from domestic changes. In that case there would have been no drift. To achieve drift of 1 per cent would have required a 6·2 per cent increase in his earnings or a cash increase of 25s.; 10s. 6d from the industry agreement and 14s. 6d from domestic changes. Consequently the official figure of drift does not give an accurate indication of the volume of domestic bargaining. In most British industries today zero drift is compatible with a powerful upward pressure on earnings in domestic bargaining, and positive drift suggests an even greater pressure. It is therefore evidence of a substantial and sustained growth of domestic bargaining that, in the fifteen years from April 1954 to April 1969, drift was positive in thirteen and negative only in two.[1]

The Royal Commission preferred to use figures for the gap between wage rates and earnings as their index of domestic

[1] The highest rate of drift was 2·7 per cent between April 1964 and April 1965

bargaining. This exaggerates the importance of the settlement and manipulation of pay at plant level. Shift differentials, for example, are not part of the minimum industry rates, and the extra earnings from shiftwork therefore help to widen the gap although they are for the most part determined by industry agreement. An increase in overtime rates by industry agreement also increases the gap although it has nothing to do with domestic bargaining. On the other hand an increase in overtime earnings will be due to workshop pressure if it is caused by work group limitations on the pace of work, or by the acceptance of a practice that an offer of overtime must be for a minimum period of so many hours. Consequently it is proper to include some overtime earnings in an index of domestic bargaining. No one could say how much.

A more fundamental objection to the use of drift or gap as indicators of the importance of workplace bargaining is that the real determinants of pay are the pressures of the labour market. On this view all that is measured by drift or gap is the opportunity given to domestic bargainers to look as though they were playing an important part in determining pay. However, it is impossible to explain many of the observed movements and relationships in pay by the demand for labour. An example is the distribution of earnings between workers in a group of forty firms from one industry in one locality studied by Derek Robinson. Of 77 occupations in these firms, "49 had a spread [in earnings] of more than 50 per cent, and 12 had a spread of more than 100 per cent. . . . In only two occupations was the spread of earnings less than 30 per cent". Changes in earnings over a period of two years were equally varied. "Increases in lorry drivers' average earnings ranged from 5·6 per cent to 38·1 per cent. . . . Bricklayers ranged from 8·4 per cent to 41·3 per cent and so on." There was no constant relationship between the size of the increase to an occupation and the changes in the numbers employed in that occupation. "Some firms were able to increase their labour force without greatly increasing wages relative to other firms, and without having to be at the top of the local earnings league-table. Some other firms did increase pay considerably and also increased their labour force, while yet other firms increased pay considerably but not the numbers employed."[1] This survey did not reveal the

---

[1] "Myths of the Local Labour Market", *Personnel*, December 1967.

labour market working according to inexorable laws of supply and demand for labour. The authors of *Labour Relations in the Motor Industry* noted that "the tendency for production operatives' earnings on payment-by-results systems to rise autonomously has pushed their wage so close to that of skilled workers that the difference is negligible, even if the latter are also on P.B.R.".[1] The National Board for Prices and Incomes has said of the engineering industry generally that "the actual structure of earnings within individual plants may give rise to differentials between different skills which may be so distorted or reversed as to cause as much concern on grounds of equity or justice as does the position of low-paid workers", and quotes several examples of "semi-skilled production workers . . . paid more than particular groups of skilled men in their plants".[2] Given the continuing shortage of skilled workers in post-war Britain it is not easy to explain these relationships as a consequence of labour market pressures.

Another instance is the relationship between men's pay and women's pay. Women's rates have risen sharply in comparison to men's rates since 1938, but in engineering and in many other manufacturing industries the relationship between the earnings of the two sexes has remained virtually unchanged.[3] This might be explained by a stable relationship between the marginal productivity of the two sexes which determines their relative pay whatever the negotiators may say. But sociologists might see the relative pay of men and women as a consequence of social values. Industry negotiators, swayed by a surface current towards equity, have sought to narrow differentials. Workshop negotiators, however, have continued to give expression to a deeply felt preference for male superiority. If the economic explanation were correct it would reveal the folly of men in striving, through pressure in piecework negotiations and control of overtime, to keep their relative earnings at a level which they were bound to retain anyway, and the wisdom of women in not concerning themselves with these matters.

However, even if the market were the only important influence determining pay movements and relationships, it would still be

---

[1] p. 158.
[2] *Pay and Conditions of Service of Engineering Workers* (First Report on the Engineering Industry), Report No. 49, Cmnd. 3495, 1967, pp. 10–11.   [3] See p. 227.

important for anyone concerned with social institutions that these movements are now more and more transmitted through plant mechanisms, for this affects the way men behave. Industry negotiators have come to concern themselves more and more with relative movements of earnings which seem to be determined at the plant. This concern is shared by governments and administrators interested in movements in pay. Newspapers, the public, employers, trade union leaders and shop stewards have all discerned an increase in the power of workshop organisation since the war, and made consequential adjustments in their behaviour.

It must also be remembered that pay is by no means the only subject of domestic bargaining. In this respect the use of drift and gap as indicators of workshop pressures exaggerate the change which has occurred since 1938. Even then workshop regulation, mainly through work group custom and practice, had a great influence on the organisation of work. Many of the developments since then can be seen as the outcome of this same work group control of the organisation of work, together with a strong managerial preference for informal arrangements, operating in an environment of full employment. And even the most convinced devotee of the iron laws of economics will admit that, by altering labour productivity, changes in the organisation of work can affect pay, and not only pay but also the whole economy.

DOMESTIC BARGAINING AMONG WHITE COLLAR WORKERS

White collar workers already constitute forty per cent of the labour force in Britain and will outnumber manual workers well before the end of the century. Although less well organised than manual workers, they provide more than a quarter of the country's trade union members and this proportion is growing rapidly. Collective bargaining among white collar workers, therefore, is bound to assume greater importance in relation to collective bargaining among manual workers; and domestic bargaining among white collar workers will also become relatively more important.

Nevertheless, very little is known about domestic bargaining among white collar workers. The Royal Commission surveys covered neither white collar unions nor the dealings between management and white collar representatatives. Their one research paper mainly concerned with white collar industrial relations[1] dealt primarily with the membership of white collar unions, the extent of their recognition by employers and the coverage of collective bargaining, but not with the content and procedures of collective bargaining. Other studies in this field, even studies of particular industries or professions, have tended to share the same interests.[2]

One reason for this neglect is the widespread view that there is little domestic bargaining on pay among white collar workers. There is some evidence for this. White collar trade unionism is heavily concentrated in national and local government service and in education. Outside the public sector, and apart from the relatively small numbers employed in "theatres, cinemas, sport, etc.", it has achieved its highest density in "insurance, banking and finance". The Royal Commission lists national and local government service and education among the industries in which "existing industry-wide rates are generally followed", and financial services among the industries for which "there is not sufficient information available to justify any estimate of the relationship between nationally determined rates and actual levels of pay".[3] Moreover, it seems that it is not the practice to appoint "shop stewards" or their equivalent in white collar unions in national and local government, and in education.[4] Such domestic bargaining as is required is carried on by branch officers. But the matter has not been investigated by any national survey, nor is anything known for certain about the extent of domestic bargaining on issues other than pay, such as recruitment, promotion, the quality, speed and distribution of work, the staffing of offices, transfers and redundancies.

There are indications that the picture is different in private manufacturing industry. Some of the white collar unions which operate there appoint office representatives, such as Draughtsmen's

---

[1] *Trade Union Growth and Recognition.*

[2] For example R. M. Blackburn's study of unionism in the banks (*Union Character and Social Class*, 1967) does not deal with the handling of individual and group grievances and problems as a matter which might influence union growth.

[3] Royal Commission, *Report*, Appendix 5.

[4] This was the finding of a survey of trade union branches in the Oxford area conducted as a pilot study for *Trade Union Officers*.

"corresponding members". The white collar sections of manual workers' unions also appoint stewards in some of the offices which they organise. The Royal Commission reported that white collar workers in those few private manufacturing industries in which there are industry agreements on white collar pay, "for example in engineering and paper and printing, usually receive actual rates of pay well in excess of basic rates".[1] Further information on this point is given in the first report of the National Board for Prices and Incomes, on the *Pay and Conditions of Service of Engineering Workers*.[2] The Board carried out an earnings survey of white collar workers in the industry during June 1967, and some of the results are set out in Table X.

It is clear that overtime is responsible for only a relatively small part of the considerable differences between the industry scales and the actual earnings, and bonus and other payments provide only a few shillings a week.[3] The remainder of the difference is accounted for by the salary scales settled in the individual firm or plant. The Board's analysis of its figures suggested that these scales differed widely from one undertaking to another. For instance, among male clerical staff described as carrying "considerable responsibility", who might therefore be expected to be at or near the top of their respective scales, 18·9 per cent earned less than £20 a week whereas 13·2 per cent earned more than £30. Similarly wide ranges of earnings were found among clerical staff with "some responsibility", among clerical staff with only "routine responsibility", among draughtsmen and technicians, and among supervisors. For supervisors, however, there is no industry scale. The agreement which covers them, negotiated with the Association of Scientific, Technical and Managerial Staffs, merely recognises the union where it has "a majority membership in a particular grade in any establishment operated by a constituent member of the Employers' Federation". Where it can prove majority membership the union is entitled to negotiate a salary scale. Otherwise supervisors' salary scales are at the discretion of the employer, as also those of clerical staff, draughtsmen and technicians where their unions have no members.

The several unions negotiate separately with the Employers'

[1] Royal Commission, *Report*, Appendix 5.
[2] *Pay and Conditions of Engineering Workers (First Report)*, Appendix J.
[3] Over all grades bonus averaged 4s. 6d. a week and "other payments" 3s. 9d.

Federation. Enquiries among a number of engineering firms suggest that separate negotiations are common also in individual plants, and that there are some plants in which scales have been negotiated for some grades while scales for other grades are laid down by management. As the best-organised grade, draughtsmen have negotiated scales even where technicians and clerical staff have not.

TABLE X

EARNINGS OF ENGINEERING WHITE COLLAR WORKS (MEN), JUNE 1967

Occupational Group	Industry Salary Scale	Average Weekly Earnings	Average Over-time Worked (hours)	Average Overtime Pay
Clerical staff	£2.18.9d at 15 years old to £10.12.6d at 21	£20.8.8d	3·3	£1.15.3d
Draughtsmen and Allied Technicians	£15 at 21 years old to £22.10.0d at 30	£25.10.8d	2·0	£1.7.1d
Other Technicians and Technologists	£10.18.0d at 21 years old to £13.6.6d at 21	£25.15.7d	2·3	£1.8.8d
Supervisors	—	£27.12.6d	4·0	£2.11.10d

We know little about the relative importance of full-time officers and office representatives in these negotiations. The impression is that full-time officers play a more important part in domestic bargaining for white collar workers than they do among manual workers. Certainly the draughtsmen, the best-organised and most "militant" group, seem to respect the official procedures far more than manual workers. They strike more frequently than other white collar workers, but their strikes are normally constitutional and official. Whereas strike pay in manual workers' unions ranges between £3 and £5 a week, the Draughts-men's and Allied Technicians' Association pays at the rate of basic salary so that its members have more to lose by striking unofficially than have manual workers. However, in 1967 the Draughtsmen developed a new technique—"work without en-thusiasm". It proved very successful in their dispute with Pressed Steel Fisher investigated by a committee of the Motor Industry Joint Labour Council in 1967. The committee reported that "the sanctions applied have been harsh and as a result it seems that in some drawing offices very little work was being produced al-though employees continued to receive full salary". The same technique was subsequently applied with success in Coventry and elsewhere in the West Midlands. The draughtsmen concerned were independent of their union's financial backing and it was not always clear that the union was in full control of the disputes.

Consequently there is no certainty that increasing unionisation among white collar workers will bring a return to industry control of pay movements. Private manufacturing industry is the most fertile area for the growth of white collar unions, and its industry agreements for white collar workers seem to be of little more importance in the determination of their salaries than are industry agreements in determining the pay of manual workers.

In one respect negotiations for white collar workers are even more fragmented than for manual workers. In engineering there is no industry agreement on conditions of service other than pay. The length of the working week and of the annual holidays are settled plant by plant. According to the National Board for Prices and Incomes, "success of the unions and in particular D.A.T.A. in conducting 'guerilla' tactics, especially in relation to the claim for a fourth week's annual holiday, influenced the [Employers'] Federation to propose a charter of standard con-ditions of employment to the staff unions at a conference on 31 August 1966. After a series of conferences no basis of agreement could be found. . . . The unions' main objection . . . is that it would rule out domestic bargaining on conditions. They say they are not prepared to have their members shackled to the pace of the slower and most inefficient firms."[1]

[1] *Pay and Conditions of Service of Engineering Workers (First Report)*, pp. 29–30.

Non-Federated Firms

For the purpose of this section a "non-federated" firm is defined as a company which is not party to an industry (or a district) agreement between an employers' association and a union or unions, whether or not the company is affiliated with an association for other purposes, and even though these purposes might include the discussion of industrial relations issues and the co-ordination of policy on personnel matters. This qualification is of some importance now that several firms, including I.C.I., are members of individual employers' associations for everything but collective negotiations with the unions, and that other firms not federated with any individual employers' association are affiliated to the Confederation of British Industry. There are many thousands of non-federated firms, the great majority of them small. Most of these and some larger non-federated firms do not recognise trade unions and have no dealings with them. It is the remainder with which this section is mainly concerned.

A few firms, again including I.C.I., have withdrawn from employers' associations in order to pursue their own industrial relations policies.[1] But most of the larger non-federated firms which have dealings with the unions have never been federated. When the occasion arose for collective dealings with trade unions they decided that they could serve their needs best by negotiating on their own. Ford is an example. Originally they were un-federated because they did not wish to deal with trade unions. Membership of the Engineering Employers' Federation would have entailed recognition of the unions. When a combination of government persuasion and trade union pressure brought Ford managers to the negotiating table, they decided that they could still do better outside the Federation. Similarly when, one after another, the oil companies began to deal with the unions concerning pay and conditions in their refineries, they did not wish to do so collectively. A number of other American-owned companies have followed the same path as Ford and Esso, in many instances for the same reasons, that union recognition came

---

[1] In 1935 I.C.I. left the Chemical and Allied Employers' Association to pay its employees rates higher than those settled by the industry's joint industrial council. After the war it allied itself with the association once more, but continued to negotiate its own agreements with the unions.

late and when it came the company decided to proceed on its own. Probably their decisions were influenced by the structure of collective bargaining in the United States, where plant or company agreements are the rule in manufacturing industry. It would, however, be unwise to conclude that American companies are implacably opposed to federation among their overseas affiliates. Many American firms with unfederated British affiliates have continental affiliates which are federated, as is Ford in Germany.

Federated firms adjust to their industry procedures as best they can. Non-federated firms can negotiate procedures to suit themselves. Consequently their procedures are generally set out in fuller detail than domestic procedures in federated firms. On the company's side the signatory is in most instances the company itself, although some companies prefer to negotiate plant by plant. On the union side it is signed by either district or national full-time officers, who are also brought into the procedure for settling disputes, whereas many industry procedures make no provision for full-time officers to come in until the issue has left the hands of the company for those of its association.

If a federated company wants to increase the level of its pay it may have to permit overtime to rise, or allow work-study standards to slacken, or grant general "merit" payments, in order to disguise its action from other employers. A non-federated firm is not under the same obligation. Incomes policy apart, it can negotiate a straight increase in wage rates when it chooses. In its report on the 1963 agreements in the engineering and shipbuilding industries, the National Incomes Commission commented on the settlements which had been made in three non-federated firms at about the same time as the industry agreements. The firms were Ford, Vauxhall and Rubery Owen. The Commission found Ford's "methods of controlling their wage structure are particularly worthy of note". There was no payment by results. Merit payments were "within the exclusive discretion of the Company", and "awarded only in respect of proved qualities which conduce to the greater productive efficiency of the concern as a whole". Consequently "any negotiated increase in rates is the increase in actual earnings and the company are free, at any rate internally, from the complication of wage drift". Similarly Vauxhall, having "changed over to a basis of fully consolidated time

rates with no provision for any form of payment by results",
was also free from internal wage drift.[1]

This account exaggerated the degree of order in the two wage
structures. Overtime was not mentioned, and, when Ford was
subsequently forced into a general merit payment for toolmakers,
it emerged that merit payments had already been made for reasons
other than the reward of "proved qualities" conducive to
efficiency. Nevertheless, the situation at Ford and Vauxhall was,
and still is, in strong contrast to that in the car firms of the West
Midlands. Not all non-federated firms, however, make use of
their freedom to negotiate well-controlled pay structures. The
Commission's third company, Rubery Owen, paid their direct
workers by results. The earnings of these workers grew until
they "substantially exceeded the earnings of the time workers
[indirect workers], with the result that the Company found
themselves compelled to increase their . . . rates for the latter . . .
in order to reach some degree of assimilation between the earnings
of the two types of worker".[2] This is a familiar situation in
federated undertakings. Before its productivity agreements of
1960 the unfederated Esso refinery at Fawley had negotiated time
rates only, but these rates did not determine the earnings of the
men. In addition there were the payments arising from substantial
overtime working, which was not "at the discretion" of the
management. In 1948 the Standard Motor Company withdrew
from the Engineering Employers' Federation and "introduced its
so-called 'large-gang' system" of piecework, the result of "two
years of negotiation with its shop stewards". The hope of management was that this group piecework arrangement "would make
it easier to introduce new production methods". One consequence was to push "average earnings at Standard substantially
above the average for the industry",[3] and since then the upward
drift of piecework earnings at Standard has not been noticeably
less than drift under other piecework systems in the Coventry
Area. The non-federated Steel Company of Wales developed a
wage structure at least as complicated, uncontrolled and fragmented as those in other steel companies.

In a federated firm this sort of pay structure might be seen as

---

[1] National Incomes Commission, *Agreements of November–December 1963 in the Engineering and Shipbuilding Industries*, Cmnd. 2583, 1965, pp. 105–7.
[2] *Ibid.*, p. 109.   [3] *Labour Relations in the Motor Industry*, 1967, pp. 97–8.

the consequence of federation in conditions of full employment. If non-federated firms are free to act differently, why do many of them not do so? One answer is that the "club spirit" of employers is not confined within employers' associations. Any firm which agrees to an exceptionally large increase in rates of pay is liable to criticism from other employers, whether the consequence is an exceptionally high level of earnings or not; and the devices which allow earnings to rise faster than rates are as available to a non-federated firm as to a federated firm, if it chooses to use them. Consequently for a non-federated firm to exercise its freedom to conduct negotiation in a manner different from federated firms requires a conscious determination to resist the pressures which operate on them both. What has distinguished industrial relations in non-federated firms in recent years is not so much that their negotiating arrangements and pay structures have been superior to those of federated firms from the beginning, but that their managers have had greater freedom to recast their industrial relations when they chose to do so. Several non-federated firms were among the pioneers of productivity bargaining.

Before turning to that subject, there are two further points to be made about non-federated firms. Firstly, no general study has been made of their industrial relations, so that although something can be said about several large non-federated firms, there is very little basis for generalisation about methods of negotiation and agreements in the general run of non-federated firms which deal with unions. Secondly non-federated firms which do not recognise trade unions may have internal representative committees elected by their employees, with which management can consult. One of the most prominent of these is Kodak, a subsidiary of an American company, which first established an elected committee in its Harrow factory in 1942, and now has seven of them in different parts of its undertaking, covering between them over twelve thousand employees. In its written evidence to the Royal Commission the company said that it was "difficult to envisage the day-to-day working of the organisation without the existence of representatives of employees, who can be consulted on matters affecting employees, or with whom negotiations can be carried out".[1] The company thus saw its dealings with these committees

[1] Royal Commission, *Minutes of Evidence*, p. 2896.

s a form of domestic bargaining, and its spokesman went on to
ell the commission that the committees "had sufficient independence to provide a safeguard" for the employees in their dealings
with managers.[1] Trade unions, however, deny this. They insist
that there can be no real bargaining except where independent
and external trade unions are recognised. As to pay, the outcome
of the 'negotiation" is a "general level of wages . . . set in relation
to wages paid in the community and nationally by companies of
similar standing to Kodak and generally known as good employers".[2] Nothing is known about the number of firms which
operate committees of this kind for manual workers. But a
considerable number operate staff associations for white collar
staff, even firms which recognise manual workers' unions.

PRODUCTIVITY BARGAINING

In the past work practices have rarely been regulated by industry
agreements, but in some industries this is not for want of trying.
Over seventy years a succession of attempts have been made in
engineering to ensure by agreement that methods of work should
be determined by management. The 1898 agreement gave
managers the "right" to determine what grade of worker should
operate a given machine. The 1915 "Treasury agreement" dealt
with the same issue by allowing unfettered "dilution" of skilled
work in munitions and by laying aside, for the duration of the
war, all pre-war practices. The 1922 agreement gave managers
the "right" to decide on overtime working (within ill-defined
over-all limits) and to introduce changes in work practices subject
to the review by procedure of any objections from the workers
—after the event. The agreement of 1957 committed the unions
to cease support for a whole list of limitations on efficient working
in return for a general increase in pay. It had no noticeable effect,
but in 1968 a so-called productivity agreement bound the unions
to put an end to a number of restrictions on the freedom of
managers to determine working methods in return for substantial
pay increases.[3]

[1] *Ibid.*, Q. 10966. The witness added "If you had to control 12,000 of them [the em-
ployees] you would soon know".
[2] *Ibid.*, p. 2897.
[3] The unions undertook "to ensure that at all levels their Committees and their members
accept all appropriate and recognised techniques for analysing and evaluating methods of

At plant level bargaining over work practices is no novelty. By itself the Treasury agreement of 1915 achieved little dilution of skilled labour, but results began to come in during the following year. Dilution Commissioners appointed to achieve progress found that they could do so only by negotiating with committees of shop stewards, plant by plant. Since then piecemeal change in working practices in return for pay concessions has been a feature of plant bargaining for many years. The acceptance of a new machine, or of a reduction in manning, has been accompanied by a slackening of piecework standards to allow earnings to increase, or by additional merit money, or by up-grading. When the National Board for Prices and Incomes began to investigate productivity agreements several companies came forward to offer evidence concerning agreements to introduce "new methods of work . . . in a single department, or for a single group of workers" which "were being made long before the term productivity agreement was coined", and to ask the Board to agree, as it did, that "it may be appropriate to reward these with increases in pay".[1]

Consequently the novelty of the 1960 productivity agreements at Esso's Fawley refinery was not that this was the first occasion on which work practices were mentioned in an agreement, or that it was the first exchange of alterations in work practices for increases in pay. What was new was the negotiation with workshop representatives of all the unions concerned, of a series of changes in work practices throughout the plant and their embodiment in a formal agreement with the unions.[2] There were also lesser novelties. It was one of the first instances of a company publicly admitting that it had been using overtime as a means of achieving an acceptable level of pay rather than to get work done. Rarely if ever before had attention been publicly drawn to opportunities

production", and "to co-operate fully in eliminating impediments to efficient utilisation of labour". Examples of such impediments were given, and included "inappropriate and uneconomic use of labour" and "resistance to the planned use of working hours". The agreement limited "improvements in pay and conditions at domestic level" to circumstances where "there is a measured increase in labour productivity or efficiency to which the efforts of the workers concerned have contributed", or a new comprehensive evaluated wage structure, or where pay is "out of line with prevailing wage patterns", but set up no machinery to enforce this limitation.

[1] *Productivity and Pay During the Period of Severe Restraint*, Report No. 23, Cmnd. 3167, 1966, p. 10.

[2] The classic account of these agreements is *The Fawley Productivity Agreements*.

'or flexibility among maintenance craftsmen. The extent of ɪnderemployment among craftsmen's mates had not previously ɔeen a matter of public debate, nor had the inefficiencies which ꞓan result from demarcation lines between process workers as well as among craftsmen.

The Fawley agreements were intended to cut overtime back from 18 per cent of total hours worked to 2 per cent among maintenance staff and 6 per cent among process workers. Hourly ɽates of pay were increased so that the average weekly earnings would be higher than before, even when the overtime cuts had been achieved. The reduction in overtime was not to lead to ɪncreased employment but was to be covered by more effective ɯse of manpower. Each craft agreed to "flexibility" whereby its members could do some jobs previously reserved for other crafts. The craftsmen also agreed to dispense with mates, who were to be retrained for other jobs. The process workers agreed ɬo versatility between grades. It was expected that improved ɛfficiency would allow a greater throughput so that the company could not only cover the increased rates of pay but also achieve a reduction in labour costs.[1] Generally all these aims were achieved after the agreement came into force, although subsequently overtime rose well above the new target.[2]

During the six years following the Fawley agreements Esso negotiated settlements on somewhat similar lines at other undertakings, and a further productivity agreement at Fawley. Meanwhile a number of other oil firms, several chemical companies, one or two transport and manufacturing concerns and the electricity supply industry had negotiated or begun to negotiate productivity agreements which contained many of the same features, several of them in conscious imitation of Fawley. Some

[1] The National Board for Prices and Incomes emphasised that this and other productivity agreements were not merely the "buying out of restrictive practices". The "starting-point of most agreements has not been a list of proposed changes in working practices and in pay, but the preparation by management of plans for new and more effective methods of operation for the whole plant or company. Only when these have been drawn up and explored can a company know what particular changes in practice are most needed and what alterations in pay are feasible" (*Productivity Agreements*, p. 3).

[2] In 1966 overtime averaged about 15 per cent among process workers and 10 per cent among maintenance staff (*Ibid.*, p. 51). The Board went on to outline the special reasons which had led the refinery management to re-introduce overtime working. It had "not been caused by pressure from the workers" (pp. 26–7).

also introduced new features. Alcan's Rogerstone plant and I.C.I. had previously made use of payment by results. They now decided that these payments were no longer justified by their incentive effects. They therefore sought to consolidate them, along with overtime earnings, in the new rates of pay. In addition, they wished to reduce the number of grades of worker and to reassess the grades, not only because separate grades lead to inflexibility in the use of labour but also because it was thought that some grades were not adequately paid in relation to the others. Job evaluation was used for the reassessments. At Rogerstone and in some other agreements the rates for the most skilled process workers were levelled up to those of the craftsmen.

In addition to their complex changes in work practices and pay structures these productivity agreements also contained several other characteristics unusual in British collective bargaining and running counter to the general trends of the last thirty years. Consolidation of overtime pay, payment by results and other additional payments have diminished or closed the gap between rates and earnings. Where the new overtime levels have been held—the National Prices and Incomes Board found no other instance of backsliding besides Fawley—further increases in earnings cannot arise from drift, but only from negotiated increases in rates of pay. Consequential benefits for workers are that that their income is more secure, not subject to fluctuation with changes in output, and that fringe benefits related to basic pay, such as holiday pay, are automatically brought nearer to actual earnings. The wage becomes more akin to "a salary". The electricity industry emphasised this feature by calling its agreements "status agreements", intended to raise the status of the manual worker to that of the white collar worker.

In most cases the negotiation of flexibility and new pay structures has involved simultaneous or common negotiations with the representatives of several different unions. Thus comprehensive agreements have replaced fragmented bargaining, at least for manual workers. Most of the companies concerned do not recognise white collar unions, and in them the reorganisation of white collar work and pay which has followed or preceded many productivity agreements has not been negotiated. In electricity supply there were consequential negotiations to increase the salaries of clerical and administrative staff, and these included some changes in methods of work. But these negotiations were quite separate from the original productivity agreements. There have also been some productivity agreements in white collar industries.[1]

Open negotiation over a wide range of work practices has made the scope of formal agreement far wider than in other undertakings. In most instances it has also brought about changes in bargaining methods. As a general rule work practices can only be effectively negotiated with the shop stewards, whereas basic rates of pay must be negotiated with full-time officers. By including both work practices and basic rates in a single agreement, productivity bargaining brings shop stewards and full-time officers together into the same bargaining. This has three consequences. Shop stewards take a recognised place in the negotiation of formal agreements, full-time officers take a more prominent part in plant negotiations than is common in British industrial relations, and full-time officers and shop stewards see more of each other than is usual. Because of this, productivity agreements "place a special strain upon internal union communications" and "make heavy demands on the time and energy of union officers".[2]

Many of the early productivity agreements were in non-federated undertakings, and some federated undertakings withdrew from their associations before opening negotiations.[3] More recently some employers' associations have re-negotiated industry agreements to offer encouragement to plant or productivity agreements.[4] In any event productivity bargaining has placed a far greater emphasis on formal agreements at plant and company level than has been common in Britain in the past.

The exception to this was the electricity supply industry in which a series of productivity agreements were signed at industry level. This, however, is a nationalised industry with only fifteen employing authorities—the Central Electricity Generating Board, twelve area distribution boards in England and Wales, and the two Scottish boards. Its industrial relations have been highly

---

[1] One of these, covering the Co-operative Insurance Society, is described in *Productivity Agreements*, p. 74. Subsequently the Board published a second report on *Productivity Agreements*, Report No. 123, Cmnd. 4136, 1969 (henceforth *Productivity Agreements, Second Report*). Chapter 5 dealt with agreements covering non-manual workers.

[2] *Productivity Agreements*, pp. 28–9.

[3] See pp. 151–2.   [4] See pp. 152–4.

L

centralised for many years. Even so the implementation of the agreement varied from one authority to another.[1]

Finally the agreements brought about changes in management. In order to prepare for them, managers had to collect information about performance in their undertakings which had previously been lacking, and turn their minds to the possibility of changing methods of work. "Because far more managers were brought into the process [of negotiation] than in conventional negotiations many of them were made closely aware for the first time of the consequences for industrial relations of technical and financial decisions." In addition, the application of the agreements brought "a revolution in managerial control over working hours and practices in many of the undertakings affected".[2]

At the end of 1966 the National Board for Prices and Incomes estimated that productivity agreements "have probably affected no more than half a million workers", and the majority of these must have been in electricity supply, chemicals and the oil industry. By that time, however, the prices and incomes policy introduced in 1965 was beginning to have an effect on the whole process of productivity bargaining. Discussion of further developments is therefore deferred to Chapter 11.

---

[1] In the Central Electricity Generating Board average hours of work fell from 51 to 39 a week. In distribution the overall average fell from almost 49 to 43, with area averages varying from 40–45 hours. Changes in working practices were fairly widely accepted in generation, and there was some changes in every distribution board, but "in a few Boards small and fragmentary gains were overshadowed by some major disappointments". (*Productivity Agreements*, pp. 59–60.)

[2] *Ibid.*, p. 25.

CHAPTER 8

STRIKES

Strike Statistics

Stoppages of work due to disputes appear to be a readily measurable aspect of industrial relations and therefore a suitable subject for statistical comparison and analysis. Consequently students of industrial relations and newspaper readers are accustomed to comparisons of the number of stoppages and the number of working days lost through stoppages[1] during a period, from one period to another, from one country to another, and from one industry to another.

This suitability for statistical handling is due to the standard units which are used. Comparisons of pay, by contrast, are tricky. If pay in one industry is higher than in another, the reason may be the higher level of overtime in the first, or the higher proportion of skilled workers in the labour force. If so it may be possible to argue that the first industry is really less well paid than the second, since a comparison of hourly earnings, or of weekly earnings grade by grade, could put it in second place. International comparisons of pay are even more troublesome, for comparisons of money units are meaningless, and there are a number of snags in converting different currencies into a common standard. But strike statistics seem to avoid these difficulties. A hundred strikers are twice fifty strikers, and a working day in one industry is much the same unit as a working day in another industry, or another country.

Nevertheless there are problems about the use of these figures. How big does a strike have to be before it is worth measuring? At what point does an argument between a dozen workers and their foreman constitute a stoppage of work? If a lunch-time

---

[1] The number of working days is obtained by multiplying the number of workers stopped at the establishment or establishments on strike by the number of working days for which the stoppage lasts.

meeting called by shop stewards runs on into working time, is it a strike? The Department of Employment and Productivity tries to record and classify all strikes which involve ten or more workers and which last for at least one day, or which lose more than a hundred working days in all. It is highly probable that many strikes too small to be caught by this net occur each year. Then there is accuracy of reporting. There is no statutory obligation upon employers to report stoppages, and each year a number of strikes which fulfil the Department's conditions escape the notice of its regional officers.

The car industry provides examples of the difference between the official figures for strikes and those known to have taken place. Professor Turner and his colleagues note that "strikes recorded over a recent twelve-month period by B.M.C. at all its plants total 226—as against thirty-seven publicly recorded."[1] They give similar figures for several other car manufacturers. In his account of the work of the Motor Industry Joint Labour Council in December 1967, Sir Jack Scamp drew upon information supplied by the eight major car firms as they then were, to report that "60 per cent of all stoppages lasted for less than four hours and nearly three-quarters for no more than one working day".[2] Clearly the official figures do not give a complete picture of disputes in this industry.

On the other hand it is believed that the reporting of stoppages which meet the Department's definitions is a good deal more thorough in the nationalised industries, including the National Coal Board, in which all stoppages are reported to its head office and thence to the Department. Consequently one of the reasons for the prominence of the coalmining industry in post-war strikes is the greater accuracy of its reporting.

If accuracy of reporting can differ from one industry to another in one country, differences between countries are even more likely, and there is also the problem that the standards adopted for a reportable strike and the industrial coverage of strike statistics differ from country to country. These differences, however, mainly affect small strikes. The larger the strike the more certain it is to be reported. Small strikes necessarily make a small contribution to the number of working days lost. Consequently,

[1] *Labour Relations in the Motor Industry*, pp. 52–3.
[2] *Report by Sir Jack Scamp, D.L., J.P., on the Activities of the Council*, 1968.

although comparisons of the number of strikes between industries and between countries must be treated with some reserve, comparisons of the number of working days lost present a more accurate picture.

At one time an attempt was made to distinguish a strike, a stoppage in which workers refuse to continue work until some demand is met, from a lockout, a stoppage in which one or more employers refuse to continue workers in employment until they agree to accept a change in their terms and conditions of employment. The attempt failed because a number of stoppages could not be classified unambiguously under the one heading or the other.[1] In any case stoppages which have any claim to be considered lockouts are rare today.

The official statistics do not cover other forms of pressure, such as the "work to rule", the "go slow" and the overtime ban. There is evidence to show that these are common in Britain today, and because much less was heard of them in the past it may be inferred that they have become more common in the post-war period. This must be true of the overtime ban, which can flourish only in a period in which regular overtime is widespread.

Examples of the use of sanctions are given in the Cameron Report. Between August 1965 and November 1966 there were six strikes at Myton's Barbican site, six go-slows, and one half-day protest march. Between March 1965 and October 1966 the Horseferry Road site experienced twenty strikes, five embargoes on overtime, two instances of "work-to-rule" and one refusal of a group of workers to operate a bonus scheme.[2] The Royal Commission's surveys provide more general information. Shop stewards were asked whether there had been any withdrawal of labour at their place of work since they became stewards,[3] and what other forms of pressure had been used. Forty per cent of them said there had been at least one strike at their place of work, 42 per cent said there had been bans on overtime, 28 per cent that working to rule had been employed, and 12 per cent that there had been "go-slows". Among managers 30 per cent had experienced strikes, and 33 per cent overtime bans, since their

---

[1] In this book the words "strike" and "stoppage of work" are synonymous. A lockout is treated as a special kind of stoppage.

[2] *Report of a Court of Inquiry into trade disputes at the Barbican and Horseferry Road construction sites in London*, pp. 23–4.

[3] The average period for which they had held office was six years.

appointment to their current posts. Working to rule and "go-slows" scored 18 per cent each.[1] The Commission concluded that "overtime bans may be as frequent as strikes—a reflection of the extensive use of overtime in this country"; and that "industrial disharmony manifests itself in overt action on the shop floor more frequently than the official statistics imply".[2]

Although not recorded as stoppages these sanctions may be almost indistinguishable from strikes in their effects. Where a go-slow, or "working without enthusiasm" among draughtsmen, results in no work being done, the sanction becomes a "stay-in" strike except that the employer is expected to continue paying wages so long as he does not dismiss the workers concerned.

Bearing in mind these qualifications, it is possible to give a rough picture of the pattern of strikes in Britain today and to make broad comparisons with the past and with other countries.

Between 1891 and 1926 a yearly average of about seventeen million working days were lost in strikes and there were on the average rather more than seven hundred strikes a year. Since 1927, although the labour force has continued to expand, the average number of working days lost has fallen to three million a year but the average number of strikes has been much higher than in earlier years, at about 1500 a year. During the twelve years 1956–68 the average loss of working days has risen a little to about four million and the number of strikes has risen considerably to nearly 2500. Before 1927 a small number of industry-wide stoppages, especially in coalmining, cotton, engineering and shipbuilding, accounted for the lion's share of working days lost. Between 1916 and 1926, for example, industry-wide stoppages accounted for 305 million working days lost out of a total of 357 million.[3] Even now a small number of major strikes account for a large share of working days lost.

One factor in the comparison between the last thirty years and the period before 1927 is the effect of unemployment. There has been a strong tendency for the loss of working days to be high in depression years when employers may not be too anxious

---

[1] *Workplace Industrial Relations*, pp. 32–4, 83–4. Among the personnel managers, employed mainly in larger plants, the proportion reporting experience of each kind of pressure was higher than among the works managers.

[2] *Report*, pp. 99–100.

[3] H. A. Clegg "Some Consequences of the General Strike", *Manchester Statistical Society*, January 1954.

to get their men back to work until stocks are depleted, and for the number of strikes to rise in years of high employment when it is easier to put pressure upon employers. But that is not the whole story, for the sharp decline in working days lost began in 1927, more than a decade before the era of full employment began. Whatever the explanation, the average strike is now very much smaller and shorter than it was before 1927, or even before the war. If the figures covered all stoppages of work, and not only those which fall within the official definition and happen to be reported, the trend towards smaller and shorter strikes would probably be even more marked. The strikes which are not reported are the smallest and shortest strikes, and if there is a notable increase in the small and short strikes which are reported, it is a reasonable inference that there is an equivalent or greater increase in the number of strikes which are so small and short as to escape the net.

The Royal Commission published a table comparing the strike record of fifteen countries[1] for the years 1964–6, together with a number of footnotes drawing attention to differences in coverage and definition.[2] The figures of strikes and of working days lost are given in Table XI.

To the extent that comparisons between these figures can be trusted they show Britain's annual loss of working days to be modest, ninth out of fifteen countries.[3] In the number of stoppages we come rather higher, sixth. A further examination of the table reveals three groups of countries. In the lower half are seven countries, Finland, Japan, Belgium, Denmark, the Netherlands, Norway and Sweden, in which strikes are relatively infrequent and losses of working days relatively small. In the top half comes another group of five countries, Australia, Italy, Ireland, Canada

[1] The Federal Republic of Germany is also included in the Royal Commission table but neither of the relevant columns of figures contain an entry for that country.

[2] p. 95.

[3] In *Is Britain Really Strike-Prone?*, 1969, H. A. Turner concluded that "the Donovan Commission's analysis of the comparative *frequency* between countries of strikes must be regarded as almost worthless" (p. 10). His main reason is that the other countries included in the table (for which the relevant information is available) "appear to define strikes in a way which is rather more restricted than the British definition" (p. 9). If this were true the application of the British definition to their experience would bring Britain lower down the table. However, it does not seem to be true. Where the information is available it shows that the definitions of the other countries are for the most part less restrictive than that of Britain, so that if a common standard had been adopted Britain might well be nearer the top of the table.

and the United States with relatively heavy losses of working days and a relatively large number of stoppages. Britain comes with France and New Zealand in the top half of the table for number of stoppages and below the middle point for working days lost.[1] For what it is worth, then, the table suggests that in recent years British strikes have been smaller and shorter than those of other countries which, like Britain, have a relatively high number of strikes a year.

TABLE XI

INTERNATIONAL COMPARISONS OF STRIKE STATISTICS,
AVERAGE ANNUAL FIGURES FOR 1964–66

Country	No. of Stoppages per 100,000 Employees	No. of Working days Lost per 1000 Employees
Australia	63·8	400
Italy	32·9	1170
New Zealand	26·8	150
Republic of Ireland	25·6	1620
France	21·8	200
United Kingdom	16·8	190
Canada	15·8	970
United States	13·2	870
Finland	10·8	80
Japan	7·6	240
Belgium	7·0	200
Denmark	5·5	160
Netherlands	2·2	20
Norway	0·6	Less than 10
Sweden	0·5	40

For several recent years the Department has distinguished between official strikes and unofficial strikes, the latter being strikes which have not been sanctioned by the appropriate union authority. Their figures show that over 95 per cent of strikes during 1964–6 were unofficial, and only about 3 per cent official.[2] The official strikes, however, accounted for 30 per cent of the working days lost. Although figures of unofficial strikes are

[1] France is actually at the middle point for working days lost.
[2] A small number were "partly official" (approved by at least one but not all of the unions concerned) or lockouts, or strikes by unorganised workers, or "unclassified" (Royal Commission, *Report*, p. 97.).

available for only two previous years,[1] there is very little doubt that the proportion of unofficial strikes has risen with the decline in the size and duration of strikes, for nearly all very large strikes have always been official, and all available information suggests that official strikes account for a disproportionate share of working days lost. It is also a reasonable inference that, although countries abroad do not make this distinction in their statistics, the unofficial strike is more common in Britain than abroad. A study of United States strike figures suggests that the unofficial (or "wildcat") strike, although not uncommon, is a good deal less common than in Britain.[2]

Unofficial strikes are those which lack the sanction of the relevant union authority. "Unconstitutional" strikes are those which are called in breach of the relevant procedure agreements. Either explicitly or implicitly these agreements oblige the parties to refrain from a stoppage until all the stages in the machinery of negotiation have been used and have demonstrably failed to settle the issue in dispute. Sometimes a union calls an official strike in breach of procedure, and occasionally workers strike unofficially over an issue which had been taken through all stages of procedure without settlement, but in fact almost all unconstitutional strikes are unofficial.

Comparisons with the past, and with foreign countries, do not reveal variations in the incidence of strikes from one class of worker to another and from one industry to another. White collar workers strike much less than manual workers. The contrast remains sharp even if it is made between organised white collar workers and organised manual workers. When white collar workers do strike, they are more likely to strike officially than

[1] Of 1101 recorded disputes from January 1935 to September 1936, at least 530 were unofficial. For the year 1936, of 818 recorded strikes, 435 were known to be unofficial and 189 were known to be official, 89 were strikes of unorganised workers, and there was no information by which the status of the remaining 115 strikes could be determined. (*Hansard*, 12 November 1936, col. 11026; July 1937, col. 2167, quoted by K. C. J. C. Knowles, *Strikes*, 1952, p. 33 f.n.).

[2] Jack Steiber, "Unauthorised strikes under the American and British Industrial Relations Systems", *British Journal of Industrial Relations*, July 1968. Having examined the available evidence, Professor Steiber concludes: "On balance, we would hazard a guess that something like 25 to 30 per cent of all strikes in the United States are unauthorised" and that they "account for perhaps 5 per cent of all man-days lost." In *Is Britain Really Strike-Prone?* Turner says "it is quite possible that if strikes in the U.S.A. were recorded in British categories, the majority of them would be found to be in breach of agreement also" (p. 21); but he appears not to understand the relevant definitions.

are manual workers, and the most strike-prone among white collar workers are the draughtsmen, many of whom are recruited from among the engineering apprentices.[1] Although there have been some famous strikes among women, from the match girls' strike of 1888 to the Ford sewing machinists' strike of 1968, women strike much less than men.[2] Indeed it may be that the propensity of women to strike has declined since the early nineteen thirties when the cotton industry, for long the predominant area of trade unionism among women, ceased to be a strike-prone industry.

Even among male manual workers, however, striking is an exceptional habit. Most of them strike rarely, if ever, and a few industries account for most of the strikes. Writing of the years 1960–4 the Ministry of Labour informed the Royal Commission that "the five or six industry groups losing most days per thousand employees have included motor vehicles, shipbuilding and port transport every year from 1960, and coalmining every year except 1962. No other group figures among the annual leaders more than once in the five years except iron and steel, which figures twice. The four worst groups accounted for about 44 per cent of the time lost in the last five years and over half the number of strikes . . ."[3]

At that time the four groups—coalmining, cars, docks and shipbuilding—included less than eight per cent of the employed population. Their predominance in strike statistics is a feature of the whole post-war period, and steel has been moving erratically towards them throughout the period. Looking further back, however, the figures show that cars is a relative newcomer to the scene. Before and during the war the industry was relatively peaceful, whereas the strike-prone record of coalmining, docks and shipbuilding stretches back into the nineteenth century. This contrast is emphasised by comparison with car manufacture abroad. In the United States the industry is only moderately strike-prone, and in Europe relatively strike-free.[4]

While cars and steel have risen in the league-table for strikes, coalmining has been losing its pre-eminent position. For decades it led the country both in the number of strikes and in working

---

[1] See pp. 299–300. [2] See pp. 26–7. [3] *Written Evidence of the Ministry of Labour*, p. 38.
[4] *Labour Relations in the Motor Industry*, Chapter X, "Industrial Relations in Foreign Car Firms".

days lost through strikes. Its loss of working days has declined throughout the post-war period, and more recently its annual number of strikes has diminished sharply, even taking into account the rapid reduction in the labour force. In 1957 there were 2224 recorded strikes in coalmining, and 635 in all other industries. Coalmining's total has diminished in every year since then except 1959 and 1964, and the figure for other industries has risen in every year except 1963 and 1966. In 1968 there were 221 strikes in coalmining and 2157 in other industries. The cut-back in coalmining has been especially sharp since 1964. This decline has been offset by a rapid rise in the number of strikes elsewhere, even excluding cars, docks and shipbuilding, which rose from 326 in 1953 to 1597 in 1968.

Even within the strike-prone industries the pattern of strikes is by no means uniform. In coalmining the Scottish, South Wales and Yorkshire coalfields account for by far the greater part of the strikes and the working days lost in the post-war period, and even so many collieries in each of these areas have been almost entirely strike-free. In car manufacture Vauxhall has been relatively peaceful throughout the post-war period, at least until 1966, whereas several of the factories which now form part of British Leyland have had poor records since the early fifties. Some docks and some shipyards are relatively strike-free.

THE STRIKE-PRONE INDUSTRIES

Commenting on the record of cars, coalmining, docks and ship-building the Ministry of Labour told the Royal Commission that there was "no one reason for the poor record of these industries, but certain factors arising from both past history and present conditions may be mentioned". These were the prevalence of payment by results, "perhaps the main common feature"; insecurity of employment; inter-union difficulties; and the "traditions and atmosphere of each industry". These last included the "strong sense of solidarity" bred by the special way of life in coalmining and in the docks; a willingness to exploit shortages of labour and key positions in the production process on the part of car workers; and the "memory of past depressions" which "still affects attitudes on both sides" in shipbuilding.[1]

[1] *Written Evidence of the Ministry of Labour*, p. 39.

There is now a good deal of evidence against which these propositions can be tested. Professor Turner and his colleagues have provided an extensive study of car strikes in their *Labour Relations in the Motor Industry*. The Devlin Committee devoted a fair part of their *Final Report* to a discussion of the reason for strikes in the docks. There have been several studies of strikes in coalmining during the post-war period;[1] and two of strikes in shipbuilding.[2] How far do they, and the other available evidence, support the Ministry's diagnosis?

To begin with, is payment by results the main common feature? The most recent survey, in 1961, returned 52 per cent of wage-earners paid by results in the vehicles industry and 65 per cent in shipbuilding and marine engineering. The survey did not include coalmining, nor did it give separate figures for docks; but the Devlin Committee estimated that 70 per cent of the work done in the docks is "paid for by the piece",[3] and before the coal industry's national powerloading agreement of 1966 almost all faceworkers were on some form of payment by results. These faceworkers were not a majority among colliery wage-earners but they dominated the union and industrial relations at the colliery and accounted for the great majority of strikes.

The four industries therefore have, or until recently had, a high proportion of workers paid by results. But other industries which pay by results have different strike records. With 51 per cent of wage earners paid by results, textiles have been relatively strike-free in the post-war period. The suspicion that payment by results does not by itself provide the explanation is reinforced by a close examination of shipbuilding experience. The industry's labour force is divided into the "black squads" who build the main structure of the ship, and the finishing trades. Traditionally the former were paid by the piece and the latter were on time-rates; the former, most of them organised in the Boilermakers' Society and the Shipwrights, accounted for the majority of strikes, and the latter, organised in a variety of engineering and building

[1] Notably, *Coal and Conflict*.
[2] G. C. Cameron, "Post-war Strikes in the North-East Shipbuilding and Shiprepairing Industry", *British Journal of Industrial Relations*, March 1964; and chapter 3 in J. E. T. Eldridge, *Industrial Disputes*, 1968.
[3] *Final Report*, p. 22. Since many pieceworking dockers spend part of their working week on time rates, the proportion of dockers who are paid in part by the piece is well above 70 per cent.

unions, were less strike-prone. In those days, therefore, the association between payment by results and strike-proneness was valid. But they are long past. During the second world war incentive bonus schemes were introduced for the finishing trades, the majority of whom are now paid by results. Meanwhile methods of payment had also been changing for their colleagues engaged in ship construction. The spokesman of the Shipbuilding Employers' Federation told the Royal Commission that "piecework practically throughout the industry is very much less than it was 40 or 50 years ago".[1] It had been replaced by lieu rates, a lieu rate being a "fixed rate . . . based upon what a man can earn on piecework", and "it has been recognised probably for the last fifty years that piecework should be something of the order of 40 or 50 per cent above the time rate."[2] This reversal does not seem to have affected the relative strike records of the two groups. The "black squads" are still well in the lead.[3]

Why then do they still strike so much, and still strike predominantly over wage issues? Cameron finds that insecurity is "a major cause of strikes in the shipbuilding industry".[4] Traditionally this insecurity has been due to the wide fluctuation in demand for the industry's products, expensive capital goods whose purchase can easily be postponed in years of depression. In the post-war period the rapid decline in the labour force, especially since 1957, has added to insecurity of employment. But this is not all. The methods of production also promote insecurity. "Shipbuilding is an assembly industry in which the skills of the many trades are used in turn, so when the work of any particular trade is finished on one vessel, there is the possibility that other vessels in the yard will not be at a stage of building which requires the skill of the particular trade which is seeking new work."[5] Moreover insecurity does not arise only from the risk of unemployment. It is also a consequence of variable earnings due to the dependence of "the earnings opportunities for any trade" upon "the changing stages of vessel assembly. Thus even

[1] Royal Commission, *Minutes of Evidence*, Q. 7828. As piecework earnings for riveting fell with the substitution of welding, riveters secured "fall-back" rates which became their actual rates. Welders, on the other hand, put "ceilings" on their rising earnings which became effectively fixed rates (Qs. 7834–5.)
[2] *Ibid.*. Qs. 7871–3. "There is no one nowadays in the industry working on a time rate, except perhaps the odd labourer, the odd sweeper-up" (7876).
[3] Cameron, p. 5. [4] *Ibid.*, p. 6. [5] *Ibid.*, p. 6.

if a trade is not paid off at the conclusion of its work on one vessel, it may have its overtime opportunities reduced or completely removed, or be under-employed." Earnings fluctuate also because of the frequent revision of piece-rates, or now more commonly lieu rates, which are fixed job by job and which can bring fluctuating earnings "as each new job is rated."[1] Besides this it is not uncommon for further adjustments to be made during the course of a job. Workers make "wage claims at a point when management greatly requires their particular skill. . . . A good example of this type of dispute is the pre-launching strike of the shipwrights. Amongst the duties of this craft is the preparation and control of the launching of each vessel, and this . . . provides a highly suitable occasion for a wage claim which can, if necessary, be backed by a short strike."[2]

Consequently the experience of shipbuilding suggests that a high propensity to strike is not associated with payment by results as such, but with a system of payment which yields variable earnings and provides frequent opportunities for the fragmented adjustment of pay of small groups of workers. These can be characteristics of a system of payment by results, but in shipbuilding they are also associated with payment by means of lieu rates.

Do pay systems in the other three industries share these characteristics? Professor Turner and his colleagues reproduce diagrams of wide fluctuations in weekly earnings for several sections of workers in one car plant in 1962–3. They show "normal" earnings for an operative on the final line of £23–4; "but on only a minority of occasions did his actual earnings come within these figures, and in particular weeks within that period his gross wage rose above £31 and fell as low as £13". In the trim shop the "normal" figure was £25–7 but earnings frequently fell below this figure, on one occasion to £11.[3] Wide fluctuations are characteristic "of earnings generally in the payment-by-results plants. . . . This is partly a consequence . . . of the general fluctuation in production to which it [the motor industry] has become liable in recent years. It is also a consequence of such more minor disturbances to output as the effects of technical hold-ups, of breakdowns, sometimes of changes in models or equipment, and of strikes in other departments or plants. Occasionally, it results

---

[1] *Ibid.*, p. 7.　　[2] *Ibid.*, p. 13.　　[3] *Labour Relations in the Motor Industry*, pp. 162–3.

from methods of bonus calculation themselves."[1] However, the entirely timeworking plants of Ford and Vauxhall were not wholly free from fluctuations in earnings, for hours worked in the industry have a range of variation nearly twice that in the whole group of engineering industries, which must lead to considerable variation in overtime earnings. This type of variation is almost certain to be greater in time-working plants, for overtime premium payments related to their relatively high base rates represent a larger sum per hour than the overtime premium payments of pieceworkers in other plants.

The pieceworking plants provide an opportunity for adjustments of pay every time a new rate is set or an old time is revised. Bargaining "tends to start from the assumption that the new task must give at least the same earnings . . . as that with which the old task ended. . . . Moreover, workers' productivity tends to rise particularly fast in the first few weeks or months after a new task is undertaken. . . . Thus, the more frequently job-rates have to be changed, the faster earnings of production workers rise";[2] and the more concerned are timeworkers in the same plant to strive to catch up by means of claims for lieu rates, or bonuses or plus-payments of one sort or another. It is significant that the two major timeworking car firms, Ford and Vauxhall, have always experienced a lower propensity to strike than the pieceworking car firms in the midlands; although the sharp reduction in stoppages at Ford after 1962, when seventeen "trouble-makers" were dismissed, shows that other factors are at work as well.

By contrast frequent changes in piece-rates are not a cause of trouble in the docks, for one of the industry's problems in recent years has been the difficulty in revising piece-rates even when revision has been patently required.[3] This failure to revise leads

---

[1] *Ibid.*, p. 159.   [2] *Ibid.*, p. 157.

[3] In December 1965 Mr Allan Flanders reported on a dispute in Bristol and Avonmouth docks. He wrote: "I am particularly concerned about the apparent state of helplessness in which both sides find themselves when confronted with the rising dissatisfaction with piecework rates at the docks, a factor which must have contributed to a ready acceptance of strike action by the men. . . . There is urgent need for a joint review of piecework rates and manning scales to bring both into line with modern requirements." (*Report by Mr Allan Flanders of a Committee of Investigation into the Bristol and Avonmouth Docks Dispute*, 1966, p. 20.) Nearly three years later the National Board for Prices and Incomes reported that "piecework rates have not been reviewed, nor have manning scales been reviewed". (*Pay Awards made by the City and County of Bristol to staff employed in its docks undertaking*, Report No. 81, Cmnd. 3752, 1968.)

to fluctuations in earnings. According to the Devlin Report: "Where mechanisation is introduced and piecework rates remain unadjusted, piecework earnings tend to 'run away' from the time rates. Attempts are then made to correct this tendency in a general way by granting wage increases which provide for a smaller percentage addition to piece-rates than to time rates. ... A consequence of this is that for many piecework operations which have remained untouched by mechanisation or by the introduction of new methods, the rate is too low and no longer offers a reasonable incentive."[1] A move from one type of cargo to another can thus bring wide fluctuations in earnings. In Liverpool, however, at least until 1968, the practice of "welting" meant that piecework earnings contributed little if anything to the pay of most dockers. The variable element was overtime, paid at higher rates than in other ports or other industries,[2] and weekly pay fluctuated according to the availability of weekend working.

Whether he relies on piecework or overtime, the docker is dependent on the volume of shipping in the port to earn his money, and before September 1967 casual employment was another cause of fluctuating earnings. Unless he was one of the minority of permanent employees, the docker was then entitled only to "attendance money" of 9s. a turn if he attended and no work was available, and to a guaranteed minimum of £9 a week.

These characteristics of dock employment have led to fluctuations in weekly earnings even wider than in the car industry. The graphs included in the Devlin Report showed variations between £11 and £47 in the weekly earnings of one London docker during the course of a year, and between £10 and £39 in those of a Liverpool docker.[3] Moreover by its system of casual employment the industry developed a class of worker—the "floater"—with a direct interest in preventing the revision of piece rates and in maintaining excessive overtime rates in Liverpool. For the floater's way of life depended on picking the jobs which he thought would bring him high earnings and on avoiding jobs with low earnings; and high and low earnings arose out of the inequitable piecework rates and the high overtime payments at Liverpool.

Because of the opposition to revision of piecework rates, adjustment of job values does not provide frequent opportunities

[1] *Final Report*, p. 23.   [2] See p. 279.   [3] *Ibid.*, p. 6 and Appendix.

for fragmented bargaining in the docks. Instead these opportunities arise in the settlement of "allowances" for handling particular cargoes, usually because poor stowing or some other unusual feature does not allow normal piecework earnings to be made, or because a cargo is unpleasant to handle.

Although coalminers have always been permanent employees, some of the problems arising out of their work and pay systems are very similar to those of the dockers. Changes in the structure of a seam and conditions of work at the coal face can be as frequent as the change from one cargo to another, and can bring wide fluctuations in earnings for the pieceworker. As in the docks the consequence has been frequent negotiations over special allowances to individual groups of workers at the face, providing a "running battle between the manager and his pieceworkers over their wages and his costs".[1] In examining disputes in four pits in the Lancashire coalfield, W. H. Scott and his colleagues found two other causes of variation in earnings which could lead to dispute. Men transferred from one face to another might suffer "a drop in wages unless they could persuade the under-manager to increase the rate"; and if the men did not complete as much work as he expected under difficult conditions, the under-manager "would pay only for the amount of work actually completed", so that they would earn less than under normal conditions.[2] Scott and his colleagues sought to test "the belief that groups whose wages fluctuated from week to week would have a greater number of wage disputes than groups whose wages were more stable" and found that their evidence went some way to support it.[3] The faceworkers accounted for the great majority of the strikes, and among them the fillers and packers were the two most strike-prone groups. In matters of pay, "for faceworkers, and particularly fillers, fluctuation of earnings was the problem", and "under variable physical conditions and with advancing mechanisation, the main causes of variability of earnings lie increasingly outside the faceworker's control".[4]

Since nationalisation there has been a reluctance on the part of colliery managers to alter piece rates, and the decision to make

---

[1] G. B. Baldwin, *Beyond Nationalisation, The Labour Problems of British Coal*, 1955, p. 176.
[2] *Coal and Conflict*, p. 124.   [3] *Ibid.*, p. 130.   [4] *Ibid.*, p. 190.

changes has been reserved to higher management. This reluctance was most evident in Yorkshire, where rates remained virtually unchanged between 1947 and 1955. The consequence was that allowances came to constitute a larger and larger part of the pay packet, and the negotiation of allowances took a larger share of the time of supervisors and managers.

It seems reasonable to conclude that all four industries share, or until recently shared, common problems in fluctuating earnings and fragmented wage-bargaining. These features are associated with payment by results in most instances, but not in all, and the Ministry of Labour may have obscured the connection between payment by results and propensity to strike when it set out payment by results and insecurity of employment as two distinct characteristics of strike-prone industries. In fact both of them can have their effect on the propensity to strike through fluctuations in earnings. In most ports and in the car industry payment by results and insecurity of employment combine to bring about extreme fluctuations in earnings. But in Liverpool high overtime earnings have taken the place of payment by results. In shipbuilding the earnings of the "black squads" continue to fluctuate despite the decline in piecework, and over most of the post-war period faceworking coalminers have experienced fluctuating earnings despite security of employment.

Since 1966 almost 90 per cent of the faceworkers in the pits have been transferred from piecework to daywork under the national powerloading agreement which applies to all mechanised coalfaces. Fluctuation in earnings has become a thing of the past for them. The time rate, which differs from one coalfield to another, is adjusted upward from time to time in industry negotiations. There are no allowances, and negotiation in the colliery is confined to settling the task which is to be expected in return for the fixed wage.

Accordingly this agreement seems to offer a neat and simple explanation for the rapid decline in the number of strikes in coalmining. But the decline began about 1958. The agreement can therefore do no more than account for the acceleration in the decline since 1965. However, the powerloading agreement was the culmination of a long process of mechanisation and of adjustment in the traditional methods of wage-settlement. The proportion of coal output which was powerloaded rose from 4 per cent in 1950 to 70 per cent in 1965. Over the period divisional powerloading agreements were negotiated coalfield by coalfield. Except for the Scottish agreement, which settled a time rate for powerloading ahead of the industry agreement, these divisional agreements contained two features. They retained a margin of pay fluctuating with output, but the major part of weekly pay was a fixed rate; and they removed the most important decisions on the pay of powerloading faceworkers from colliery bargaining to discussions between divisional coal boards and the area officials of the National Union of Mineworkers. Without detailed investigation of the effect of these agreements on the number of disputes, division by division, it is not possible to link the two with certainty, but it is at least plausible to suggest that the agreements led to a progressive reduction in the propensity of faceworkers to strike by diminishing the range of fluctuations in earnings and the scope for fragmented bargaining over pay in the colliery.

If these changes in pay structure can help to explain the declining propensity to strike in the coalmining industry, what about the rising propensity to strike among steelworkers? Payment by results is common in steel. The 1961 survey showed 59 per cent of workers in metal manufacture paid by results. Traditionally process workers have been paid by the ton, the tonnage rates for the all-important heavy steel section being contained in an industry list, and maintenance workers have been paid by time. But technical development, which has simplified the coalmining pay structure, has brought added complexity to pay structure in steel. Rising productivity rendered the old tonnage rates obsolete and new rates were settled mill by mill, and section by section. At the same time increasing mechanisation raised the proportion of maintenance workers in the labour force while rising productivity widened the gap between their pay and the earnings of the process workers paid by results. Consequently various schemes of incentive payment were introduced for maintenance workers to diminish the gap, but this has not prevented unrest among them. The rising propensity to strike has therefore been associated with a fragmentation of the methods of pay determination in the industry leading to competitive wage-bargaining inside the plant.

Not all strikes, however, are about pay. The Royal Commission gave an analysis of unofficial strikes for 1964–6 based on the official classification of recorded strikes by "principal cause". This showed that "wages" accounted for 48 per cent of all unofficial strikes; "working arrangements, rules and discipline" for 29 per, cent; and "redundancy, dismissal, suspension etc." for 15 per cent. The remaining causes—including demarcation, trade union recognition and victimisation, as well as "hours of work" and sympathetic strikes accounted for only 8 per cent between them.[1]

It is not easy to determine the principal cause of a dispute since the overt cause may be less important than other grievances among the strikers. For all that it is important for the hypothesis just advanced that the analysis showed wage strikes to be far more numerous than any other sort of strike. Otherwise it would hardly be plausible to explain the propensity to strike in terms of wage structure and methods of negotiating pay. The official figures do not permit any useful distinction between different types of wage dispute,[2] but Turner's reclassification of car strikes shows that "straight wage-increase demands or wage reductions" accounted for 13 per cent of the strikes and 14 per cent of the days lost between 1946 and 1964, whereas 39 per cent of the strikes and 30 per cent of the days lost came under the heading of "wage-structure and work loads".[3]

It might appear that a comparison between the causes of strikes in different industries should provide a fruitful line of inquiry in explaining propensity to strike. In fact industries are remarkably uniform in this respect. From 1964 to 1966 wages were everywhere the largest single cause of strikes, except for coalmining where working arrangements, rules and discipline (49 per cent) came marginally ahead of wages (47 per cent). Otherwise the figures show that the craft-ridden shipbuilding industry has a higher incidence of demarcation disputes than other industries, and (perhaps a more interesting observation) that in the nationalised coalmining industry, with its industry redundancy agreement, few strikes were caused by "redundancy, dismissal, suspension etc."

[1] *Report*, p. 101.

[2] The Department's returns distinguish between "claims for increases" and "other wage disputes", but the very marked difference between coalmining and other industries in this respect suggests a difference in usage between the Coal Board and departmental officials, rather than a difference in the pay structures themselves.

[3] *Labour Relations in the Motor Industry*, p. 65, Turner and his colleagues classify disputes about the task to be done for a given wage together with disputes about the pay for a given task as about "wage-structure and work loads."

What the figures do show, however, is that remarkably few strikes are ascribed to any cause directly related to multi-unionism. Demarcation strikes are almost invariably disputes between unions, for although there may be arguments between two groups within a single union over which of them is entitled to a given class of work, such arguments are usually settled without a stoppage. Demarcation accounted for 2·5 per cent of all strikes and 12 per cent of shipbuilding strikes. Disputes over trade union recognition may arise from competition between one union and another, but they can equally well arise from the demand of one union alone to be recognised in a field in which no other union is operating. In any event, recognition disputes accounted for less than one per cent of all strikes. It is possible that a closed-shop dispute might arise out of the desire of one union to close the door to others. Closed-shop disputes accounted for rather more than one per cent of strikes. Even on the most generous interpretation, therefore, inter-union difficulties have accounted directly for no more than 5 per cent of the strikes.

Multi-unionism, however, could still be an important background factor in strike-prone industries. It unquestionably exacerbates the conflicts over pay in the steel industry. In the car industry Turner and his colleagues suggest that the weaknesses of trade union organisation have prevented "the national unions" from having much "impact on the detailed determination of car industry employment conditions and labour relations" so that "in this respect the shop steward organisation has become the real union". However, they do not attribute the industry's high rate of unofficial strikes to the strength of shop-steward organisation, for they also suggest that the "unofficial-unofficial strike" which lacks the approval of the "shop stewards' leaders" as well as the sanction of the unions themselves now "appears to be becoming the norm" in the car industry.[1]

Other considerations also suggest that it is possible to exaggerate the importance of multi-unionism as a cause of strikes. Apart from a few skirmishes with a breakaway organisation of colliery enginemen, coalmining has been virtually free from inter-union conflict because it has virtually one union for manual workers, so that multi-unionism cannot explain its high rate of strikes in the past, nor the recent decline. In recent years the ports of

[1] *Ibid.*, pp. 222–3.

Liverpool and Hull have been riven by conflict between the Transport and General Workers and the National Amalgamated Stevedores' and Dockers' Union (the blue union). But these two ports were equally strike-prone before 1954 when the blue union first broke into the northern ports.

Accordingly the evidence suggests that, although multi-unionism is a contributory cause of strikes, the explanation for the relatively high propensity to strike shown by five British industries must be mainly in terms of their fluctuating earnings and fragmented methods of bargaining over pay. But can this explanation apply to the strikes which are not classified as wage strikes and which account for about half of all recorded strikes in these industries as elsewhere?

There are two parts to the answer. The first and less important is that working rules and arrangements, the major cause of "non-wage" strikes, can have as much effect on pay as the determination of a piece rate or a lieu rate, for example by boosting overtime earnings. The second, and more important, is that if the increase in the number of strikes over pay in these industries is due to the informality and fragmentation of pay settlements and pay systems, then the rising number of strikes over non-wage issues may be attributed to the settlement of these issues in the same fashion. In Britain working rules and arrangements—whether they affect pay or not—and redundancy, dismissal and discipline are generally settled in the plant or the workshop, and often by custom, or by *ad hoc* decisions applying to particular groups or individual workers. If the pattern of strikes over pay in these industries is due to the way that pay is determined, then their pattern of strikes in general is due to the way that they go about the business of regulating employment in general.

However, these five industries employ no more than ten per cent of the labour force. Can the explanation of their propensity to strike also account for the three-fold increase in strikes in other industries over the last ten years? This question could be answered only by a series of detailed investigations, but it is at least plausible to suggest that there is a connection between wage drift and strikes. Over the last ten years the earnings of manual workers have diverged from agreed rates in almost every industry in the country. Much of the growing "gap" which results from the divergence consists of payment by results, overtime earnings and ther forms of pay which can fluctuate from week to week. These elements are generally settled within the plant and provide a field in which fragmented bargaining over the pay of small groups of workers can flourish.

Their origin in fragmented bargaining explains why the great majority of strikes are unofficial and unconstitutional. It is probable that most strikes have been both unofficial and unconstitutional ever since industry bargaining procedures were instituted. The proportion has always risen rapidly in periods of full employment when strikes have been shorter and smaller than at other times, and it has risen even further as strikes have continued to become smaller and shorter in the post-war period. So long as union officials withhold approval from strikes on issues which have not been through procedure a country with industry-wide procedures and a high incidence of strikes is bound to have a high incidence of unofficial strikes. Sweden, with industry procedures, has few unofficial strikes because there are few strikes. The United States can have a relatively high rate of official strikes because in most industries the procedures terminate within the plant.

An unofficial strike is a strike which has not received the approval of the appropriate union authority. But it is not necessarily a strike of which the union authority disapproves. In most instances the strike is over before there has been any opportunity for approval or disapproval to be expressed. In 1964–6 over half of all unofficial strikes lasted less than two days, and four-fifths were over within the week.

Furthermore the Royal Commission discovered that most union executives have power to pay benefit in respect of strikes which did not have authorisation. The records of the fourteen largest unions in the country showed that benefit was paid in nearly 200 such strikes in 1965, and probably more than 150 in 1966. In these instances the executives presumably had some sympathy with the strikers. The Royal Commission concludes "that in the majority of unofficial strikes the unions do not officially declare an attitude and that in a substantial proportion of the remainder they are prepared to pay strike benefit after the event".[1]

[1] *Report*, p. 109.

REVOLT AGAINST LEADERSHIP

However, the Commission also pointed out that "in some cases" unofficial and unconstitutional strikes "are demonstrations against the official policies of trade unions", and instances the London dock strike in September 1967 when decasualisation was introduced.[1]

Unlike the majority of unofficial strikes, many of these demonstrations are concerned with issues dealt with in industry agreements. Where negotiations are in progress, they are aimed to put pressure on the negotiators. Where a settlement has been made, they are intended to express a protest and, if possible, to force the negotiators to reverse what they have done.

The docks provide several examples. In 1951 Manchester and London dockers struck against a settlement just made, demanding much larger concessions which were set out in an unofficial document called the "Dockers' Charter".[2] In 1960 the "Seamen's Reform Movement" organised strikes in several northern ports to protest against an industry settlement and to publicise their demand for the resignation of the general secretary, Sir Thomas Yates. Early in 1961 an unofficial strike of London Underground workers almost brought London traffic to a halt for a day. It was followed by a decision of the executive of the National Union of Railwaymen to call an official strike for an interim increase in wages pending the report of the Guillebaud Committee on Railway Pay. In fact the increase was conceded without a national stoppage. In the summer of 1964 unofficial action by London postmen helped to push the executive of the Union of Post Office Workers into a one-day national strike on 16 July and into calling a further strike, averted at the last minute, to start on 25 July.[3] During 1965 there was a series of "four-night week" disputes in the midlands car plants in protest against the industry agreement in engineering of December 1964 which reduced the working week to 40 hours to be worked in five days or nights. The strikers wanted four nights of ten hours each and their action was "less a strike than a mass abstention from Friday-night

[1] *Ibid.*, p. 108.
[2] An account of this dispute is given in Appendix 1 of the *Dock Worker*.
[3] A brief account of these events can be found in the *British Journal of Industrial Relations*, November 1964, pp. 432–4.

shifts".[1] In October 1968 midlands lorry drivers struck for forty-eight hours against the clause in the Transport Bill then before parliament concerning the installation of a measuring device known as the "tachograph" in road haulage vehicles. They felt that the Transport and General Workers' Union was showing too much tolerance towards the proposal.

It is tempting to perceive a link between this type of strike and the more common unofficial and unconstitutional stoppages over plant issues. If car workers, especially in the midlands, frequently stop work to press work group claims, is it not natural that they should stop work to show their dislike of an industry agreement which disregards their wishes? Dockers, and to a lesser degree road haulage drivers, are given to unofficial strikes about matters which arise on the job, and it is not surprising that the habit of striking should spill over to those occasions in which they wish to influence their leaders, or to protest against what their leaders have done. But the frequent occurrence of unofficial and unconstitutional strikes on domestic issues is not a necessary condition of their use to bring pressure to bear on union leaders over issues in industry negotiations and settlements. Railway workers rarely strike on domestic issues and post office workers almost never. It would also be a mistake to see these demonstrations against union leadership as a product of the post-war years of full employment, or even of the era of industry bargaining since the first world war. Conflict between union leaders and groups of members over negotiations and settlements affecting those members is almost as old as trade unionism itself. Examples are scattered through the nineteenth century,[2] although the subsequent development of industry procedure agreements and industry pay agreements added to the likelihood of conflict.

Disputes between members and leaders offer rich opportunities to any opposition faction within a union. Successful championship of the members' cause is a wonderful advertisement for an opposition, and even if they fail the attempt draws attention to

---

[1] *Labour Relations in the Motor Industry*, pp. 204–5. Professor Turner and his colleagues suggest that the union leaders should have been made aware of the night-shift workers' preference, "if by no other means, by several previous unofficial strikes and at least one major plant agreement on the same issue".

[2] One instance is the strike of 1891 of Clydeside boilermakers "against a wage reduction negotiated by the Society's executive after district bargaining had failed". (Clegg, Fox and Thompson, *A History of British Trade Unions*, Vol. I, p. 150.)

them. For their part, union leaders are ready to emphasise the part played by opposition factions in fomenting disputes in order to distract attention from their own failings. Both sides therefore have an interest in magnifying the importance of "trouble-makers" in causing industrial unrest. In 1917 many sections of the munitions industry were shut down in what came to be known as the "May strikes". Union leaders, parliament and the press attributed much of the responsibility to a group called the Shop Stewards' and Workers' Committee Movement. Its prominent members were revolutionaries whose philosophy committed them to a class struggle against capitalism. Strikes were necessary weapons in the struggle and agreements were no more than temporary truces to be broken whenever the cause could draw advantage from so doing. However, subsequent examination has shown that the revolutionary group was pitifully weak and incom-petent,[1] and that the grievances of the strikers were enough to provoke a good deal of trouble without the intervention of agitators.

In recent years it has been customary to ascribe unrest in the docks to those "more concerned to disrupt the working of the port as often and as seriously as possible than . . . to improve dock workers' conditions".[2] It is not easy to judge the strength of the successive "liaison committees" which have provided unofficial leadership for London dockers, but a more accurate assessment can be made of the strength of the blue union, which has taken the lead in unofficial strikes in the northern ports. Previously a small London union, the National Amalgamated Stevedores and Dockers began recruiting in the northern ports in 1954 and launched a major strike for recognition in 1955. This failed, and with failure most of its recruits returned to the Transport and General Workers' Union, or lapsed from union membership. In 1965 the blue union claimed to have 12 per cent of Liverpool dockers in membership, but both the Transport and General Workers and the employers regarded this claim as greatly exaggerated.[3] Such a small group could not regularly take the lead in major stoppages unless there were real grievances in the

---

[1] Branko Pribićević, *The Shop Steward Movement and Workers' Control 1910-22*, 1959, pp. 100–2.

[2] *Report of a Court of Inquiry into Unofficial Stoppages in the London Docks* (Leggett Report), Cmd. 8236, 1951. p. 10.

[3] Devlin Committee, *Final Report*, pp. 38–9.

ocks. But for many years successive governments, and the Transport and General Workers, regarded the Dock Labour Scheme, introduced as a temporary measure by Ernest Bevin as Minister of Labour during the war and embodied in permanent form under the National Dock Labour Board after the war, as an exemplary method of organising dock labour. Continued unrest could therefore be explained only by the machinations of trouble-makers, and for a long time there was little serious effort to discover the cause of the trouble. In 1965, however, the Devlin Committee found grave defects in the scheme. The "decasualisa-tion" which it had been supposed to accomplish had left most dock workers still casually employed. Among the features which "make the docker more strike-prone than the ordinary worker" the committee included the activities of "wreckers", but also listed four characteristics inherent in the scheme. These were "lack of security", the "preferential treatment" accorded to certain groups of workers, "irresponsibility" due to casual employment, and "casual management".[1]

Another instance of an opposition group promoting strikes comes from the building industry. The inquiry into the Barbican and Horseferry Road strikes emphasised the influence of the London Building Workers' Joint Sites Committee and demon-strated its close links with the Communist Party. In fact the report does no more than draw attention to the continued efforts by the Communist Party to exploit trade union difficulties and industrial disputes.[2] But the evidence on this subject has piled high over the years. It does not prove that the Communist Party can make trouble over nothing, and in building there is plenty of material on hand. There is the inadequacy of the machinery for regulating industrial relations on the site;[3] the chaos of incentive payment schemes in the industry which gives "ample opportunity for those who wish to foster discontent to do so";[4] the fact that "men are often paid on a basis which bears no relation to the rates prescribed in the Working Rule" and that "in many cases the craftsmen may make his private bargain" with the employer;[5] and the inadequacy of the official disputes

[1] *Ibid.*, pp. 5–11.
[2] *Report of a Court of Inquiry into trade disputes at the Barbican and Horseferry Road con-struction sites in London, part 7.*   [3] *Ibid.*, pp. 65–9.   [4] *Ibid.*, p. 25.
[5] *Report of a Committee of Inquiry under Professor E. H. Phelps Brown into Certain Matters concerning Labour in Building and Civil Engineering, p. 162.*

machinery which "keeps the volume of its business at a low level by handling a diminishing proportion of the real industrial relations of the industry".[1]

The use of the unofficial strike as a means of putting pressure on union leaders is a long-established device of British trade unionism employed in industries which are otherwise strike-free as well as in the strike-prone industries. This kind of unofficial strike is naturally associated with factional conflict in the unions, but experience shows that it is common to exaggerate the importance of the trouble-makers and to neglect the other causes of trouble.

OFFICIAL STRIKES

Between 1960 and 1966 the annual number of official strikes fluctuated between 49 and 97 without showing a definite trend in either direction. Some of them arose out of domestic issues which had been processed through the relevant industry procedure without settlement. At that point the union or unions concerned had to decide whether to let the matter rest or to give notice of a strike, taking into account such considerations as their view of the justice of the case, the strength of feeling among their members and their chances of success. However, although there has been no upward trend on the general figures of official stoppages, there has been a sharp increase in the number of constitutional stoppages in engineering. From 1954 to 1958 there were none except for the national engineering strike of 1957. In 1959 there were three and the number rose to 29 in 1965 and 28 in 1966.[2]

There have also been some major official strikes in non-federated undertakings with their own procedures. The biggest of all was the London bus strike in the summer of 1958 which cost over 1·6 million working days. Another was the stoppage of maintenance craftsmen in the Steel Company of Wales during the winter of 1963–4. Both arose out of claims for increased pay.

Occasionally trade unions give official backing to disputes in breach of procedure. In the summer of 1968 the Vehicle Builders and the Engineers officially recognised a strike of Ford women

---

[1] Royal Commission, *Report*, p. 18.

[2] *Disputes Procedures in Britain*, p. 25. Some of these stoppages may have been unofficial for there can be unauthorised strikes on matters which the procedure has failed to settle if the union takes the view that the issue does not warrant a stoppage.

orkers at Dagenham which had begun as an unofficial stoppage.
1 other instances trade unions may consider the procedure so
ieffective in dealing with a particular type of dispute as to make
virtually irrelevant. This can happen in victimisation disputes.

There have also been some official strikes for recognition. Such
trikes cannot be unconstitutional, for a union cannot break a
rocedure to which it is not a party. Even so a majority of
ecognition strikes are unofficial.[1]

However, the bulk of working days lost in official disputes
ince the war has been due to a small number of stoppages over
laims affecting a whole industry. In May 1955 there was a
iational strike of the Associated Society of Locomotive Engineers
nd Firemen on the railways, which cost nearly a million working
lays. In the spring of 1957 a national shipbuilding stoppage cost
wo million working days and a concurrent stoppage over a
imilar claim in engineering four million days, although the
vhole industry was not stopped. The unions had arranged to call
iut the districts in stages and a settlement was reached before
hey had all been affected. Shortly afterwards a strike in company
ius undertakings throughout the country cost three-quarters of a
nillion days. In 1959 a printing stoppage accounted for 3·5
nillion days. The losses in the 1966 shipping strike amounted
o almost a million days.

In 1962 the engineering unions called two one-day stoppages
vhich lost 3·5 million days between them, and another one-day
trike in 1968 lost two million working days. These were "token"
toppages, intended to show the employers that the unions meant
iusiness. There was a similar one-day stoppage on the railways
n 1962 and another in the Post Office in 1964.

These ten stoppages cost almost eighteen million working days,
iearly two-fifths of the total losses in recorded strikes in the
ieriod 1955–68. There have also been several instances in which
inions have ordered a work-to-rule and banned overtime during
he course of industry negotiations. They include the dispute over
he "status" agreement in the electricity supply industry in March
1964 and the dispute over a national productivity agreement on
he railways in the summer of 1968. The second ran for several
veeks and must have cost the country the equivalent of several
iundred thousand lost working days. In addition there have

[1] Royal Commission, *Report*, p. 102.

been a number of instances in which unions have threatene
national strikes, but a settlement has been reached before th
threat has been carried out. In this respect the Railwaymen hol
the record for the post-war period. Since the war their unio
has issued notices of national railway stoppages in Decembe
1953, in January 1955, in October 1958, in February 1960 and i
December 1965; and has taken action on several other occasions
including 1967 and 1968, which implied the threat of a nationa
stoppage. In the autumn of 1968 negotiations for an engineering
settlement took place under the threat of a strike. Notices wer
issued, but postponed to permit further negotiations.

From 1919 to 1926 national stoppages were common in Britain
and the losses in working days were colossal by any standards
After 1926 trade union attitudes changed. More leaders wer
cautious, and cautious leaders found it easier to hold their member
in check. But caution could not prevent four national stoppage
in the textile industries during the years 1929–32, one in woo
and three in cotton.[1] From 1932 to 1954 there were no nationa
stoppages. For part of the period, from 1940 to 1951, the Con
ditions of Employment and National Arbitration Order placed
ban on all strikes and lockouts. This had no visible effect o
trends of unofficial strikes, but it almost certainly added to th
caution of trade union leaders, which was in any case reinforce
by patriotism during the war. There were hardly any officia
strikes while the order was in force.[2] From 1933 to 1939, however
these considerations did not apply, but there were no nationa
stoppages; the largest single strike being the London bus strike o
1937. Why then did national stoppages return after 1951?

The main background factor has been the higher level o
employment in the post-war period which increased the bargaining strength of the unions and made it less easy for trade unior
leaders to control their followers. But all leaders have not beer
equally anxious for restraint. There have been policy difference
and factional conflicts between the advocates of caution and thos
who wish to replace caution by aggression. For nearly twenty
years the Railwaymen's executive has been a battleground fo

[1] During the "great depression" of 1929–33 the textile workers suffered wage cut
more severe than those in any other major industry.

[2] On occasion, however, other sanctions were officially authorised. In 1950 a London
printing dispute led to an official union decision to ban overtime and work to rule. The
employers replied with a threat to dismiss any worker who obeyed these instructions.

moderate and militant factions. In 1956 Cousins took over the general secretaryship of the Transport and General Workers with the avowed intention of reversing the moderate policies of his predecessors. The conduct of the 1957 strikes in engineering and shipbuilding was a contest between him and William (later Lord) Carron, president of the Engineers. In the end Carron used his casting vote on the Engineers' executive in favour of a settlement, and then used his union's vote to carry the Confederation of Shipbuilding and Engineering Unions for a settlement against the opposition of Cousins. The Transport and General Workers' new policies were evident in the company bus strike in the same year, and in the London Transport strike in 1958. Shortly before the threatened engineering strike of 1968 Carron had been replaced by Hugh Scanlon. He had won the election caused by Carron's retirement on a platform of militant policies.

However, the most significant common feature of most of the post-war national strikes has been government intervention in industrial relations. The 1957 engineering and shipbuilding strikes followed an announcement by the Engineering Employers' Federation almost a year earlier that they would resist any wage claim which was "contrary to national policy". National policy on the matter was defined by the Chancellor of the Exchequer who stated that "another round of wage increases such as there had been in the last two years could be disastrous", and one of his colleagues promised "the strongest possible government support . . . to arrest any further increases in wages unless the rise is coupled with increased productivity".[1] A few weeks later the government instituted a voluntary price freeze intended to prevent wage increases not covered by rising productivity. The resistance of the engineering employers lasted through wearisome negotiations during the following winter, but the strike persuaded them to be more conciliatory, and they were also influenced by a change of heart on the part of the government who decided that the country would suffer more damage from a prolonged strike than from continued inflation.[2]

From 1964 onwards the Labour government developed the most thorough prices and incomes policy Britain has seen, and in

[1] *The Times*, 27 April 1956 and 26 May 1956.
[2] A full account of these events is given in *The Employers' Challenge* by H. A. Clegg and Rex Adams, 1957.

1966 supported it with statutory penalties. Every wage-negotiation took place in the shadow of the policy, including the negotiations before and after the railway strike notices were issued in December 1965, the negotiations before and during the shipping strike of 1966, the railway negotiations of the summer of 1968 during which orders to ban overtime and work to rule were issued, and the engineering negotiations of the autumn.

With the railways running at a heavy loss ever since nationalisation, increases in pay have depended on the willingness of the government to meet the bill. Railway negotiations have therefore come under particular government surveillance since nationalisation, to such an extent that several series of negotiations have terminated with talks at Downing Street.

If the major national strikes of post-war Britain have arisen from differences between moderates and militants, the pressures of incomes policy and the extent of government intervention in industrial relations, then they have been concerned with some of the central problems of post-war industrial relations. They are issues on which opinions differ widely, and it is not surprising that these differences should occasionally break out in open conflict.

THE COST OF STRIKES

So far the importance of a strike has been measured by the loss of working days. This is better than no measure at all, but it is a poor guide in many instances. A strike of two million engineering workers for one day may cause little loss to anyone. Workers paid by results can make up for it over the next few days so that the employer gets his output and the worker his pay. Time-workers can make up output in overtime hours. Delay in deliveries will be negligible. On the other hand a strike of ten thousand dockers for two weeks adds up to only one-twentieth of the total working days lost in a one-day national engineering strike, but the loss in wages and profits may be irrecoverable if cargoes are diverted to other ports, and could lead to a continuing loss if some of the shipowners decide to continue to use these other ports. In addition there are the losses suffered by other employers who cannot continue in full production because of lack of supplies from the port, and by their employees who may be put on short time or laid off as a consequence. These losses, in their turn, may be partly or wholly recoverable according to the nature of the business and its circumstances.

Consequently the real losses incurred by a strike may be very much less than indicated by the cost in working days, and they can also be very much more. In some instances some of the factors in the account can be measured. The national coal strike of 1912, for example, cost the industry 11 per cent of its annual working time, but only 4 per cent of its expected annual output.[1] The official returns in Britain include time lost by workers at the establishment or establishments in which the strike takes place, regardless of whether they are on strike themselves, so some of the consequential losses are included in these figures. They exclude time lost in other establishments, but the Ministry of Labour calculated that from 1960 to 1964, when 480,000 days were returned as lost in car strikes, a further 260,000 were lost in other establishments. Car plants are particularly vulnerable to shortage of supplies.

In general, however, figures are lacking, and where they exist they may be deceptively accurate. Professor Turner and his colleagues suggest that the figures given by car firms for production lost due to strikes are the difference between "planned" output and actual output, and that the plan is based on a number of assumptions about the resources available, the organisation of work and demand which may be falsified by many other factors besides strikes.[2]

The Royal Commission attached great importance to consequences of unofficial strikes which are even less susceptible of measurement than those so far mentioned. An unofficial strike, they say, "may face a manager with a sudden and acute dilemma. He may be under severe pressure from customers to produce goods or materials by a particular deadline, and in a competitive market such pressure is not easy to resist. . . . It is not surprising if managers sometimes make unwise concessions . . . at the cost of storing up trouble for the future. This situation is found in its

---

[1] "Owing to the increased activity both before and after the dispute." (*Report on the Strikes and Lockouts of 1912*, Cd. 7089, 1914, p. 11.)

[2] *Labour Relations in the Motor Industry*, pp. 45–50, gives a detailed examination of the cost of car strikes. The general question of the consequences of strikes is discussed in K. G. J. C. Knowles, *Strikes, A Study in Industrial Conflict*, chapter V.

M

most acute form in the small number of establishments where there is what might be termed an "endemic strike situation".[1]

Even though they pay benefit in a substantial number of unofficial stoppages as well as in official stoppages, strikes are today relatively inexpensive for the unions. In 1963 registered trade unions,[2] which cover over 85 per cent of all trade union members, paid £464,000 in dispute benefit, less than 3 per cent of their total expenditure. This amounts to about 5s. for each working day lost through recorded strikes during the year, and less than £1 for each day lost in official strikes. In most major manual workers' unions the rates of strike benefit for a man vary between £3 and £5 a week. The Draughtsmen are rare, if not unique, in paying the full rate of salary to their members on official strike.

Strikers can draw any income tax rebates to which they are entitled. The Royal Commission calculated that a man normally earning £21 a week might be entitled, according to the number of his dependents, to between £2 10s. od and £4 a week "in the first few weeks of the strike (provided it began some considerable time after the start, and before the end, of the tax year)". In addition the families of strikers are eligible for supplementary benefit. In 1962–6 the average number of workers involved in strikes[3] who received payments in respect of their dependants was 5266, and the average annual cost was £64,678.[4] In 1967 the figures were higher due to prolonged unofficial dock strikes in London and Liverpool.

---

[1] *Report*, p. 111–12.

[2] The only information published on trade union finances is contained in the reports of the Chief Registrar of Friendly Societies which deal with registered trade unions alone.

[3] Most of them were undoubtedly strikers, but some workers put out of work as a consequence of strikes are not eligible for unemployment benefit, and their dependants might qualify for supplementary benefit. The provisions on this point are intended to ensure that workers who are directly supporting a strike, or directly profit from it, are excluded from unemployment benefit, but the details are exceedingly complicated. (Royal Commission, *Report*, pp. 246–56.)

[4] *Ibid.*, Appendix 8, pp. 345–6.

CHAPTER 9

THE STATE IN INDUSTRIAL RELATIONS:
THE TRADITIONAL PATTERN[1]

Up to this point the business of industrial relations in Britain has been discussed as if it were a matter of voluntary dealings between workers and managers and between trade unions and employers' associations. Particular statutes and government actions have been mentioned, but only incidentally. There have been more frequent references to industrial relations in various public undertakings, but mainly as examples, sometimes as extreme cases, of what can happen in collective bargaining anywhere. This simplification, useful for the purpose of exposition, must now be set aside so that the intervention of the state in industrial relations can be given systematic treatment.

The starting-point is the law. This is no place for an account of the legal framework of British industrial relations. That requires a book of its own,[2] and is entirely beyond the competence of the author. What is attempted here is an outline of how the law bears upon those aspects of industrial relations which are outside the law.

THE LAW

The British system of industrial relations is often characterised as a voluntary system. In the previous volume entitled *The System of Industrial Relations in Great Britain* Professor Kahn-Freund wrote: "There is, perhaps, no major country in the world in which the law has played a less significant role in the shaping of [industrial] relations than in Great Britain and in which today the law and the legal profession have less to do with labour relations".[3] This

---

[1] This chapter outlines the law as it stood before the Industrial Relations Act, 1971. That Act is discussed in Chapter 12.

[2] By far the best available for the general reader is K. W. Wedderburn, *The Worker and the Law*, 1965.

[3] Flanders and Clegg, p. 44.

remains true despite substantial additions to statute law on labour matters since those words were written; and even then the body of statutory labour law was substantial. The point is that the great bulk of industrial relations lies outside the scope of these statutes.

Traditionally the most important of them are the Factories Acts. These have dealt with health, laying down minimum standards on matters such as ventilation and sanitation; with safety, requiring the guarding and proper maintenance of certain types of machinery and other apparatus; with welfare, such as the provision of drinking water; with the notification of accidents and industrial diseases; and with the employment of women and young persons. The present Factories Act (1961) limits the working hours of women in factories to nine a day and forty-eight a week (with overtime allowed up to six hours a week) and bans the employment of women at night. It also places restrictions on the employment of young persons under eighteen years of age.

In 1963 the Offices, Shops and Railways Premises Act extended restrictions similar to those of certain sections of the Factories Act to establishments outside its scope. In addition there are statutes applying to particular industries—the Mines and Quarries Acts, the Merchant Shipping Acts, the Agriculture Acts, the Road Traffic Acts and so on. Some of these restrict men's working hours. The maximum daily period permitted for underground work in the mines is now seven hours (excluding "winding" times from pit bottom to the surface). But in contrast to most other countries the legal regulation of hours of work for men is still exceptional.

The Factories Acts are enforced by a professional inspectorate, and there is special provision for inspection in most industries in which safety, health and welfare are regulated by separate statutes. In addition workers who suffer industrial accidents or contract industrial diseases may sue their employers for damages, and their rights in this regard were extended by statute in 1948. Apart from such common-law action the system of national insurance provides benefits in case of injury or disease arising out of employment.

Unemployment insurance provides for workers who lose their jobs and in 1965 the Redundancy Payments Act entitled a worker with a minimum period of service to compensation if he lost his job through redundancy.

All this legislation is of great importance to workers and managers and to their representative organisations, but it does not impinge much upon the main business of industrial relations, for three reasons. Firstly the pursuit of legislative protection now plays a less important part in British trade unionism than it did earlier in the century. Before 1914 the movement was dominated by the coal and cotton unions, the former demanding an eight-hour day by legislation, which they achieved in 1908, and the latter seeking more modest reductions in the working hours of women and children which, because of the organisation of the labour force in the mills, governed the hours of the men as well. Other unions, such as railway unions, also sought the protection of the law, and the movement as a whole was deeply concerned with the introduction and extension of unemployment insurance and the improvement of legislation on industrial injuries and diseases. The distribution of trade union membership has greatly changed since then, and over the last twenty years further change in these areas of legislation has appeared to most unions as a matter of marginal adjustment.

Secondly, although the work arising out of this legislation is increasing, it is still for the most part fairly separate from other aspects of industrial relations. Injuries at work can serve as an example. In most unions stewards and branch officers are expected to have a general acquaintance with the main requirements of the law so that they can give advice to injured members on what forms to fill in and how to do it. Greater expertise is expected of full-time officers, many of whom are called upon to represent their members before industrial injuries tribunals, and may have to decide whether an injured member should be referred to the union's solicitors so that the likelihood of a successful claim for damages can be examined. Within the plant, shop stewards may take an active part in safety committees concerned among other things with the enforcement of the law, or may use other joint committees for this purpose. If a union pursues this part of its work actively and intelligently it will help to cement the loyalty of its members; but otherwise the business could all be transferred to some other agency without much effect on the rest of industrial relations.

Thirdly, many of the limits imposed by the law do not now have much practical effect. Legislative control of the working hours of women does not seem to have much effect upon the hours which women work. The law allows forty-eight hours a week, with six hours overtime, and average working hours for women in manufacturing industries are about thirty-eight a week. They do not exceed forty in any manufacturing group. Special dispensation is available to allow women to work shifts. With the extension of continuous shift working the restrictions on the employment of women at night could become a serious limitation in the future, but it has not been so in the past. The restrictions on working hours in road transport are liberal and not easily enforced. Road haulage records the highest average working hours of any British industry or service covered by the periodic inquiries of the Department of Employment and Productivity,[1] and overtime is a central feature of its industrial relations.

The Industrial Training Act, 1964, could have a profound effect on British industrial relations. The reform of methods of training which are being undertaken or contemplated by the training boards set up under the Act could substantially modify, or indeed destroy, the system of apprenticeship as it has operated in the past. Since this system has been among the most important agencies determining the present shape of British industrial relations, the consequences of its reform could be immense. But that lies in the future.

For the rest the law affecting industrial relations comes under six headings: the contract of employment, the law on collective agreements, trade union law, the law on strikes, Wages Council legislation, and the law on conciliation, arbitration and inquiry.

THE CONTRACT OF EMPLOYMENT

Employees and employers are in a contractual relationship with each other. The contract includes the pay and conditions of the employee and his obligations of service to the employer, and the notice required to terminate the contract. In the past the rate of pay and the conditions were frequently not written down nor even mentioned when the employee was taken on. They were assumed to be determined by custom, and where there existed a

---

[1] Overtime in the merchant navy is even higher. In 1966 "ratings on foreign-going ships average a 66-hour week and those in the home trade average about 74 hours". Pearson Inquiry, *Final Report*, p. 27.

collective agreement covering the relevant trade in that district the courts, in the absence of any evidence to the contrary, would hold that its provisions determined the contract. Notice was also commonly a matter of custom.

The Contracts of Employment Act, 1963, radically changed the situation by laying down minimum periods of notice ranging from one week after six months' continuous employment to four weeks after five years' employment,[1] and by requiring employers, with certain exceptions, to give each employee "written particulars" of certain terms of his employment after he has been employed for thirteen weeks. This requirement can be met by referring the employee to some document containing the particulars which may be, and often is, a collective agreement. If the employer is federated the pay and conditions of his employees will in any case be expected to be those contained in the relevant agreement or more favourable terms.

The contract of employment might therefore figure more prominently in industrial relations if employers frequently offered terms less favourable than those specified in collective agreements. But many of the relevant agreements are industry or district agreements, and pay is in most industries in excess of these agreements in both federated and non-federated firms. The contract might figure more prominently in industrial relations if the employer were required to give, and if need be justify, reasons for terminating employment, so that disciplinary dismissals could be subject to the review of a tribunal. But this can now happen only in cases of summary dismissal where the employer claims that the employee has violated his contract. Such dismissals are rare, and damages are limited by the period of notice required. The contract might also figure more prominently if employers were in the habit of suing their employees for damages when they strike without giving due notice, for with rare exceptions notice is not given in unofficial strikes, and 95 per cent of our strikes are unofficial. Employers have occasionally sued, but only in an infinitesimal proportion of cases. They may be deterred by the need to sue each striker individually and by the relatively small amount of damages which could be exacted from each of them.

---

[1] After six months' service the employee must give a week's notice. This period is not increased for longer service by the Act, but it may be increased by agreement between the employer and employee.

It is more likely, however, that the reason is that "the main interest of the employer is in the resumption of work and preservation of good will".[1] However, what has been said so far in this paragraph requires a qualification which may grow in importance. Managers and professional employees in private industry commonly have their own individually agreed contracts. Since their numbers are growing fast with increasing size of firm and technological change, more may be heard of these contracts in the future, especially if union organisation makes headway among this class of employee.

COLLECTIVE AGREEMENTS

Although the substantive clauses of collective agreements generally form part of the contract of employment of the workers they cover, collective agreements themselves are not treated as legally binding contracts in Britain as they are in most countries abroad. One reason for this is section 4 of the Trade Union Act, 1871, which debars the courts from "enforcing directly" any agreement between one trade union and another, for many employers' associations, if not all of them, are trade unions in the eyes of the law. This would not affect an agreement between a union and an individual company or a plant manager, but both these and agreements which would come within the scope of the 1871 Act are generally regarded as "gentlemen's agreements", outside the scope of the courts because that is the intention of the parties. "They do not intend to make a legally binding contract, and without both parties intending to be legally bound there can be no contract in the legal sense."[2] There has been some controversy among lawyers over this issue,[3] but in March 1969 the decision in the *Ford* case confirmed the predominant opinion.[4]

In certain circumstances, however, the terms of collective agreements can be made binding on employers. The first "fair wages resolution", setting out the conditions of employment which must be observed by firms awarded government contracts, was

[1] Royal Commission, *Written Evidence of the Confederation of British Industry* (*Selected Written Evidence*, p. 290).
[2] Royal Commission, *Report*, p. 126.
[3] *The Worker and the Law*, pp. 105–11.
[4] *Ford Motor Co. Ltd. v. Amalgamated Union of Engineering and Foundry Workers and Others*, 1969/1 W.L.R. 339.

passed by the House of Commons in 1891, and about the same time local authorities began to pass similar resolutions. The current House of Commons resolution obliges the contractor to observe terms and conditions of employment not less favourable than those laid down in agreements between the unions and employers' associations for that trade or industry. Strictly speaking the resolution is not a law, but a direction to government departments to award contracts only on these terms. However, the principle has been extended by statute to certain other industries. For example, the observation of "fair wages" is a condition of obtaining a licence to operate a passenger bus service, and the failure to observe the appropriate agreements for road haulage drivers can be a criminal offence for a company which is not a common carrier but transports its own products by road. Similar provisions apply in certain other industries.

The Terms and Conditions of Employment Act, 1959, provides another means of obliging employers to observe collective agreements. Besides providing for binding arbitration awards in disputes, the arbitration arrangements in force from 1940 to 1959 empowered the National Arbitration Tribunal (and subsequently the Industrial Disputes Tribunal) to compel an employer to provide pay and conditions at least as favourable as those in the relevant agreement, by awarding that the terms of the agreement should be implied terms of all the relevant contracts of employment. When the Industrial Disputes Order was revoked in 1959 the Industrial Court was empowered to deal with complaints that an employer is not recognising the relevant agreements, and to compel him to observe them in the same way.

Since pay in most industries is now in excess of the industry (or district) agreements which can be enforced under fair wages resolutions and the 1959 Act, they do not play such an important part in industrial relations as they might otherwise do. When the question of enforcing collective agreements is discussed today the issue is generally not the enforcement of the substantive term of agreement on the employer, but the enforcement on unions (or workers) of the obligation, whether stated or implied, not to strike until the issue in dispute has been through the various stages laid down in the procedure agreement. This was the issue in the *Ford* case, which showed that, as things stand, the courts will not enforce this obligation on trade unions.

TRADE UNION LAW

The foundation of modern trade union law in Britain is the Trade Union Act, 1871. Prior to the Act most trade unions were considered to be unlawful bodies because they were "in restraint of trade". The Act freed them from the liabilities and disabilities to which this had exposed them, and also made it possible for trade unions to register if they wished. Registration imposed obligations upon unions to make returns and to include certain provisions in their rules, and conferred upon them certain financial advantages, but both obligations and advantages are marginal. About two-thirds of trade unions, other than employers' associations, are registered and they cover 85 per cent of trade union members.

The total number of trade unions is therefore uncertain because there is no official list of unions. Any organisation is a trade union if it meets the requirements of the definition which can be derived from the 1871 and subsequent Acts. It is, in essence, "any combination, whether temporary or permanent, the principal objects of which are under its constitution statutory objects, namely, the regulation of relations between workmen and masters, or between workmen and workmen, or between masters and masters, or the imposing of restrictive conditions on the conduct of any trade or business, and also the provision of benefits to members. . . ."[1]

This clearly includes some employers' associations. Others are registered as companies,[2] and this cannot, according to the provisions of the Trade Union Acts, be done by trade unions. Consequently it must be supposed that they have "principal objects" over and above those contained in the definition. Some professional associations are in the same position although they appear to act as trade unions by taking part in collective bargaining.[3] The status of subordinate and ephemeral trade union organisations, such as branches, shop stewards' committees and strike committees, is not clear. All of them might well claim to be trade unions. But all these complications and obscurities have caused remarkably little trouble.

Neither the 1871 Act nor subsequent statutes established the legal status of trade unions clearly and unambiguously. In the

---

[1] Royal Commission, *Report*, p. 205.
[2] See p. 143.
[3] *Wage Policy and the Health Service*, pp. 10–12.

Taff Vale case and the *Bonsor* case the House of Lords decided that a registered trade union could sue and be sued as if it were a corporate body, and that it was capable of being a contracting party at law. It seems probable that unregistered unions cannot be contracting parties at law and can only sue and be sued by the unsatisfactory device of a "representative action".[1]

The authors of the 1871 Act were anxious to exclude the courts from certain trade union activities, and section 4 was intended to accomplish this. It said that nothing in the Act should enable a court "to entertain any legal proceeding instituted with the object of directly enforcing or recovering damages for the breach of" restrictive practices, trade union rules on subscriptions, on fines and on benefits, and agreements between unions. However, the consequences of this section are not as sweeping as it might seem. It does not restrain the courts from interpreting trade union constitutions on any point; it has no effect on unions whose purposes are not in restraint of trade and are therefore outside the scope of the Act; and in a long series of cases the courts have permitted proceedings concerning matters included in the section on the grounds that they did not ask for "direct enforcement". These include cases seeking to restrain unions from raising money and spending money contrary to their rules, cases to restrain unions from expelling members in violation of the rules, and cases to recover damages for wrongful expulsion. The view of the majority of the Royal Commission was that the scope of the section had been "very greatly cut down by judicial decisions".[2]

Some of these decisions may have done the unions little harm. There seems to be nothing to be gained by preventing an official of a union recovering a salary which the union owes him. Similarly it would seem to be in the interests of justice to restrain a union from expelling a member in violation of its rules, especially if his livelihood is thereby taken from him. Indeed it might be argued that the courts have insufficient authority to review expulsions, since they cannot interfere so long as the union observes the rules of natural justice in dealing with an expulsion, and so long as its rules are not infringed. Most British unions of any size have armed themselves with a general power to suspend, expel or otherwise penalise a member who acts detrimentally to

---

[1] The "formidable difficulties" facing such proceedings against trade unions are set out in the Royal Commission's *Report*, pp. 208–9.   [2] *Ibid.*, p. 218.

the union as seen by the tribunal set up in the union to adjudicate upon alleged offences.

Potentially the most important limitation upon the unions which has resulted from the interpretation of section 4 by the courts is the possibility of actions to restrain unions from paying benefit in strikes called in violation of their rules. Whether to put a curb on rash ardour or in the interests of democracy, many unions require a ballot to be held before a major strike is called. This takes time, and in an emergency the choice before the executive may be to call a strike at once or not at all. Many unions were in this position at the time of the General Strike in 1926, and almost all of them decided to disregard their rules. Similarly in the national shipbuilding and engineering strikes of 1957 several unions apparently ordered their members out in violation of their rules.[1] However, an action could be brought before the courts only by a union member, and so far unions seem to have been able to rely on their members' loyalty in such emergencies.

The Trade Union Act, 1913, was mainly concerned with the right of trade unions to spend money on political activities. They were permitted to do so provided that they secured the authorisation of a ballot of members, that they established separate funds for the purpose, and that members could "opt out" of contributing. Most manual workers' unions of any size have established a fund under these conditions, although several important white collar unions have not done so.

THE LAW ON STRIKES

The rights given to the unions by the 1913 Act were rights which they had supposed they already possessed until the House of Lords decided in 1909 that they did not. Similarly before 1867 trade unions had supposed they could prosecute members or officers who embezzled their funds. In that year a court decided that a union whose purposes were in restraint of trade could not do so, and the Act of 1871 was needed to put the matter right. The most important limitations of the scope of trade union action by the courts, however, have been over the right to strike.

They have turned largely on the doctrine of conspiracy. One aspect of this doctrine is that certain acts which would not be

[1] *The Employers' Challenge*, pp. 99–102.

criminal, nor actionable in a civil court, if performed by a single person, may nevertheless become criminal or actionable when performed by a combination; and that a combination which threatens these acts may also be liable to ciminal or civil proceedings. The sort of action to which this aspect of the doctrine can apply in the use of economic power by a group to further their own interests at someone else's expense, and a strike is an obvious example. The unions were first brought up against the doctrine in criminal cases. They sought the aid of parliament and the Conspiracy and Protection of Property Act, 1875, laid down that an agreement or combination to do an act "in contemplation or furtherance of a trade dispute" could only be indicted as a conspiracy if the act would have been punishable as a crime when committed by one person. Subsequently the courts brought the doctrine of conspiracy into play in civil actions, and the Trade Disputes Act, 1906, laid down that acts done in pursuance of an agreement or combination "in contemplation or furtherance of a trade dispute" should be protected from civil proceedings unless they would have been actionable without any combination.

The 1906 Act also gave trade unions complete immunity from civil actions of this kind by forbidding the courts to entertain "any action against a trade union . . . in respect of any tortious act alleged to have been committed by or on behalf of the trade union". This was not confined to actions in contemplation or furtherance of a trade dispute. In addition it gave protection to strike leaders, whether unofficial or official, in strikes in which workers ceased work in breach of their individual contracts of employment. The workers themselves remain liable, but the strike leader who "induces" them to break their contracts of employment is protected under section 3.

A "second limb" of the same section made clear that, if acting "in contemplation or furtherance of a trade dispute" no one could be made liable merely for "interference with the trade, business, or employment of some other person, or with the right of some other person to dispose of his capital or his labour as he wills", although the extent of the protection offered by this limb is not entirely clear.

In 1965 another Trade Disputes Act was passed to deal with loopholes in the 1906 Act to which the case of *Rookes v. Barnard* had drawn attention. This case turned on the tort of intimidation, which is threatening an unlawful act. The unlawful act in this instance was the breach by the strikers of their contract of employment. It is unlawful when committed by a single person, and consequently the strike leaders were not protected from an action for conspiracy although there was no doubt that they were acting in furtherance or contemplation of a trade dispute. Moreover they were not protected by section 3 of the 1906 Act for the case against them was not that they had "induced" their members to break their contracts of employment but that they had intimidated the employer. Complete immunity from tort still protected the trade union itself, but since one of the defendants was a full-time official of the union, the union could not easily deny moral responsibility for meeting the damages and costs arising out of the case. The 1965 Act specifically protects a threat that a contract of employment will be broken and a threat to induce another to break a contract of employment, provided the threat is made "in contemplation or furtherance of a trade dispute".

There remain some problems. All the statutes give protection to acts "in contemplation or furtherance of a trade dispute". They do not apply where there is no trade dispute. The definition of a trade dispute in the Acts of 1875 and 1906 is therefore of great importance. Probably a strike called wholly for political purposes would not be covered by it, and there has been some doubt as to whether it covers a dispute over recognition. The Royal Commission held that it did cover recognition, but that if they were mistaken "such a provision can easily be made".[1]

Section 3 of the 1906 Act gives protection to those who induce breaches of contracts of employment in a trade dispute, but strikes may also lead to a breach of commercial contracts by the employer when he is unable to fulfil his obligations to his customers. Indeed in some instances it may be the intention of the strikers to exploit this to bring pressure to bear on his customers with whom they are in dispute. In several instances in recent years strike leaders have been sued for "inducing" a breach of commercial contract, and this type of action is of special importance for strikes against "labour-only sub-contractors" in the

---

[1] *Report*, p. 220. In Torquay Hotel Co. Ltd. v. Cousins (1969/2 W.L.R. 289; 1969/1 All E.R. 675) the Court of Appeal has now made clear that a recognition dispute (even if it is a dispute between unions for recognition) is a trade dispute.

building industry. The Royal Commission found the law "upon this subject is far from clear", and recommended that protection should be given by omitting the words "of employment" after "contract" in section 3 of the 1906 Act so that, in a trade dispute, an act should not be actionable "on the ground only that it induces some other persons to break a contract". They were, however, divided over the question of limiting this clause to the protection of official strikes.[1]

Where there is reasonable ground for supposing that an action against a strike might succeed, it is possible for the courts to grant an "interlocutory injunction" restraining the strike leaders while the substance of the matter is settled. This is of primary importance in an official strike where the leaders are easily identifiable. Since it may be very difficult to re-impose a strike once it has been called off, the injunction may damage the union's cause even if the ultimate decision is in its favour.

The rights of strike pickets were defined in the 1875 Act and extended by the 1906 Act. From time to time cases still reach the courts, and the Royal Commission heard evidence both for a further extension and for restriction. A majority decided that neither was required. The Royal Commission also recommended that the liability of employees in gas, water and electricity under-takings to criminal proceedings for breaking their contracts of employment, originally created by the 1875 Act, should remain as it is. They made no comment on the special restrictions on the right to strike in the police force and among seamen. The Pearson Inquiry suggested that in amending the Merchant Shipping Acts, parliament would have to include "safeguards for the seamen's right to strike in the United Kingdom", but did not state what these should be.[2]

The main outlines of the "voluntarism" of British industrial relations have now been exposed. The provisions of the Factories Act and similar legislation have little impact on the central business of industrial relations. Collective agreements, as such, are outside the law. The Acts regulating trade unions require very little of them. Although the courts have circumvented the prohibition in the 1871 Act on "direct" interference in certain aspects of trade

[1] *Report*, pp. 231–7.
[2] *Final Report*, p. 94. The question, said the *Report*, extended "far beyond the scope of our Inquiry".

union business, their intervention on most of these points has not been of crucial significance. Of far greater importance has been the intervention of the courts in trade disputes, but parliament has stepped in on three occasions to push the courts back. The protection thus afforded to trade unions and to strikers are often described as "trade union immunities", because instead of creating a positive "right to strike" the Acts have removed from unions and strikers liabilities which would otherwise have been theirs. In addition the unenforceability of collective agreements as such might be considered a further immunity allowing trade unions and their members to break agreements without incurring legal penalties.

WAGES COUNCILS

Statutory regulation of pay in modern Britain dates back to the Trade Boards Act, 1909. Originally intended to protect workers against the evils of "sweating", the scope of the Boards was extended, following the reports of the Whitley Committee, to industries in which organisation was too weak to support effective voluntary collective bargaining. The committee looked forward to a post-war world in which all well-organised industries would regulate their industrial relations by voluntary agreements, and elsewhere Trade Boards would protect the unorganised and foster the habit of collective regulation, so that ultimately voluntary collective bargaining would be universal.

Now renamed Wages Councils, these bodies consist of equal numbers of representatives of such trade unions and employers' associations as exist, together with not more than three independent members, all of them appointed by the Secretary of State for Employment and Productivity. One of the independent members is chairman. The councils are empowered to make proposals about remuneration and holidays in the industries they cover. These they submit to the Secretary of State, who can refer them back but, if the council insists, embodies them in an order. Provided the representatives of the two sides can agree, the independent members have little to do. Otherwise they can try to bring the two sides closer together and finally cast their votes with the one or the other to make up a majority.

The Wages Councils cover about three and a half million

workers. In addition there are two Agricultural Wages Boards, one for England and Wales and the other for Scotland. The main difference between their powers and those of the councils is that the decisions of the two Agricultural Boards are not subject to ministerial consent. Enforcement is the responsibility of two inspectorates, one for Wages Councils and the other for the Agricultural Wages Boards.

It is easier to judge the success of the councils in promoting organisation than in stamping out "sweating", for the evidence on organisation is more readily available and less difficult to interpret. Firstly, in several industries where organisation was weak before councils were established, voluntary organisation developed after the councils began their work and has continued to function effectively since the councils have been abolished. Examples are the Sugar, Confectionery and Food Preserving Council, the Tin Box Council and the Tobacco Council. In all three industries the development of effective organisation was aided by the domination of the employers' side by a few large companies, and probably also by technological developments affecting the character of the labour force.

Equally impressive as an example of assistance to effective organisation is the experience of the Furniture Council. Furniture-making has a long history of collective organisation and collective bargaining, but in 1938 the employers were able to show that 96 per cent of the workers employed in cabinet-making in London were receiving less than the agreed rates.[1] A council was established in 1940, organisation and control improved, and in 1947 both employers and unions felt sufficiently confident to ask for its abolition.

The Rubber Manufacturing and Rubber Reclamation Councils, both established in 1939, and abolished in 1958 and 1955 respectively, fall somewhere between these two types. A joint industrial council had been set up in rubber manufacture shortly after the first world war, but it collapsed within a year or so, and was reconstructed only in the second world war with the support of the Wages Council. The industry had briefly shown some capacity for organisation in favourable circumstances, but could not sustain it in a period of heavy unemployment. In baking separate councils were established for England and Wales (1938) and

[1] F. J. Bayliss, *British Wages Councils*, 1962, pp. 35–6.

for Scotland (1939), not because voluntary organisation was generally weak, but because collective bargaining had failed to find a way to control night work in bakeries. It was thought that a satisfactory solution could be found to this problem only with statutory support.[1] In 1948 the Scottish section of the industry, which has long been the best organised, signed a voluntary agreement to regulate night work, and the Scottish Council has since been abolished.

In most instances in which the abolition of a council has been under discussion the employers have been more reluctant than the unions. This is because they feared that without legal enforcement of the rates of pay and hours of work some of the smaller firms might resort to undercutting in both wages and prices, and their organisation would not be able to put a stop to it. The unions with their membership concentrated in the larger firms were confident that they could ensure that voluntary agreements would be followed there, and were less concerned about the small fry. The procedure for abolition is complicated, but it has always been possible to set it in motion on a joint request from the two sides of the industry concerned, and since 1959 the Secretary of State has had authority to initiate proceedings on his own. In either event it must be shown that there is voluntary machinery substantially representative of the two sides, and capable of effective regulation of pay and conditions of work. The main union in the Paper Bag and Paper Box Councils, the Society of Graphical and Allied Trades, takes the view that technological change has made these industries virtually part of printing, whose agreements could easily be extended to it. In their opinion, "the councils are being used by the employers to obstruct the extension of collective bargaining".[2] It was because of this and similar circumstances in other councils that the Department of Employment and Productivity asked the Royal Commission, and the Commission agreed, that the Secretary of State should be empowered "to abolish any Wages Council where satisfied, on the application of a trade union which is representative of a substantial proportion of the workers concerned, that the wages and conditions of the workpeople would not be adversely affected if the Council ceased to exist".[3]

---

[1] *Ibid.*, p. 36.   [2] *Ibid.*, p. 147.   [3] Royal Commission, *Report*, p. 66.

The Agricultural Wages Boards are examples of a different relationship between statutory enforcement and effective organisation. The National Farmers' Union and the National Union of Agricultural Workers are bodies of considerable strength, but both take the view that effective regulation of pay and conditions would be impossible except through the machinery of the Boards. "Because employment is spread over a very large number of small and scattered units . . . statutory regulation is needed to secure adequate enforcement."[1] Some Wages Councils operate in somewhat similar circumstances. Those in the clothing trades cover many small and scattered units as well as some big firms, yet their workers are relatively well organised for a Wages Council industry. The Tailors and Garment Workers have about a quarter of all clothing workers in membership. However, there are important differences between clothing and agriculture. In agriculture negotiation takes place through the Board. In clothing there are a number of voluntary agreements, the most important of them between the Clothing Manufacturers' Federation and the Tailors and Garment Workers. It provides that: "In the absence of any agreement to the contrary no alteration in rates of wages or conditions of employment shall become operative unless and until such alteration shall have become obligatory under the Orders of the Ready-made and Wholesale Bespoke Tailoring Wages Council and the Wholesale Mantle and Costume Wages Council". Consequently these councils are bodies for endorsing and enforcing voluntary agreements, and their decisions are closely followed by the other clothing Wages Councils.[2] With this and similar instances in mind the Royal Commission recommended, on the advice of the Department of Employment and Productivity, that the Secretary of State should be empowered "to continue to use the inspectorate for a limited period after the abolition of a Council".[3] Subsequently the National Board for Prices and Incomes recommended a timetable for the abolition of the clothing Wages Councils, starting with the well-organised Rubber Proofed Garment Council, and the merging of the separate Scottish Councils for dressmaking and retail bespoke

---

[1] *Ibid.*, p. 66.
[2] National Board for Prices and Incomes, *Pay and Conditions in the Clothing Manufacturing Industries*, Report No. 110, Cmnd. 4002, 1969, pp. 12–15.
[3] Royal Commission, *Report*, p. 67.

tailoring with their counterparts for England and Wales. The relatively well-organised Ready-made and Wholesale Bespoke Tailoring Council, Corset Council and Shirtmaking Council should follow in 1971, and the remaining four councils (dressmaking; wholesale mantle; retail bespoke tailoring; and hat, cap and millinery) should follow in 1973.[1]

In these instances statutory machinery has given some assistance to organisation. There are, however, two classes of Wages Councils in which statutory machinery has done little for voluntary organisation.

A considerable number of councils in manufacturing industries are "characterised by large numbers of small employers, many of whom are hostile to any form of association, by a very high proportion of women employees for factory trades, and by the prevalence of piece-work and home-work". The unions concerned, mainly the Transport and General Workers and the General and Municipal Workers, keep the councils going, waiting "for a general movement of wages to take place before bringing these councils into line",[2] but their membership is thin. Most of these councils have been in existence for almost fifty years without making a significant contribution to voluntary organisation.

In numbers employed this group is overshadowed by the councils in road haulage, catering, retail distribution, laundries and hairdressing, all of which suffer from defective organisation. Of the $3\frac{1}{2}$ million workers covered by Wages Councils, over $2\frac{1}{2}$ million are in these areas.

On the trade union side, road haulage is perhaps the best organised of the Wages Council industries, but the employers have not been able to develop organisation with a capacity for voluntary collective bargaining. Following the first report of the National Board for Prices and Incomes,[3] the Transport and General Workers and the other unions made one of their periodic efforts to established voluntary machinery with the Road Haulage Association. A National Negotiating Committee was set up. In 1966 it negotiated an agreement, but next year it failed to reach a settlement on a claim from the unions, and the claim went to the Wages Council instead. The Negotiating Committee has

[1] *Pay and Conditions in the Clothing Manufacturing Industries*, pp. 38–9.
[2] *British Wages Councils*, pp. 146–7.
[3] *Road Haulage Rates*, Report No. 1, Cmnd. 2695, 1965.

"shown no signs of revival since then. The main reason for this would seem to be a refusal on the part of the unions to negotiate with the R.H.A. on the grounds that the Association could not bind its members to any agreements reached between the two sides."[1] By that time, however, the unions were having some success in negotiating agreements with individual firms.

The Royal Commission published an estimate of the number of trade unionists in the distributive trades which indicated that about 13 per cent of the labour force was organised. Most of the trade union members are employed in the co-operative sector in which the closed shop generally applies. Outside the co-operatives, union membership in retail distribution is probably little more than 5 per cent. Nevertheless there are other voluntary agreements besides those negotiated by the Co-operative Union on behalf of the co-operative societies. In 1967 the National Board for Prices and Incomes estimated that "about 90,000 full and part-time workers, over a quarter of those within the scope of the Drapery Wages Council, are covered by voluntarily negotiated wage agreements". Most of them were covered by the agreements negotiated with the Co-operative Union, the Multiple Shoe Retailers' Association and the Multiple Tailors' Association, but the Union of Shop, Distributive and Allied Workers also "has agreements or less formal arrangements with a few individual companies operating departmental stores".[2] Drapery is probably rather better organised than most other sections of retail distribution, and than hairdressing and laundries; but the over-all picture is of a well-organised co-operative sector, a few voluntary agreements in large organisations outside, and trade union membership spread very thinly outside the co-operative societies.

In catering, the Royal Commission's estimate of trade union membership was 4 per cent of the labour force, and there are very few voluntary agreements, although the General and Municipal Workers made a colourful attempt to organise the London hotels in 1947–8,[3] and the Transport and General Workers made another flamboyant gesture in Torquay in 1968, which in the

---

[1] National Board for Prices and Incomes, *Productivity Agreements in the Road Haulage Industry*, Report No. 94, Cmnd. 3847, 1968, p. 7.

[2] *Pay of Workers in the Retail Drapery, Outfitting and Footwear Trades*, Report No. 27, Cmnd. 3224, 1967, pp. 10–11.

[3] *General Union*, pp. 124–30.

end led to a local agreement with the General and Municipal Workers.

In 1964 the Wages Council inspectorate detected arrears of wages amounting to £134,672 and affecting 10,335 workers, and arrears of holiday pay of £26,736 and affecting 5635.[1] The recovery of these sums, with the aid of legal proceedings in six instances, was an important although costly service. But the aim of introducing statutory regulation into "sweated" trades was not only to bring increased pay to the worst-paid workers in these trades, but also to raise the average level of pay in each trade because it was felt to be too low in relation to pay elsewhere. Figures of arrears recovered have little bearing on this point. Whether the objective has been met could be demonstrated only by showing that the effect of fixing Wages Council rates has been to raise earnings higher than they would otherwise have been.

Quite apart from the difficulty of knowing what earnings might have been, it was impossible until 1969 to discover what earnings actually were in a good many Wages Council Industries. The Royal Commission commented that there were "no official figures at all relating to catering . . . and those relating to other sectors, especially retailing, are patchy and difficult or impossible to relate to the coverage of individual Councils". Of the 22 Wages Councils for which the Commission found "sufficiently relevant figures", four—cutlery, paper bag, paper box and road haulage—had earnings for men above the national average. Most of the rest were well below the national average. The Commission concluded that pay in Wages Council industries did not "seem to have improved significantly in relation to that of other industries".[2] The fuller information made available by the Department of Employment and Productivity's new survey of earnings in 1969[3] is not inconsistent with this tentative verdict.

The Ministry of Agriculture maintains excellent records of agricultural earnings. In 1966 the National Board for Prices and Incomes compared the average for men in agriculture, £14 9s. 4d,

---

[1] *Written Evidence of the Ministry of Labour*, p. 119. In 1968 the inspectorate recovered £8,849 for 1398 workers in the clothing industry, at an estimated cost of about £100,000 most of the infractions arising from regulations on holiday pay. "Serious infractions are extremely rare." (*Pay and Conditions in the Clothing Manufacturing Industries*, p. 31.)

[2] *Report*, p. 66.

[3] Published in the *Employment and Productivity Gazette*, May-August, 1969.

with a national average for men of £20 5s. od. At 68 per cent of
the national average this is rather better than the 60 per cent or
so recorded in 1910,[1] although all sorts of factors besides statutory
regulation might account for the improvement. In 1966 the
statutory minimum rate for agriculture was £10 10s. od. Most
of the difference between this figure and average earnings is
accounted for by overtime, leaving £1 11s. 5d per worker to
cover all payments for special skill and responsibility.[2] In the
following September the National Board for Prices and Incomes
surveyed the earnings of road haulage drivers and found an
average of £22 7s. 9d of which £1 5s. 9d was bonus and other
payments, and £8 8s. 8d was recorded as overtime payments.[3]
Little overtime is worked in retail distribution, and a survey of
earnings in drapery conducted by the Board in 1966 found that
the earnings of male shop assistants and cashiers, with statutory
minimum rates of £10 16s. od in London, and of £10 8s. 6d or
£9 15s. od in the provinces, were £15 16s. 1d, made up of
£14 1s. 6d as basic rates, £1 11s. 2d commission, and 3s. 5d "overtime and other earnings". Retail distribution, however, is predominantly a woman's trade. For women in these grades the
statutory minima ranged from £7 5s. od to £8 1s. od. Their basic
pay rates averaged £9 os. 9d with 15s. 11d commission and 7d
overtime and other earnings, making £9 17s. 3d in all.[4] Workers
with greater skill and responsibility had higher statutory minimum
rates and earned more. In 1968 the Board discovered that 51 per
cent of men in clothing, and 11 per cent of full-time women,
had hourly earnings 4s. or more over the hourly statutory minimum.[5]

An increase in the statutory minimum rates in agriculture
inevitably increases the actual pay of agricultural workers, for
most of them earn little over the minimum apart from overtime.

[1] Clegg, Fox and Thompson give earnings for agricultural labourers as 18s. 4d. in
1910 compared with a " 'good average' wage-packet for a man" of 30s. (pp. 481–2).

[2] National Board for Prices and Incomes, *Pay of Workers in Agriculture in England and
Wales*, Report No. 25, Cmnd. 3199, 1967, pp. 13–15. The pattern of agricultural pay was
little changed when the Board issued another report two years later. (*Pay of Workers in
Agriculture in England and Wales*, Report No. 101, Cmnd. 3911, 1969.)

[3] *Charges, Costs and Wages in the Road Haulage Industry*, Report No. 48, Cmnd. 3482,
1967, pp. 10–13.

[4] *Pay of Workers in the Retail Drapery, Outfitting and Footwear Trades*, Statistical Supplement, Cmnd. 3224–I.

[5] *Pay and Conditions in the Clothing Manufacturing Industries*, p. 27.

This is also true of road haulage, but only because of the way in which the employers choose to record payment in that industry. In fact many of the workers actually earn well above their statutory minimum rates during the agreed forty-hour week. In drapery and clothing, however, there is room for considerable increases in the statutory minimum remuneration without affecting the pay of most workers. This is particularly true of men, but it is also true of women. In fact, however, it is customary in drapery "for nearly all employers to pass on an increase agreed by the Wages Council to most, if not all of their employees";[1] and this seems to be true of many of the clothing councils, especially the Ready-made and Wholesale Bespoke Council.[2] The Royal Commission found that it was generally the case in Wages Council industries.[3]

Accordingly many Wages Councils no longer set minimum rates which have much affect as minima. Instead they have become mechanisms for settling increases in pay which apply throughout their industries, to those workers, if any, on the minimum, and to other workers as well, however high their earnings; and there are wide variations in earnings in most Wages Councils industries as in other industries.[4] Sometimes this process works in a bizarre fashion. In drapery the first step is usually an increase agreed by the Co-operative Union, followed first by other voluntary agreements and subsequently by the Wages Council. The exact terms of the co-operative settlement "are not always followed", but "it sets a standard". However, the survey of the National Board for Prices and Incomes showed that earnings in the co-operative sector were well below the rest of the trade, and in the multiple shops with voluntary agreements they were rather below the shops with no agreements at all. Consequently "the normal process of decision-making begins with the negotiations for workers in Co-operative Societies' shops, which are the lowest-paid sector of the drapery trade. The results are then transmitted to the higher-paid and unorganised sectors

---

[1] *Pay of Workers in the Retail Drapery, Outfitting and Footwear Trades*, p. 18.
[2] *Pay and Conditions in the Clothing Manufacturing Industries*, pp. 28–9.
[3] *Report*, p. 71.
[4] With average earnings for men in clothing at £20 19s. 2d the Board found that 5 per cent of adult male operatives and 19 per cent of adult male ancillary workers earned less than £14 a week (*Pay and Conditions in the Clothing Manufacturing Industries*, pp. 24,30).

of drapery by means of a statutory machinery intended to avoid low pay and to promote organisation".[1]

This aspect of pay movements in Wages Council industries is very similar to the relationship between industry-wide agreements and actual earnings in better-organised industries, but there is one important difference. In these other industries the elements of pay over and above the minimum rate are generally controlled by domestic bargaining. In weakly-organised Wages Council industries, they are at the discretion of the employer. If domestic bargaining could be substituted for the employers' discretion, trade union organisation might be expected to benefit very considerably. But the machinery of the Wages Council is confined to the level of the industry. It has no means of intervening in matters domestic to the firms, and lacks even the industry disputes procedures which provide a link in other industries. Consequently, as the settlement of pay shifts from the industry to the plant, so the machinery of the Wages Council becomes less relevant both to the problem of low pay and to the problem of inadequate organisation. The National Board for Prices and Incomes found this to be true even in the relatively well-organised clothing Wages Councils. "Outside a few large firms" collective bargaining at plant level "is non-existent. This means that the two sides are unable through negotiations to deal effectively with the industry's low pay problems and cannot develop productivity bargaining. In the present situation the workers have no effective voice in the establishment of payment systems, wages structures and conditions of work. Normally the only course open to workers who fail to obtain redress for their grievances is to leave their jobs and go elsewhere." The voluntary industry agreements have not established effective disputes procedures, and "shop stewards, where they exist at all, tend to accept a narrow view of their function and are often merely collectors of union subscriptions".[2]

In 1954 Professor Kahn-Freund wrote that in Britain "the law seeks to stimulate collective bargaining and the application of collective agreements by indirect inducements in preference to direct compulsion, and, where this fails, to provide substitute standards enforceable by legal sanctions. . . . Minimum wage

[1] *Pay of Workers in the Retail Drapery, Outfitting and Footwear Trades,* pp. 23–4.
[2] *Pay and Conditions in the Clothing Manufacturing Industries,* pp. 17–18.

legislation is much the most important substitute for collective bargaining."[1] This is still true, but minimum wage legislation is a substitute only for industry bargaining. In the past Wages Councils provided an effective means of regulating pay, and helped to develop effective industry bargaining in some industries. But as voluntary industry bargaining has become a less effective mechanism for regulating pay, Wages Councils have also lost much of their regulatory effect and such ability as they had to promote organisation.

Another limitation of British minimum wage legislation is its assumption that low pay is a problem of agriculture and of industries covered by Wages Councils but not of other industries. This assumption is incorrect. Nearly every industry has pockets of low-paid workers. In 1968 the Department of Employment and Productivity conducted a new earnings survey designed to discover not only average earnings but also how earnings were distributed. New methods of analysis were applied to the results, and for the first time showed the distribution of earnings under each major national agreement (and Wages Council). This showed a concentration of low earnings in agriculture and catering. Over a third of the male manual workers in agriculture earned less than 6s. a hour, and over half of those employed in licensed residential establishments and licensed restaurants. But there were some men earning less than 6s. an hour under ten of the 21 national agreements in the private sector and under twelve of the 21 national agreements in the public sector. Under several of the national agreements in both sectors the proportion of men earning less than 6s. an hour was higher than under the Wages Councils for milk distribution and road haulage. Similarly there was a higher proportion of women earning less than 4s. an hour under several national agreements than under the Wages Councils for dressmaking and ready-made and wholesale bespoke tailoring.

Findings such as these have led to the suggestion that the system of Wages Councils should be replaced by a national minimum wage applying to all industries. Besides the administrative burden, however, there would be several other problems to be solved. It would be necessary to decide whether the minimum was to apply on a weekly or hourly basis, whether it should include overtime earnings or not, and whether it should apply to

[1] Flanders and Clegg, pp. 65-6.

rates or earnings. In 1969 a government committee reported in favour of minimum hourly earnings, with the same rate applying to overtime hours as to normal hours.[1] They also drew attention to the high cost of applying the same national minimum to both men and women, noting that "the Government are fully committed to the application of the principle of equal pay".[2] Besides this the cost would depend upon the extent to which workers above the minimum insisted on retaining their differentials. "The higher the level of the minimum at its introduction, the greater the risk seems of it setting off pressures for the maintenance of differentials."[3] There is also the risk that the periodic adjustments of the minimum would be influenced by electoral consideration.

CONCILIATION, ARBITRATION AND INQUIRY

The Labour Department of the Board of Trade was set up in 1886, in the first instance mainly to collect information on trade unions, strikes, rates of wages and similar topics. Gradually it began to play some part in trying to assist the parties to a dispute to reach a settlement. Following the report of the Royal Commission on Labour, the Conciliation Act of 1896 empowered the Board of Trade to appoint arbitrators at the request of both sides and conciliators at the request of either side, and to inquire into disputes. "Even if this amounted to little more than what the Board's Labour Department was already doing, the Act established its authority beyond doubt."[4] During the early years of the present century, and particularly 1910–14, the department provided an active conciliation service to deal with a rapidly rising number of strikes, with arbitration where appropriate and acceptable.

Following the Whitley reports, the Industrial Courts Act, 1919, set up the Industrial Court as a permanent independent tribunal for voluntary arbitration at the request of the parties. Initially it took over some of the personnel and procedures of the Committee on Production which since 1915 had served as a temporary war-time tribunal for compulsory arbitration, hearing cases whether the parties wished it or not, and handing down

[1] Department of Employment and Productivity, *A National Minimum Wage* (*Report of an Inter-Departmental Working Party*).
[2] *Ibid.*, p. 54.   [3] *Ibid.*, p. 53.   [4] Clegg, Fox and Thompson, p. 263.

awards which could be enforced in the courts. In addition the Act empowered the Minister of Labour, whose department had now taken over the Board of Trade's responsibilities in the labour field, to set up courts of inquiry to investigate the causes and circumstances of industrial disputes.

In 1893 the Prime Minister, Gladstone, asked the two sides in the great coal lockout of that year to meet under the chairmanship of Lord Rosebery to try to reach a settlement. In 1907 Lloyd George added to his reputation by his skilful handling of a threatened railway strike which led to the setting up of the first formal conciliation scheme on the railways, although without formal recognition for the unions. Thereafter ministerial intervention in major disputes became almost a matter of course, and in the 1912 dock strike the Prime Minister, Asquith, had to chide ministers for flocking in to try to produce a settlement. Since 1919 the normal method of handling intractable major disputes has been for the Minister of Labour to begin talks with the parties when his officials seem to be unable to find a way of avoiding a stoppage, and, as often as not, for the Prime Minister to take over if the Minister of Labour fails.

Today the Ministry of Labour has become the Department of Employment and Productivity, the Minister is a Secretary of State, and the conciliation service (later the industrial relations service) is now part of the manpower and productivity service. Both in the regions and at headquarters the service tries "to keep in close touch with leading representatives of employers and trade unions", and the practice of appointing departmental liaison officers to sit on the national negotiating bodies of about sixty industries helps to keep the service informed.[1] Normally conciliation follows on the application of one or both parties, but if there is no approach the department can indicate to the parties that its services are available. Once the conciliator has informed himself of the facts he may proceed by separate talks with each side, but more commonly by joint meetings at which he takes the chair. Either way, the discussions are intended to be "a continuation of the process of collective bargaining with outside assistance" in which an "essential feature" is "the independence and impartiality of the conciliator".[2] If the conciliator cannot persuade the parties into a settlement, he may suggest arbitration.

[1] *Written Evidence of the Ministry of Labour*, p. 97.   [2] *Ibid.*, p. 95.

In 1964 the conciliation service was used on 408 occasions. In 90 instances the approach came from the unions and in 72 from the employers. There were 37 joint approaches, and in nine instances the department took the initiative. Over the years 1960–4 a stoppage of work took place in "about 20–25 per cent" of the disputes in which the conciliation service was used.[1] The total number of stoppages in 1964 was 2524, but only seventy of these were official and in the remainder "conciliation has commonly been inhibited by the concern that nothing should be done which might appear to condone or even encourage breaches of agreements. . . . Exceptionally . . . conciliation action is taken while such strikes are in progress", but the department "never deals with unofficial strike leaders but only with authorised officers of the trade unions concerned", and even so usually intervenes only where it seems likely that the stoppage might have "a seriously damaging effect on the economy".[2] Thus what might appear to be the success of the service in keeping official stoppages down to a modest level must be weighed against the severe limitations under which it works in dealing with the overwhelming majority of strikes which are unofficial and unconstitutional. In its evidence to the Royal Commission, the department asked whether it "should intervene more frequently in circumstances of this kind".[3]

The Industrial Court includes a full-time president, other independent members, and representatives of employers' associations and trade unions. In practice the court consists of three members, an independent chairman (usually the president), an employer and a trade unionist. The court decides whether the parties can be represented by lawyers, and whether to sit in public or in private. Normally its decisions are the agreed award of the three members of the court, but exceptionally the award is the chairman's decision. Awards are not binding on the parties, but as "they result from a joint desire for settlement by arbitration, the question of enforcement does not generally arise".[4]

The court has other functions besides voluntary arbitration. Under the Terms and Conditions of Employment Act it adjudicates on whether an employer is observing terms of employment not less favourable than those in the relevant collective agreement, and claims arising out of its decision can be enforced in the courts.

[1] *Ibid.*, p. 96.   [2] *Ibid.*, p. 98.   [3] *Ibid.*, p. 98.   [4] *Ibid.*, p. 104.

It exercises powers with a similar purpose under the Road Haulage Wages Act, 1938, the Fair Wages Resolution of the House of Commons and the Civil Aviation Act, 1949. Setting these functions aside, the court dealt with 203 cases during the years 1960–4, an average of about forty a year. This compares with about sixteen references a year over the same period to the Civil Service Arbitration Tribunal whose jurisdiction is confined to about half a million employees.[1] Taking into account the fact that most of the cases heard by the court concern relatively small groups of employees, it can be seen that its work as a voluntary arbitration tribunal is a marginal element in the system of industrial relations as a whole. Its scope has been limited by the creation of separate tribunals for several public industries and services. While compulsory arbitration was available, from 1940–59, private and public industry could turn to it as an alternative, without the need for both sides to consent and in the knowledge that awards could be enforced. Even after the war-time ban on strikes and lockouts was terminated in 1951 the number of references to the Industrial Disputes Tribunal ran at about 140 a year. Since the tribunal was dissolved in 1959 private industry generally has been slow to make use of arbitration.

The court shares some of the objectives of the conciliation service, particularly its determination to maintain a scrupulous independence, and its concern that whatever is done should be acceptable to the parties and should tend to retain their good will. In his evidence to the Royal Commission the president of the court, Sir Roy Wilson, referred to the impression that the government was interfering with the independence of arbitrators during the period of the pay pause in 1961. In his view there had been no interference, but "the impression was widely gained that that independence was being interfered with; and the result was, in my opinion, disastrous". He went on to suggest that it led to a decline in the number of references to the court.[2]

Both independence and acceptability are argued in support of the general practice (with some exceptions) of giving no reason for awards. The first president, Sir William Mackenzie (later Lord Amulree) gave reasons and hoped to build up a body of

---

[1] *Ibid.*, p. 111. In addition single arbitrators (including independent chairmen empowered to act as arbitrators) were dealing with twenty-five cases a year.

[2] *Minutes of Evidence*, p. 1938.

"case law". Sir Roy initially shared this view but after careful consideration came down on the other side. His first reason was that an award was intended to terminate a dispute whereas giving reasons would "result in prolonging and possibly even exacerbating the differences between the parties, or in transferring the area of controversy from one topic or topics to another". In addition case law would restrict the court in subsequent decisions, the members might be able to agree on an award but not on their reasons for it, and giving reasons might be embarrassing for the employer and trade union members of the court.[1] He thought "it would greatly decrease the popularity of arbitration and the confidence the parties have in arbitration if we had to give reasons".[2] However, on a change of chairmanship, it was agreed with the concurrence of the Treasury and the civil service unions that the Civil Service Arbitration Tribunal should henceforth normally give reasons for its awards, although it would not be bound to do so.

No statistical study of the court's decisions has yet been published, and the only detailed investigation of the work of a major British arbitration tribunal which is available deals with the Industrial Disputes Tribunal.[3] The distribution of its awards between industries shows the attraction of arbitration for the public services. Local authority services came first and the health services third. Between them they accounted for 341 awards over nine years, over a quarter of the total. Some of the reasons for this have already been given. In addition the National and Local Government Officers' Association had been able to use the tribunal's predecessor, the National Arbitration Tribunal, to enforce agreed salaries and conditions on authorities which were unwilling to negotiate with them, and even after 1951 it still found this support helpful in dealing with claims on behalf of small groups, mainly of senior officers.

The evidence suggests some unions in private industry also used the tribunal mainly to deal with disputes concerning relatively weak groups of membership. Most cases in the vehicles and engineering industries "involved non-federated firms—i.e. firms

---

[1] *Ibid.*, pp. 1935–6.   [2] *Ibid.*, Q. 7223.
[3] W. E. J. McCarthy, "Compulsory Arbitration in Britain: The Work of the Industrial Disputes Tribunal", in *Three Studies in Collective Bargaining*, Royal Commission Research Papers No. 8. This is largely based on M. Reiss, *Compulsory Arbitration as a Method of Settling Industrial Disputes* (Unpublished B.Litt. thesis, Oxford, 1964)

where the unions are known to be generally far less well-organised".[1]

The tribunal was composed of five members, three of them including the chairman being independent, but it followed much the same procedures as the Industrial Court. Its chairman throughout was Lord Terrington. Most of its awards concerned pay, and an investigation of the amounts awarded suggests that, although the tribunal followed the general practice of not publishing reasons for its decisions, it nevertheless had a policy. "Essentially the Tribunal granted wage increases that did not differ significantly from those obtained by other methods—e.g. negotiation, recourse to the Industrial Court, and so on. . . . Terrington was concerned to settle references according to what appeared to be 'the going rate'."[2]

Arbitration is even more severely limited to official disputes than is the conciliation service. To allow the leaders of an unofficial dispute to present their case to a tribunal would be to put them on a par with the authorised officers of the union.

When a public inquiry into a dispute seems to be needed, the Secretary of State is not limited to courts of inquiry under the 1919 Act. In addition, committees of investigation, normally used for less important and far-reaching disputes, can be set up under the 1896 Act, and committees of inquiry can be appointed under general powers. The use of general powers is essential where the inquiry is instituted jointly with another minister and may be preferred where it is thought that the terms of reference should be drawn more widely than is possible under the 1919 Act. In the years 1960–4 there were two courts, three committees of investigation and five committees of inquiry. Nevertheless, over the years the great majority of investigations into major disputes have been conducted by courts of inquiry.

"A Court is generally appointed only as a last resort when no agreed settlement of a dispute seems possible, and when an unbiased and independent examination of the facts is considered to be in the public interest."[3] There is no need for the consent of the parties as there is with a reference to the Industrial Court. Very occasionally the court consists of a chairman alone, but normally an independent chairman—usually a judge, a practising lawyer or an academic—sits along with an employer and a trade

[1] *Ibid.*, p. 37.   [2] *Ibid.*, p. 39.   [3] *Written Evidence of the Ministry of Labour*, p. 106.

unionist, neither of them with a direct interest in the dispute. On several occasions in recent years when the chairman has been a judge, an academic specialising in industrial relations has made a fourth member of the court.[1]

Besides their normal usage to deal with official disputes which affect very large numbers of employees or which might lead to widespread disruption of industry and services because of the key position of the workers concerned, courts and other forms of inquiry can be used in disputes where arbitration would be out of the question, for example in unofficial stoppages, and in particular to investigate an unofficial dispute in "a highly publicised and notorious 'trouble spot'", such as "the 1957 inquiry at Briggs Motor Bodies, and its sequel at Fords in 1963".[2] On these occasions the court can interrogate the leaders of an unofficial dispute without seeming to accord them parity of status with the full-time officials. The unofficial leaders can be asked to attend as individuals who can give the court information of relevance to their inquiry without imparting to them a formal status as representing anyone.

The contrasts between arbitration and inquiry must not be exaggerated. Although there is no need to consult the parties before a court is appointed, careful soundings are usually taken and the department is "unlikely to set the machinery in motion if they have reason to believe that either party would regard this as unhelpful".[3] In this respect the preliminaries are not so very different from those which precede the use of voluntary arbitration. Nor are courts necessarily expected to do a different job from arbitration tribunals. Normally a court's terms of reference instruct it to inquire into the causes and circumstances of a dispute and to report, but with rare exceptions courts have also made recommendations for a settlement. McCarthy and Clifford explain the "frequent use of courts to settle national wages and conditions in engineering, shipbuilding and printing" by the dislike of both sides of these industries for arbitration. "By contrast, both sides have found the court of inquiry machinery more acceptable."[4]

---

[1] For example, the courts of inquiry into the electricity supply dispute 1964 and the shipping dispute 1966, both chaired by Lord Pearson.

[2] W. E. J. McCarthy and B. A. Clifford, "The Work of Industrial Courts of Inquiry" *British Journal of Industrial Relations*, March 1966, pp. 43–4.

[3] *Ibid.*, p. 42. [4] *Ibid.*, p. 51.

N

Moreover, so far as pay is concerned, courts of inquiry follow much the same criteria as arbitration tribunals. Many of them "justify the increases by reference to so-called 'comparability' arguments". Some have recommended adjustments of pay in line with other workers doing similar work, and others have favoured "equal increases for groups traditionally linked together in some customary 'wage-round' process".[1]

On the other hand, the similarity between inquiries and tribunals can be pressed too far. Courts normally accept a responsibility to give reasons for their proposals, and they usually respect the obligation to comment on the causes and circumstances of the dispute. Frequently this leads a court outside the substantive points at issue between the parties—which would be the sole concern of a tribunal—into the procedures for collective bargaining in the industry or undertaking under examination. In a number of instances the courts have recommended procedural changes. Where this is so, "the strongest impression one gets from reading the reports of courts of inquiry is that, in general, their members have been strong constitutionalists—i.e. they have believed that industrial relations can be improved by the establishment and observance of joint procedures for dealing with union grievances and claims". These procedures are, of course, the recognised procedures, normally at industry level. Where action is taken outside them, an "uncompromisingly hostile attitude" has been "adopted to unconstitutional action of any kind".[2]

Recommendations on procedural points, however, appear to win less acceptance than proposals on pay. McCarthy and Clifford point to several courts appointed to deal with disputes in engineering, shipbuilding and printing in which the parties accepted the substantive recommendations but ignored those on procedure; and to the 1957 inquiry at Briggs, where the recommendations were entirely procedural and completely ignored.[3]

Why should proposals on procedure not win acceptance? Two reasons can be offered to explain how courts can miss the mark in dealing with these issues. Firstly, some courts appear to work on unrealistic assumptions about the nature of industrial relations. They seem "to assume that it cannot really be in the interests of any group to act unconstitutionally, and in every case have certainly concluded that the specific action complained of was

[1] *Ibid.*, p. 47.   [2] *Ibid.*, p. 46.   [3] *Ibid.*, pp. 52–3.

quite unjustifiable. It is arguable that this naïve and legalistic approach has militated against attempts to analyse and prescribe for problems such as some of those existing in, say, Fords in 1957, and London Airport in 1958."[1] Secondly, although commissioned to discover causes and circumstances, they have in the past often relied on inadequate means of informing themselves and therefore others. Normally the sole methods have been to request evidence from the parties and to interrogate witnesses. This is likely to be effective only when the parties know the facts, and are reasonably willing to disclose them. In many of the procedural problems with which courts have to wrestle the parties may not be anxious to tell all that they know, but it is even more likely that they do not possess much of the information necessary for a solution. If they had understood the problem they might have done something about it before. Most courts have neglected the techniques of social investigation developed in the behavioural sciences.

The traditional work of conciliation, arbitration and inquiry has been described and analysed so far by means of published evidence and studies. Perhaps a personal comment may not be out of place. It is based on participation in arbitration tribunals and in courts and committees of inquiry and on some acquaintance with the work of the Department of Employment and Productivity and of Wages Councils. The principles of independence and impartiality have, in my opinion, often led to narrow-minded obscurantism. The procedure of arbitration tribunals has often been reduced to a lengthy recital of written cases, which the tribunal and the opposing party have already had the opportunity to study, followed by a few perfunctory questions. Courts of inquiry have often confined themselves to the examination of witnesses who can plainly tell them little of what they need to know to unravel the problems before them. Awards and recommendations have been based on unquestioned assumptions and on rule-of-thumb applications of comparability. Many Wages Councils have bumbled through the process of setting minimum rates for industries of whose actual earnings and pay movements they were content to remain in ignorance.

These things have been accepted because they helped to support the system of industrial relations; their justification has been that they worked. But what the participants failed to realise for too

[1] *Ibid.*, pp. 53–4.

long was that the system was changing. What they were support-ing was a structure of forms and practices which were less relevant to actual behaviour in industrial relations with each year that passed. But the strength of their assumptions and the poverty of their information kept them from observing this change. If they came across behaviour outside the rules, their natural reaction was to demand that it cease forthwith, for it was in conflict with the system which they were engaged to support. However, the changes are now beginning to be recognised, and reform of the institutions for state intervention in industrial relations has begun. How this has happened is the subject of Chapters 11 and 12.

GOVERNMENT EMPLOYMENT

In developing their policies on industrial relations it has often been an embarrassment to governments that they also are em-ployers of labour, and, in addition to that, among the biggest employers in the country. Already in 1900 the Post Office, with 167,000 employees, was by far the largest enterprise in Britain.

However, it was not so much the number of its employees that separated the government from other employers in the conduct of its industrial relations. The distinction was due mainly to the doctrine of the "sovereign employer". In its extreme form this doctrine states that the legislature is supreme, and cannot be bound by any other person or body, even by its own agent. Consequently collective bargaining is impossible. Joining with other employers in dealing with trade unions is ruled out because the sovereign legislature cannot delegate authority to an employers' association to take decisions on its behalf. But domestic bargaining is also out of the question for the legislature cannot itself conduct negotia-tions and equally cannot be bound by its agents, whether ministers or senior civil servants.

The ban on joint action with other employers applied at that time to such establishments as the ordnance factories and the Stationery Office, which employed the same classes of worker as outside establishments. But most departments, including the Post Office, had no outside counterparts with whom they could have associated even if they had wished to do so. This was emphasised by the structure of civil service trade unionism. If they belonged to unions, most government engineering workers and printers were members of the unions which catered for the same type of worker outside. But towards the end of the century unions began to emerge in other departments, either confined to a single department like the Postmen's Federation and the Tax Clerks' Association, or covering a class of civil servants employed in several departments like the Second Division Clerks' Association.

It was recognised that civil servants might have grievances. If so, they could "memorialise" the heads of their departments or "their lordships of the Treasury". These gentlemen, if impressed by the arguments, might try to persuade parliament to provide money to meet the prayers of the memorialists, or part of them. This procedure did not recommend itself to the unions. Over a period of some years, with the Post Office unions in the forefront of the struggle, they established that civil servants had a clear right to join unions and to take part in union business. One Postmaster General agreed to receive union deputations and another to meet full-time union officers.[1] Meanwhile the civil service unions organised lobbying of parliament so successfully that a series of committees was set up to investigate postal pay, and in 1912 a Royal Commission established to enquire into the organisation of the civil service undertook to receive evidence from the major civil service associations.

Lobbying and giving evidence to committees and commissions provided a channel for trade union action, but did not give the unions a direct part in the final decisions. Moreover, lobbying had its drawbacks for the government. One Postmaster General described it as "nothing more nor less than asking Members to purchase votes for themselves at the general election at the expense of the public Exchequer".[2] It was partly in order to avoid this that a major step towards collective bargaining was taken in 1914 when a further committee appointed to investigate Post Office pay included two officials of Post Office unions among its five members.

The rapid increase in retail prices during the war brought a drastic reduction in the living standards of civil servants and added to agitation for a satisfactory method of settling their pay.

---

[1] Clegg, Fox and Thompson, pp. 215–20.
[2] *Hansard*, 6 July 1905, col. 1365.

In 1917 the government established a Civil Service Arbitration Board as a temporary war-time concession to deal with the claims of civil servants earning less than £500 a year, and when the Whitley reports were given official blessing, the civil service unions were quick to demand that the government should grant to them the same machinery for negotiation as it was recommending to private industry. After some argument the principle was established so far as government "industrial" employees were concerned, but at first it was proposed that the new "Whitley" committees which were to be established in the rest of the civil service should be allowed no more than the "consideration of the general principles" which should govern pay and conditions of service.[1] The union response was sharp and unanimous. They would accept nothing short of authoritative collective bargaining. A joint committee was set up to devise a scheme, and it soon proposed the substitution of "determination" for "consideration", with decisions made "by agreement between the two sides" and "reported to the Cabinet, and thereupon shall become operative".[2] Thus the doctrine of the sovereign employer was laid to rest. In fact it is an essential element in public employment only where a government is not assured that its decisions will be upheld by the legislature, as is the case in the United States. But in Britain, with a system of cabinet government, it is even less likely that an agreement between the Treasury and the unions will be rejected by parliament than that the agreements of the most disciplined of employers' associations will be rejected by its members.

Following the decision to introduce full collective bargaining for non-industrial staff, a National Whitley Council for the Civil Service was instituted to deal with general issues, including the pay of general classes of civil servants employed in a number of departments. The "official" side now consists of senior civil servants appointed by the Civil Service Department which has taken over from the Treasury, and the "staff" side of representatives of the civil service unions. Departmental Whitley Councils deal with departmental issues, including the pay of "departmental classes", without reference to the National Council. Each Council

---

[1] *Report on the Application of the Whitley Report to the Administrative Departments*, Cmd. 9, 1919.

[2] *Report of the National Provisional Joint Committee on the Application of the Whitley Report to the Administrative Departments*, Cmd. 198, 1919.

draws its members from the unions recognised as representing the staff of the department, and from the senior officials of the department.

The erection of this elaborate structure of councils did not solve all the problems of collective bargaining in government service. There remained the question of what was to happen if the two sides could not agree. An appeal to force was hardly conceivable. Although there has now been a Post Office strike, most civil service unions are extremely reluctant to consider the use of a strike; and "it is clear that striking, even if not illegal, is a disciplinary offence on the part of a civil servant".[1] In 1919 there was still the war-time Arbitration Board, but this was abolished by the government in 1922, leaving no appeal against the final decision of the Treasury. This was clearly unacceptable, and in 1925 the government agreed to put arbitration on a permanent footing, at first through the Industrial Court, and from 1936 by means of a separate Civil Service Arbitration Tribunal. Certain subjects, such as salaries above a specified level, superannuation and the granting or withholding of established status, were excluded from arbitration, and there were two further conditions: that "the Government will give effect to the awards of the Court ... subject to the overriding authority of parliament"; and that the government "must also reserve to itself the right to refuse arbitration 'on grounds of policy'."[2] The first proviso has never been used, and the second only to exclude the issue of equal pay for men and women, but in the 1961 "pay pause" the Chancellor of the Exchequer took it upon himself to postpone the operation of awards of the Civil Service Arbitration Tribunal until the end of the "pause".[3]

There remained still another question to be settled if civil service negotiations were to run smoothly; on what principle should the pay of government employees be settled? Since the ability of the official side to meet claims for higher pay is limited only by the government's capacity to raise taxes, they require some other criterion for their offers than ability to pay. It needs a defence against the accusation that it is squandering the nation's resources by over-paying civil servants. On the other hand governments are open to the charge of niggardliness; they may

[1] H.M. Treasury, *Staff Relations in the Civil Service*, 1965 edition, p. 20.
[2] *Ibid.*, p. 24.   [3] See p. 415.

be accused of encouraging others to be good employers while dealing harshly with their own employees. To defend themselves against these attacks from both sides, before 1914 ministers and committees generally laid considerable weight on pay in comparable occupations outside the service. A Royal Commission on the Civil Service which reported in 1931 (the Tomlin Commission) raised these comparisons into a general principle by laying down that "broad general comparison between classes in the Service and outside occupations are possible and should be made".[1] There is, however, wide scope for argument over the application of broad general comparisons, and in 1955 another Royal Commission on the Civil Service (the Priestley Commission) not only reiterated the view that the pay of civil servants should be settled by "fair comparison with current remuneration of outside staffs employed on broadly comparable work, taking account of differences in other conditions of service", but also recommended that a specialised unit should be set up to discover staffs employed on comparable work and to investigate their pay and conditions of service.[2] As a result the Civil Service Pay Research Unit was formed to carry out a fact-finding task. The evaluation of the information they supply is, however, left to the negotiators, with reference to the Civil Service Arbitration Tribunal when they cannot agree.

This device can only be applied to those classes of civil servants for whom "outside analogues" can be discovered, and there are many of them, such as tax inspectors and tax officers, whose jobs have no close counterparts outside. For them the Priestley Commission recommended the use of "internal relativities" whereby their pay could be related to the pay of some other class of civil servants for whom outside analogues could be found.

On this basis the official side and the unions have elaborated a system of periodic "pay reviews" on the basis of Research Unit investigations for classes with outside analogues, leading also to pay adjustments for "child grades" attached to these "parent grades". In between the reviews, upward adjustments can be provided by general agreements covering the whole service. Another report on the Civil Service (the report of the Fulton Committee), published in 1968, gave general approval to the principle of fair comparisons, but also made two recommendations

[1] *Report*, Cmd. 3909, 1931, p. 85.   [2] *Report*, Cmd. 9631, 1955, pp. 25, 27.

which could lead to radical changes in the existing methods of applying the principle. The first is the absorption of the hundreds of existing grades of civil servants, many of them consisting of relatively small numbers attached to a single department, into a severely limited number of general grades; and the second is that the techniques of job evaluation should be used in dealing with civil service pay. It is not yet known how these recommendations will be implemented.

Methods of collective bargaining do not extend to the pay of the highest grades of the service, which include about eight thousand administrative, executive, professional and scientific officers. Following the Priestley Report, in 1957 an independent Standing Advisory Committee was established to review their pay either on its own initiative or at the request of the government. In order to inform its decisions, the committee collects "information about how salaries in other public services and in broadly comparable employment outside the public services [has] moved since its last general review."[1]

By 1955 civil servants generally, despite the Tomlin formula, had lost ground in pay relationships compared with 1938.[2] Since the Priestley Commission reported, however, many grades have received larger increases of pay than other wage- and salary-earners and most of their unions are warmly favourable towards the machinery and principles which have been derived from its reports. There is, however, one important exception. Postmen have no obvious outside analogue, and there is no other grade within the service which would make a convenient "parent" for them. In the year following the Priestley Commission their grievances over their pay settlements contrasted strongly with the satisfaction of the Post Office Engineers with the outcome of comparisons between themselves and skilled engineers and technicians outside. Eventually a special inquiry reported in favour of "factor" comparisons with outside occupations whereby pay could be related to that of occupations whose work included elements similar to that of postmen, even though the job as a whole was not a close counterpart.[3] Publication was followed

---

[1] National Board for Prices and Incomes, *Pay of Higher Civil Servants*, Report No. 11, Cmnd. 2882, 1966, p. 2.

[2] *Occupation and Pay in Great Britain 1906–60*, pp. 124–5.

[3] Committee on the Pay of Postmen, *Report*, 1964.

by a one-day strike and the threat of a longer stoppage which gained a substantial interim increase for postmen pending the application of the new method of comparison.

The machinery established in 1919 for settling the pay and conditions of industrial civil servants was on a different pattern. Three Trade Joint Councils, one for shipbuilding, one for engineering, and one for miscellaneous trades, dealt with common conditions of service; and departmental councils dealt with domestic matters such as the arrangement of holidays. Where the two sides could not agree, they could, if they chose, submit the issue to arbitration by the Industrial Court. The principle of settling the pay of industrial civil servants by comparison with outside occupations had been laid down before the first world war. In 1910 the government undertook to apply the terms of the "fair wages" resolution of the House of Commons to its own employees. This obligation was carried over into the Trade Joint Councils.

A relatively small number of industrial civil servants are "trade-rated", and paid strictly according to agreements negotiated in private industry. They include printing workers at the Stationery Office and building workers employed by the Ministry of Public Building and Works. The majority, however, were until recently paid rates adjusted according to average movements of outside rates. Up to 1940 district averages were used for each separate establishment, but in that year it was agreed that rates should be settled nationally. Two craft rates, one for London and the other for the provinces, were fixed by averaging the minimum time-work craft rates paid in 22 outside industries (21 for London); and two "M" rates for labourers were similarly settled by averaging rates paid in 34 outside industries (32 for London). These four rates were adjusted every six months.

This system might have been expected to yield much the same results as the more sophisticated methods of the Civil Service Pay Research Unit. In fact they were very different. The earnings of most salaried employees, both inside and outside government service, are largely determined by the rates of salary laid down for them, and in any case the Pay Research Unit investigates remuneration, not merely minimum rates. Consequently the process of "fair comparison" provides the non-industrial civil servant with much the same income as his outside analogue. But systems of payment by results, plus rates and overtime can bring the earnings of manual workers to a level far above the minimum time rates which were the basis of comparison for industrial civil servants. Consequently a comparison based on averaging these rates did not guarantee the industrial civil servant an income on anything like the same level as those of the workers with whom his own basic pay was compared. Moreover, most industrial civil servants were paid above the craft and M rates which resulted from the comparison. Craftsmen were paid supplementary rates according to their skill and experience, and most of the remainder were semi-skilled workers receiving "lead" rates added to the M rate. Many of them worked overtime and in 1966 it was reported that "about 15 per cent of the total labour force are on payment-by-results schemes of various kinds".[1] Accordingly the pay of industrial civil servants could be at the same level as that of their outside counterparts only if the average additional payments to each group came to the same figure. In fact the National Board for Prices and Incomes found that earnings were generally lower in the industrial civil service. The evidence suggested that "although the present system is designed to give industrial civil servants pay comparable with that of their counterparts in private industry, it often fails to do so".[2]

The Board suggested a thorough overhaul of the system. Industrial civil servants should, they suggested, be grouped according to the type of work on which they were employed—engineering, chemicals, dockyards, building, vehicle maintenance and so on. Then the rates of pay for the key occupations should be settled initially with regard to "the actual levels of wages (not the basic rates) for a 40-hour week of timeworkers engaged in similar activities in outside employment."[3] Thereafter there should be separate pay negotiations for each industrial group concerned not with statistical comparison with outside basic rates, but with the needs of each group assessed in the light of government incomes policy, including the possibility of exceptional pay increases for special contributions towards increasing productivity. The re-grouping and initial reform of the pay structure was carried out in 1967, yielding considerable increases to most grades of industrial civil servant. It has not yet proved possible for the

---

[1] National Board for Prices and Incomes, *Pay of Industrial Civil Servants*, Report No. 18, Cmnd. 3034, 1966, p. 4.   [2] *Ibid.*, p. 9.   [3] *Ibid.*, p. 11.

separate industrial groups to take over their own negotiations so that the long-run effects of the reform cannot be assessed. Initially the report has led to a method of "fair comparison" for industrial civil servants more closely akin to that which has operated for non-industrial civil servants since the Priestley report.

Thus there have been developed increasingly more accurate devices for transferring the pay decisions of private industry into the wages and salaries of government employees. It has sometimes been argued that the government should set an example to private employers. In Britain the government has preferred to avoid trouble and criticism by taking private employers as the model which they should follow, at least in questions of pay.

OTHER PUBLIC EMPLOYMENT

Besides being the direct employer of some half million industrial and non-industrial civil servants, the government also plays an important part in negotiating the pay and conditions of employees in other publicly owned industries and services.

The National Health Service provides an example. The Health Service Act of 1946 nationalised private hospitals and brought them into a single national system along with hospitals previously run by the local authorities. Assurances were given that there would be "set up some machinery of the Whitley Council type"[1] for dealing with pay. Collective bargaining was then relatively new in the hospital service, machinery having been only recently established for the two largest groups of employees, the nurses and the manual staffs, and some other groups having no machinery at all. Consequently the system of "functional councils"[2] was an innovation and had to face a number of unusual problems. One of these was the representation of staff in the many grades among which unions had few or no members. This was solved by pressing into service the representatives of professional associations.[3] Another was to determine with whom the unions and professional associations should negotiate.

Along with representatives of the hospital authorities created by the Act the management sides of most of the functional councils included representatives of the local authority associations, for local authorities continued to administer some branches

---

[1] *Hansard*, 2 May 1946, col. 402.   [2] See p. 210.   [3] See p. 350.

of the health service. Where appropriate, representation was also accorded to the committees established by the Act to run the various practitioner services. All these bodies were employing authorities within the service. In addition, however, there were officials from the Ministry of Health and the Scottish Department for Health, although neither of these bodies had any claim to be health service employers. The reason was evident. Although the hospital and other authorities are in law the employers of their staffs, almost all their income comes from the Exchequer. Consequently the departmental representatives are there to protect public funds. Moreover, although they are in a minority, they are normally bound to have the last word on major issues of pay since they have the power of the purse. More exactly, the last word lies with the Treasury, which they must inevitably consult before agreeing to substantial increases in government expenditure. Consequently there have from time to time been complaints that the management sides are subject to "remote control".[1] Even so the Minister of Health was given powers to confirm the decisions of the councils by embodying them in regulations.[2] In 1958 the then Minister refused to confirm an agreement reached in the functional council for administrative and clerical staffs, so that it remained inoperative. There is no obligation on either side in the health service to accept arbitration, but normally the management sides have been willing to allow disagreements to be referred to the Industrial Court. Indeed at one time it was suggested that the frequent recourse of the health service to arbitration showed that in times of financial stringency the government preferred to have even justified pay increases awarded by arbitration, so as to shift the responsibility.[3]

There are closely similar arrangements for negotiations for the police and the probation service. Representatives of the relevant department sit alongside representatives of the employing authorities on the negotiating bodies, and the decisions of these bodies require confirmation by a Minister. The National Joint Council for Fire Brigades, on the other hand, does not include

---

[1] *Report of the Committee of Enquiry into the Cost of the National Health Service* (Guillebaud Committee), Cmd. 9663, 1956, p. 233. "Decisions reached in Whitley Council procedure must", said the report, "be acceptable to the Government if they are to be approved by Ministers for general application throughout the Health Service."

[2] S.I.1373 of 1951, made under Section 66 of the 1946 Act.

[3] *Wage Policy and the Health Service*, p. 94.

departmental representatives although its decisions require confirmation.

Until 1965 the Burnham Committees, established in 1920 to settle teachers' pay, were in the same constitutional position as the National Joint Council for Fire Brigades. However, a dispute in 1963 revealed the difficulties of this relationship. The Minister decided that an agreement reached by the Main Burnham Committee, which deals with schoolteachers' pay, was unacceptable, but he could not persuade the committee to amend their proposals to his liking. Deadlock ensued, for the Minister's legal advisers had ruled that it would be *ultra vires* for the Burnham Committees to have recourse to arbitration.[1] In the end the Minister imposed his own scales. This drastic action seems to have been taken as much to force a reorganisation of the system as to alter the agreement which the committee had made, undesirable though it was in his eyes. In 1965 the Remuneration of Teachers Act introduced departmental representatives into the employers' sides of the Burnham Committees, and also established an arbitral body for settling unresolved disputes. Consequently the Minister's views can be heard in the process of negotiation, and there is a device for clearing deadlocks.

The devices just described are not used to control the negotiations covering the main bodies of local authority staffs. Before 1914 the local authorities regarded themselves, like the central government, as sovereign employers. This did not mean that they refused to deal with unions. As organisation spread among local government staffs, union officials were often permitted to meet the chief officer of the relevant department, and also, if need be, the committee to which he was responsible. Their dealings came very close to bargaining, even if the ratification of the full council was required. But at that time the local authorities would not accept an association among themselves to deal jointly with the unions. Each was determined to retain its own sovereignty.

During the first world war, however, a number of authorities in Lancashire and Cheshire formed an association to deal with the unions over wartime wage increases. After the war the principle of collective bargaining for wage-earners was accepted also in other parts of the country. Pay was to be settled by provincial

---

[1] Although the Main Burnham Committee had managed on more than one occasion to introduce a form of arbitration by referring an issue to "independent advisers".

councils whose employers' sides were directly representative of the individual authorities in the region. The employers' side of the National Council, which dealt with disputes that the provincial councils could not settle, consisted in part of representatives of the provincial councils and in part of representatives of the local authority associations—such as the Association of Municipal Corporations—which had hitherto not been concerned in labour matters. This structure, which gave a degree of protection to the autonomy of individual authorities, was continued after the second world war when the responsibility for negotiating pay was transferred from the provincial councils to the National Council. Its advantages had been demonstrated by the collapse, early in the 'twenties, of a national council for local authority white collar staffs whose employers' side had been based on the local authority associations alone. A second attempt, made during the second world war, followed the partially federal structure of the councils for manual workers, and successfully established the National Joint Council for Local Authorities' Administrative, Professional, Technical and Clerical Staffs.

Soon afterwards the Local Authorities' Conditions of Service Advisory Board for England and Wales was set up by the local authority associations and the employers' sides of these and the many other joint councils dealing with local authority employees, such as land drainage workers, building craftsmen and town clerks. Its function is to provide co-ordination and advice. With growing centralisation, the associations and the Advisory Board have come to play a larger part in the decisions of the various councils, and the once-prized autonomy of the individual authorities is now almost forgotten. Nevertheless the central government plays no official part in the work of these councils or of the Advisory Board. Whatever discussions there may be between the Board's officers and government officials are private and have no official standing. However, it would be surprising if the view of the government were unknown or disregarded in the pay decisions of important public services which draw heavily on Exchequer grants.

The Labour Government which took office in 1945 greatly extended the area of public employment by a series of nationalisation Acts, but most of the new public corporations which they established—the Coal Board, the Transport Commission, the

Airways Corporations and the various boards in gas and electricity —inherited labour problems very different from those of either central and local government or the health services. The manual employees of most of these boards have been strongly organised in unions for decades, and collective bargaining had long been established; on the railways this was also true of white collar employees.

A model for this situation had been established in 1934 when the London Passenger Transport Board took over, not only London's Underground and its buses and trams, but also, with only slight alterations, the complex network of collective bargaining arrangements covering the staff employed to operate them. The post-war nationalisation Acts laid a statutory duty on the boards to make provisions for collective bargaining. Section 46 of the Coal Industry Nationalisation Act of 1946 obliged the Coal Board to draw up with the unions joint machinery for "the settlement by negotiation of terms and conditions of employment, with provision for reference to arbitration in default of such settlement. . . ." Similar words were inserted in the other nationalisation Acts. In most instances the obligation to bargain over the pay and conditions of wage-earners was met by taking over the existing machinery, although some new features were added, notably in coalmining. For white collar employees, however, most of the nationalised industries had to set about devising industry negotiating procedures for the first time, and there were substantial increases in the membership of the relevant unions.

It has never been easy to gauge the degree of government intervention in collective bargaining in the nationalised industries. Formally the responsible minister has the power to give "directions of a general character as to the exercise and performance by the Board of their functions in relation to matters appearing to the Minister to affect the national interest",[1] but this power has been used only once, in relation to transport charges. Indirectly, however, the minister has great power over the boards whose members he appoints and may decide not to reappoint at the end of their terms. One cogent instance of this was the humiliation of Mr. Steven Hardie, chairman of the Iron and Steel Corporation, in 1952, following which he was forced to resign.[2] Government

[1] This is the wording of the Coal Industry Nationalisation Act.
[2] W. A. Robson, *Nationalised Industry and Public Ownership*, 1960, pp. 238–40.

influence has been felt in many pay settlements in nationalised industries, which normally require the blessing of the cabinet, if not its formal approval. For some years ministers tried to maintain the fiction that labour matters were entirely within the managerial discretion of the boards, and board chairmen were required to support this pretence. Ridiculous subterfuges were employed. Since 1958, however, successive Prime Ministers have themselves conducted the final discussions with the railway unions at crises in railway negotiations,[1] and the secret is less well kept.

The heavy losses suffered by the railways ever since nationalisation have made its pay settlements of particular concern to the government which has, one way or another, to finance them. The Coal Board has not lost money continuously, but has accumulated substantial deficits. Other nationalised industries, however, including gas and electricity, have generally paid their way. It might be supposed that these boards could be permitted to devise and apply their own pay policies so long as they could meet the cost, especially when every government since the publication of the White Paper on the *Financial and Economic Obligations of the Nationalised Industries*[2] in 1961 has avowed the intention of equating their conditions more closely to those of private competitive industry. But it is doubtful whether this degree of independence can ever be achieved. The political importance of pay decisions in nationalised industries is bound to attract ministerial intervention, and there is no means to protect the boards against their influence. The uproar which arose during the "pay pause" when the negotiators for the electricity industry settled on a date of application for a pay settlement without ministerial sanction[3] showed that government supervision operates in nationalised industries which pay their way as well as those which run a deficit.

With government influence playing a considerable part in

[1] For example in May 1958, February 1962 and December 1965.

[2] Cmnd. 1337, 1961.

[3] In a statement to the House of Commons just after the settlement, Mr. Macmillan, the Prime Minister, said: "the decision . . . rested with the Electricity Council, but the Government had left the Council under no doubt as to the importance which the Government attached to the pay pause. . . . Accordingly, when my right honourable friend the Minister of Power was informed, late on Thursday evening, that a final offer was about to be made, he expressed grave disquiet and anxiety and emphasised the damage that a settlement in the terms proposed would do." (*Hansard*, 21 November 1961, col. 1146.)

their pay settlements it is not surprising that a number of these public services and nationalised industries have experienced some of the pressures at work on central government pay policies. In 1960 there appeared three reports dealing with pay in public employment, from the Royal Commission on Doctors' and Dentists' Remuneration (the Pilkington Commission),[1] the Royal Commission on the Police (the Willink Commission)[2] and the Railway Pay Committee of Inquiry (the Guillebaud Committee).[3] The Guillebaud Committee was expressly instructed "to conduct an investigation into the relativity of pay" of railway workers compared with other workers and to "establish the degree of job comparability" between them. The Pilkington Commission was asked to compare the remuneration of doctors and dentists with that of other professions. The Willink Commission expressly rejected "fair comparisons" as a method of settling police pay, but went on to recommend that the pay of the constable should be related to that of wage rates in selected skilled occupations.

None of the three bodies was able to find a method of comparison as straightforward as that used in the civil service. Having argued that the work of doctors and dentists could not be compared with that of any other profession, the Pilkington Commission decided that comparison should be made with those professions which compete with the medical and dental professions for able young men and women. On this basis they found that average remuneration was higher among doctors and dentists than in any other profession, although doctors came slightly below actuaries if allowance was made for a different age distribution.[4] They held, however, that the disadvantages inherent in the working lives of doctors and dentists warranted an even higher differential over other professions, and recommended substantial increases in their remuneration. Their report was accepted, and a review body was established, similar to the Standing Advisory Committee for higher civil servants, to review their pay from time to time and to propose further adjustments.

[1] *Report*, Cmnd. 939, 1960. [2] *Report*, Cmnd. 1222, 1960. [3] *Report*, 1960.
[4] There is a widespread impression that the medical profession is inadequately paid. This could be due to the structure of remuneration in the profession. Junior and middle-grade hospital doctors have always received far less than the majority of their colleagues, and their working conditions are often onerous. It is their plight which is advertised when the pay of doctors is subject to public discussion.

Having decided that the constable's pay should be related to an average of the minimum rates of skilled craftsmen, the Willink Commission proposed to add 45 per cent to the average to take account of supplementary earnings of skilled craftsmen, and a further 25 per cent for the dangers and drawbacks of the policeman's job. They did not reveal the formulae whereby these percentages were derived. The outcome was a substantial pay rise for the police.

The Guillebaud Committee made straight comparisons between a number of railway jobs and outside jobs, much on the lines of the Civil Service Pay Research Unit, and tried by a crude method of job evaluation to relate the pay of other railway grades to those for which outside analogues could be found. But pay comparisons were on the basis of minimum rates, neglecting substantial supplementary earnings on both sides of the comparison. Once more the consequence was a substantial pay rise. Over the next five years there was a controversy between the railway unions and the government as to whether the Guillebaud comparisons should be applied in subsequent negotiations. Consequently railway pay fell behind in one negotiation and then, with the aid of a strike threat, caught up again in the next.

Generally speaking the subjects of these inquiries have been well satisfied with the results. University teachers were likewise pleased by the recommendations of the National Incomes Commission concerning their salaries in 1964.[1] Subsequently, however, they were made the subject of a standing reference to the National Board for Prices and Incomes whose first report on their pay aroused bitter hostility among them.[2] Other groups of public employees have also failed to secure similar treatment to that accorded to doctors and civil servants. No method of fair comparison has been agreed for schoolteachers. Their unions emphasise the continuing decline in their average salaries

[1] National Incomes Commission, *Remuneration of Academic Staff in Universities and Colleges of Advanced Technology*, Report No. 3, Cmnd. 2317, 1964. The Commission rejected the suggestion that academic salaries should be determined by "fair comparison", but were "satisfied that over the years there has been a decline in the position occupied by university salaries in the overall pattern of relativities" (p. 17) which ought to be reversed.

[2] Not only did it recommend considerably smaller increases than they believed they deserved, but it proposed methods of relating pay to performance which they held to be unworkable and undesirable (National Board for Prices and Incomes, *Standing Reference on the Pay of University Teachers in Great Britain*, Report No. 98, Cmnd. 3866, 1968).

compared with the average earnings of male wage-earners, but the argument that their pay should be determined on this basis has not won acceptance, and for many years teachers' pay has been a controversial issue. If anything nurses' pay is even more of a problem. A reference to the National Board for Prices and Incomes did not lead to any form of fair comparison for dealing with their pay. The Board's report found a need to improve their salary structure and made proposals for increases in salaries over two years which, as it turned out, yielded salary advances for most nurses below the general rise in earnings over the same period.[1] Most other subordinate health service professions share some of the nurses' grievances, although their complaints have received less attention.

PAY AND PERFORMANCE IN PUBLIC EMPLOYMENT

The method of fair comparison has not been applied to wage-earners outside central government service except for police and railwaymen. It would be difficult to find outside analogues for coalminers. The face-workers, the dominant group in the National Union of Mineworkers, have been relatively high-paid since nationalisation, and confident in their own bargaining strength without recourse to the support of statistical formulae. Fair comparison could be more easily applied to wage-earners in gas and electricity supply, but their unions also have preferred other methods, with reasonable success. In October 1966 the National Board for Prices and Incomes found that average earnings of adult male wage-earners in the gas industry, at £20 5s. 2d a week, were "not far from the average in the economy". Overtime (£4 10s. 5d a week) was the main supplement to basic pay (£13 5s. 9d) but incentive payments were worth £4 19s. 0d a week to the 17 per cent of the employees who received them, and "the industry is now strongly committed to the spread of incentive bonus schemes".[2]

However, workers in some other public services have been less fortunate. In the October 1967 survey of average weekly

---

[1] *Pay of Nurses and Midwives in the National Health Service*, Report No. 60, Cmnd. 3585, 1968.

[2] *Pay and Conditions of Manual Workers in Local Authorities, the National Health Service, Gas and Water Supply*, pp. 13, 44–5.

earnings of manual workers, taken before the recommendations of the National Board for Prices and Incomes on industrial civil servants had been put into effect, men in national government service (£16 2s. 2d) and in local government service (£17 0s. 0d) came below men in every other industry included in the survey, the national average for men being £21 7s. 6d. The national health service was not included in the survey, but a year earlier at the time of the Board's inquiry into the *Pay and Conditions of Manual Workers in Local Authorities, the National Health Service, Gas and Water Supply*, the earnings of men in the health service were about 15s. above those of men in the local authorities (mainly due to a higher incidence of shift working) and at that time only six of the 129 industries in the official survey came below the health service.[1] The relative position of the three services had been much the same for many years before that. It is a matter for some surprise that these large bodies of public servants should not have made a greater outcry about such a state of affairs, and that their grievances were not pressed upon the public with the same force as the complaints of nurses and teachers, especially as all three groups are strongly unionised.

In its investigation into "the problem of low pay" among manual workers in the local authorities and the health service, the National Board for Prices and Incomes concluded that "the root cause of the problem is low productivity". With special reference to local authority employees, the Board admitted that "the potential of some may not be high and the average age of the labour force is higher than in industry generally", but they did not accept these as the main causes of poor performance. They assembled figures for increases in labour productivity achieved in a small number of authorities by means of work study and incentive-payment schemes and suggested that "the more important reason for inefficiency is the acceptance by management of low standards of performance as normal and a failure to take sufficient steps to realise the full potential of the labour force".[2] The Board went on to detail some of the defects of local authority management, and found that most of them could be matched in the health service. Many of their observations recalled their earlier report on the industrial civil service in which they had also diagnosed managerial inefficiency and had suggested that

[1] *Ibid.*, pp. 11, 13.   [2] *Ibid.*, pp. 22–5, 32.

"the combined use of a broad arithmetic average for determining pay and of a central budget for determining numbers does not necessarily result in the most economic running of establishments".[1]

In many respects these services are models of the system of industrial relations recommended by the Whitley Committee. With pay and conditions settled by centralised bargaining, away from the individual establishment, industrial relations within the establishment had to be largely confined to consultation (apart from the relatively small numbers covered by payment-by-results schemes). But the reports of the National Board for Prices and Incomes suggest that the centralised settlement of pay and conditions may hinder the effective use of manpower in the establishment. Rather than strive for improvement, it may be easier to allow managerial performance and labour productivity to find a level which those in the establishment are willing to accept as a reasonable return for the pay and conditions which are outside their control. It does not follow that undertakings in higher-paid industries and services, with a considerable volume of domestic bargaining over pay, are bound to be more efficient than these public services. But if they are not more efficient, the remedy lies within their grasp.

In this connection the experience of the nationalised industries is also relevant, for they have devoted a good deal of effort to developing joint consultative committees. The most consistent effort to render these committees effective has been made by the management of the electricity supply industry. Lord Citrine, the first chairman of the Central Electricity Authority (as it then was), gave the effort his full support. Full-time officers were appointed to serve the National Joint Advisory Councils and the Area Councils. In 1958 the Yorkshire Division of the Generating Board introduced "informal" departmental meetings, because "while employees are primarily interested in the functions and responsibilities of their own groups, the L.A.C.s are primarily interested in station affairs as a whole".[2] The National Council described these "meetings of working groups held on a systematic but informal basis" as "an attempt to carry consultation . . . to

---

[1] *Pay of Industrial Civil Servants*, p. 15.
[2] C. G. Richards and H. Sallis, "The Joint Consultative Committee and the Working Group: A Power Station Experiment", *Public Administration*, Winter 1961.

he 'shop-floor' ",[1] and other parts of the country followed York-
hire's example.

This was the most large-scale and sustained attempt in Britain
o associate manual workers and junior clerical and technical
grades with the management of industry. Nevertheless in 1960
"a number of the committees in London and South-East England"
were "virtually immobilised by attacks from the unofficial shop
tewards' movement".[2] As for their affect on performance, it was
possible for the productivity agreements of 1965-6 to cut back
average hours worked from 51 to 39 in generation and from 49
to 43 in distribution without a decline in average earnings, while
at the same time accomplishing, according to the National Board
for Prices and Incomes, "an over-all saving to the industry".[3]
Only two years later the industry negotiated an incentive payment system to apply to virtually all its wage-earners. A bonus
above the agreed rate was to be paid starting at a performance
of 65 "as against the 100 equivalent to standard performance".
The National Board for Prices and Incomes reported that "this
starting point is itself low by comparison with schemes that exist
in some other industries. In addition the general performance in
this industry is certainly below 65. In most cases, therefore, an
improvement in performance will have to be achieved before
payments start, even at 65."[4] It is possible that, before this series
of agreements began, the effect of centralised settlement of all
aspects of pay and conditions on performance in the electrical
supply industry was not very different from its effect in the
industrial civil service, in local government and in the health
service, despite the industry's highly developed system of consultation. The most obvious difference was the high level of
overtime which then sustained earnings in electricity supply
compared with the relatively low levels of overtime and low
earnings of the other three services.

[1] *Annual Report of the National Joint Advisory Council of the Electricity Supply Industry*,
1962–3, p. 45.

[2] Michael Shanks (ed.), *Lessons of Public Enterprise*, 1963, p. 119.

[3] *Productivity Agreements*, p. 20.

[4] *Electricity Supply Industry National Guidelines Covering Productivity Payments*, Report
No. 79, Cmnd. 3726, 1968, p. 4.

CHAPTER 10

THE TRADES UNION CONGRESS AND THE CONFEDERATION OF BRITISH INDUSTRY

Mention has already been made of the Disputes Committee of the Trades Union Congress in dealing with union structure, and of the part played by the British Employers' Confederation in the Mond-Turner discussions, but so far no systematic discussion of the central organisations of the two sides of industry has been necessary. Since their constituents allow them only a peripheral part in the process of collective bargaining, their importance lies mainly in their dealings with the government. For this reason the treatment given to them in these pages is brief. Most of their work belongs to a study of political pressure groups rather than to a book on industrial relations. The severe limitation of their powers is in large measure due to the date of their creation. Each was established at a time when many of its constituents were already developed and mature. They wished to guard against any encroachment on their own autonomy and they had the strength to do so.

THE TRADES UNION CONGRESS

This is true of the Trades Union Congress although it came into being in the late eighteen-sixties. The unions had already burned their fingers in earlier experiments with central organisations possessing wide powers. The title which they gave to the executive body of Congress—the Parliamentary Committee—made plain that its main function was to lobby parliament to secure support for those resolutions of Congress which required legislation. Only slowly and with great caution did Congress venture into other fields, such as collecting funds for unions involved in major stoppages, and when bold extensions of common action were demanded Congress sought to avoid responsibility by calling new agencies into being.

The first of these was the General Federation of Trade Unions, formed in 1899 to provide central strike insurance for all unions who wished to join. For nearly two decades it cut a considerable figure in the trade union movement, even on occasion challenging the leadership of Congress, but one by one its major constituents found its benefits unnecessary or its policies unattractive and withdrew, until today it provides insurance and common services for a group of smaller unions.

By 1900 the unions had been sending representatives to parliament for a quarter of a century, and had already made more than one attempt to create their own electoral organisation. In that year they joined with three socialist groups to found the Labour Representation Committee. The Committee prospered and became the modern Labour Party. For decades now the party and Congress have kept their distance from each other but most major unions and many smaller unions are affiliated to both bodies, and the party still bears the mark of its origin in the powers which its constitution grants to the unions.

While Labour was replacing the Liberals as the country's major left-wing party, Congress was beginning to acquire the confidence to widen its own powers. During and immediately after the first world war several other bodies, including the Triple Alliance and the workers' side of the 1919 National Industrial Conference, were in competition with the Congress as the central representative organisation of the unions. But in a major reorganisation in 1921 Congress reasserted its authority as spokesman for the industrial side of the labour movement, substituting a General Council for the Parliamentary Committee and increasing its resources and its staff. Many of those who took part in the reorganisation hoped to centralise the movement's industrial policies, and since the years following the first world war brought the heaviest incidence of industry-wide strikes that this country has ever experienced, centralisation of industrial policy was seen at that time in terms of the co-ordination of industrial disputes. In 1924 Congress empowered the General Council to intervene in a dispute if negotiations broke down and other workers were likely to be involved or affected by the outcome. If such a dispute led to a stoppage and the union concerned had followed the Council's advice, the Council was to "take steps to organise on behalf of the union or unions concerned all such moral and material support as the circumstances of the dispute may appear to justify". Even so the unions protected their autonomy by inserting a clause stipulating that "unless requested to do so by the affiliated union or unions concerned, the Council shall not intervene so long as there is a prospect of whatever difference may exist on the matters in question being amicably settled by the machinery of negotiation existing in the trades affected".[1]

It was under this rule that the General Council arranged an embargo on the transport of coal in 1925, thus forcing the government to intervene in the current coal dispute by offering a subsidy to maintain miners' wages. The rule provided such constitutional authority as the Council had to call a General Strike nine months later, when the subsidy came to an end. Thereafter the rule fell into disuse for many years, but in 1955, and on several occasions since then, the General Council has intervened in an actual or threatened stoppage to promote a settlement, adding its influence to that of the Ministry of Labour as a peacemaker. Indeed its powers have been extended to allow it to intervene in the early stages. The only occasion since the war on which the General Council has been asked to muster "material resources" on behalf of strikers was by the Transport and General Workers during the London busmen's strike in 1958. The Council sponsored a financial appeal but advised "against any extension of the stoppage to other groups of workpeople".[2] After 1926, however, the attention of Congress and the General Council was no longer concentrated on strikes, and the Council sought to extend its authority in other fields. Guided by Walter (later Lord) Citrine they paid less attention to increasing their formal powers than to extending their influence. They first attempted to achieve this by co-operating with the central employers' organisations through the Mond-Turner talks. When these failed they turned again to their traditional activity of exerting pressure on legislation and government action. Citrine insisted that governments should deal with the trade union movement only through the General Council, and that dealings between individual unions and the government should be under the Council's control. The access of union leaders to honours and to

---

[1] The constitution of Congress is set out as an appendix to each year's *Annual Report*.

[2] Trades Union Congress, *Annual Report*, 1958, p. 137.

places on government committees was controlled by the Council and therefore by Citrine.

Because the nineteen-thirties was a period of gradually extending government intervention in the economy, this policy led to a steady increase in the standing of Congress up to the outbreak of the second world war. During the war, government intervention reached out to most aspects of economic affairs and the standing of Congress rose to a peak with Ernest Bevin at the Ministry of Labour. The basic compact in domestic affairs was an understanding on the part of the unions that they would avoid official strikes, support measures for expediting the output of munitions and exercise restraint in their wage claims, provided that the government did not intervene openly in the process of wage settlement and stabilised the official cost of living index by means of subsidies. This compact was reached in discussions between the government and the Council, and by increasing the real earnings of manual workers at a time of rationing and high taxation it achieved the greatest advance towards economic equality that Britain has ever experienced in such a short period.

After the return of a Labour Government in 1945 the standing of Congress was at first almost as high as during the war. But as war-time controls and policies were abandoned and the government turned to methods of wage restraint less to the taste of the unions, differences developed both between the government and the unions, and between the unions and the General Council. The decline continued under Conservative governments after 1951, and the influence of Congress reached perhaps its lowest post-war trough in 1958–9 when the government put an end to the Industrial Disputes Tribunal against its wishes. In doing so the government broke a convention honoured since before the war, that governments should not make radical changes in labour legislation and regulations without the consent of both sides of industry.[1] Within a year or so, however, the Conservatives had

[1] The government's excuse was that they proposed to terminate the wartime Order from which the tribunal's powers were derived. This meant that the tribunal could continue only if it was embodied in permanent legislation, and consequently, according to the government, the existing state of affairs could only be continued if both the unions and the employers were agreeable to introducing a statute. With some reluctance the employers decided against continuing the tribunal in this way. Some of its powers were, however, passed to the Industrial Court under the Terms and Conditions of Employment Act, 1959.

become converts to economic planning, and were seeking the support of the General Council for their projects.

With the National Union of Teachers the only major absentee, Congress is now the unchallenged central organisation of British trade unions. Its 155 affiliates include nearly 90 per cent of British trade union members. These affiliates send about a thousand delegates to the annual meeting, held in the first full week in September at a major seaside resort. The three main functions of this meeting are to elect the General Council for the forthcoming year, to discuss the report of the retiring Council, and to debate resolutions submitted by the Council or by constituent unions, the latter almost invariably "composited" by the standing orders committee. Although unions are entitled to delegations according to their size, important or controversial issues are decided by "card votes" at which each union casts the votes of its entire membership in one direction. The General Council dominates Congress, a good deal of the time being occupied by its members introducing reports and resolutions, and intervening in, or replying to debates. Congress cannot initiate policy, for if it were to pass a positive resolution contrary to the Council's wishes, the Council could ignore it or make only the smallest gestures towards its fulfilment. On the other hand, Congress can effectively censure the Council which is sensitive to the "reference back" of part of its report. A reference back will almost certainly lead to a modification in the Council's line. A favourite device for dealing with potentially dangerous resolutions is to ask for their reference to the Council for examination.

The Council of thirty-nine members is elected in twenty groups (nineteen on an industrial basis and one for women) but by the whole vote of Congress. Consequently, if a majority of the large unions act together, they can determine the composition of the whole Council. The other major unions, for instance, consistently refused to vote for two successive general secretaries of the National Union of Mineworkers, Arthur Horner and Will Paynter, because of their membership of the Communist Party. In 1968–9 the Council consisted of the chief officers of all but one of the seventeen largest affiliated unions, together with fourteen chief officers of smaller unions and nine other representatives of major unions. Within the Council the lead is normally taken by its general secretary and by the chief officers of the larger unions, but one or two subordinate officers of major unions have played important roles, as did Arthur Hayday between the wars and more recently his son, Fred Hayday.[1]

In addition to its general secretary and assistant general secretary the Council employs a headquarters staff of about seventy, organised into eight departments. Most of the officers of these departments—as opposed to the clerical staff—are university graduates, and form by far the largest group of specialists in the trade union movement. In 1963 the Council took over responsibility for trade union education from the National Council of Labour Colleges and the Workers' Educational Trade Union Committee. This opportunity has not been exploited but at least it has equipped the council with its first full-time regional officers. These are education officers, most of whom have been taken over from the National Council of Labour Colleges.[2]

Otherwise the Regional Advisory Committees, formed of full-time officers of affiliated unions, lead but a shadowy existence; and local co-ordination of the trade union movement is the job of the trades councils and their regional federations. Many of the trades councils of major cities can trace their history back before the foundation of Congress, but the growing centralisation of the unions has robbed them of many of their former functions. They have a number of administrative jobs, such as nominating trade unionists to local committees and tribunals, and they provide a forum for the discussion of any issues which local trade unionists wish to air. They have always offered generous facilities for the expression of radical opinions, but since they were brought under the control of the Trades Union Congress in 1926, the opportunity for Communist infiltration has been limited. A council whose activities seriously embarrass Congress is threatened with the withdrawal of official recognition. Where this threat has been carried out it has proved an effective death warrant. In return the General Council allows the trades councils a one-day annual conference at which they can put forward their views for consideration.

The services which Congress can offer trade unions either

[1] Arthur Hayday was a district secretary, and his son is a national officer of the General and Municipal Workers.

[2] Shortley after the war Congress began to provide training courses as a service to affiliated unions, and these were much expanded when handsome new headquarters were opened in 1957.

centrally or locally are limited by its income. Between 1952 and 1968 annual affiliation fees rose from 6d. to 1s. 6d. a member but a large part of the increase was earmarked for the educational work which Congress had taken over. The 1968 figure was less than 2 per cent of the average contribution per member received by British trade unions. The equivalent figure in Western Germany is 12 per cent and German trade union contributions are substantially higher than British. Its limited resources mean that Congress and the General Council must have their effect within the movement mainly through their influence on the individual unions, and not through what they do themselves.

The General Council meets monthly, mainly to approve the work of its numerous committees,[1] whose membership and chairmen are selected with close regard for seniority—as is the chairman of the Council itself. His tenure is limited to one year. The former Parliamentary Committee's task of influencing legislation and the administration of government departments remains an important function for the General Council, although methods have changed with the times. With the rise of the Labour Party and union-sponsored Members of Parliament there is no need to cultivate friendly Members to sponsor measures. With tight government control on legislation and the growing importance of government administrative action in many industrial and economic spheres, contacts with government departments have become all-important, at the expense of action in the House of Commons. The original practice of sending deputations to ministers to put forward relevant Congress resolutions is still in use, but in addition the General Council now nominates members to all relevant Royal Commissions and departmental committees of inquiry, and also to a large number of permanent committees which give direct access to the main government departments.

The constitutional powers of the General Council are set out in Rules 11, 12 and 13 of Congress. Rule 11 covers industrial disputes and Rule 13 "disputes between affiliated organisations". The limit of the Council's authority in inter-union disputes is its

---

[1] One of these, the International Committee, deals with relations between Congress and the international trade union movement, representing Congress in the International Confederation of Free Trade Unions and other international organisations, and running an advisory service for unions in under-developed Commonwealth countries.

power to suspend a union and to recommend its expulsion to Congress; and this limit applies equally to Rule 12 which empowers it to enquire into the "conduct of affiliated unions". The major instance is the investigation of the Electrical Trades Union in 1959–60 in which the Council proceeded with obvious reluctance. Expulsion was recommended to Congress in 1961 only after the Electricians' malpractices had been exposed and condemned by the courts, and they were re-admitted with obvious relief as soon as they had changed their leaders. Although the Council has been ready to propose the expulsion of minor unions for disregarding its decisions, it has always recognised that to expel a major union could harm Congress as much as the union. Congress's main strength is its representative character, and this could be destroyed by the loss of a few major unions.

However, the rules of Congress are not the chief source of power. When the moment is ripe, the General Council can commit the movement to a course of action by calling a conference of trade union executives, who have the power to act on behalf of their members, or are willing to usurp it. Such a meeting authorised the General Strike in 1926; another supported wage restraint in 1948; and from 1965 a series of them first gave support to the prices and incomes policy of the Labour Government elected in 1964, and then to the General Council's own policies on prices and incomes. What the Council lacks is any means to keep an unwilling union in line. In 1926 the Miners refused to accept the terms on which the General Strike was called off. The General Council has no power to prevent a union entering upon a settlement for an increase in pay in excess of the amount sanctioned either by the government's incomes policy or by the Council's own incomes policy.

Some of the weaknesses and strengths of Congress can be seen in the several attempts to take new initiatives in the period since 1955, most of them associated with George Woodcock, who became assistant general secretary in 1946 when Vincent Tewson succeeded Citrine as general secretary, and then succeeded Tewson in 1960. The further initiatives of 1969, after Woodcock's departure, are discussed in Chapter 12.

In 1955 the General Council took up the issue of trade union finance. A limited survey revealed that a "number of unions spent more than they received in contributions"; that "the real

value of reserves per member is lower today than it was in 1939";
and "that the increases that have taken place in contributions are
inadequate to meet the increased costs of administration".[1] A
wider survey in 1956 confirmed the findings,[2] and another in
1969 revealed that "there was little improvement in the financial
health of trade unionism as a whole and in many respects there
was a distinct worsening".[3] Since 1955 was the year in which
the rate of increase in union contributions began to accelerate, it
may well be that the Council's surveys helped to hasten the
change, although financial pressures must have had their effect
in the end.

The next important innovation came in 1959 when the Council
undertook an investigation into "the broad problem of disputes,
workshop representation and related matters". Their interim
report, published the following year, seemed to promise bold
recommendations. It did not burke the difficulties, and even went
so far as to suggest that "it would . . . be attractive to recommend
direct communication between the secretary of a joint committee
of unions nationally and the officers of joint stewards committees
within the industry concerned", although it added that "this is
impractical for a number of reasons at this stage".[4] However,
even the idea of an invasion of individual union autonomy was
too much and next year's report failed to live up to the promises
of the first, merely informing Congress that the General Council
would continue its discussions.[5]

Next the General Council took up the vexed question of
trade union structure. Twice before, in 1927 and 1947, the
General Council had issued carefully-drafted reports on this
issue. Both of them made clear that radical reorganisation on the
lines of "industrial unionism" was out of the question, and
reform would have to be by means of amalgamations, federations
and working arrangements. When the subject came up at the
1962 Congress, George Woodcock argued the case for industrial
unionism, but in the end the Council's report drew attention to
"the severely practical limits within which . . . it might be
possible and desirable for some unions to come more closely to an
industrial basis of organisation".[6]

---

[1] *Annual Report*, 1955, pp. 304–5.   [2] *Ibid.*, 1956, p. 305.
[3] *Ibid.*, 1960, p. 307.   [4] *Ibid.*, 1960, pp. 124–30.
[5] *Ibid.*, 1961, pp. 134–6.   [6] *Ibid.*, 1963, pp. 122–5.

Nevertheless the investigation was not without effect. The General Council began actively to promote amalgamations, and perhaps some of the mergers of the last six years owe something to the Council's prodding. More important, however, was the Council's decision to take up the legal obstacles to amalgamation with the Minister of Labour. The barriers were lowered by the Trade Union (Amalgamation etc.) Act, 1964, without which most of the amalgamations since then would probably have fallen through.

The unions reacted strongly against the pay pause of 1961. Many of their members retained a deep hostility to any kind of government wage policy acquired from their experience in the years 1948–50. Others saw this as the wrong kind of pay policy maladroitly applied. It did not seem an auspicious occasion for the government to seek the Council's co-operation in a new venture in economic planning. Nevertheless, at the end of the year the government invited them to participate in the proposed National Economic Development Council. Woodcock and those of his colleagues who were concerned with the public image of the trade union movement and the authority of Congress persuaded the remaining members of the Council that "they should put to a practical test the question whether participation would give them a genuine opportunity of influencing the Government's policies in ways which would help trade unionists".[1] Six members of the General Council were appointed to the National Economic Development Council, and Congress ratified the decision. This was done in spite of the General Council's strong disapproval, shared by the movement as a whole, of the government's next venture in pay policy, the National Incomes Commission of 1962, which the Council considered to be as inept as the pay pause, if less damaging to the unions, since they could ignore it with impunity. In 1963 Congress approved a report from the Council on *Economic Development and Planning*, which contained several innovations in trade union thinking although the section on "prices and incomes" had to be revised to make plain that there was no commitment to "wage restraint".[2] This led up to the pay policies of the Labour Government elected in October 1964, which are examined in the next chapter.

The standing of Congress therefore depends on the extent and

[1] *Ibid.*, 1962, p. 254.   [2] *Ibid.*, 1963, pp. 480–95.

direction of government intervention in the economy, and on the ability of the General Council both to influence the government's actions and to bring the unions along with them. The degree of government intervention is largely outside the control of the Council, but their influence on the government and their own members must reflect their competence and leadership. Most important are the qualities of the general secretary, but the chief officer of one of the major unions can also exercise great authority within the Council. Congress has flourished most when a shrewd general secretary has co-operated with the capable leader of a major union. From 1926 to 1940 there was such an alliance between Citrine and Bevin. With Bevin as Minister of Labour during the war the alliance gained new resources, and Bevin's successor at the Transport and General Workers, Arthur Deakin, showed himself a man of character and courage though without Bevin's genius. Even when Citrine was succeeded in 1946 by Vincent Tewson, with little of Citrine's ability, some authority was preserved up to Deakin's death, but then the Council was left leaderless, divided and ineffective. Tewson's successor, Woodcock, had both the intelligence and courage which the job demands. But he found no ally of Bevin's stature, nor even of Deakin's.

THE CONFEDERATION OF BRITISH INDUSTRY

Central organisation among employers in Britain was a much later development than among trade unions. There were several attempts before 1914, but all of them failed. It required the first world war and large-scale government intervention in private industry to provide British employers with the National Union of Manufacturers, founded in 1915, and the more weighty Federation of British Industries, founded in 1917, both intended primarily to deal with commercial matters. The National Confederation of Employers' Organisations developed out of the employers' side of the National Industrial Conference summoned by the government early in 1919, and was therefore even more clearly a child of government intervention. Later its name was changed to the British Employers' Confederation.

The Confederation's rejection of the Mond-Turner proposals was the most important event in its early years, and probably in its whole history, for it was that decision which prevented the Confederation playing a major formative part in British industrial relations. Otherwise in its early years the Confederation made representations to the government of the day on legislative proposals concerning labour matters, and represented British employers at the International Labour Organisation. In the economic crisis of 1931 it issued two statements, one on the general situation, the other on unemployment insurance, making proposals for wage cuts. Thereafter its voice was not heard in public for twenty-four years. During and after the war the Confederation provided its representatives to sit alongside those of the Trades Union Congress on the manifold advisory committees set up by the government on industrial matters. But they played a subordinate role to that of the trade union members, under the war-time coalition, under the post-war Labour Government, and even in the first years of Conservative administration which took office in 1951. The spirit which breathed in them was the spirit of Sir Allan Smith who had dominated the early years of the Confederation. Change in industrial relations was likely to be for the worse. Employers should not therefore promote change; they should prevent change if they could; but if there had to be change they should accept it quietly.

In 1955, however, there were signs of a fresh approach. Under a new director, Sir George Pollock, the Confederation announced its views to the world in a pamphlet, *Britain's Industrial Future*, which dealt mainly with the problem of inflation. There were proposals for a reduction in government spending, but responsibility for moderation also rested on "employers and workers and their organisations and members of arbitration tribunals and statutory wage-fixing bodies". The Confederation began to circulate a fortnightly *Bulletin* to its affiliates and their members. This gave brief accounts of current events of interest to employers, but its editorials were plainly intended to mould opinion. In 1959 it was made available to the press.

In 1956 a voluntary "price-freeze" emerged from discussions between the government, the nationalised industries, the Federation of British Industries, the National Union of Manufacturers, the British Employers' Confederation and the Associated British Chambers of Commerce. Price stability was intended to bring wage stability, and led to the engineering and shipbuilding strikes of 1957. This attempt to control inflation through the concerted efforts of employers' organisations was unique in British history, and revealed an unusual spirit of enterprise on their part, but even so they played a secondary role. The government had initiated the talks on price stability and the government ended the strikes by prevailing upon the employers to make an offer.

During the next few years the Confederation made two attempts to crystallise opinion among employers by holding conferences. The first, in October 1958, dealt mainly with the effect of wage settlements on inflation. At the second, in May 1961, several academic specialists in industrial relations were present and an official of the Trades Union Congress gave a talk. The main topic on this occasion was the development of "plant-by-plant negotiation", and whether it should be encouraged, or countered by more "centralisation and co-ordination between industries". No bold new ideas emerged, and the press notice reported "the broad conclusion . . . that, though the present system . . . is the most appropriate system for this country, it will require constant review and modification from time to time".[1]

This conclusion might have been acceptable to Sir Allan Smith, but he would not have approved the direct approaches to the General Council of the Trades Union Congress initiated by Pollock. After a working party had considered unconstitutional strikes, the Confederation concluded that "certain aspects of the problem could best be dealt with by a joint examination by the B.E.C. and the T.U.C.".[2] Talks yielded no positive results at that time, but in 1964 the two bodies undertook "a joint experimental investigation into strikes in breach of procedure, or called at little notice, as a fact-finding exercise".[3] Further discussions in 1962 dealt with three issues; the training of shop stewards, dismissal procedure, and payments during sickness. On the first there was agreement that stewards should be helped "to carry out their functions as responsible officers of their unions" and that "it was in the interests of employers that stewards should represent their unions and the members of those unions effectively". The Confederation undertook to "recommend their members to con-

---

[1] British Employers' Confederation, *Bulletin*, 31 May 1961.

[2] *Ibid.*, 16 November 1960.

[3] Royal Commission, *Evidence of the Confederation of British Industry, Selected Written Evidence*, pp. 252–3.

sider the possibility of extending the co-operation between employers, unions and educational organisations . . . with the object of providing more courses . . . for attendance at which stewards might be released with pay".[1]

For all its new-found vigour, however, the Confederation was very dependent on the government for achievement. In 1958 the need for improved industrial training led to the formation of the Industrial Training Council with representatives from the Confederation and the General Council, from the nationalised industries and from the government, and a secretariat provided by the Confederation. The results of this voluntary effort fell so far short of what was required that the Industrial Training Act, 1964, set up statutory training boards financed by compulsory levies. Similarly the Redundancy Payments Act, 1965, was evidence of the failure of collective bargaining to provide effective incentives to industrial mobility. In both these instances the Confederation and the General Council supported legislation. By contrast they both opposed the Contracts of Employment Bill in 1963, aimed to provide a modest increase in security for employees. The Confederation had found the Bill "complex and in places unintelligible".[2] Nevertheless the Bill became the Contracts of Employment Act, 1963, another token of the failure of voluntary action.

Even where no government action has yet been taken on one of the issues on which the Confederation has striven to achieve progress, opinion has been gaining ground that something more than voluntary action is required. In 1968 the Royal Commission found the need for shop-steward training was still "immense" with "no general agreement on what should be taught", and suggested that grants from the industrial training boards could be used "to increase the number of day-release courses and to improve their standard".[3] Talks on dismissals led to an investigation by a committee of the National Joint Advisory Council which revealed a disagreement between the unions and the employers. The General Council representatives favoured a statutory right of appeal against dismissal. The employers were against it. The Royal Commission decided that the "balance of advantage greatly favours the establishment of statutory

---

[1] British Employers Confederation, *Bulletin*, 8 May 1963.
[2] *Ibid.*, 13 February 1963.   [3] *Report*, p. 191.

machinery",[1] and the government has announced its intention to legislate.[2]

From time to time proposals had been made for an amalgamation between the Confederation and the Federation of British Industries. A decision in principle for fusion in 1946 became ensnared in the details of working out a constitution acceptable to both, but in 1962 the formation of the National Economic Development Council emphasised the drawbacks of division. Since the Council's work covered both commercial and labour matters it included the spheres of interest of both organisations; and the National Association of British Manufacturers (as the National Union of Manufacturers was now called) might also have had a claim to a seat as the representative of the interests of small firms. Consequently, whereas the six trade union members of the Council were the nominees of the General Council, the Chancellor of the Exchequer chose six individual employers as broadly representative of private industry. The nationalised industries were separately represented.

Under this spur the three central employers' organisations agreed on the objectives of an amalgamated organisation and appointed a Commission of two to advise on a suitable constitution. Their report,[3] which was presented and accepted in 1964, led to the formation of the Confederation of British Industry by Royal Charter[4] in 1965. In addition to the members of the three amalgamating bodies the new organisation included the main nationalised industries. It therefore had a strong claim to be considered widely representative of employers.

The main difficulty in devising a constitution was to reconcile the structure of the Confederation, which had encompassed only employers' associations, with that of the Federation of British Industries and the Association of British Manufacturers, each of which had included both trade associations and individual firms. The new Confederation admits companies, employers' associa-

[1] *Ibid.*, p. 146.

[2] *In Place of Strife*, Cmnd. 3888, 1969, p. 31.

[3] Sir Henry Benson and Sir Sam Brown, *Report on the Formation of a National Industrial Organisation*, 1964.

[4] The British Employers' Confederation was unincorporated and understood to be a trade union, although unregistered. The Confederation of British Industry with its Royal Charter is not a trade union "as its labour and social activities, although of great importance, do not constitute its principal object". (Royal Commission, *Selected Written Evidence*, p. 247).

tions and trade associations to membership, along with the nationalised industries. On its Council of four hundred sit representatives of about a hundred employers' associations and 150 trade associations, along with representatives of the regional councils of the Confederation and elected representative of the individual companies. Labour matters, however, are handled by the Labour and Social Affairs Committee. Its "about 130 members" include at least one representative from each employers' association, and up to four from the largest. In addition there are representatives of the nationalised industries and of those "large individual company members which negotiate direct with the unions".[1] Thus the members of the old Confederation retain a firm grip on this side of the work of the Confederation.

The new body's "main functions in the labour and social affairs field are to formulate general employer policy for implementation by its members and for expression to the Government, to the public and (to a lesser extent) to the T.U.C.".[2] Because of its coverage, its leaders can speak to the government, the public and the General Council more authoritatively than any of its predecessors. But in dealing with the implementation of policy by members they are in much the same position as the leaders of the old Confederation. They can only give advice.

The amalgamation has not even equipped them with powers equivalent to those of the General Council. The General Council is authorised to intervene in major industrial disputes when these seem likely to affect other workers, and since 1955 it has done so on several occasions. The Confederation has no such power. The General Council has taken upon itself to call together executives of the unions in order to persuade them to commit themselves to a common course of action. The Confederation has developed no equivalent mechanism. Nor has it yet equalled the public standing of Congress and the General Council. The annual meetings of Congress are great events in the British calendar, and the meetings of the General Council receive far greater attention from the press than the meetings of the Council and the Labour and Social Affairs Committee of the Confederation. In part the difference arises from the greater reticence of employers' organisations, but it also reflects their relative importance in the eyes of the press and the public.

[1] *Ibid.*, p. 248. [2] *Ibid.*, p. 248.

Just as the constitutional changes brought about by the amalgamation can be exaggerated, so can its effect on the spirit of organised employers. It had been the hope of some of those who supported the amalgamation that the bringing together of trade associations and individual companies with employers' associations would imbue the latter with more progressive and bolder ideas. The fusion of trade associations and employers' associations in some individual industries has had just this effect.[1] But the structure of the Labour and Social Affairs Committee has minimised the chance of a similar effect on the Confederation. The employers' associations control the committee and its subordinate committees. Among them the Engineering Employers' Federation retains the dominating position that it held throughout the life of the old Confederation, and the National Federation of Building Trades Employers comes next to it both in numbers and in influence. Between them they possess an ascendancy even greater than that of the two largest unions, the Transport and General Workers and the Engineers within the Trades Union Congress. Neither is noted for its progressive ideas or its adaptability, although the Engineering Employers are now beginning to change.

However, the Confederation was formed to meet the need for a fully representative organisation of employers to play its part in the business of economic planning and in the prices and incomes policy which was expected to grow out of it. It must be judged mainly by what it has achieved in this respect.

[1] See p. 151.

CHAPTER II

INCOMES POLICY

EARLY ATTEMPTS

An incomes policy may be defined as an attempt by a government to alter the level of wages and salaries, or to alter the pace of their change. There have been occasions when governments have made a conscious effort to raise wages as did Roosevelt's New Deal administration in its attempt to reduce unemployment in in the United States in the thirties. But such policies are far less common than attempts to hold back the rate of increase in incomes at times of rising or full employment. At such times the price level is usually increasing. Costs are the biggest element in most prices, and wages and salaries are by the far largest element in costs in an advanced economy. Consequently it is not difficult to argue that (ignoring import prices) if the increase in wages and salaries keep pace with the growth in goods and services available for consumption there is no need for prices to rise, whereas a continued increase in incomes above that rate must push up prices.

Rising prices cause difficulties. They redistribute incomes, and they may diminish savings and weaken confidence. These disadvantages have been sufficient to induce governments to devise incomes policies, although other countries have adjusted themselves to a continuously rising price level. Differences between the rate of increase in price levels from one country to another, however, cause more intractable problems. A country whose price level is rising faster than the average becomes less competitive in export markets at the same time as its imports tend to rise. If the situation persists the country must run into a balance-of-payments crisis. There are several well-known remedies, including devaluation and deflation, but they also have drawbacks, and there is attraction in an incomes policy which could slow down the increase in costs, and therefore of prices. Indeed, an incomes

policy might be a means of remedying an imbalance in pri
levels even when prices generally are not rising. In 1926 it w
widely held that the British government wanted to see wag
reduced throughout British industry so as to adjust costs to tl
high rate of exchange at which the pound had been fixed on tl
return to the gold standard in the previous year.

Britain's first attempt at incomes policy in modern times can
in 1916 when the Asquith coalition tried to halt the tide of w
bonuses, but the attempt was abandoned within a few month
In the second world war the government avoided open inte
vention in collective bargaining by a combination of voluntar
restraint and a stabilising of the official cost of living index,[1] at
time when the lend-lease arrangements with the United Stat
diminished concern with the balance of payments. There is roo
to argue whether this was an incomes policy or not, but confusic
can be avoided if the term is confined to those occasions on whic
governments issue clear guidance on the limits within which the
think incomes should be permitted to move, and take overt ste
to try to keep incomes within those limits.

Within this definition there were three attempts at an incom
policy in post-war Britain before 1965: wage restraint under tl
Attlee administration in 1948–50, the price freeze of 1956–7, ar
the pay pause of 1961–2. Of these the price freeze was the lea
important, and there is no need to add to what has already bee
said about it.[2] The others deserve a little more attention.

The first was, to all appearances, the more successful of the tw
It lasted from the publication of the White Paper on *Person*
Incomes, Costs and Prices[3] in February 1948 until 1950 when
crumbled away during the course of the year. Increases in week
and hourly earnings were a good deal less than they had been i
the previous year or so, and than they were to be over the ne:
two or three years. This by itself does not prove that the polic
was effective, since other factors like the level of employment ar
the terms of trade also affect changes in incomes, but econometr
cians try to include the relevant variables in their equations, ar
they find that it slowed down pay increases. Moreover, at tl
time everyone, including government, employers, trade unioi
and workers, believed that it was having an effect. At the outs
most unions gave grudging support to the policy, but one by or

---

[1] See p. 399.   [2] See pp. 407–8.   [3] Cmd. 7321, 1948.

they turned against it because of the effect that it was having on their members' pay.

The pay pause was relatively short-lived. On 20 July 1961 the Chancellor of the Exchequer, Selwyn Lloyd, announced a temporary pause in pay increases in the public sector, and asked private industry to follow suit. The pause came to an end after eight months, in March 1962. During the period it was unquestionably successful in holding up the application of awards and agreements in the public sector, and probably slowed down the pace of pay increases in private industry. It was intended to allow time for the government to work out a longer-term policy, and a White Paper on *Incomes Policy: The Next Step*[1] appeared towards the end of the pause. This gave guidance on the rate at which pay should be permitted to increase thereafter, but it had no visible effect. The unions which had protested against the pause soon ceased to criticise the White Paper. They ignored it.

On the other hand this White Paper showed a more sophisticated approach to the problems of incomes policy than had the Labour Government's White Paper in 1948. The latter document laid down that, with the possible exception of undermanned industries, there was "no justification for any general increase of individual money incomes". At the conference of trade union executives called by the General Council to discuss the policy it was decided to give approval on the understanding that exception would also be made for claims based on increased output, for adjustments for those "below a reasonable standard of subsistence" and for increases needed to safeguard "essential" differentials. Fortunately for the success of the policy little attempt was made to apply these sweeping exceptions, and wage restraint worked by holding back on claims and, when claims were made, on concessions. Some industries, such as the railways, received no general increase at all during the period of more than two years, and others, such as the engineers, received only one.

No specific guidance was given as to whether any particular increase in the cost of living would justify a general increase in pay, and industries with cost-of-living sliding scales continued to apply them. Following devaluation at the end of 1949 the Chancellor of the Exchequer, Stafford Cripps, sought to safeguard its advantages by securing trade union agreement to a

[1] Cmnd. 1626, 1962.

"wage-freeze" so long as the retail price index did not rise b
more than a specified number of points. This would have mean
the voluntary suspension of the sliding scales. The Genera
Council gave its approval, but the unions directly concerned di
not. At a further conference of trade union executives the majorit
for the freeze was so small as to foreshadow the end of the whol
policy.

Having given notice of the end of the temporary pause, th
Conservative White Paper of 1962 looked forward to an annua
increase of between 2 and 2·5 per cent in overall productivity, an
held that average increases in pay should be kept within thes
limits, so that prices could be stable. However, all pay claim
should not be treated alike. "In many cases there may indeed b
no justification at present for any increases at all. In others ther
may be particular circumstances which point the other way.
One such circumstance could be a manpower shortage wher
"the building up of manpower in one industry relatively t
others, or the prevention of a threatened decline" made it "plainl
necessary that an increase on those grounds could be justified'
Another was a "direct contribution . . . to an increase of prod
uctivity and a reduction of costs". In addition, "comparisons
would "still have a part to play" although "in the immediat
future more regard will have to be given to the general economi
considerations". There was room for differences of interpretatio
in the application of the White Paper, and to meet this th
government set up the National Incomes Commission in Novem
ber 1962. They were to examine pay claims under negotiatio
provided the parties agreed, to review settlements already mad
whether the parties agreed or not, and to investigate the pay o
public servants. During the two years of their existence th
Commission conducted retrospective inquiries into three agree
ments, and reported on a pay claim for university teachers. In th
circumstances they were "unable to make any effective con
tribution towards the development of an agreed wages policy".
Moreover they were overshadowed by the National Economi
Development Council, set up a few months earlier in Februar
1962. Since the unions would have nothing to do with th
National Incomes Commission, neither trade unionists nor in
dustrialists were included among its members, none of whon

[1] C. W. Guillebaud, *Wage Determination and Wage Policy*, 1967 ed., p. 42.

were well-known public figures. The National Economic Development Council, by contrast, included representatives of the General Council, leading industrialists, senior ministers and two well-known independents, served by a powerful staff of experts. In March 1963 their report on the *Growth of the United Kingdom to 1966* made the assumption that a growth rate of 4 per cent in production was a feasible objective. This was accepted by the government and the "guiding light" on permissible increases in pay was altered from 2–2·5 per cent to 3–3·5 per cent. This change brought no greater degree of observance, but the participation of General Council representatives in the work and reports of the National Economic Development Council gave grounds for supposing that a more effective incomes policy might develop out of economic planning.

Wage restraint in 1948–50 had been concerned with agreed rates of pay. It is possible that the policy's emphasis on increased production tended to enlarge the gap between rates and earnings by the impetus which it gave to overtime working and to the extension of payment by results. The major study of the subject, unfortunately unpublished,[1] found that differential movements in earnings hastened the downfall of the policy. Railwaymen on time rates envied engineering workers paid by results. Day-workers in the collieries envied the upward creep in face-workers' earnings. The easiest means available to the unions for assuaging these jealousies was to seek general increases in time rates, industry by industry.

The 1962 White Paper noted that what matters is not the agreed rate but "the amount actually paid" and pointed to the likelihood "that basic rates will in practice be supplemented in certain employments by local or special payments". This was a step forward, but it showed no grasp of the parts played in earnings movements by overtime and payment by results, nor of the importance of domestic bargaining.

Neither wage restraint nor the pay pause brought permanent changes in collective bargaining. They were not intended to do so. The proposals of the 1962 White Paper might, if observed, have led to changes; but they were ignored.

[1] John Corina, *The British Experiment in Wage Restraint with Special Reference to 1948–50*, Oxford D.Phil. thesis, 1961.

PRICES AND INCOMES POLICY 1965–9

The Labour Government which took office in October 196.
showed its concern for economic planning by establishing a
new Ministry, the Department of Economic Affairs headed by
Mr. George Brown, deputy leader of the party. Faced by the
immediate balance-of-payments crisis, the department rapidly
developed a new incomes policy which appeared to combine the
advantages of wage restraint in 1948–50 with the approach of the
White Paper of 1962 and to show that the lessons of the National
Economic Development Council had been learned.

The unions were fully committed to the new policy. In December 1964 there appeared a *Declaration of Intent* signed by representatives of the government, the General Council and the
central employers' organisations (not yet amalgamated) which
committed them to:

"urgent and vigorous action
  (i) to raise productivity throughout industry and commerce;
 (ii) to keep increases in total money incomes in line with
      increases in real national output;
(iii) to maintain a stable price level".

Two White Papers,[1] published in February and April 1965
after consultation with the General Council and the employers'
organisations, told the country how this was to be done. The
second, on *Prices and Incomes Policy*, laid down the criteria which
should govern changes in prices and incomes. General movements
in prices and incomes were to be kept under review by the
National Economic Development Council. Particular cases were
to be investigated by a National Board for Prices and Incomes.

At first sight the White Paper and the Board bore a close
resemblance to the White Paper of 1962 and the National Incomes
Commission. The guiding light was replaced by a "norm", but
the figure remained that of the former White Paper, as subsequently amended, 3–3·5 per cent. "Exceptional pay increases"
could be permitted:

"(i) where the employees concerned, for example by accepting
     more exacting work or a major change in working

---

[1] Cmnd. 2577 and Cmnd. 2639, 1965. The title of the first was *Machinery of Prices and
Incomes Policy*.

practices, make a direct contribution towards increasing productivity in the particular firm or industry. Even in such cases some of the benefits should accrue to the community as a whole in the form of lower prices;

(ii) where it is essential in the national interest to secure a change in the distribution of manpower (or to prevent a change which would otherwise take place) and a pay increase would be both necessary and effective for this purpose;

(iii) where there is general recognition that existing wage and salary levels are too low to maintain a reasonable standard of living;

(iv) where there is widespread recognition that the pay of a certain group of workers has fallen seriously out of line with the level of remuneration for similar work and needs in the national interest to be improved."

Nevertheless there were important differences from 1962. Prices were included along with pay in the White Paper, and so far as possible accorded parallel treatment. The general objective was to be price stability, but four circumstances were set out in which prices could be raised, and four circumstances in which "enterprises will be expected to reduced their prices". In this the treatment of prices was more systematic than the treatment of pay, for the White Paper gave no explicit guidance on which groups should receive increases in pay below the norm.[1] There was no direct guidance on dividends, but "where the growth of profits or dividends is based on excessive market power this could indicate scope for price reductions and such cases would be referred to the National Board for Prices and Incomes for examination". The Board, like the National Incomes Commission, could institute inquiries only on a reference from the government, but the scope for references was far wider. Not only could prices and other money incomes besides wages and salaries be referred to the Board, but references on pay could include "claims, settlements or questions relating to pay or other conditions of service or employment", without any mention of the

---

[1] On this point it proposed only that exceptional increases in pay "should be kept to a minimum, bearing in mind that they will need to be balanced by lower than average increases to other groups if the increase in wages and salaries over the economy as a whole is to be within the norm".

consent of the parties. The General Council was explicitly committed to the policy, and a member of the Council, Robert Willis, secretary of the National Graphical Association, was given leave of absence by his union to serve as a full-time member of the Board and vacated his seat on the Council in order to take up the post. The Board's chairman, Aubrey Jones, was a former Conservative cabinet minister and a considerable public figure. The remaining three full-time members and four part-time members of the Board included several industrialists, and a staff of civil servants, larger and more high-powered than that of the National Incomes Commission, worked alongside a staff of professional advisers in economics and industrial relations.

The Board set to work with a will, and within its first year had produced fourteen reports, but the results of the policy as a whole were disappointing. Between April 1965 and April 1966 retail prices rose by about 3·5 per cent, weekly wage rates by about 5·5 per cent, and weekly earnings by nearly 8 per cent. Because the general movement to a forty-hour working week was still taking effect, average increases in hourly rates and hourly earnings were even higher. It is possible that, given the high level of employment, pay might have been expected to rise by marginally more than this without the policy, but against this hypothetical advantage were arrayed the facts that pay and prices seemed to be rising as rapidly as in the last two years of economic boom and far faster than in previous periods of incomes policy, and that the criteria of the White Paper were manifestly not observed in most pay settlements. In addition the government's forecasts of economic growth proved to be too high and their expectations of improvement in the balance of payments too optimistic.

One obvious weakness was that there was no way of ensuring that the policy was applied to any particular pay or price increase except by a reference to the Board, and the Board could evidently handle no more than a small fraction of the total increases. Accordingly in September 1965 the government announced its intention to introduce a compulsory "early warning" system whereby there would have to be advance notification of price and pay increases. If an increase appeared likely to breach the policy the government would be able to take appropriate action to contain it. In November, after consultations with both sides of industry, a voluntary early warning system was established pending the introduction of legislation. Initially, however, this did not seem to check increases in either pay or prices.

Of the Board's first seven reports, four dealt with price references, two with pay settlements already reached, and one with a pay claim for clerical and administrative staffs in electricity supply. In them the Board began to show an ability for rapid collection of the salient information, an understanding of the nature of movements in earnings, and an eagerness to relate increases in pay to changes in working practices which would increase productivity. Its eighth report was a far sterner test. In September 1965 the railway unions had rejected offers of pay increases of 3·5 per cent each in October 1965 and October 1966 together with the introduction of a forty-hour week and improvements in holidays and pensions. They were persuaded to agree to the immediate introduction of the first 3·5 per cent increase, and a reference of their claims, based on the "Guillebaud formula",[1] to the Board, with the promise of a report by the end of the year.

The Board faced an impossible task. Including the reduction in the working week, the offer which the Railways Board had made for 1966 was already well outside the norm. The Board estimated that it would lead to an increase in earnings of between 6·5 and 7·5 per cent, leaving aside improvements in holidays and pensions. There were no proposals for meeting the cost by changes in working practice leading to increased efficiency. On the other hand a failure on the part of the Board to improve upon the Railways Board's offer would almost certainly lead to rejection of their report by the unions, and perhaps a railway strike.

The Board stood their ground. They roundly condemned the use of the Guillebaud formula. They would allow no general increase above the offer for manual railway workers.[2] In addition they suggested that the introduction of the forty-hour week should be accompanied by "flexibility in the planning of hours worked". For the future they recommended pay and productivity councils to negotiate productivity increments in return for more flexible

[1] See p. 391.
[2] The earnings of clerical staff were found to have fallen behind those of manual workers and clerical staff elsewhere, and for them the Board recommended a salary increase of 5 per cent.

use of manpower and reduction in overtime.[1] The National Union of Railwaymen rejected the report and issued strike notices. The strike was called off at the last moment following the intervention of the Prime Minister. The dates of the 1966 concessions were advanced, but the main concession was a promise of a further review of the whole question of railway pay under the aegis of the Prime Minister, and outside the scope of the Board. Disaster had been avoided, but the Board's value as an instrument for securing the acceptance of the policy had diminished, at least for the time being.

The next challenge came in the spring of 1966, from the National Union of Seamen. In 1965 the Seamen had recognised that they were required to work every day while at sea by increasing the agreed working week at sea from 44 hours to 56 hours, the loss in overtime earnings being more than compensated by an advance in basic rates. The owners estimated the increase in their costs at 13·5 per cent. Now the Seamen asked for the introduction of a forty-hour week while retaining the new basic rate. This, the owners estimated, would cost a further 17 per cent on their wage bills, which they were prepared to meet only if the change was made in three stages over two years. This was unacceptable and in April the union gave a month's notice of a strike.

The dispute did not come before the Board, but one of its members was included in the Court of Inquiry appointed after the strike had begun. The court recommended that the change should be introduced in two stages. The additional costs compared with introduction in three stages were to be met mainly by a reduction in overtime working (which was in the end achieved).[2] Initially these proposals were rejected by the Seamen, but with some further adjustments they formed the basis of an agreement reached in July after the strike had lasted for almost two months.

By that time Britain was in the middle of another severe balance-of-payments crisis. At least one reason for lack of confidence abroad was an impression that the incomes policy was a failure. Since the short-run solution of the crisis involved borrowing

[1] *Pay and Conditions of Service of British Railways Staff*, Report No. 8, Cmnd. 2873, 1966, pp. 25–6.
[2] *First Report of the Court of Inquiry into Certain matters concerning the Shipping Industry*, Cmnd. 3025, 1966.

additional sums from other countries, reinforcement of the policy held an immediate political advantage in facilitating loans, quite apart from its ultimate effect on pay and prices. On 20 July the Prime Minister announced a complete standstill on pay increases, and on price increases except for those arising out of increases in import prices or taxation. The standstill included pay increases already negotiated but not yet applied. A new White Paper, *Prices and Incomes Standstill*,[1] gave further details and announced that the standstill would be followed by six months of "severe restraint" during which the norm would be zero, and the requirements for improvements in pay would be "much more stringent" than before. There was to be a standstill on dividends for twelve months.

Action on these proposals was not to be voluntary. They were to be enforced by a Prices and Incomes Act whose passage was hurried through by 12 August. The Act had three main sections. Part I established the Board, originally constituted by Royal Warrant, on a statutory basis. Part II gave legal force to the early warning system. After notification the government had thirty days in which to decide on a reference to the Board, and, if a reference was made, the increase should not be put into effect until the Board reported, which they should do within three months. But it would then be applied even if the report was unfavourable. Part IV gave statutory force to the standstill, whether or not a reference was made to the Board. Both Parts II and IV provided for fines of up to £500 where increases were put into effect contrary to their provisions, or where strikes attempted to persuade employers to breach them; and neither was to operate unless brought into force by an Order in Council.

The standstill was a success. For the first time for many years the index of weekly wage rates stood still for five months. From April 1966 to April 1967 weekly earnings rose by just over 2 per cent, but this change can be almost entirely explained by increases in rates before and after the freeze. Part IV of the Act had to be brought into force after two months, primarily to prevent the application of agreements reached before the standstill. The General Council did not give its approval but, "after the most scrupulous examination of the alternative courses of action genuinely open to them" they "reached the conclusion that the

[1] Cmnd. 3073, 1966.

interests both of trade unionists and of the nation as a whole . . . compelled them to acquiese in the Government's proposal".[1]

It seemed that the policy was effective at last, and that there was an opportunity to maintain its ascendancy after the end of the standstill by a rigorous application of the criteria through the early warning system and the penalties which lay behind it. In December the Board issued *Productivity and Pay During the Period of Severe Restraint*, with seven tests of a pay agreement which set out to reward "a direct contribution towards increasing productivity", and another White Paper, published in November, restated the three other grounds for exceptional pay increases in language which was patently intended to narrow their application. Increases on grounds of inadequate living standards, for example, must be "confined to the lowest-paid workers", and an increase on grounds of comparability could be justified only where it was "imperative to correct a gross anomaly".[2]

Such expectations, however, were disappointed. Immediately following its application of the tests of a sound productivity agreement, the Board reported on the three-year agreement in the electrical contracting industry which provided increases in wage rates over two years of up to a third.[3] Because it eliminated the grade of electrician's mate and provided for the grading of skilled electricians, the agreement was expected to lead to some economies, but the Board held that these proposals "have not yet been worked out in detail and do no more, in our view, than provide a framework within which proper measures to increase productivity can be taken". The Board nevertheless recommended that the initial increase of 13 per cent, which had been held up by the standstill, should be paid at the end of six months, although the remaining stages should be re-negotiated "nearer the date of implementation in the light of progress made in ensuring increases in productivity and of economic conditions at the time".[4] The first recommendation was not justified by the Board's severe tests, but by a legalistic interpretation of the relevant White Paper.[5] Moreover electrical contracting rates

---

[1] Trades Union Congress, *Annual Report*, 1966, p. 326.
[2] *Prices and Incomes Standstill: Period of Severe Restraint*, Cmnd. 3150, 1966.
[3] See p. 225.
[4] *Wages and Conditions in the Electrical Contracting Industry*, Report No. 24, Cmnd. 3172, 1966, p. 27.
[5] The Board held that the paragraph in the White Paper on *Prices and Incomes Standstill*:

were widely followed by employers in other industries for the payment of their electricians. The Board recommended that the 13 per cent increase should not extend outside electrical contracting. The government, however, decided that it should apply to hospital electricians, and many private employers found themselves under pressure to make a similar extension. Some of them gave way. These decisions set the scene for what was to follow—generous and occasionally ingenious interpretations of the policy by the Board, and a tolerant attitude on the part of the Ministry of Labour, which had been given the responsibility for "vetting" claims reported under the early warning system.

Since then the policy has been redefined on more than one occasion. A White Paper on *Prices and Incomes Policy After 30 June 1967*[1] appeared in March 1967. By asserting that "no-one can be entitled to a minimum increase" in pay, and that "any proposed increase (or other significant improvement) will need to be justified against the criteria", it seemed to foreshadow rigorous restraint. But this promise was tarnished by the reintroduction of the whole range of justifications for exceptional increases contained in the original policy of April 1965, under which pay increases had been so plentiful. Following devaluation new distinctions were introduced by a further White Paper early in 1968 dealing with *Productivity, Prices and Incomes Policy in 1968 and 1969*.[2] The norm was now replaced by a "ceiling", at the same figure as the original norm—3·5 per cent, but all increases however small were required "to be justified against the criteria and considerations of the policy", the four criteria for exceptional increases in pay remaining unchanged. In addition, however, the ceiling might be exceeded by "agreements which genuinely raise productivity and increase efficiency sufficiently to justify a pay increase above $3\frac{1}{2}$ per cent" and by "major reorganisations of wage and salary structures which can be justified on productivity and efficiency grounds".

These refinements did not appear to have much effect on actual movements in pay. Over 1967 as a whole, starting with a zero norm and ending with all pay increases requiring justification

Period of Severe Restraint which provided that the operative date of increases agreed before 20 July 1966 should be delayed for six months made it obligatory to permit their payment at the end of six months.

[1] Cmnd. 3235, 1967.   [2] Cmnd. 3590, 1968.

against the criteria, the increase in weekly wage rates was nearly 6 per cent. Prices rose by 2·5 per cent and the increase in weekly earnings from October 1966 to October 1967 was also about 6 per cent. These rates of income growth were more modest than in the period before the standstill, but this probably has more to do with the level of unemployment, which was running well above the earlier period, and the index of production, which was static through most of the year, than with the effect of the policy. From April 1967 to April 1968 the increase in weekly earnings was 8·5 per cent, and from April 1968 to April 1969 it was 7·5 per cent. Throughout the years 1967–9 it was evident that pay increases were running well in excess of the limits prescribed by the policy.

This gap between policy and practice was emphasised by several notorious agreements which were not referred to the National Board for Prices and Incomes. The most notable stoppage of 1967 was in the docks. Decasualisation arrangements negotiated over the two years since the publication of the Devlin report were applied on 18 September. They included "modernisation" payments of 1s. an hour and guaranteed minimum earnings of £16 in London and £15 elsewhere in return for changes in working practices which varied from port to port. There followed a general unofficial stoppage in Liverpool for further increases in pay and a partial unofficial stoppage in London against the application of some of the agreed changes in working practices. The main grievances of the Liverpool dockers were that their guarantee was lower than the London guarantee and that their piecework earnings were also relatively low. Their settlement, reached at the end of six weeks after the intervention of the Prime Minister, gave Liverpool dockers on piecework a three-months guarantee of a further 2s. an hour, thus raising their guaranteed minimum to more than £17 a week so long as they were employed on piecework. Meanwhile piece rates were to be revised. No justification in terms of the incomes policy was published. The London strike lasted for two months and led to a revision of the new working arrangements. During the year the Ministry of Labour sanctioned the second-stage payments under the electrical contracting agreement.

The major dispute of 1968 was in engineering. Negotiations dragged on through most of the year, punctuated by a one-day stoppage in May and leading up to a decision to call a full-scale strike throughout the industry in October. A settlement was reached after the strike had been first postponed and then abandoned. Since it was a three-stage agreement spread over two years and the most important pay clauses dealt, not with wage rates, but with minimum levels of pay, the effects of the agreement cannot easily be compared with the requirements of the pay policy. However, the Board had discovered that under the previous long-term engineering agreement (the "package deal" of December 1964) average earnings had risen as rapidly as minimum earnings levels. If this relationship persists under the new agreement, with its 30 per cent increase in minimum earnings levels, the agreement will prove to have been a colossal breach of the policy.[1]

After two years of negotiation on pay and productivity, British Overseas Airways pilots struck at the end of March 1969. The settlement on 5 April increased the salaries of senior pilots from £5880 a year to £6750. Overtime provisions made possible even larger increases in earnings. Since it was a productivity agreement there was some justification for exceeding the ceiling laid down in the policy, but the excess was far more than the employers or the government had originally been willing to envisage as appropriate to the changes in working arrangements.

These major agreements were matched by a number of settlements in companies, plants and sections of plants which attracted less attention but could be equally at variance with the policy. At first the part played by the Ministry of Labour's industrial relations service (re-christened the manpower and productivity service from the beginning of 1969) seemed to be one of the successes of the policy. Claims or proposed settlements affecting relatively small numbers of employees could not be effectively handled from London. Consequently the officers of the regional service were brought into discussions on pay claims and pay structures in firms and plants. In many instances companies and local union officers found their advice helpful, and the Ministry

---

[1] *Pay and Conditions of Service of Engineering Workers* (*Second Report on the Engineering Industry*), Report No. 104, Cmnd. 3931, 1969. Between January 1965 and January 1968 the increase in minimum earnings levels for skilled workers was 21·7 per cent. Excluding overtime, average earnings rose by 21·1 per cent for skilled timeworkers and 20·7 per cent for skilled workers paid by results (p. 12).

was for the first time brought into the processes of domestic bargaining as part of its regular business. But as time passed and pay rose well in excess of the prescribed limits a good deal of the energy of everyone concerned was absorbed in finding justification for pay adjustments which appeared to make sense in the circumstances but did not seem to conform to the policy. Although it is impossible to give figures of failure to report agreements on pay, it is recognised that there was a growing reluctance among some employers to submit claims or agreements, and through 1968 and 1969 an increasing number of companies failed to do so. Some unions encouraged the practice. If the vetting arrangements had really established control over domestic bargaining the result should have been a check to earnings drift. In 1967 drift was indeed "negative", but this was probably due to the relatively high level of unemployment, and it rose sharply in 1968. Between April and October weekly earnings rose by more than 3 per cent while weekly wage rates increased by less than 1·5 per cent.

Meanwhile there were moves towards a trade union incomes policy administered by the General Council. When the voluntary early warning system was developed in the autumn of 1965 the Council undertook to deal with the claims of affiliated unions. They asked the unions to inform them of all impending claims and set up a special committee to review them. If the committee did not wish to comment the union or unions would be informed within a month. Otherwise the committee would make written observations or arrange for a discussion. The Council undertook to "keep the Government informed of developments".[1] This arrangement ceased with the standstill, after which the government required notification of claims and settlements direct to the Ministry of Labour, a process later enforced by activating Part II of the 1966 Act. However, the Council decided to retain its own vetting arrangements, looking forward to a stage in which there would be "a transition from a largely Government-determined policy to a policy of which the ingredients were determined by the trade union Movement". Between November 1966 and the following July, 340 claims were notified, covering just over 4 million workers. Approval was withheld from 40 per cent of the claims covering 40 per cent of the workers. "In other cases the committee indicated that they would have no objections to

---

[1] *Prices and Incomes Policy: An "Early Warning" System*, Cmnd. 2808, 1965.

negotiations proceeding on part or all of the claims, but in many instances indicated modifications which they considered should be made."[1] One observer remarked that the committee had "been acting with vigour and determination" and had "shown that it takes seriously the implications of its contention that voluntary action within the Trade Union movement is capable of exercising an effective measure of control over wage increases which could be detrimental to the national interest".[2]

The distinction between the government's policy and that of the General Council was emphasised by conference votes. At a conference of trade union executives on 2 March 1967, the Council's policy was endorsed by a vote of eight to one. Congress confirmed the decision in September, but agreed that "the Prices and Incomes Acts have been detrimental to the best interests of trade unionists" and asked for their repeal.[3]

However, the rapid growth of earnings revealed the weaknesses of the General Council's policy as well as those of the government's policy. As time passed it became evident that the vetting of claims gave the Incomes Policy Committee little control over actual negotiations, as in those affecting dockers and draughtsmen in 1967 and manual engineering workers in 1968. In attempting to develop its own policy the Council had in mind the example of the Swedish central confederation of unions which exercises considerable control over the claims and settlements of its constituent unions. But its ability to do so is largely due to the extreme centralisation of power in the Swedish confederation of employers' associations. Close co-operation between the two bodies enables them jointly to influence both negotiations and settlements. The new Confederation of British Industry was unwilling to accept any responsibility for administering the new policy so far as it affected prices, and undertook to play only a limited part in the voluntary scheme for notifying pay claims and settlements.[4]

---

[1] Trades Union Congress, *Annual Report*, 1967, pp. 328, 332–3.

[2] *Wage Determination and Wage Policy*, p. 54.

[3] Trades Union Congress, *Annual Report*, 1967, pp. 536–43.

[4] "The Confederation of British Industry is arranging to provide the Government with information about claims, formal offers, references to arbitration and terms of settlement reported by their members. So far as national claims and settlements are concerned, the Confederation of British Industry will itself collect the information and pass it on to the Ministry of Labour. Information about local and company negotiations will be supplied

For all these disappointments the government did not abandc
the policy. On the contrary it extended its powers of enforc
ment. When Part IV of the 1966 Act lapsed in 1967, Part II w
activated for a period of twelve months. A new Prices an
Incomes Act, 1967, stopped up loopholes which had been di
covered in the original measure and provided that where th
Board reported adversely on a proposed increase in pay or pric
its application could be deferred for a period of six months fro1
the date of reference to the Board. Next year a further A
extended the period of delay to a maximum of a year. Moreov
the Acts were used to some effect.

In a series of reports on the bus industry beginning in Ma
1966 the Board tried to devise serviceable productivity agre
ments for its various sections. In December 1967 one of the:
reports condemned an agreement reached in the municipal sectc
the week before. Since the parties would not withdraw, th
Minister of Labour placed a standstill order on the agreemen
When the new Act became law in July there was still no accep
able agreement and the order was renewed for a further si
months. On both occasions the Transport and General Worke
debated a strike, but decided instead to concentrate on securin
local agreements providing for back pay to the date of th
original agreement, to be paid when the standstill order ran ou
In November the Board reported on the building industry, an
found that an increase in pay which had already been applie
was in excess of the 3·5 per cent ceiling. By threatening a stand
still on the whole increase, the Secretary of State was able t
persuade the unions to renegotiate a more modest rise, agai
after talk of a strike. In both instances the unions were in wea
bargaining positions, and there have been many occasions whe
the government might have used their powers against stronge
unions and have not done so. But it is clear that the powers ca
be persuasive in some circumstances, although there have bee
no prosecutions as yet.

Moreover the government continued to place considerabl
reliance on the National Board for Prices and Incomes, whos
standing has remained remarkably high throughout the perioc
not only with the public, but also with the unions. The numbe

to the Ministry of Labour direct by the firms and employers' organisations concerned'
(*Prices and Incomes Policy: An "Early Warning" System*).

ɔf references to the Board rose through 1966 and 1967 to a peak
n 1968, and one of the most interesting aspects of the policy has
ɔeen the attempt of the Board to develop and apply the criteria
.aid down in the several White Papers to the cases which have
ɔome before them.

THE CRITERIA OF PAY SETTLEMENTS

For most of the period covered by the policy there has been
some guidance on the norm or ceiling for pay increases, the figure
being either 3·5 per cent or zero. This might have been expected
to reinforce the existing tendency in industry agreements towards
uniform increases and the maintenance of differentials, with the
"exceptions" clauses handling rare cases. In fact other influences
were at work. Apart from the standstill, rates of pay generally
were rising faster than the current policy allowed. This meant
that few settlements could be justified in terms of the policy
without recourse to one or more of the criteria supposedly
reserved for exceptional cases. Similarly when the Board dealt
with a pay reference, they were also under pressure to recommend
an increase not too far out of line with the general movement
of rates, and therefore they also worked the exceptional critieria
hard.

The four critieria were used to very differing extents. In its first
General Report[1] the Board argued strongly for a very restricted
use of the second criterion dealing with the distribution of manpower. Their investigation of the *Salaries of Midlands Bank Staff*[2]
"showed that adjustments in pay designed to remedy a labour
shortage were subsequently followed by other employers with
the result that no redistribution of labour was achieved". Nevertheless they were prepared to use the criterion to justify a pay
increase. In their report on the *Pay of the Higher Civil Service*,[3]
they approved an exceptional pay increase for Under Secretaries
on the grounds that without an improvement in the salary
structure of the administrative class, the civil service would not be
able "to compete fairly with others for its share of talented people";
and they recommended an exceptional increase in *Fire Service Pay*

[1] Report No. 19, Cmnd. 3087, 1966, pp. 15–16.
[2] Report No. 6, Cmnd. 2839, 1965.
[3] Report No. 11, Cmnd. 2882, 1966.

because the "failure of firemen's earnings to keep pace with other earnings has led to a significant increase in wastage. It has led also to an inability to recruit sufficient men to meet all the Service's requirements, both in numbers and in quality."[1] By this time, however, the Board had derived a general rule from their investigations of the *Pay of Busmen*,[2] that "at a time of full employment the most effective protection from scarcity of labour is for the employer to make more effective use of the labour he has".[3] Moreover, this could justify an exceptional pay increase on productivity grounds, thus protecting the employer from further loss of labour.

Although the fourth criterion allowed exceptional increases where pay had "fallen seriously out of line with the level of remuneration for similar work", the original White Paper on Prices and Incomes had asserted that "less weight than hitherto will have to be given" to certain influences on pay determination, among which it included "comparisons with levels or trends of incomes in other employments". The Board took up the point in their first *General Report* in which they argued that formulae for linking the pay increases of certain groups with pay increases elsewhere "provide a mechanism for spreading increases in wage rates from one group to another, regardless of the reasons for which the original increases were given". In general, they said, "the doctrine of comparisons . . . can in fact frustrate the social case for special treatment for particular groups".

Where formulae for "fair comparison" had come to their attention, said the Board, they had "recommended that they should no longer be used".[4] They instanced the "Guillebaud" formula on the railways, the "Phelps Brown" formula for London busmen and the system for adjusting the pay of industrial civil servants. However, their recommendations for industrial civil servants led, at least initially, to a more precise form of fair comparison.[5] Moreover, the most important of all the formulae, that of the non-industrial civil service, has never been brought to the attention of the Board. In 1968 a general agreement provided for pay increases based on Civil Service Pay Research Unit investigations. Each grade was to receive up to 7 per cent from the

---

[1] Report No. 32, Cmnd. 3287, 1967, p. 11.
[2] Report No. 16, Cmnd. 3012, 1966.
[3] *First General Report*, p. 16.   [4] *Ibid.*, p. 16.   [5] See pp. 383–4.

beginning of that year (representing a 3·5 per cent ceiling over the two years since the previous increases) and the balance, if any and whatever it might be, was to be paid a year later. Thus fair comparison continued to apply, but only after a delay.

In dealing with comparisons, as in dealing with labour shortages, the Board continued to keep efficiency in mind. In their report on the *Pay and Conditions of Merchant Navy Officers*,[1] they recommended an exceptional increase to keep the pay of officers in line with that of ratings, but argued that it was "incumbent on the industry to search for ways in which this increase can be used to develop more effective teams of officers and thus lead to ultimate reductions in cost", and made suggestions to help the search.

Thus the Board tried to restrict the criteria of manpower shortage and comparability within narrow limits, although they did not define the limits clearly. The third criterion, low pay, was more of a problem. Since both the government and the unions emphasised that social justice was a central objective of the policy, this criterion was expected to figure prominently in the Board's work. At the end of 1966 the Board had before them three references dealing with relatively low-paid groups which seemed to offer an opportunity for developing a plan to lead to a more equitable distribution of earned incomes. In their report on the first of them, *Pay of Workers in Agriculture in England and Wales*, they found that farm workers generally were among the lowest paid and that an increase recommended by the Agricultural Wages Board was justifiable even in a period of severe restraint.[2] The second report, on the *Pay of Workers in the Retail Drapery, Outfitting and Footwear Trades*, reported that an earnings survey had shown that "workers in these trades as a whole are not among the lowest paid in the community".[3] Accordingly the industry should abandon the practice of passing on increases in

---

[1] Report No. 35, Cmnd. 3302, 1967, p. 14. The increase followed on the agreement for ratings at the end of the 1966 shipping strike. It was not justified by the fourth criterion, since the pay of officers had not fallen out of line with remuneration for similar work, "but rather with the remuneration of those whose work they supervise and direct" (p. 13). It was therefore related to a paragraph in the White Paper on *Prices and Incomes Policy after 30 June 1967*, which stated that "it is important in the interests of economic efficiency that there should be a proper development of salary structures which provide incentives to improved performance".

[2] There were some small groups of relatively high-paid farmworkers to which the Board thought the increase should not apply.   [3] p. 25.

the minimum to all or almost all workers, regardless of their current levels of pay. Increases should be confined to workers at or near the minimum by a system of tapered additions.

In the third report the Board found that the manual workers employed by the local authorities included "large concentrations of workers who are among the lowest paid in the country". However, the low earnings here and in the health service were not a consequence of low wage rates, for rates were substantially higher than in agriculture and in the retail trades, and "compare favourably with those negotiated elsewhere". Consequently "given their present wage structures and limited earnings opportunities, there is no scope for wage increases confined to or weighted in favour of the lowest paid".[1] The Board diagnosed low productivity as the "root cause" of low pay and recommended shorter-term and longer-term devices for linking pay increases with improved efficiency which would have to be justified in terms of productivity.[2] Thus wherever they started the Board seemed to end up with the productivity criterion.

These reports provided ideas for dealing with the problem of low pay, but no clear definition of the low paid, and no clear guidance as to the appropriate remedy for a particular case. In the first of them the Board had given its view that, "at any rate for the purpose of settling pay", it was impossible to lay down "a 'standard of need' at some particular figure in pounds, shillings and pence to divide the lowest-paid from the rest. . . . The identification of the lowest-paid worker requires an examination of average earnings in the industry concerned compared with average earnings in other industries, of the distribution of earnings in that industry and of other items of relevance to remuneration such as fringe benefits".

The General Council were bolder. Having set up their own vetting arrangements they also developed their own critieria for pay changes early in 1967. In most respects these did not differ materially from those of the government, but they included a clear definition of low pay. The Council decided "to aim at progressively raising national minimum rates to a level of £15 a week" and as a first step to allow "claims for increases of up to £1

---

[1] *The Pay and Conditions of Manual Workers in Local Authorities, the National Health Service, Gas and Water Supply*, p. 48.
[2] See p. 393.

week in national minimum rates which were less than £14 a week, on condition that the full increases were applicable only to those workers who were on or near the existing minimum, with tapering increases to those whose current earnings (excluding overtime) were not more than £15 a week".[1] But this ran into trouble with unions of skilled workers who feared their differentials might be whittled away, and in the following year the definition of low pay was abandoned. Instead the General Council's *Economic Review*, 1968, which set out new guidelines, argued for uniform money increases which would yield higher percentage increases for the lower-paid.[2] Soon afterwards the government downgraded the criterion of low pay, along with the manpower and comparability criteria, when the White Paper on *Productivity, Prices and Incomes Policy in 1968 and 1969* insisted that increases granted under these three headings should be contained within the annual ceiling of 3·5 per cent.

The development of price policy brought further pressure on the Board to concentrate its efforts in improvements in the use of labour. The White Papers assumed that criteria of acceptable price adjustments could be applied in the same way as criteria of acceptable pay adjustments. In fact this assumption proved to be false. The notion of a "fair wage", differing for different levels of skill, responsibility and efficiency, and for different working conditions, forms part of most negotiations over pay. But the notion of a "just price" has a medieval ring about it. It implies that there is a fair level of return on capital which is another concept difficult to reconcile with the working of a competitive economic system. Consequently in most price references, and there have been fewer references on prices than on pay, the Board has been tempted to sidestep this issue by arguing that price increases could be avoided or could be less than otherwise if costs could be reduced, and to make proposals for changes in labour utilisation which might form the basis of a productivity agreement.

---

[1] Trades Union Congress, *Annual Report*, 1967, pp. 328–9.

[2] Looking forward to an increase of "5 per cent or rather more" in productivity from mid-1968 to mid-1969, the Council foresaw a "tolerable increase of five per cent or somewhat more in earnings per head". Of this they expected about 1·5 per cent to be absorbed by local productivity bargaining, leaving 3·5–4 per cent for general increases. Excluding juveniles and part-time workers, this would amount to 14s. a week on the average (p. 70).

The tests of a productivity agreement, originally set out in December 1966, were slightly revised in a report on *Productivity Agreements* published six months later and containing detailed studies of seven agreements. Both reports stressed the importance of accurate calculations based on the application of "proper work standards", the need for controls to ensure that the projected changes were achieved, the necessity to take into account consequential pay increases elsewhere in the undertaking and the importance of avoiding "extravagant levels of pay which would provoke resentment outside".[1] The only significant difference was over benefit to the consumer.[2] In August 1969 another report on the same subject, based on wider enquiries, made considerable changes in the wording of the guidelines, but only one alteration of substance. This was to extend them to cover all kinds of "efficiency agreements" including those in which no changes in working practice or method were specified. Consequently the first test which had formerly reproduced the working of the White Papers ("It should be shown that the workers are making a direct contribution towards increasing productivity by accepting more exacting work or a major change in working practices") was revised to read:

"It should be shown that the workers are contributing to the achievement of constantly rising levels of efficiency. Where appropriate, major changes in working practice or working methods should be specified in the agreement."[3]

Several subsequent references required the Board to apply its own guidelines to particular cases, such as local bus agreements and an agreement covering *Pay and Productivity of Industrial Employees of the United Kingdom Atomic Energy Authority*.[4] But the most important references to the Board were claims and settlements at industry level. Although there have been a few important productivity agreements at this level, including the "status" agreement in electricity supply, and a railway agreement in 1968, industry bargaining is generally unsuited to the successful

---

[1] *Productivity Agreements*, p. 45.

[2] The first had required "clear benefit to the consumer, in lower prices or in improved quality". The second, noting that an important economy in one plant "may contribute only a fractional saving in relation to the price of the product", required only "a contribution to stable prices."

[3] *Productivity Agreements (Second Report)*, p. 39.

[4] Report No. 51, Cmnd. 3499, 1968.

negotiation of changes in working practices. Consequently in dealing with these references the Board could generally do no more than suggest that clauses should be introduced to encourage individual firms to set about preparing their own productivity agreements. The report on *Productivity Agreements* had already advised employers' associations "to issue guidelines suitably modified to suit the industry's own circumstances", and to agree them with the unions.[1]

The productivity criterion was intended to apply to systems of payment by results as well as to productivity agreements. Recognising this, the Board took the view that proposals for introducing new systems of payment by results should also satisfy the seven rules. They should be based on proper work standards, should be accurately costed, should contribute to stable prices, and should cover consequential increases in pay to timeworkers within the undertaking. These tests, however, could apply only where new systems were introduced, and the Board noted that about $4\frac{1}{2}$ million workers were already paid by results. There was, they said, "an element of looseness inherent in most systems of payment by results which cannot be controlled merely by seeing that the agreement is followed". Consequently they would "welcome an early Reference from the Government which enabled us to examine systems of payment by results in depth".[2]

The reference was made, and in May 1968 the Board published *Payment by Results Systems*,[3] based on the most thorough-going examination of the subject undertaken in Britain. Its main achievement was to show how these systems actually worked and the wide range between the best and the worst, but the Board also set out tests which could be applied to payment-by-results systems to show whether they were working effectively or were in urgent need of overhaul. There could, however, be no certainty that managers would apply the tests, still less that they would set about remedying any fault thereby revealed. The Board therefore looked to changes in the structure of industrial relations to assist in applying the remedies. Their "main hope" was "that collective bargaining at the plant or company level will become increasingly stronger in relation to fragmented workplace bargaining"; but

[1] *Productivity Agreements*, pp. 36–7.
[2] *Productivity and Pay During the Period of Severe Restraint*, p. 20.
[3] Report No. 65, Cmnd. 3627, 1968.

P

they also argued that "industry-wide negotiating and conciliation systems can serve a valuable purpose" in relation to payment by results. Industry agreements, they suggested, should settle "standard procedures for bargaining at the enterprise level"; should "lay down guidance for plant payment systems"; and should "provide a means of correcting faults in such systems as they arise".[1]

ACHIEVEMENTS

In their *Third General Report* the Board set out some calculations of "what the movement in prices and incomes would have been in the absence of the policy. The first results . . . indicate that the average annual increase in earnings in recent years may have been just under 1 per cent less than it otherwise would have been."[2] The calculations are complex for they involve taking into account changes in all the important factors which might influence pay movements, such as prices, employment and so on, but independent calculations by several econometricians seem to confirm the Board's findings. However, the major effect was the impact of the 1966 standstill and since than the calculations appear to show that the effect has been falling off. This might be taken to confirm John Corina's view that incomes policy "is a socio-economic instrument of extreme instability. But it is possible that it is workable if this fact is accepted; and if policy-makers work on a basis of forecasting its rate of breakdown and attempt to contain it within bounds. This makes it possible to enter upon another experiment after a length of time has elapsed".[3] In 1950 the government persisted so long with a fractured policy that the next serious experiment was postponed for more than a decade. In 1969 the announcement by the Chancellor of the Exchequer in his budget speech that the government proposed to return to the four-month delay of the 1966 legislation in place of the twelve-month delay of the 1968 Act seemed to foreshadow a phasing out of the policy before equivalent harm had been done. But the pace of retreat was limited by international commitments

---

[1] *Ibid.*, pp. 59, 66.
[2] Report No. 77, Cmnd. 3715, 1968, p. 12 and Appendix A.
[3] "Can an Incomes Policy be administered?" *British Journal of Industrial Relations* November 1967.

in return for overseas loans. At the Trades Union Congress of 1969 a majority rejected the advice of the General Council by condemning not only all statutory control over pay but also the National Board for Prices and Incomes itself. This revolt indicated that there might not be much time left for an orderly withdrawal.

The Board's *Fourth General Report* suggested that the policy may have had more lasting effects on the growth of productivity. It found that since the war productivity has normally risen faster in a period of economic recovery when unemployment has been falling, but "the rate of increase which developed in 1967 and continued in 1968 was higher than average and singular in that it was not accompanied by a rise in demand reflected in lower unemployment".[1] In other words productivity was advancing more rapidly than might have been expected in the circumstances. This could be related to the spread of productivity bargaining under pressure of the incomes policy. By June 1969 the register of productivity cases kept by the Department of Employment and Productivity recorded some 3000 cases covering about 6 million workers or 25 per cent of all employed workers.[2] Most of these were not, of course, "comprehensive" agreements of the type examined in the report on *Productivity Agreements*. Many were partial agreements affecting "only one practice and often only a single group of workers".[3] The Department strove to apply the seven tests to these agreements, but in many instances the application had to use rule-of-thumb checks because detailed figures were not available, and often the sheer weight of work meant that examination was cursory. In relation to the share of the reduction in costs which should accrue to the workers, the Department's officials developed standards of their own which had no basis in the Board's reports. The number of rejections (130 covering 48,000 workers) suggests that the Department's decisions were generous. The Board noted that "a few companies seem deliberately to have misled the D.E.P. Two granted a wage increase following, or to stave off, industrial unrest, and productivity agreements were presented on the basis of figures which had little foundation in fact."[4] One agreement submitted by a

[1] Report No. 122, Cmnd. 4130, 1969, p. 5.
[2] *Productivity Agreements (Second Report)*, p. 3.
[3] *Productivity Agreements*, p. 2.
[4] *Productivity Agreements (Second Report)*, pp. 3–5.

major engineering firm and approved by the Department was a scrap-saving bonus. The bonus increased as scrap fell but a basic bonus of 10s. a week was paid whether scrap fell, stayed put or rose. However, the evidence that many bogus agreements have slipped through does not prove that the movement towards productivity agreements has not made a contribution to economic growth, and it is evident that the pressure of the policy has been at least partly responsible for the rapid development of productivity bargaining.

The influence of comparability in the settlement of wage rates has apparently been reduced. There is less "bunching" of settlements over time, and there is wider variation in the amounts of increases than in the past. But it does not follow that the influence of comparability has been replaced only by considerations of productivity, labour shortage and low pay. Since the government intervenes in settlements more than ever before, the dispersion of pay increases might reflect their views on the advisability of concessions in one instance and the chance of success with a firm stand in another. Moreover, the downgrading of comparability has affected rates rather than earnings. It seems that the average earnings of manual workers, industry by industry, have kept in step about as much as they did before 1965.[1] If so this could reflect the irrelevance of the policy to the real determinants of pay.

One consequence of the policy is not in doubt. The 1965 White Paper included changes in the cost of living among those factors affecting pay which would have to be given "less weight than hitherto". Over the next three years the two largest industries with cost-of-living sliding scales agreed to terminate them. These were building and printing. It was an achievement which had eluded Stafford Cripps in 1950.

Finally, many of the Board's reports diagnosed a need for radical overhaul in the structure of collective bargaining so as to allow the policy to take effect and to make room for productivity bargaining. In the long run the policy and the Board may be judged by their achievements in this field.

[1] For this information I am indebted to Dr. Corina of St. Peter's College, Oxford, who is conducting a detailed statistical investigation of the effects of the policy.

CHAPTER 12

THE REFORM OF INDUSTRIAL RELATIONS

The Structure and Working of the System

The Board's suggestions for the reform of collective bargaining had to compete with several other proposals for reforming industrial relations. In June 1968 there appeared the report of the Royal Commission on Trade Unions and Employers' Associations, chaired by Lord Donovan, with most of its space devoted to consideration of the problems and the law of collective bargaining. In January 1969 the Labour government issued its proposals for legislation in a White Paper entitled *In Place of Strife*, followed by an abortive draft Bill and an abortive Bill. Meanwhile, in *Fair Deal at Work*,[1] the Conservative Party had been developing their own scheme which ultimately resulted in the Industrial Relations Act, 1971.

These various proposals can only be understood by reference to the problems of the British system of industrial relations, as it exists and as their authors saw it. A summary of the structure and working of the system as set out in the previous eleven chapters will therefore serve as an introduction to a discussion of schemes for reform.

In 1965, just before the schemes began to appear, industry bargaining was still seen as the main feature of the British system. Although everyone realised that there had been changes since the Whitley Report in 1917, there was nothing available to replace the model which the Whitley Committee then constructed to guide public policy, and which for many years thereafter provided a fair first approximation to the working of the system. In the Whitley model, unions and employers' associations negotiate through industry procedures to arrive at substantive agreements regulating those aspects of employment which are subject to collective bargaining. They provide a disputes procedure

[1] Conservative Political Centre, 1968.

through which their members in the firms and the branches can raise difficulties and controversies relating to the agreements. It is also recognised that there may be issues not subject to agreement which can nevertheless usefully be discussed between managers and men in the plant, the assumption being that management bears the responsibility for the final decision. Each side is responsible for controlling its own members, and strikes and lockouts should occur only after the procedure has been used and has failed to bring agreement. Consequently, the model must allow for official strikes and lockouts with the risk that they may close down a whole industry, but the government provides a range of services—conciliation, arbitration and inquiry—designed to help with unresolved disputes before stoppages occur, and to bring stoppages to an end as soon as possible. Stoppages in the public services are to be particularly deplored, but so is the subjection of the pay of public servants to political debate and lobbying. Consequently, it is accepted by all concerned that negotiations in the public service should follow the standards agreed in private employment. Industries with defective organisation among employers or workers, or both, are served by statutory Wages Councils intended in the short run to provide a substitute for collective bargaining, and in the long run to promote organisation, with a view to replacing the Councils by voluntary machinery.

Although the Whitley model had not been replaced, there were by 1965 at least eleven respects in which the system had moved a considerable distance away from its assumptions:

(1) Employers' associations had lost authority. For several reasons, which include a remarkable growth in the size of firms, changing expectations of what a company should provide for its employees, and a long period of full employment, many more decisions about the rules governing employment were taken within the firm without reference to employers' associations.

(2) At the same time there had been a growing fragmentation of decisions on labour matters within the firm. Because most firms lacked coherent labour policies and effective manpower controls, issues were settled piecemeal by departmental managers and by foremen. Pay structures and manpower utilisation in the plant were the consequence of a large number of unco-ordinated sectional decisions.

(3) In plants with a high degree of trade union organisation these decisions were commonly shared with shop stewards, but as understandings much more often than as written agreements. The motive for dealing with the stewards was that workers would be likely to accept an arrangement that the stewards approved, and, indeed, stewards usually referred important decisions to the groups of workers whom they represented. But this led on to situations in which arrangements which suited the work group were accepted by foremen and managers who had not formally consented to them.

(4) Consequently, shop steward organisation in the plant replaced the branch as the basic unit of union organisation in many industries—in practice, but not in the union rule book. It followed that a hierarchical model of organisation was no longer applicable to the unions, if it ever had been. The full-time officer came into domestic bargaining as an occasional adviser or as the route to the official disputes procedure. Otherwise he had not the time, or the knowledge, or the authority to control domestic bargaining.

(5) Trade union democracy has always leaned heavily upon the decentralisation of authority to districts or branches, or other forms of local organisation. By 1965 the predominant form of decentralisation in many unions had come to be the transfer of authority in collective bargaining to shop stewards and their workshop organisations.

These first five developments were closely linked to each other. Together with fragmentation of decision-making within the firm, the decline of authority of employers' associations enhanced the power of work groups and shop stewards, thus encouraging the new form of decentralisation within the unions. But these associated developments had proceeded at widely differing speeds in different industries and in different undertakings within each industry. Thus there were industry agreements which still exercised effective control over most issues subject to any form of collective bargaining, so that domestic bargaining was little developed in those industries, and, even in industries where domestic bargaining predominated, the industry-wide agreements were followed to some extent in all federated firms, and to a greater extent in some of them than in others. These variations were reflected in the authority of shop stewards and in the distribution of power within the unions. But, even so, we now know that by 1965 the five changes had progressed further than almost anyone was then prepared to admit.

(6) Where domestic bargaining predominated, disputes procedures tended either to become overloaded with domestic disputes or to fall into disuse because they would only handle disputes concerning industry agreements.

(7) These circumstances help to explain why the proportion of strikes in breach of procedure had risen to about 95 per cent of recorded strikes, and the number of strikes per worker had been growing in almost every industry except mining. There had probably been an even more rapid growth of unrecorded strikes, overtime bans, work-to-rules and other sanctions. Virtually all of these were in breach of procedure, as were the great majority of recorded strikes.

(8) Consultative arrangements in the plant tended to be transformed into bargaining bodies or to fall into disuse because shop stewards preferred a more authoritative method of participating in managerial decisions.

(9) The changing pattern of strikes and other sanctions had limited the effectiveness of the government's services to industrial relations. It was considered improper for the government to recognise unofficial leaders, so conciliation and arbitration could be used only in official disputes and not to avoid or contain unofficial action.

(10) As the volume of domestic bargaining increased, so the gap widened between earnings and the rates negotiated in industry agreements. Public employees began to take steps to relate their pay to earnings in private industry rather than to negotiated rates.

(11) Most industry agreements on pay did no more than provide periodic increases in rates of pay effectively settled in domestic bargaining. This trend was most evident in manufacturing industry, but was also visible in other industries and services. Similarly Wages Councils no longer set effective minimum rates, but instead provided periodic upward adjustments in pay for the workers they covered. Meanwhile, since the Councils lacked any authority to promote negotiating machinery within the plant, they had no means of encouraging within their industries the developments in bargaining and union organisation which were occurring in the well-organised industries. This further reduced

their already limited ability to promote organisation among workers.

Thus every element included in the Whitley model was operating in a different way from the model's prescriptions. In addition the system included elements, notably domestic bargaining and the new distribution of power within the unions, which had no place in the model despite the prodigious importance that they had acquired in practice. The Whitley model was, therefore, of little help in understanding the system and its working in 1965, and a new model was already urgently needed.

One new model, suggested by the earlier chapters of this book, begins with the plant, and particularly with sizeable and strongly unionised plants where managerial co-ordination and control are weak. Most of these plants are subject to industry agreements, but these exercise little control over industrial relations in the plants. Most decisions on industrial relations matters are taken by foremen and shop stewards, acting separately or in concert, by work groups, and by individual workers in setting piecework values, with occasional incursions by higher management. These decisions have led to a mass of custom and practice and informal arrangements which, together with such formal rules as exist, regulate employment in the plants. They determine how work is done, the levels and ranges of earnings, the range of decisions in which workers and their representatives have an acknowledged share, and the ways in which disagreements will be handled.

Trade union officers and employers' associations play a severely limited part in the affairs of these plants. Their industry agreements fix minimum standards for certain aspects of employment. They can offer advice and draw up guidelines to try to influence plant behaviour. They may be called in to handle unresolved disagreements in the plants, but even so their decisions are limited to what will be acceptable and workable in the particular plant.

Most of the other elements of the system serve to pass on the results of these plant dealings. In industries where such plants are common, industry negotiations drag minimum standards of pay and conditions along behind the levels achieved in the plants so that the weaker brethren shall not fall too far behind. Occasionally they attempt, usually without success, to pull the minimum nearer the average by "consolidating" part of the pay packet. Wages

Councils transmit pay increases from these industries to the badly-organised industries.

Even industries where control over labour matters is more centralised are subject to the influence of pacemaking plants elsewhere. Their carefully designed pay structures must yield earnings not too far behind the levels in those plants, lest they be eroded by the introduction of schemes of payment by results or rising overtime. In some public services the arrangements for following the pacemakers are formally recognised and systematised by formulae for establishing fair wage comparisons.

In this model the most effective point to apply the pressure of strikes or other sanctions is within the plant, probably on issues which directly affect only a section, and unofficially and unconstitutionally. There is also room for the large-scale official strike, but as part of the transmission process, to put pressure on employers who are reluctant to follow plant earnings levels elsewhere.

Through Wages Councils, public service negotiations, conciliation and arbitration, the government has a considerable part to play in the transmission process, but the working of industrial relations in the plants, and therefore the dynamics of the system, are beyond the reach of the government. Nor can the government exercise indirect control over plant industrial relations through employers' associations and trade unions. Employers' associations have little authority within the plant, and in the unions which organise in the pacemaking plants there has been a substantial redistribution of power to shop stewards and their committees.

The Donovan Commission saw the contrast between the two models as a conflict between two systems of industrial relations, "the formal system embodied in the official institutions" and "the informal system created by the actual behaviour of trade unions and employers' associations, of managers, shop stewards and workers".[1]

However, in 1965 the changes since the inter-war period could also be seen as an impressive instance of unconscious adaptation. The official institutions continued relatively undisturbed in their structure and methods while the system of industrial relations experienced massive readjustment to accommodate new elements. At that time a debate between these two views could have pro-

[1] *Report*, p. 12.

duced telling arguments on both sides. Forerunners of the Donovan Report could have pointed to the growth in unofficial strikes (outside coalmining) and to the wide disparity between the managerial prerogatives assumed by industry agreements and the practical limitations placed upon them in many plants. For their part, the adaptation school could point to the great changes in collective bargaining, pay systems and union behaviour which had gone on largely unobserved and without obvious disruption of the official institutions. But looking back from 1972, the signs of conflict and disruption can be seen to have multiplied, together with demands for radical reform.

For one thing, the pace of change appears to have been accelerated. If the number of recorded strikes (all but a tiny proportion of them unofficial and unconstitutional) can be taken as an index, the acceleration can be seen in the rapid rate of increase of strikes in Britain from 1968 to 1970.[1] If the rate of increase in pay can serve as a measure, the acceleration can be seen in the upward surge of wages and salaries from 1969 to 1971, almost unprecedented in peacetime, which came to be known as the wage explosion.[2]

It could also be argued that the adaptation theory had been disproved long before 1965 by the successive attempts of post-war governments to apply an incomes policy. Once governments accept responsibility for management of the economy they must have a view on the proper level and rate of change in incomes, and therefore in negotiated pay and in gross earnings. A rate of change in agreed rates or earnings which differs widely and persistently from the government's intentions is evidence of conflict within the system, and an attempt by government to close the gap by imposing an incomes policy is a bid to make radical alterations to the system.

However, fragmented plant bargaining is not only a menace to a government incomes policy, but also a challenge to managerial authority; for how, in such conditions, can the management of a company frame and apply a manpower policy? This challenge has most commonly been identified in the obstacles to efficient

---

[1] The number of recorded strikes rose from 2378 in 1968 to 3116 in 1969 and 3906 in 1970. In 1971, with rising unemployment the figure fell to 2223, but the number of working days lost through strikes rose to 13·5 million, the highest figure since 1926.

[2] Average hourly earnings of manual workers which had been rising by about 6 per cent a year in the decade 1959–69, rose by 15·4 per cent from October 1969 to October 1970.

operation provided by restrictive practices embedded in custom and practice and in workshop agreements and understandings. The process of reform in plant relations which came to be known as "productivity bargaining", and which attracted widespread attention during the sixties, was a managerial attempt to make radical changes in the system.

Accordingly the conflict hypothesis now has the best of the argument. But that does not mean that its supporters agree on the nature of the conflict or on the remedy which should be prescribed. The Donovan Report concentrated primarily on the failings of managers and governments, but the unions have increasingly come under attack. Decentralisation of power to the work groups and shop stewards has been castigated as the abnegation of effective trade union government, with the complexities of union structure adding further obstacles to successful control by union executives and officers, and to dependable dealings between managers and trade unions. Thus defects within the unions are identified as a major cause, sometimes the sole cause, of the failures of incomes policy, of faulty manpower management, and of a rapidly rising rate of unconstitutional strikes.

Small wonder in these circumstances that there has been a variety of proposals for a thoroughgoing overhaul of the system of industrial relations. The first of them was never set out in a single document, but emerged from a number of major reports of the National Board for Prices and Incomes.

THE NATIONAL BOARD FOR PRICES AND INCOMES

The Board argued for a reform of domestic pay structures in a number of reports, for example in their general reports on *Productivity Agreements*, *Payment by Results Systems*, and *Job Evaluation*, and in their reports on the country's two largest industries, engineering and building. But they realised that the negotiation of satisfactory pay structures depends upon the existence of satisfactory domestic negotiating arrangements. Thus they recommended that "appropriate joint negotiating machinery" should be set up "in every plant or company" in engineering;[1] and that the larger building firms at least should "enter into

[1] *Pay and Conditions of Service of Engineering Workers (First Report)*, p. 41.

company agreements with the unions" dealing with facilities for stewards, for union officials and for union meetings on site, and with the handling of grievances and discipline, as well as with "the content of P.B.R. schemes" and "the regulation of overtime working".[1]

They were less confident, however, when it came to recommending how these changes should be brought about. Ideally an incomes policy should have been able to prevent pay increases in firms which failed to adopt such recommendations, thus building up pressure for reform. But in fact the reverse was true. The policy was unable to do much about domestic pay increases so long as domestic pay structures and procedures were fragmented and informal. The reports on payment by results and engineering recorded wage drift, unrelated to productivity improvements, taking pay well above the limits of the policy.[2] Ill-regulated productivity agreements could produce similar results. In 1968 the Board investigated a number of productivity agreements in road haulage and found a sorry state of affairs. "It can be said of all the Birmingham agreements that the only element in them which specifically aimed at offsetting the increase in rates paid is the provision for increasing maximum running speed from 30 to 40 m.p.h. In every case, however, the controls necessary to ensure that this improvement in speed is realised are lacking. . . . In many cases, in Birmingham, Merseyside and in Scotland, we found that the drivers themselves did not know what was expected from them by way of cost decreases in return for wage increases."[3] The Board wanted to reform domestic bargaining in order to increase the regulatory effect of the policy. The easiest way of achieving pay increases was to stay unreformed.

Consequently the Board had to look for some other instrument for promoting reform, and they turned to industry bargaining, for which they proposed new functions and responsibilities. The two sides should adapt to their own circumstances the guidelines and tests of satisfactory payment systems and procedures suggested by the Board, and embody them in agreements; and they

---

[1] *Pay and Conditions in the Building Industry*, p. 49.

[2] *Payment by Results Systems*, Chapter 3; *Payment by Results Systems (Supplement)*, Papers 7 and 9; *Pay and Conditions of Service of Engineering Workers (First Report)*, Chapter 3.

[3] *Productivity Agreements in the Road Haulage Industry*, Report No. 94, Cmnd. 3847, 1968, pp. 10, 12.

should accept responsibility for seeing that domestic arrangements conformed to the guidelines and satisfied the tests.

The Board's confidence in this instrument appears to have fluctuated. In dealing with payment by results they wrote: "It has to be recognised from the outset that the contribution of industry negotiating bodies to the reform of payment systems is likely to have rather limited effect in the short run. It involves a fairly radical adaptation in institutions to meet needs which are not yet generally recognised."[1] Again in *Productivity Agreements* (*Second Report*) they found that relatively few framework agreements to regulate domestic productivity bargaining had been negotiated at industry level, and went on to say that the success of such agreements would depend, not on tight central control, but on the creation by the employers' associations of "an effective and influential advisory service".[2] But at other times their expectations were pitched a good deal higher.

They found the two main shortcomings of the building industry's pay structure to be defective systems of payment by results and fluctuating overtime. Their recommendation was that the National Joint Council should foster approved company agreements among the large firms, bring out guidelines and model agreements for payment by results, negotiate a new structure of rates and subscribe to the principle "that overtime working should be limited to the minimum essential to meet operational requirements". Thus they hoped to narrow the "wide discrepancy between earnings and nationally agreed rates".[3] But this discrepancy had arisen despite the National Joint Council's efforts to maintain standard rates, to regulate overtime and to guide payment by results. The Board did not make apparent how the Council was to succeed where it had failed before. The engineering industry was advised to establish a Joint National Council with an independent chairman who "would need to have in mind coordination both between grade and grade and between actual earnings and nationally agreed minima, and would also have regard to the requirements of the national policy for productivity, prices and incomes".[4] To help police productivity agreements in

---

[1] *Payment by Results Systems*, p. 61.
[2] p. 25.
[3] *Pay and conditions in the Building Industry*, pp.56–62.
[4] *Pay and Conditions of Service of Engineering Workers* (*First Report*), p. 41. These proposals were not repeated in the *Second Report* published over a year later.

road haulage the Board wanted to revivify the industry's National Negotiating Committee,[1] established following the Board's first report on Road Haulage,[2] although the committee was already defunct, and there was no reason to believe that the feeble Road Haulage Association could exert effective control over its members' payment systems.

These bold proposals give the impression that the Board were whistling to keep up their courage. In general their concern for the reform of domestic industrial relations was evident, but it was far from clear that they had devised satisfactory means to achieve it. Nor should they have been expected to do so, for their prime concern was with the particular cases and problems referred to them.

THE DONOVAN COMMISSION

On the same day as the Board came into being, the Labour government appointed the Donovan Commission "to consider relations between managements and employees and the role of trade unions and employers' associations in promoting the interests of their members and in accelerating the social and economic advance of the nation, with particular reference to the Law affecting the activities of these bodies". With such wide terms of reference, and three years to develop and formulate their ideas, the Commission had a far better opportunity to work out a far-reaching analysis of the defects of British industrial relations and a consistent set of remedies for them than had the Board, which was under continuous pressure to produce reports on a variety of topics.

The Commission's analysis rested on the conflict between the formal and informal systems which they diagnosed as the cause of the "central defect . . . the disorder in factory and workshop relations and pay structures. . . . Any suggestion that conflict between the two systems can be resolved by forcing the informal system to comply with the assumptions of the formal system should be set aside. Reality cannot be forced to comply with pretences."

The Commission asserted that "most industry-wide agreements cannot provide effective regulation of industrial relations and

[1] *Productivity Agreements in the Road Haulage Industry*, p. 76.
[2] *Road Haulage Rates*, Report No. 1 (Interim), Cmnd. 2695.

could not be made to do so". Consequently the instrument of reform was to be the "factory-wide agreement", although in a multi-plant company a company agreement might serve the purpose equally well if it allowed scope for factory negotiating bodies. These agreements were to provide "comprehensive and authoritative collective bargaining machinery", and "joint procedures for the rapid and equitable settlement of grievances"; and to regulate the rights, duties and work of shop stewards. They should deal with redundancy, discipline and safety, and assist "companies to work towards the negotiation of pay structures which are comprehensive, fair and conducive to efficiency".[1]

This proposal has a good deal in common with some of the pronouncements of the Board, but the Commission diverged more clearly from the Board when it came to suggesting how the new factory agreements were to be brought about. The Commission allowed a place for employers' associations and industry agreements. Many companies, poorly equipped to negotiate on their own, would need the advice of their associations; and industry agreements could set out "guidelines for acceptable company or factory agreements", and settle "minimum earnings levels for a standard working week". But neither employers' associations nor industry agreements could bring about the change; nor, for that matter could the unions. "If Britain is to shift to factory agreements therefore the change must be accomplished by boards of directors. . . . At present boards can leave industry-wide agreement to their employers' associations, and the task of dealing with workers within those agreements to subordinate managers. Removing this protection will direct the attention of companies to the need to develop their own personnel policies."[2]

The Commission, then, accepted that the Whitley model was no longer valid. "The practices of the formal system have become increasingly empty." They saw that fragmented bargaining was now the dynamic of the system. "The practices of the informal system have come to exert an ever greater influence on the conduct of industrial relations throughout the country."[3] But the system could be reformed. If most industry agreements were incapable of regulating workshop relations, the job could never-

[1] *Report*, pp. 36–45.   [2] *Ibid.*, pp. 41–6.   [3] *Ibid.*, p. 37.

theless be done by properly-constructed plant or company agreements, provided that companies would take upon themselves the responsibility of planning and negotiating these agreements. For the Commission's model did not place management and unions upon an equal footing of responsibility; companies should be primarily accountable for industrial relations in their own undertaking.

Once the reform was carried out, the Commission expected the rate of unofficial and unconstitutional strikes to fall off substantially. The new agreements would also permit the more effective use of manpower, for they would "get rid of assumptions and attitudes to collective bargaining which have allowed restrictive labour practices to grow and efficiency to languish".[1] Moreover, they would offer firm ground for government intervention in industrial relations. "Incomes policy must continue a lame and halting exercise so long as it consists in the planning of industry-wide agreements most of which exercise an inadequate control over pay."[2]

But how were companies to be persuaded to set about the reform of their industrial relations? There was to be an Industrial Relations Act obliging companies, initially those with more than five thousand employees, to register their agreements with the Department of Employment and Productivity, or to report that they had none. The Department was to handle queries and problems as far as it could, but the Secretary of State was to be empowered to refer cases and general issues for investigation by a Commission on Industrial Relations,[3] to be established by the Act with responsibility for the long-run reconstruction of British industrial relations.

Although the Commission placed the primary responsibility for reform upon companies, they also gave attention to the defects of multi-unionism which they considered to be a serious obstacle to the reconstruction of industrial relations. They thought the most helpful means of reducing multi-unionism was "by agreements between unions on recruiting rights and negotiating rights" in the plant, suggesting that the Trades Union Congress should adopt the principle of "one union for one grade of worker within one

[1] *Ibid.*, p. 85.   [2] *Ibid.*, p. 53.
[3] The title suggested in the report was "Industrial Relations Commission", but this was altered to avoid confusion of initials with the Industrial Reconstruction Corporation.

factory" as a guide for the movement.[1] In addition, they proposed that the new Commission on Industrial Relations should deal with recognition disputes, including disputes between unions.

Apart from the proposal that companies should be liable to a monetary penalty if they failed to register their agreements, or to report that they had no agreements and why, the Donovan Commission did not suggest penalties for failure to carry out the recommendations of the new Commission, whether the fault lay with the company or with the unions. This was because they felt that the defects of existing industrial relations were "primarily due to widespread ignorance about the most sensible and effective means of conducting industrial relations, and to the very considerable obstacles to the use of sensible and effective methods contained in our present system of industrial relations".[2] The job to be done, therefore, was educational, beginning with the Donovan Report itself, and subsequently to be carried on by the new Commission. When managers and trade unionists saw that current ideas about industrial relations were out of touch with reality, and had become props for outworn institutions, they would be ready to carry out the reforms which were needed.

This emphasis on education went along with a pessimistic view of the efficacy of legal sanctions in industrial relations, and a good deal of the report was taken up with arguing that particular proposals for introducing sanctions were unnecessary, or would not work. The Commission were not in principle opposed to the legal enforcement of collective agreements. If the reform of industrial relations was carried out it would "be possible to identify the situations in which it would be neither unjust nor futile to apply legal sanctions".[3] But existing agreements would not serve the purpose. The parties' intention that they should not be contracts was "manifest from the style in which those agreements are expressed. To make them enforceable would in the first place require their redrafting." But even if that were done, "the root of the evil is in our present methods of collective bargaining and especially our methods of workshop bargaining. . . . Until this defect is remedied, all attempts to make procedure agreements legally binding are bound to defeat themselves."[4] Remedying this defect would create a new situation in which the incidence of

---

[1] *Ibid.*, pp. 182–4.   [2] *Ibid.*, p. 51.
[3] *Ibid.*, p. 137.   [4] *Ibid.*, pp. 126–8.

unconstitutional strikes would be greatly diminished. "It is impossible at the present time to say whether in this situation any further sanctions will be required."[1]

However, the Commissioners were not opposed to making changes in the law or to extending its scope. They proposed to sweep away doubts about the legal status of unions by granting them full corporate personality and by making it incumbent on them to register. This would extend legal requirements concerning union rules to all trade unions, and the Commission suggested additional requirements on admissions, discipline, disputes between members and their unions, elections and shop stewards.[2] They argued there was no case for legislation against the closed shop as such, but the widespread use of the closed shop meant that "trade unions cannot be regarded simply as voluntary clubs from the members' point of view".[3] Consequently they proposed a review body of two trade unionists with a lawyer as chairman to review complaints against disciplinary action by trade unions, and against election malpractices. The review body were also to deal with disputes between the Registrar and a trade union as to whether its rules met the requirements of the law.[4]

At this point the Commissioners diverged. A majority of seven wished to see trade unions induced to register by confining to registered trade unions the immunity, granted in section 3 of the Trade Disputes Act, 1906, from action for inducing a breach of contract of employment in a trade dispute. The minority of five could not see "any justification for exposing unofficial strikers to a measure of this kind . . . as long as our system of collective bargaining is in its present state", and thought that registration should be made obligatory by making "the members of the Executive Committee of a body which should, but does not, register as a trade union . . . liable to a penalty".[5]

Other changes in the law were suggested to help in extending the scope of collective bargaining which, wrote the Commission, if "properly conducted, . . . is the most effective means of giving workers the right to representation in decisions affecting their working lives, a right which is or should be the prerogative of every worker in a democratic society".[6] Henceforth any stipulation in a contract of employment that an employee should not

---

[1] *Ibid.*, p. 137.   [2] *Ibid.*, pp. 174–6, p. 212.   [3] *Ibid.*, p. 170.
[4] *Ibid.*, pp. 176–8.   [5] *Ibid.*, pp. 214–15.   [6] *Ibid.*, p. 54.

belong to a trade union ought to be void. To assist the Commission on Industrial Relations in securing recognition of unions where they felt this was justified, the Secretary of State should be empowered to make unilateral arbitration by the Industrial Court available to "industries, sections of industry or undertakings" where employers refused to recognise trade unions or refused to bargain effectively.[1] The Commission made a series of proposals designed to make the abolition of Wages Councils easier and to give those which remained greater powers to promote voluntary domestic bargaining.[2]

A further major revision in the law proposed by the Commission was an enactment that employment should be terminated only where there was a valid reason "connected with the capacity or conduct of the worker or based on the operational requirements of the undertaking", and certain reasons for dismissal, such as race, sex and trade union membership and activity, should be specifically declared invalid. A dismissed employee was to be entitled to complain to a tribunal, which would try to reach an amicable settlement, and hold a hearing only if these efforts failed. The tribunal should be empowered to order reinstatement, with compensation as an alternative if either party preferred it. Voluntary disciplinary procedures could be exempted if they were collectively agreed and were judged to come up to the required standard.[3]

LABOUR'S LEGISLATIVE PROPOSALS

Despite these far-reaching proposals for changes in the law, the Donovan Commission rejected legal sanctions as a means of accomplishing the major reforms which they thought were needed, placing their hopes in voluntary action once government, managers and trade unions realised the defects of existing institutions. Thereby they disappointed the press, the politicians and probably the public too. Within a year or two the Donovan analysis had generally come to be recognised as an acute elucidation of the complexities and defects of British industrial relations, but at the time reaction was predominantly hostile. The press neglected the analysis for the proposed changes in the law, which were condemned as "weak", when firm measures were said to be

[1] *Ibid.*, pp. 69–70.   [2] *Ibid.*, pp. 65–8.   [3] *Ibid.*, chapter 9.

required, in particular to curb unconstitutional strikes and to enforce union discipline. The government also had hoped for a report which would be "tougher" in these respects. When their proposals appeared in a White Paper entitled *In Place of Strife* in January 1969, they followed the diagnosis and the proposals of the Donovan Report fairly closely, but with the addition of "tough" measures of their own.

The White Paper accepted that there was "no institution primarily concerned with the reform of collective bargaining".[1] The gap was to be filled by setting up a Commission on Industrial Relations, whose functions were to include investigating inter-union disputes which the Trades Union Congress could not resolve. Going beyond the Donovan Report, the White Paper proposed to empower the Secretary of State to give effect to the Commission's recommendations in such disputes by means of an order, so that unions failing to comply would be liable to a fine.[2] Moreover, the Donovan Report had not gone "far enough in its recommendations for modernising the trade union movement", so there was to be a scheme for grants and loans to unions to assist mergers, training, research and the employment of management consultants.[3]

On strikes the White Paper began by accepting the Donovan thesis that "the fundamental solution lies in the re-structuring of our present system of collective bargaining when it is disordered and defective". But it went on to say that strikes in breach of procedure "are increasing in many industries and their effect can be very serious", so that there were grounds for requiring "that groups of employees shall not take precipitate strike action, which may seriously damage the economy and their fellow employees, before they have used the machinery of discussion to which they themselves have agreed or which may be made available by the government".[4] Consequently the government proposed that the Secretary of State should have a "discretionary reserve power to secure 'a conciliation pause' in unconstitutional strikes and in strikes where, because there is no agreed procedure or for other reasons, adequate joint discussions have not taken place". The normal conciliation services were to be tried first, and in such cases as victimisation or where the employer had "introduced a change in working methods without adequate notice and discussion"

[1] p. 13.   [2] *Ibid.*, p. 20.   [3] *Ibid.*, pp. 23–4.   [4] *Ibid.*, pp. 25–8.

he would be required to restore the status quo. When all this had been done the Secretary of State could issue a warning, followed by an order (backed by financial penalties) to return to work for twenty-eight days to allow adequate discussions to take place.[1]

In addition, although the government accepted the view that unofficial and unconstitutional strikes were the main problem, they were concerned that a major official strike could "be called when the support of those involved may be in doubt" and proposed discretionary power to require a ballot before an official strike which "would involve a serious threat to the economy or public interest".[2]

Although these passages threw the trade union movement into an uproar, they proposed discretionary powers only, and could be interpreted as relatively marginal adjustments to the Donovan recommendations. This interpretation was supported by the first practical steps which the government took, which were to introduce a scheme for the voluntary registration of procedures by undertakings with more than 5000 employees,[3] and the establishment by Royal Warrant, without statutory powers, of a Commission on Industrial Relations with George Woodcock, until then general secretary of the Trades Union Congress, as chairman. But in April 1969 the government demonstrated that their additions constituted the heart of their proposals. They announced their intention of leaving the main Bill until the next session in order to push through the most urgent of their reforms as soon as possible, including their proposals on inter-union disputes and the conciliation pause. In marked contrast to the Donovan Report, which had put the reform of company and plant industrial relations in the forefront and left the question of new legal sanctions until after these reforms had been carried out, the government now placed legal sanctions and checks on the unions in the foreground, suggesting that they too believed that these would get at the roots of the problem.

[1] *Ibid.*, pp. 28–9.   [2] *Ibid.*, pp. 29–30.

[3] The Donovan Report had recommended the compulsory registration of collective agreements, as a means of encouraging companies to enter into written collective agreements. The government narrowed this to procedures, to assure the unions and employers that the Commission would not meddle with pay, and extended it to "arrangements" as well as "agreements". As a voluntary register of any kind of procedure the scheme exerted little or no pressure on companies to enter into written agreements, and became a massive exercise in collecting information whose purpose is not evident.

The next chapter in the story opened up even wider the rift between the government's ideas and the Donovan analysis. The government said they would be willing to consider any alternatives which the trade unions had to offer. The General Council drafted amendments to rules 11 and 12 of the Trades Union Congress forbidding stoppages in inter-union disputes until after investigation by themselves or their Disputes Committee, and giving themselves power to intervene in "unauthorised and unconstitutional stoppages of work" with authority to use rule 13 on the conduct of affiliated organisations to deal with unions which refused to assist them in the exercise of their new powers.[1] A special meeting of Congress on 5 June agreed to submit these proposals to the annual meeting in September, on condition the government withdrew all proposals for financial penalties on individuals and unions either in connection with strikes or with the registration of union rules.

At first the government were dissatisfied with the General Council's proposals on unconstitutional strikes. However, by this time they were under pressure from many members of the Parliamentary Labour Party who wanted to avoid a complete breach with the unions. Consequently on 18 June they dropped "the so-called penal sanctions" in return for a "solemn and binding undertaking" from the General Council. When faced with a dispute which might have "serious consequences" and where they found "there should be no stoppage of work before procedure is exhausted", the General Council undertook to oblige the union or unions to take "immediate and energetic steps to obtain a resumption of work, including action within their rules if necessary", and to deal with them under rule 13 if they did not comply.[2] Thereafter the government prepared a new Bill, far "weaker" than the Donovan Report, but it was overtaken by the general election of 1970.

The government's actions suggested not only that they considered that new sanctions against unconstitutional strikers could make a major contribution to reducing the number of unconstitutional strikes, but also that they thought the trade union movement was a hierarchical organisation with sufficient power at the centre to impose effective sanctions. If so, they must have

[1] Trades Union Congress, *Industrial Relations, a Programme for Action*, 1969.
[2] Trades Union Congress, *Annual Report*, 1969, pp. 145–7.

had in their minds a model of British industrial relations markedly
different from the model delineated in the Donovan Report. An
alternative explanation of the government's behaviour is that
when they failed to deliver the "penal sanctions" which they
thought the electorate wanted, they grasped at the only available
alternative—a "solemn and binding undertaking" from the
Trades Union Congress.

The Industrial Relations Act

The Conservative victors of the 1970 election took office pledged
to reform industrial relations on lines very different from those of
the Donovan Report. Their proposals had appeared before the
publication of the report, in *Fair Deal at Work*. Its diagnosis was
that the main cause of the defects of British industrial relations was
the unregulated power of the trade unions. In addition to endow-
ing unions with full corporate status, new legal obligations were
to be placed upon the unions in three ways. Firstly, existing
collective agreements were to be made legally binding,[1] with
special courts, including "side" members with industrial experience, to hear suits for breach. There was to be a statutory limit
to the amount of damages. Secondly, registered unions would
have immunity from civil proceedings in a lawful trade dispute
and a legal right to recognition, and the Registrar was to have
wide powers to vet rules and investigate their application. Union
rules, for example, should not impose an obligation to restrict
output, and union members should not be penalised for failing
to take an action which would have been in breach of an agreement. The Registrar would be empowered to strike unions off
the register, with an appeal to the courts. Managers were assured
that "the basic functions of shop stewards would be clearly laid
down in union rules, and since the Registrar would have a
responsibility to ensure that the rules were adhered to in practice,
management could expect full union co-operation if shop
stewards attempted to exceed their authority". Thirdly, certain
forms of collective action, currently within the law, were to be
made unlawful. These included the pre-entry closed shop—and
there was provision for exemption on grounds of conscience from

[1] At this time the Conservatives supposed that this could be accomplished by repeal of
Section 4 of the 1871 Act.

the post-entry closed shop—and inter-union disputes, rendered unlawful by narrowing the definition of a trade dispute. In addition there were to be discretionary powers for the government to intervene in stoppages by imposing a "cooling-off" period, and by requiring a secret ballot on the employer's "last offer".

New obligations were to be imposed upon employers also. There was to be a statutory right of appeal against unfair dismissal, and employers would have a legal duty to recognise and bargain with registered trade unions subject to a ballot to determine the wishes of the employees. A Code of Industrial Relations Practice was to be drawn up for approval by Parliament to guide the behaviour of managers, unions and employees.

For the authors of *Fair Deal at Work* the high and rising rate of unconstitutional strikes was a consequence of the failure of the unions to keep their members to their agreements, and this could be remedied by imposing legal sanctions against unions which failed in their obligations. These sanctions would compel the unions to exercise their authority over their members (authority which the authors assumed that the unions had or could have). Although they welcomed "the trend to local bargaining", the authors did not appreciate the effects of domestic bargaining upon the unions. The Whitley model had put employers' associations and trade unions on an equal footing, jointly responsible for their agreements. But domestic agreements are outside the scope of employers' associations. In domestic bargaining with managers the unions are on their own up to the point at which the joint procedure is invoked, if it is invoked, and up to this point most of the union work is generally carried out by shop stewards. Thus *Fair Deal at Work* recognised that firms which belonged to employers' associations still retained a good deal of authority for themselves, but assumed that unions were unitary bodies fully responsible for the actions of their shop stewards.

In the two years between the publication of the Donovan Report and the 1970 election the Conservatives had time to study the report's analysis and to incorporate into their scheme any elements in the report which they wanted to take over. The opportunity was taken. Revised proposals emerged in a *Consultative Document* in the autumn of 1970, then in a Bill and finally in the Industrial Relations Act which received royal assent on 5 August 1971.

The main changes are to be found in Part III of the Act entitle "Collective Bargaining" and in sections 121-2. These last tw sections provide for the Secretary of State to refer "any questio relating to industrial relations generally or to industrial relations i any particular industry or in any particular undertaking or part c an undertaking" to the Commission on Industrial Relations, an for the Commission to investigate and report. This procedure which is closely in line with the Donovan recommendations an the work of the Commission prior to the Act, has already becom known as a "voluntary reference" because there is no provision a this stage for the enforcement of the Commission's findings Thus the government showed their appreciation of the need fo reform in industrial relations, and of the advantages of reform which is undertaken voluntarily.

At this point, however, the government faced a problem whicl had worried several members of the Donovan Commission, les optimistic than their colleagues about the prospects of voluntar reform.[1] What is to be done if companies and trade unions or some of them, make no effort to improve industrial rela tions?

Part III of the Act contains the government's answer. It takes uj the proposal that collective agreements should be made legall enforceable, but in view of the Donovan Commission's stricture on the current state of collective agreements, there is no attemp to enforce agreements made before the passage of the Act. Agree ments made in writing after the Act came into force are legall enforceable contracts except in so far as the parties expressly provid to the contrary.

Consequently, if they choose, the parties can carry on with thei unreformed and unenforceable agreements. To deal with thi possibility, the Commission on Industrial Relations is empowered on a reference from the Industrial Court, to investigate "units o employment" which lack procedure agreements, or suitable procedure agreements, or where the procedures do not preven unconstitutional strikes; and to propose new or revised procedures Going far beyond the Donovan Report, the Act provides tha within six months of the publication of the Commission's repor

---

[1] These reservations were expressed in *Supplementary Notes* by Lord Tangley, and b Lord Robens, Sir George Pollock and Mr. John Thompson, and in a *Note of Reservatio* by Mr. Andrew Shonfield, Royal Commission, *Report*, pp. 282-302.

an employer or a registered trade union can ask the Industrial Court[1] for an order giving the Commission's proposals the effect of a legally enforceable contract "as if a contract consisting of those provisions had been made between those parties". These provisions do not apply to industry procedures, for the "unit of employment" is confined to a company or a group of companies associated by ownership, and does not extend to an employers' association.

The government also perceived that the problems of multi-unionism were a good deal more complex than had been appreciated in *Fair Deal at Work*. As the Donovan Report had pointed out,[2] there was more to it than just taking a ballot. There was the problem of deciding which employees should vote; there was the question of whether the union or unions would have the support of a substantial proportion of the employees if they were recognised (which is not the same as support before recognition); and there was the question of whether the union had the resources to bargain effectively on their behalf. The Act makes it the job of the Commission to investigate these matters.

In addition the government borrowed from North America the notions of a "bargaining unit" and "exclusive representation", and converted them to apply to British multi-unionism by allowing for a joint negotiating panel of unions to be recognised as the "sole bargaining agent" for a bargaining unit, provided that the unions have authorised the panel to enter into collective agreements on their behalf. Enforcement is only possible in relation to a registered union or a joint negotiating panel consisting entirely of registered unions. In those circumstances the Commission's proposals can be put to the vote of the employees comprised in the bargaining unit. Where a majority of those voting favour the proposals, the Industrial Court is to make an order defining the bargaining unit and specifying the sole bargaining agent. If the employer fails to comply with the order, the union's claims against him can be submitted to unilateral arbitration with enforceable awards. On the other hand a union, whether registered or unregistered, becomes liable to an injunction and damages if it does not accept the order, or if it tries to secure recognition by a

---

[1] The National Industrial Relations Court is a specialist court created by the Act. The old Industrial Court has become the "Industrial Arbitration Board".

[2] Royal Commission, *Report*, pp. 64–5.

strike or "irregular industrial action"[1] while the issue is unde investigation. The bargaining unit is confined to a company or group of companies, or a section of employees in a company o group.[2]

The Act renders any party to a legally enforceable agreemen liable to an action before the Industrial Court if they do not "tak all such steps as are reasonably practicable" to prevent anyon purporting to act on their behalf from acting contrary to the undertaking. But this provides sanctions against unconstitution: strikes only when the agreement is a legal contract. Otherwise th principal threat against unconstitutional strikes is contained in th provisions dealing with inducing breaches of contract. A registere trade union is protected from an action for inducing a breach c contract (whether a contract of employment or a commerci contract) if it is acting in contemplation or furtherance of a industrial dispute; but an unregistered trade union has no suc protection, and an officer or member of a registered union i protected only if he is acting "within the scope of his authorit on behalf of a trade union". In the past, nearly all unofficial an unconstitutional strikers have come out without giving prope notice, and have therefore broken their contracts. If they do no change their ways, their leaders will henceforth be liable befor the Industrial Court unless the strike has been expressly authorise(by a registered trade union.

The requirements relating to the rules of registered unions ar set out in Schedule 4 of the Act. Paragraph 10 says that "the rule must specify any body by which, and any official by whom instructions may be given to members of the organisation on it behalf for any kind of industrial action, and the circumstances ii which any such instructions may be so given". It would b(possible for union rules to give wide scope to union officers, anc even to shop stewards, in calling strikes, although a clear definitioi of the "circumstances" in which they could call a strike might ta:

---

[1] This is an action, short of a strike, taken in contemplation or furtherance of an industria dispute, in which workers interfere with production, *and* break their contracts. Whethe an overtime ban is included thus depends on whether the employees are contractuall bound to work overtime.

[2] However, the Act recognises industry agreements by defining a bargaining unit a dealing with "such matters as are not dealt with under more extensive bargaining arrange ments"; and a "voluntary reference" of a recognition issue to the Commission could lea(to a recommendation for recognition at industry level.

the ingenuity of those who have to draft the rules. But it follows that if an authorised officer or shop steward calls a strike which turns out to involve one of the many other "unfair industrial practices" created by the Act, the union would then be liable. It is unlikely that unions will be prepared to face that risk. They will prefer to put close limits on the authority to call a strike. Consequently the effect of the Act on unofficial and unconstitutional strikes is likely to depend largely upon the willingness of employers to sue unofficial strike leaders for bringing out employees without giving due notice.[1]

Most of the rest of the Act is designed to give effect to the proposals of *Fair Deal at Work*. It is based upon the distinction between an unregistered union and a registered union; and also upon the new concept of an "unfair industrial practice", which is actionable before the industrial tribunals[2] and the new Industrial Court, but not before the ordinary courts except by way of an appeal on a point of law. Damages awarded against registered unions are limited to maximum figures varying according to the size of union, with £100,000 as the outside limit for the largest unions, but there is no limit for unregistered unions. [The Act uses the term "organisation of workers" to cover registered and unregistered unions, whereas a registered union is called a "trade union". It remains to be seen whether this new nomenclature catches on.]

These distinctions provide part of the explanation for the extreme complexity of the Act, which has 170 sections and 9 schedules compared with the 24 sections and one schedule of the 1871 Act, and the five sections of the 1906 Act. For example, the requirements of registration are confined to registered unions, and so is the supervision of the Registrar, but the government wished also to provide some control over the conduct of unregistered unions. Consequently the Act includes a set of principles with

[1] Due notice in a strike is defined as notice of the same period as would be required to terminate the contract of employment or longer (section 147). But the position is complicated by section 20 which may have the effect of incorporating procedure agreements into the contracts of employment of the workers to whom they apply. If it does have this effect, a strike before the procedure had been exhausted might be held to be a breach of the contract of employment.

[2] These are the tribunals created by the Industrial Training Act, 1964. Their scope was extended by the Redundancy Payments Act, and is now further widened by the Industrial Relations Act.

which all "organisations of workers" must comply, with pro
vision for complaint to the industrial tribunals, and, for registered
unions, also to the Industrial Court. There is a special register fo
organisations, such as professional associations, which are debarred
by charter or by registration under the Companies Act from bein
trade unions. A number of these organisations undertake som
trade union functions; and henceforth, if they apply for inclusio
on the special register and fulfil the relevant conditions, the
will have the same protection and privileges as registered trad
unions.

Some of the most tortuous complexities arise out of the govern
ment's concern to protect the individual worker's right to belon
to a trade union or not, as he chooses, and at the same time t
provide means whereby registered unions can protect thei
membership and their bargaining strength in accordance with th
law. Thus it is not an unfair industrial practice for an employer t
encourage his employees to join a registered trade union. Beyon
that, he can agree with a registered union or unions to establis
an "agency shop" in which workers who refuse to join the unio
or unions are obliged to pay the equivalent of the union sub
scription into union funds, unless they can establish a conscien
tious objection, in which event the money goes to an agree
charity. Under such an agreement the employer can lawfully dis
miss the employee who refuses to pay the appropriate contri
butions, and the union (after due notice) can apply pressure o
the employer to do so. If the employer refuses to grant an agenc
shop, the union or unions can invoke a procedure which leads to
ballot under the auspices of the Commission on Industria
Relations. If the vote of the workers affected favours an agenc
shop either by a majority of those eligible to vote or by a two
thirds majority of those voting, then it becomes the legal duty o
the employer to make and implement an agency shop agreemen
In addition, during the passage of the Act the government'
attention was drawn to the plight of certain unions, such as th
National Union of Seamen and Actors' Equity, whose existenc
as effective bodies was said to depend upon a closed shop. Conse
quently, when the Commission on Industrial Relations is satisfie
that certain stringent conditions are fulfilled (amounting to thei
being convinced that the viability of collective bargaining depend
on the existence of a closed shop), and after a ballot has favoured

closed shop, an "approved closed shop" can lawfully be implemented, provided the Industrial Court has given permission. Here the only alternative to union membership is to qualify as a conscientious objector so as to be allowed to pay to an agreed charity. As the argument concerning shipping and the theatre is that the unions cannot continue to exist as effective bodies there without a closed shop throughout their industries, the approved closed shop can apply to the whole industry by agreement with an employer's association, and so can an agency shop. A bargaining unit, by contrast, cannot extend beyond the boundaries of a company or a group of companies.

This, however, is not the end of the complications. Since the Act provides the way into a legally enforceable closed shop or agency shop, then the Act must provide a way out again. Accordingly further sections, and Part III of Schedule I, provide that where one-fifth of the workers concerned make a written application to be rid of a closed shop or an agency shop, and two years has elapsed since the last ballot, there shall be another ballot. If this ballot does not give the required majority in favour of continuation, the agreement loses the support of the law, and any further action to enforce it becomes unlawful.

There is much more to the Act than has been mentioned so far. There are emergency procedures for enforcing a cooling-off period of up to sixty days, and for requiring a strike ballot. There are sections providing that employers must disclose information to their employees and to trade union representatives, and another section protecting the immunity of confidential information. The Secretary of State is empowered to require employers to notify procedures. Several sections are taken up with excluding courts other than the Industrial Court from interfering in industrial relations business. But several volumes would be required to give a full account of the Act; sufficient detail has already been given for the purpose of this chapter except on two points.

Firstly, the Act follows the proposals of *Fair Deal at Work* in making certain forms of collective action unlawful. These include action to enforce the pre-entry closed shop, many cases of secondary action in industrial disputes, and probably some types of dispute between workers (or their unions). The last restriction is achieved by narrowing the definition of what used to be a "trade dispute" and is now called an "industrial dispute".

Secondly, the Act provides that a code of practice shall be lai
before Parliament for approval within a year of the passage of th
Act. Failure to observe the code will not lead to liability t
proceedings, but the Industrial Court and the tribunals are t
take it into account, where relevant, in reaching their decision
This code, published in January 1972, gives far more space to th
duties of managers, to their employment policies and to industri
relations and procedures in the plant than to duties of the union
and there is only brief mention of employers' associations an
negotiations at industry level. Generally, if not always in detai
the document is close to the spirit of the Donovan Report.

What model of industrial relations can be discerned in the Ac
The Whitley model has gone. It could be argued that, taking th
Act and the code together, the "two systems" model of the Dono
van Report has been accepted, along with its major recommenda
tions. The difference, it might be said, lies in the realism of th
government in appreciating the conditions in which thes
recommendations can be carried out with success. Industri
relations, it is agreed, must be reformed by means of effectiv
policies, procedures and agreements at the level of the plant an
the company. Senior managers and boards of companies must tak
the initiative and accept major responsibility for carrying out th
reform. But they cannot achieve reform by themselves. They ma
propose new procedures, but the unions could refuse to accep
them, or even to negotiate realistically about them. The Commis
sion on Industrial Relations can be brought in, but even they ma
fail to win the unions' agreement to their expert proposal
Accordingly, at this stage the Act makes it possible for the In
dustrial Court to impose a procedure. Furthermore, mult
unionism may constitute an insuperable obstacle to management
efforts at reform. Consequently the Act allows for the proposa
of the Commission on Industrial Relations concerning bargainin
units and sole bargaining agencies to be imposed, provided tha
sufficient workers will vote for them. In addition, there may b
unofficial and unconstitutional strikes while reform is going or
or even after it has been completed. In so far as this is not dea
with by the provision that agreements shall henceforth be enforce
able contracts except when the parties specify otherwise, th
protection from action for inducement of breach of contract
limited to registered unions and their accredited officers. Th

limitation will normally permit employers to sue unofficial strike leaders.

This is one possible interpretation, but a closer reading of the Act shows that it is implausible. The main thrust of the Act is not to encourage managers to reform industrial relations, but to restrict trade unions. It is true that the Act renders employers liable to compensate employees whom they dismiss unfairly; submits them to compulsory arbitration where they fail to recognise registered trade unions which have demonstrated in a ballot that they have the support of the employees; compels them to disclose information; and even, in certain circumstances, obliges them to accept an agency shop. It is also true that employers will be liable to damages if, by locking out their employees, they commit one of the many unfair industrial practices specified in the Act. But all this has little relevance to the well-organised centres of British industrial relations. There is not one lockout to a thousand strikes and instances of "irregular industrial action" by workers. Most employers in these areas are reluctant to dismiss an employee where they think it likely that other employees will consider their action unfair, if only for fear of the con-sequences.[1] It is uncommon in Britain for employers to refuse to recognise strongly-organised unions, even in the white-collar field.

By contrast the provisions for regulating trade unions are directed at the centre of organised industrial relations, not at the periphery. The closed shop exists where unions are strong, not where they are weak. Strong unions are at least as likely as weak unions to compete for membership and recognition, and more likely to compete effectively. Those groups of workers who make relatively frequent use of unofficial, unconstitutional strikes are almost all in the well-organised sectors. It will be possible for a registered union to have a procedure imposed on a recalcitrant employer, but it is much more likely that employers will use the Act to impose procedures on trade unions.

The Donovan proposal for compulsory registration of trade unions was intended to impose higher standards of clarity and consistency on union rule books, and to provide easier remedies for those who complained that they had been unfairly excluded

---

[1] This part of the Act is likely to have more effect where trade union organisation is relatively weak.

Q

from trade unions, or that there had been malpractices in union elections. The cumbersome proposals of the Act seem designed to lay such a large number of liabilities and disabilities on unregistered trade unions that unions would prefer to be registered despite the detailed supervision which the Act prescribes over the internal affairs of registered unions. In addition, it seems to be the aim of this detailed supervision to force unions to exercise over their workshop representatives that degree of discipline which *Fair Deal at Work* proclaimed to be practicable and desirable. This objective had no place in the Donovan scheme for registration.

If all this is true it suggests that the Act's model of industrial relations is very different from the model of the Donovan Report. It is common ground to both that the system has moved far away from the Whitley model, but whereas the Donovan Commission saw the cause in the growth in the size of firms, the loss of authority in employers' associations, and the failure of managers to develop effective policies and procedures, the Act appears to infer that the main cause has been a decline in trade union discipline and standards.

This, however, is inference, and in any case the Act will in the end be judged, not by the model of industrial relations which its authors may have had in their minds, but by its effects. While it is not the business of a textbook to speculate upon the effects of an untested statute, the consequences which this Act is intended to have on British industrial relations are so profound that a textbook on industrial relations must pay some attention to the problems which may arise in its application.

PROBLEMS IN THE APPLICATION OF THE ACT

In January 1972 the first question to be asked about the application of the Act is whether trade unions and employers will be able to prevent its operation. During 1971 the Trades Union Congress instructed constituent unions not to co-operate in the implementation of the Act. This meant that trade unionists should not accept posts on the Commission on Industrial Relations[1] and the new

[1] William Paynter, formerly general secretary of the Mineworkers, and Alfred Allen, general secretary of the Shop Distributive and Allied Workers, resigned from the Commission in 1970 shortly after the publication of the Consultative Document; and George Woodcock resigned in 1971 before the Act was passed.

Industrial Court, and that those who were already members of industrial tribunals should resign from them; that unions should not sign new agreements unless they include clauses expressing the intention of the parties that they should not be legally binding; that unions should boycott the procedures and institutions established by the Act, including the Commission on Industrial Relations; and, above all, that unions should refuse to register. Meanwhile many employers, encouraged by official guidance from the Confederation of British Industry advising them to think carefully before setting the procedures of the Act in motion,[1] were preparing plans to minimise the impact of the Act on their own industrial relations.

It lies with the parties to decide whether agreements should be made legally enforceable or not. They can avoid enforceability by including an appropriate disclaimer in every written agreement. Even the power of the Industrial Court to impose a procedure recommended by the Commission is dependent on an application from one or other of the parties, for the procedure can be invoked only by one of the employers or unions concerned. Consequently it seems probable that there will be few enforceable agreements for some time to come. The unions have set their faces against such agreements, and most employers and employers' associations seem to be willing to acquiesce. Even the nationalised industries appear to be ready to include disclaimers in their agreements.

There are, however, other parts of the Act which do not depend upon unions and employers to bring them into operation. Section 65 lays down "guiding principles" for "organisations of workers". Persons eligible for membership must not be excluded "by way of any arbitrary or unreasonable discrimination"; members must not be arbitrarily or unreasonably excluded from their rights to attend meetings, to vote and to offer themselves as candidates, nor subjected to unfair or unreasonable disciplinary action; there are minimum requirements for the conduct of ballots and disciplinary proceedings; and members must not be disciplined for refusing to take part in an unfair industrial practice. It is an unfair industrial practice for any organisation of workers or its officials to fail to apply these principles in dealings with members and applicants for membership; and aggrieved members and applicants can

---

[1] Confederation of British Industry, *Guidance to Employers on Industrial Relations Bill,* June 1971.

complain to an industrial tribunal. Consequently these sections of the Act can be invoked without reference to unions or employers and a union which has infringed the principles of section 65 can be compelled to pay compensation to the complainant who has suffered in consequence. The only protection is for a union to have rules in accordance with the principles and to carry them out. Many unions are contemplating alterations in their rules to bring them into conformity with the prescribed principles. But revision of the rules in this way will not bring a union any further within the scope of other sections of the Act, and there is nothing in section 65 to induce a union to register. Registration would bring with it the supervision of the Registrar, as well as the possibility of intervention by the Industrial Court.

The sections of the Act dealing with the closed shop and the agency shop may have more far-reaching consequences. Although pre-entry closed shop agreements become void, and employers must notify their employees of their rights in relation to union membership and non-membership, unions and employers are not obliged to take direct steps to undermine any existing closed shop, whether by agreement or by custom. An existing closed shop may be threatened when an applicant for a job is rejected because he has not an appropriate union card and refuses to apply for it, since he can complain to an industrial tribunal. But in these circumstances the employer will probably produce evidence to show that the reason for rejection is nothing to do with trade union membership, an argument not easily refuted if the original interview has been conducted with care. The greater risk is therefore a disgruntled member who resigns from the union. If dismissed, he has the same right of complaint to the tribunal, where the employer will be hard pressed to disguise the reason for dismissal, especially if he acted on a request from the union.

Compensation for dismissal is normally limited to the expenses incurred and the loss of expected benefits (with a duty on the part of the complainant to mitigate his losses), up to a maximum of two years' pay or £4160, whichever is less. But where the dismissal is in support of a closed shop, a tribunal may decide to recommend reinstatement and, if the employer refuses to reinstate, the assessment can be increased. A high assessment for one disgruntled member could encourage others to express their disgruntlement. A queue at the tribunal might persuade an employer that the price of trade union goodwill can be too high. The employer can, of course, try to reduce his losses by claiming that the union should make a contribution to the amount of compensation, but this will relieve pressure on the employer only by transferring it to the union.

The likelihood of disgruntled members; the willingness of employers to pay for union goodwill; and the extent to which unions face losses of membership if closed shops are opened: these are all matters of conjecture. But at least many unions face serious risks. By means of the agency shop and the approved closed shop the Act provides protection for unions and employers, but that protection is available only where unions are registered. Unions may regard registration as a lesser evil than large-scale loss of members; and even employers who place a high value on union goodwill may not appreciate why they should meet part of the cost of a union's refusal to register.

Other risks come from unions outside the Trades Union Congress which choose to register, and feel free to use the procedures of the Act, and from professional associations which qualify for the Special Register. Being registered, these bodies will be able to use the Act to try to secure sole bargaining agencies and agency shops. They may do this in areas where unregistered trade unions have membership. Then, if they are successful, the unregistered unions will suffer the indignity of having their members represented by another body, and forced to pay contributions to it. Being unregistered, these unions will not be able to take positive steps under the Act to protect their members. The alternative is to register and use the procedures of the Act to claim recognition and agency shops for themselves.

In this connection a great deal depends on the Commission, for the Commission determines the boundaries of bargaining units and the classes of workers to be included in a ballot for an agency shop. In determining a bargaining unit, the Commission is instructed to consider "the nature of the work" and the "training, experience and professional or other qualifications" of the workers, and further criteria are suggested in the Code of Industrial Relations Practice, including the location of work, payment systems, management and union structure, and the wishes of the employees. With freedom to pick and choose among all these criteria the Commission will be able to do very much as it pleases.

Generally speaking, larger bargaining units favour the established unions, and smaller bargaining units will allow independent unions and professional associations to establish a foothold. In engineering, for example, separate bargaining units for professionally-qualified engineers would allow the United Kingdom Association of Professional Engineers to gain recognition in a number of firms, and this recognition would promote recruitment elsewhere. On the other hand, bargaining units which included technicians together with qualified engineers would favour the established unions, the Draughtsmen and the Scientific, Technical and Managerial Staffs.

The original Commission showed their preference for comprehensive bargaining units, notably in their report on the Medical Research Council[1] where they rejected the claims of separate organisations to represent particular groups of employees. In addition they concluded that a staff association recently formed among the Council's employees would not be able to support an effective bargaining organisation despite its considerable membership. Consequently they recommended that one union, the Scientific, Managerial and Technical Staffs, should represent all grades of employee. However, the sweeping changes in the membership of the Commission since that decision detract from the value of the report as a guide to future decisions on bargaining units.

If fragmentation of bargaining units permits outside organisations to gain a foothold, and the established unions which are threatened by the recognition of these bodies respond by registering in self-defence, the consequence could be a chain reaction throughout the trade union movement. For an established union which registered and began to use the procedures of the Act against outside organisations might be tempted to use them also against unregistered unions affiliated to the Trades Union Congress. If the union yielded to the temptation—and the competitive instinct runs deep in British trade unions—its competitors would in their turn be under pressure to protect themselves by registration, and the chain reaction would follow.

Even if most major firms are anxious to co-operate with the unions in minimising the effects of the Act, there may be occasions

---

[1] Commission on Industrial Relations, *Medical Research Council*, Report No. 12, Cmnd. 4531, 1970.

when a particular firm will find it very much to its advantage to use the Act's procedures against the unions. This will be the case if a firm is suffering heavy losses from a strike which appears to constitute one of the many unfair industrial practices specified in the Act. Then the firm's legal advisers may point out that if the union can be shown to be responsible for the strike, and the unfair industrial practice can be proved, the firm will not only be able to obtain an injunction against the union ordering it to end the strike, but is also entitled to claim damages, provided the union is unregistered, up to the full value of its loss.

During recent years some employers have been willing to sue union leaders for injunctions against strikes despite the bias of legislation towards keeping the courts out of trade disputes. The *Torquay* case, the *Emerald* case, the *Stratford* case and the *Ford* case prove the point. It is likely that there will be more instances under the new Act, for it provides very many more occasions for going to court, and employers are entitled to sue the union directly, so long as it can be shown to be responsible for the stoppage. It is, of course, impossible to calculate strike losses exactly, but in many prolonged stoppages the employer will be able to demonstrate heavy losses, in some instances running into millions of pounds. If damages on anything like this scale were awarded, the union concerned would be under great pressure to register so as to limit its liability in the future, and other unregistered unions would be under pressure to register so as to avoid suffering a like fate. After all, it was not the original *Taff Vale* decision in 1901, which settled liability, so much as the agreement on the amount of the damages a year later, that threw the trade union movement into an uproar, and set the unions clamouring for a wholesale revision of the law.[1]

The Act provides for unions already registered under the 1871 Act to be transferred automatically to a provisional register for an initial period of six months. The question of transfer to the new permanent register depends on the conformity of the rules to the requirements for registration. All but a few of the unions affiliated to the Trades Union Congress were registered under the 1871 Act. To comply with the instructions of Congress these unions must apply to be withdrawn from the provisional register. Some union constitutions require that such a decision be approved by a

[1] Clegg, Fox and Thompson, pp. 313-25.

special conference or by a ballot of the members, and unions are not permitted to withdraw from the provisional register unless the decision to withdraw is taken in accordance with their rules. Consequently the operation may run on well beyond the initial six months.

A union which has an application pending to withdraw from registration is not likely to use the procedures of the Act. Consequently the important decision, in the short run, is the application to withdraw. Although a number of the unions have still to make this decision, it now seems that the majority of affiliated unions may follow the policy of Congress, despite the liability to additional tax that this may entail. Even unions which think the policy mistaken may comply, in the interests of solidarity, leaving a few unions with particular urgent reasons for staying on the register to be granted a special dispensation by the General Council. On the other hand, a sizeable minority may yet choose to stay on the register.

If most unions come off the register, the important question is how soon the pressures to register again will build up through defections from the closed shop, through the recognition of organisations on the register, and because of heavy damages awarded against unregistered unions. Probably Congress does not believe that the unions can hold out for ever. Their hope is that the Act can be held at arm's length until the next election, after which a Labour Government, if returned, might be expected to cobble together pieces of the several statutes repealed by the Industrial Relations Act to put a Bill through Parliament in order to return as near as possible to the *status quo*.[1] But for this strategy to work, the Act must be held at bay. For once the unions are enmeshed in its operation the temptation will be for a future Labour government to amend it rather than return to the *status quo*. After all, a number of its provisions bear a close resemblance to the measures which the last Labour government proposed to Parliament but were forced to withdraw. If a future Labour government found them operating successfully, they might decide to let them stay.

However, the strategy of Congress may fail. The Conservatives

---

[1] A simple repeal of the Act is out of the question. Because the Act has repealed earlier statutes, its repeal would leave wide gaps in statute law, and expose unions to the full rigour of common law.

may win the next election, or the pressures on the unions may drive them, or most of them, to register before the election. Then the Act will be in operation, and will be judged by the extent to which it fulfils its authors' intentions, especially in relation to curbing the effects of multi-unionism, to reducing the number of unofficial, unconstitutional strikes, and to improving the procedures and pay structures in use in British firms.

Prime responsibility for curbing the effects of multi-unionism now lies with the Commission. They can either discourage minority unions by establishing bargaining units in which a single union is able to win the sole negotiating agency, or recommend that the agency go to a joint bargaining panel of unions, provided that the unions are willing to hand over authority to a joint panel. Although each reference they handle might bring no more than a modest improvement, a series of references, together with their effect on the attitudes of unions and employers, could transform union structure, provided that there were no contrary pressures. But there may be contrary pressures. The inter-union dispute in the steel industry, described on pp. 67–70, provides an example of what might happen. The Pearson Court of Inquiry recommended the recognition of the Clerical and Administrative Workers and the Scientific, Managerial and Technical Staffs by the British Steel Corporation because of their strong following among some grades of the Corporation's staff. Backed by the Trades Union Congress, the established unions rejected the recommendation, and their will has so far prevailed. But if a similar issue was referred to the Commission, their view might follow the Pearson Report. Indeed, as the Pearson Report was the outcome of an informed and independent review of the matter, the odds are that the Commission, another independent and informed body, would arrive at a similar conclusion. If the ballot supported their decision, it would, unlike the Pearson Report, have legal sanctions behind it, and the consequence would be the recognition of additional unions in an already confused multi-union situation.

Another example is the revolt in 1954 of the dockers in the northern ports against the Transport and General Workers, which introduced multi-unionism into Liverpool, Manchester and Hull. If the machinery of the Act had been available at that time, and the "blue" union had chosen to register, then the Commission could hardly have denied them the opportunity to establish their position by a ballot. Multi-unionism would probably have been confirmed, whereas, as it happened, the combined opposition of the employers, the Transport and General Workers and the Trades Union Congress finally reduced the blue union's membership in the northern ports to negligible numbers.

Accordingly, there are likely to be occasions on which the Act promotes multi-unionism. Moreover, if this happens unrecognised unions will be encouraged to work harder for recognition, and potential breakaways will be encouraged to carry through their defection in the hope of using the Act to secure recognition as separate unions. Multi-unionism will breed multi-unionism.

It would be silly to try to guess whether the Commission's efforts to create greater order will prevail over the tendency in the Act to encourage multi-unionism. It is sufficient to show that both trends will be there and that the issue is uncertain.

Until and unless enforceable agreements are signed, the sanction against unconstitutional strikes is the removal of immunity from those who induce breaches of contract, unless they are registered unions or their accredited agents. Since nearly all unconstitutional strikes are unofficial and bring workers out in breach of their contracts of employment, the Act would appear to give employers ample opportunity to sue the leaders of unconstitutional strikes, if they choose to do so. But they may choose not to do so. Employers are notoriously reluctant to sue their own employees for striking. Nearly all unconstitutional strikers in Britain break their own contracts, but, with few exceptions, employers do not sue. If the employer decides to sue for inducing a breach, he has to name the leaders and prove that they called the strike. It is not difficult for unofficial leaders to take a public stance against a strike while at the same time letting their followers know that they should leave work. If the employer sues, his intention may be to secure an injunction, or damages, or both. But an injunction against one strike leader, or a group, may simply lead to their replacement; and an employer is not likely to recoup his costs, let alone his losses, from unofficial strike leaders. For all these reasons, there may be very few court cases against unofficial leaders of unconstitutional strikes, if any at all.

It should be noted that none of these reasons apply to court actions by employers against trade unions. A union is an impersonal organisation, not a group of employees, so that an employer who sues the union is not making a personal attack on his employees; if the union calls the strike officially, there can be no doubt about its responsibility for the stoppage; a trade union normally complies with an injunction because the union's funds are at risk; and most unions have considerable funds available to meet damages and costs awarded against them.

Employers and the government may suppose that the number of unofficial strikes could be reduced by stricter trade union discipline, and the Act may well influence unions to review their rules and practices in relation to strikes. But in both registered and unregistered unions these reviews are likely to lead them to tighter limitation of the authority to call strikes, and strict instructions to officers and committees to avoid any connection with an unauthorised strike lest the union be implicated too. The consequence could be that strikes, if they occur, will be even more likely to be unofficial than in the past.

Where there are legally enforceable agreements, the Industrial Court may take a strict view of the duty of the unions concerned "to take all such steps as are reasonably practicable" for the purpose of preventing breaches of the agreements, but, even so, the Court would probably not go so far as to require unions to take disciplinary action against unofficial strikers or their leaders as one of the "reasonably practicable" steps. In the end discipline in a union can be enforced only by expulsion, and expulsions can lead to breakaway organisations, which in their turn might use the procedures of the Act to try to secure recognition for themselves.

Conservative spokesmen claim that the Act is intended to provide a "framework of law", which will guide the actions of participants in industrial relations without the need for many court cases, especially in relation to strikes. But this is only likely to be true if the participants know when the law could be invoked, and expect that it will be invoked if they disregard it. If action is not taken against unofficial and unconstitutional strike-leaders when their action constitutes an unfair industrial practice, then the framework of law is not likely to be an effective guide to behaviour in industrial relations. Virtually every strike between 1940 and 1951 was a criminal offence under the Conditions of Employment and National Arbitration Order, but the order was

rarely invoked, and proved difficult to enforce even when it wa
invoked. It appeared to have very little effect on the number o
unofficial strikes.

However, more thoughtful supporters of the Act may expect i
to have its main effect on unofficial and unconstitutional strike
through promoting the reform of procedures and pay systems. I
would be possible for them to defend sanctions against such strike
as likely to exercise a restraining effect, while at the same tim
agreeing with the Donovan Report's diagnosis of the cause an
the means to effect a permanent cure.

Guidance to employers on the reform of procedures and pa
structures is contained in the code rather than in the Act, althoug
the admissibility of the code as evidence in proceedings under th
Act may add to its force, and the knowledge that he can turn fo
support to the Commission on Industrial Relations and th
Industrial Court may encourage an employer to challeng
obstructive trade unions. Thus the Act and the code together ma
provide pressure for reform. On the other hand, it is possible tha
some employers will feel that the provisions of the Act intended t
limit strikes and to control unions make it less necessary for then
to pay attention to their own industrial relations. Here again th
question is: which tendency will prevail?

By contrast the immediate effect of the Bill and the Act o
union attitudes is not in doubt. It has been to diminish thei
interest in co-operation with employers in reforming industria
relations at plant and company level, and it may take som
considerable time to dispel their resentment. Employers are no
likely to gain union goodwill by resorting to the Commissio
on Industrial Relations for help, at least in the short run. It i
possible that success by one company in invoking that part of th
Act which provides for the enforcement of a procedure recom
mended by the Commission would give other unions an incentiv
to co-operate in reform lest they too suffer an imposed procedure
But this is one of the most novel and complex provisions of th
Act; there are no clear precedents in this country or abroad t
suggest whether it will work successfully if it is invoked; an
employers may be shy of invoking it.

The preceding paragraphs may appear to suggest that th
Industrial Relations Act will have little effect even if the union
register and are brought within its scope, and even if it remains o

the statute book for many years to come. But in fact, if the Act remains, it must have a profound effect upon British industrial relations. It will transform the world's most voluntary system of industrial relations into a system whose formal aspects are largely regulated by the courts. Courts and lawyers will come to play a much larger part in the affairs of unions and employers, and in their dealings with each other. This development may be most evident when the unions threaten or use strikes or other sanctions. Then both sides will have to turn to their lawyers, and from time to time they will find themselves testing the meaning of the Act before the Industrial Court. But lawyers will also find themselves in demand to help unions revise their rules and to deal with complaints against unions before the Registrar and the industrial tribunals. Complaints against allegedly unfair dismissals are expected to generate a large volume of business for the tribunals.[1] Lawyers and the courts will also play a larger part in the business of negotiating agreements. Their part will be further enhanced if the parties allow their agreements to become legally enforceable, but it will grow even without that. As the Act takes effect, collective bargaining will be conducted more and more by legally defined bargaining agents for legally specified bargaining units. There will be legally defined agency shops, and perhaps legally approved closed shops. The definition of units, shops and agents will bring the lawyers and the courts into the regulation of inter-union relations. In many instances legally supervised ballots will be required, and the experience of the United States suggests that the conditions under which such ballots are conducted, and the regulation of canvassing, can be expected to provide a large volume of legal business.

Consequently there can be no doubt that, if the Act remains in force, it will transform many of the ways in which business is done in British industrial relations. What has been argued in the preceding paragraphs is that it is by no means certain that this transformation will lead to a major reduction in unofficial and unconstitutional strikes, to the reform of union structure and government, and to the reconstruction of industrial relations at plant and company level which is generally agreed to be needed.

[1] This is the reason for the exclusion of employees with less than two years' service, except where the alleged unfairness concerns union membership or non-membership, or union activities.

It is possible to foresee ways in which the Act will hinder development in these directions. Only time can tell which tendency will predominate—provided that the Act is given time. Consequently the prospect for reform in British industrial relations may depend more on the underlying trends existing within the system before the Act was passed than upon the Act itself.

THE PROSPECT FOR REFORM

Although there is no numerical index of the progress of reform of industrial relations in plants and companies, its scope was extended through 1970 and 1971. The most notable instance in 1970 was the negotiation in the London docks of "Stage Two" of the Devlin proposals which substituted flat rate payments for piecework and introduced double-shift working. In 1971 came Liverpool's "Stage Two" agreement—on a somewhat different basis—and the piecemeal reform of pay structures at a number of British Leyland plants. But if these are the most notable events, there are others which may in the long run turn out to have greater significance, such as the increase in the number of separate "terminal" agreements with individual companies in the London and Tilbury docks, and the piecemeal reform of plant and company procedures, especially in engineering. One instance is the reconstruction of procedures in the Rod Division of Delta Metal.[1] The pace of procedural reform in engineering is likely to be hastened by the termination of the industry's national disputes procedure at the end of 1971 after long negotiations had failed to resolve disagreements over "managerial prerogative". British Leyland has already revealed its intention of negotiating its own company procedure agreement, and other federated firms may follow. The prospect for continued reform in pay structures and procedures is therefore relatively bright.

There is also good reason to expect that this reform will lead to a reduction in unofficial and unconstitutional strikes. In addition to the sharp decline in the number of strikes per worker in the coal-mining industry since, the national powerloading agreement,[2]

[1] Richard O'Brien, "Plant Procedures and Agreements—A Case Study" in Sidney Kessler and Brian Weekes (eds.), *Conflict at Work*, 1971.

[2] These were large individual unofficial strikes in coalmining in 1970 and 1971, and an official national strike in 1972, but the number of strikes has continued to fall.

there is the evidence of the London and Liverpool docks which have been almost strike-free since the negotiation of their "Stage Two" agreements, and there are indications already that the reform of pay structures in British Leyland is being accompanied by a diminishing number of strikes. Three of the most strike-prone industries in post-war Britain—coalmining, docks and cars—have therefore provided further evidence of the close connection between procedures and pay structures on the one hand and the rate of unofficial and unconstitutional strikes on the other. The fourth industry, shipbuilding, has experienced no improvement and its machinery of industrial relations remains largely unreformed. Productivity agreements have, it is true, been negotiated in most shipyards of any size, but in their report on the industry the Commission on Industrial Relations found that these agreements had "not generally been as successful in a number of respects as was originally hoped". The Commission felt that "in a number of places both sides entered into negotiations with inadequate understanding of what was involved in bringing about the changes envisaged". In particular they had failed to establish satisfactory joint machinery at company and shipyard level to overcome the tradition whereby both unions and employers attempt to act independently of the other without joint negotiations; and they had failed "in most companies and yards" to overcome union sectionalism by "an agreed wages structure across all the occupations", with the result that "conflicts between groups over relativities have been sharpened".[1] The experience of shipbuilding is therefore further confirmation of the effect of procedures and pay structures on the rate of strikes.

During 1969 and 1970 the Department of Employment carried out a series of studies in eleven firms "where more formal bargaining arrangements had been introduced at the level of individual enterprise". One of the main findings was that "on the union side, the main burden at almost all stages of the move to plant bargaining fell upon chief lay officials" (senior stewards or convenors of stewards), and "in the operation of factory agreements it was again the lay official rather than the full-time officer who played the major part. . . . Indeed lay officials appeared reluctant to call in their full-time officers, preferring to settle

---

[1] Commission on Industrial Relations, *Shipbuilding and Shiprepairing*, Report No. 22, Cmnd. 4756, 1971, pp. 120–1.

differences within the factory if they could. Only when disputes reached major proportions was it common for the assistance of the local full-time union officer to be requested. Thus his formal involvement in plant industrial relations was virtually unchanged following the move to plant bargaining".[1] This suggests that the reform of industrial relations in the plant and the company does not alter the relation between shop stewards and their unions. On the contrary, reform confirms the authority of senior stewards within the plant, and their considerable degree of independence from their unions. There are therefore no grounds for supposing that the reconstruction of industrial relations will lead to a more hierarchical power-structure within the unions, with greater scope for the use of central disciplinary powers. Instead the devolution of union power to stop stewards is likely to be reinforced by the change.

There is a good deal of evidence that reform on these lines is associated with improved co-operation between unions in the plant, but no movement can be discerned towards a reconstruction of trade unions on a more rational pattern. Amalgamations have continued apace, but they have brought further complication rather than simplification. With the adhesion of the Draughtsmen and the Constructional Engineers, the Amalgamated Union of Engineering and Foundry Workers has become the Amalgamated Union of Engineering Workers, and a powerful force in the white collar field as well as among manual workers in most industries in the country. The amalgamation of the Woodworkers with the Painters and subsequently with the Building Trade Workers has produced a consolidation of union strength in the building industry, but the new union faces strong competition from the Transport and General Workers on its home territory, and brings together a ramshackle empire of outside interests in steel, engineering, shipbuilding and many other industries. Moreover, the dissolution of the Society of Graphical and Allied Trades has shown the insecurity of an amalgamation which allows the constituent unions to operate as independent organisations in all but a few limited matters. Because they retained their identity, the Society of Operative Printers and Assistants was able to pull out of the amalgamated organisation when they decided it was in

[1] Department of Employment, *The Reform of Collective Bargaining at Plant and Company Level*, 1971, p. iii, 84–5.

their interest to do so. The Engineering Workers' merger, and many other amalgamations, have been constructed on a similar pattern.

Accordingly, neglecting the effects of the Act for good or ill, the prospect of continued reform of plant and company industrial relations appears to be favourable. While this reform seems likely to bring a diminution of unofficial and unconstitutional strikes, it also seems likely to confirm the devolution of power to shop stewards in many British industries, and no strong trend towards a more rationalised trade union structure can be discerned.

However, this discussion of the prospect for reform in industrial relations leaves out of account what many observers consider to be the most important issue in British industrial relations, and the overriding aspect of the relationship between trade unions and the state—namely, incomes policy. Labour's incomes policy, which was described at length in the previous chapter, finally collapsed in 1970. Since then the Conservative government have sought, without any joint machinery or understanding with the unions, to reduce the amounts of industry-wide increases in rates of pay below the high figures of 10–15 per cent or more common during 1970. Figures of pay settlements have come down, especially in public services, but this does not necessarily demonstrate that the policy has been a success, for two reasons. In the first place, unemployment was rising rapidly through 1971, and this might have been expected to lead to an even more rapid decline in the level of pay settlements; and, secondly, average earnings in private industry, including engineering and building, rose much faster than the general level of pay settlements at industry level. Consequently, the problems which create pressure for an incomes policy have not yet been finally resolved, and it is pertinent to ask whether the Act will make it easier for governments to apply overt incomes policies in the future, if they choose to do so.

There are three ways in which legislation might be expected to facilitate incomes policies. Firstly, its effect might be so to weaken trade unions that they would be unable to resist a government determined to impose a policy on them. Secondly, it might bring about such a revolution in British trade union structure that any policy agreed between a government and the Trades Union Congress could be applied to the unions through a centralised system of trade union organisation. Thirdly, the reform of plant industrial relations might lead to well-regulated plant pay structures and negotiating procedures more amenable to external control than existing methods of settling pay in the plant. The previous discussion suggests that the Act is unlikely to lead either to a drastic weakening of trade unionism or to a centralisation of power in the trade union movement; but, whether promoted by the Act or not, reform of plant pay structures and negotiating arrangements seems likely to continue. This reform could assist the operation of an incomes policy provided the administrators of the policy learned how to influence the decisions of the managers and shop stewards who negotiate in the plant, but there is no reason to suppose that the Act will make it easier for the administrators to exercise the requisite influence. Consequently the Act appears to leave the problems of administering an overt incomes policy just about where they were when the Conservatives came to power.

INDEX OF AUTHORITIES CITED

(The full reference is given at the first entry in the text)

GENERAL INDEX